AF545073

THE GREAT AMERICAN PAINT IN®

THE GREAT AMERICAN
PAINT IN®
Artists sharing their pandemic stories

ACC Art Books

ISBN 978 1 78884 196 2

British Library Cataloguing-in-Publication Data
A catalogue record for this book is available from the British Library

Front cover: Art by Mary Jane Volkmann.

"...I am hopeful that in some way, this pandemic is reorienting our lives and that we are becoming more attentive to each other and to this beautiful trust in our midst: the children."

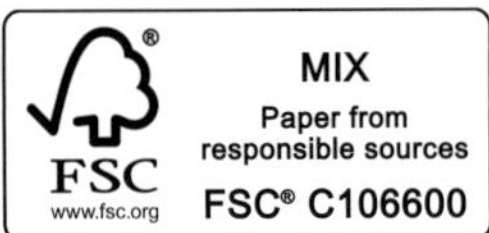

Printed in Slovenia
for ACC Art Books Ltd, Woodbridge, Suffolk, IP12 4SD, UK
www.accartbooks.com

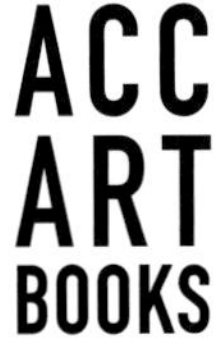

DEDICATION

This book is dedicated to all the loved ones we've lost, including the three artists from this project named below, and the healthcare professionals who have worked so tirelessly to keep us safe, putting their lives at risk every day during this worldwide pandemic.

John Deckert
Kim Minichiello
Kurt Mitchell

FOREWORD

Gallery CERO is the underwriter of The Great American Paint In® project. The goal was to collect great art from every state in the nation via social media and word-of-mouth campaigns among the artists. Ashley Weinaug steered the project with paid advertisements in art magazines and online publications.

The Great American Paint In® was birthed to create a plein-air "Paint In®" event that would allow artists to paint their emotions from their boundaries during the pandemic and allow us to share these stories for all time to come, through this curated book.

After returning to a state of normalcy, Wekiva Island showcased these historical stories online, at Gallery CERO, and around the country in several traveling art exhibits.

A heartfelt thanks to the high-caliber artists who have joined this project to share the real grit and backbone of the American pandemic 2020 story. Like so many enduring these difficult times, they discovered a whole new world and a brand "new normal" that allowed them to live, work, survive—and most importantly, create.

"We are living history right now. I believe we need to do more to document this unique moment in America, and who better to convey what we all are feeling than our country's greatest artists? It is my hope that in 50 years, art history classes will pull this book off the shelf and understand the deep emotion of this time."—William Weinaug

THE COLLECTION

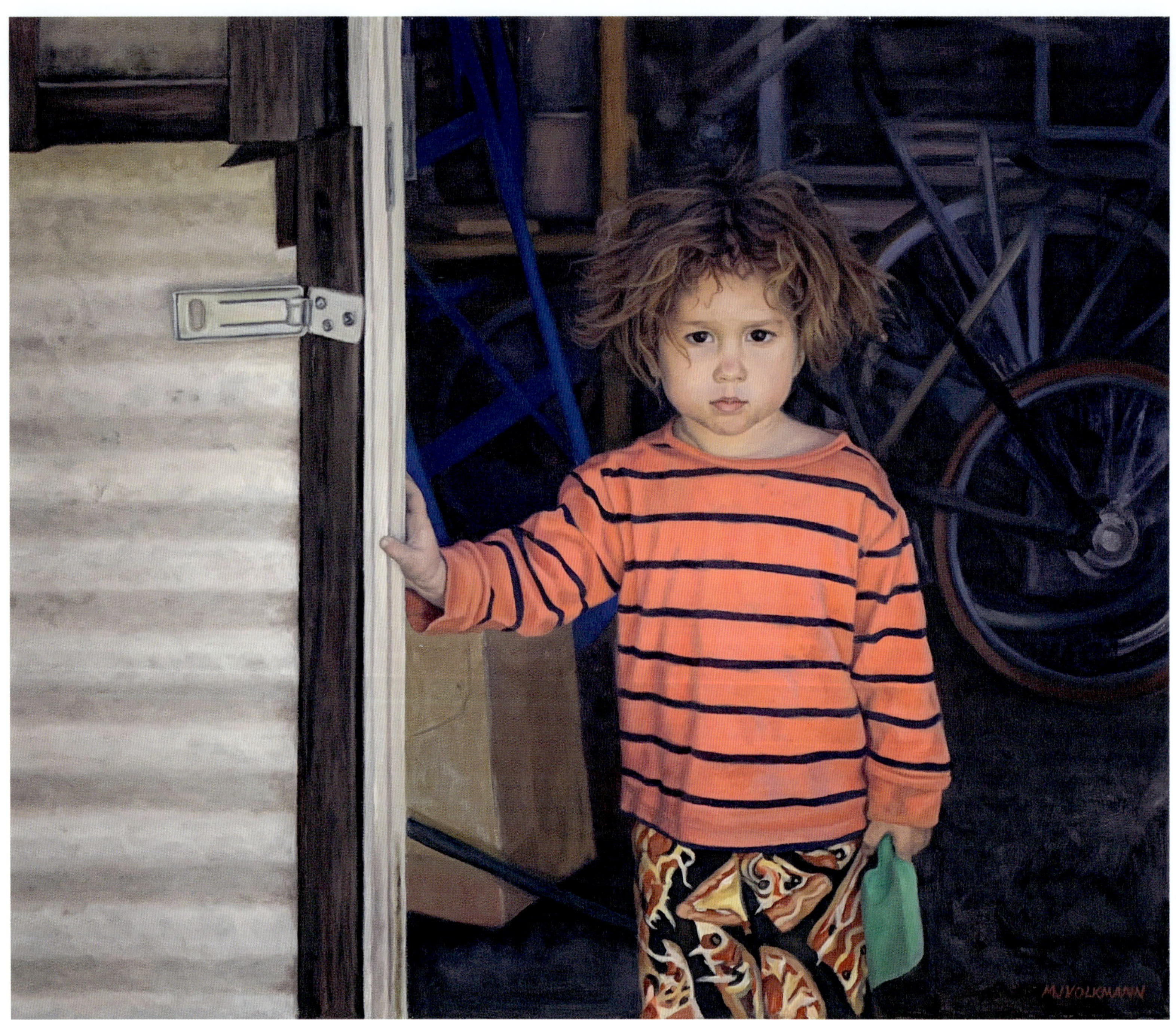
MJVOLKMANN

COVER ART

MARY JANE VOLKMANN, FLORIDA

THE POUT OF A HUNDRED POSSIBLE MEANINGS

Prior to the pandemic, this photo of one of my friend's children caught my eye. It touched my heart, and I couldn't get it out of my mind, so I called her and asked if I could use it as material for a painting. Everything about it made me think of children: a universal love for pizza; the abandonment of restraint when they can freely dig in the dirt; their curiosity in secretly exploring places they aren't supposed to be; their delight when you play a game with them that they like and for which they ask again and again, even though you've just finished the 20th round; and, of course, that perfect pout, cloaking a hundred possible meanings while grabbing your heartstrings.

Then the pandemic hit. It pulled the rug out from under our lives, threw dire uncertainty into our paths, and confined us to home. The streets became eerily empty, but I continued my daily walk around the neighborhood. Initially, there were only a few other people out walking, and when we encountered each other, we awkwardly left a careful six-foot circle of distance. Then I began noticing laughter. I saw parents in their gardens playing clever and imaginative games with their delighted children.

Gradually, more families started coming out for walks, pulling children in wagons, running together, riding all sorts of bikes, or assisting the little ones in walking their dogs. Even though we would be walking in opposite directions, from across the street, we met each other with friendly greetings and smiles and even some sweet conversations. I do not doubt that many of these families are under tremendous strain and worry, having lost jobs and income and not knowing how the future will unfold, but despite this, there seems to be a desire to reach out. Given what I'm seeing, the thoughtful conversations I am witnessing online and the number of offers of free and creative programs for children that are being shared, I am hopeful that in some way, this pandemic is reorienting our lives and that we are becoming more attentive to each other and to this beautiful trust in our midst: the children.

1 OUR SITUATION

I have always felt immensely fortunate to be an artist, to be able to create art, and to be able to make a career of it. This has been the result of some basic, natural talent, and a huge and unwavering amount of hard work, stubbornness, and determination. I have always believed that art is all about communicating: telling visual stories; expressing feelings and ideas; reaching into my viewers' brains, hearts, memories, and emotions. Likewise, it is about sharing ideas, strategies, and techniques with my students, and helping them to communicate even more. Pay it forward. During the pandemic—"Our Situation"—my art, my studio work, my collectors, students and classes, and countless associated strangers, all coalesced into one gigantic, brilliant, comforting network of communication.

As COVID-19 marched on its inevitable pathway to American shores, and then steadily traveled to every state, county, and municipality within, I watched our world and our lives shut down, as never before in my lifetime. It was bewildering, bizarre, frightening, horrifying, lonely, stultifying, crippling. Bam! Everything stopped.

After a brief pause to catch my breath, gather my wits, and regain my bearings, I just kept painting. I sent out hundreds of emails to students, artists, collectors, and strangers, checking on their health and wellbeing, and offering free instruction, inspiration, and artistic advice. I learned how to Zoom and transformed my in-person watercolor classes into online watercolor classes. Within a year I had taught nearly 200 classes online, reaching many more hundreds of people. I turned what could have been a disastrous ghost-town of a gallery exhibition into a lively, well-appreciated event, by zooming a series of online receptions.

And it all came down to communicating! Being an artist and communicating. The artists, whom you will see and experience within these pages have all been doing just that, each in their own way. Reaching out to people, collectors, readers, appreciators. Communicating via lines, shapes, colors, spaces, textures. And yes, using words as well. We were indeed all clobbered by this situation, but we are using our art to fight back, to remain strong and alert, to stay engaged with people, and to remain *in* the world, beyond our individual studios. We, the creators of watercolors, oil paintings, acrylics, pastels, and drawings, are immensely fortunate to be artists and communicators. This has helped us, and many others, to make sense of Our Situation and to navigate our way through it. Please keep reading, look, and savor. Appreciate, laugh, cry, remember. And remain ever hopeful and grateful.

Alexis Lavine, NWS, WHS, TWSA
Greensboro, North Carolina

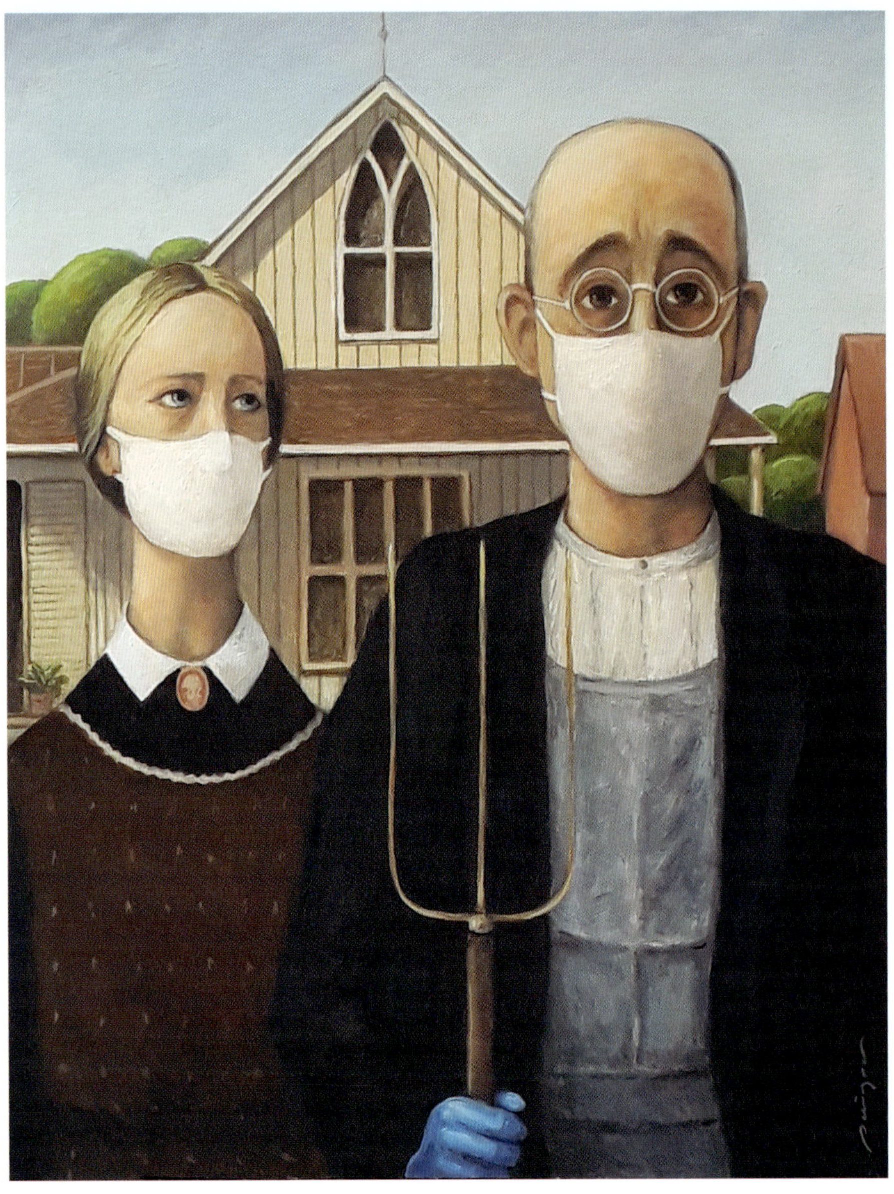

Peter Pettegrew, Florida

AMERICAN SITUATION

I have found it interesting how COVID-19 went from a problem in a distant country to a problem in the heartland of America in such a short period of time. All 50 states are now affected. It has changed everything we know so profoundly. I decided to take an American Icon—*American Gothic* by Grant Wood—and re-paint it under our current situation. In doing so, our country's great iconic artwork would be affected as well.

Not exactly my normal genre—I printed off a picture of *American Gothic* on copy paper and in pencil, made a grid over the top of it. Then I made a corresponding grid on the surface of a primed painting panel. From there, I carefully drew out the image, using the grid to keep it proportionally correct. Then, using a brush that I would normally sign my looser landscapes with, I began putting color into the drawing. It was almost like putting a puzzle together and just as mesmerizing to do. Then, I began to make my changes... In the end, *American Situation* sums up the way I feel about this thing. The wife looks very concerned, gazing at her husband for answers. He in turn looks bewildered, perhaps sliding towards bankruptcy. I'm certain that I am not too far off from what probably summarizes much of how many families are feeling at this very moment.

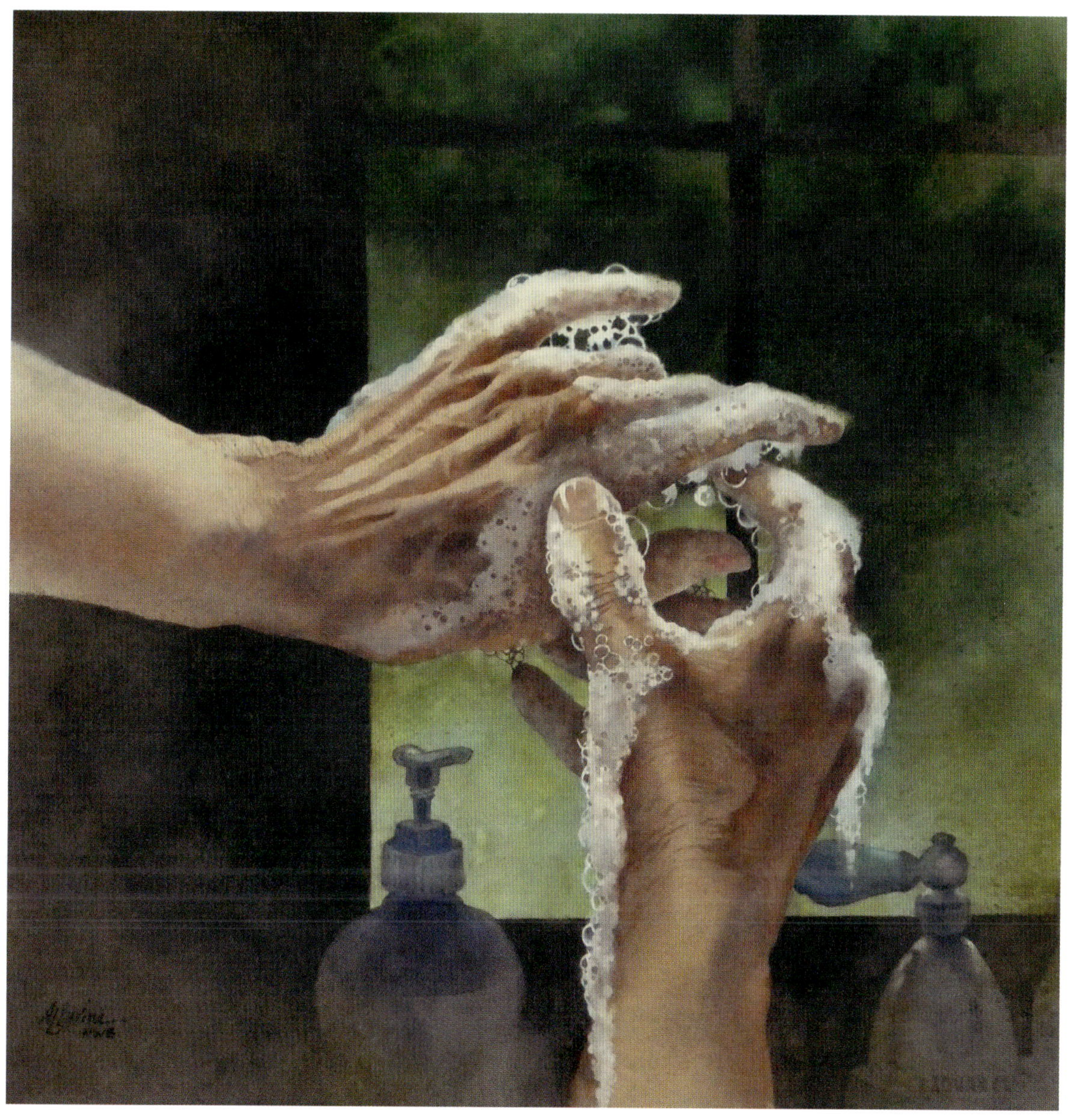

Alexis Lavine, North Carolina
TWENTY SECONDS

How many times a day, since the pandemic began, have we spent 20 seconds washing our hands? We lather up, hum the Happy Birthday song, or whatever we do to measure the time, and then hope that this will magically keep us healthy. I was standing at my sink one day, humming away when I got kind of mesmerized watching my hands, their tandem movement, the slip of the bubbles, the sound of the running water, the scent of the soap. It was a transfixing and transformative moment. And it made me realize that this image—this totally ordinary moment of handwashing—was completely iconic for this weird and scary time we are experiencing.

So, I decided that I wanted to paint my hands. Yes, those are my hands in the painting. I wanted to make them look graceful and even prayerful. I chose to put the window behind them, to remind us of the bigger world beyond this intimate moment and perhaps suggest a bit of hopefulness out there. All that green outside the window—the world is indeed alive! I want my viewers to see my painting and contemplate the various levels of meaning within it, not just the picture. And the next time they wash their hands, perhaps they will experience it in a new way. When art can communicate the beauty and the wonder in an ordinary moment, which we usually don't even think about...that really elevates art to a much more meaningful position.

Kevin McEvoy, New York

THE WINDOW

My family and I moved abroad to Europe for an undetermined period of time, leaving our home in New York with a willed intention to "live deliberately," as Thoreau had done a couple of centuries or so ago. For Thoreau, his was a desire to front only the essential facts of life; however, for my wife, three sons, and myself, our act of living deliberately was to move beyond a painful chapter in our life. We were grieving over a great loss and wanted to remind ourselves that life is beautiful, that the world is big, and that our light and momentary pain was a mere blip in the broad arc of time. London welcomed us with open arms, and thanks to the generosity of a wonderful and gifted artist friend, Josephine, we were able to live and work in her stunning painting studio. Jo is a gifted artist who had custom-tailored everything in her studio for her own painting and sculpting purposes, and so everything was ready to go for me.

The St. Paul's studios are a series of wrought iron and glass painting studios in the heart of London, renowned throughout the world for their design. The uppermost floors feature a soaring north-facing window and a massive studio, while the lower two floors consist of bedrooms, baths, and living areas, and yet another smaller painting studio. The best news was that my good friend, James Hayes, owns the painting studio a few doors down from where we were staying. I have the deepest respect for James as an artist; his work is beautiful, his knowledge of the craftsmanship of oil painting is rare, and his work ethic is indefatigable. Not to mention, he is a member of the rarest breed of artist—a generous and uplifting soul who defines his own success not only by what he himself produces but also by how much he can lift up all other artists around him. I am lucky to call him my friend, and I was extremely fortunate to be painting a few doors down from him.

Much of a professional oil painter's life consists of wrestling with logistics: Where can I find a studio? How can I get better lighting? Where can I find better materials? How can I reach my audience? How can I eliminate distraction? But in this studio, my Walden Pond, none of these problems were facing me—with the greatest art supply stores in the world just a few blocks away, with models abundant, with the problems of lighting completely solved for me, I could just paint. And then came whispers of the Coronavirus. As I set up my canvas on the easel, there was news of the spread of the virus in Italy, and the grim toll it was taking on the population. As I mixed my paints, the newspapers were relaying mounting fears daily. As I tinted my canvas, the first wave of patients was flooding the hospitals of northern Italy.

It was at this time that my family and I visited the Churchill War Rooms. Originally just basement storage rooms with low ceilings, these rooms were repurposed into underground bunkers. While bombs fell from overhead and wiped out entire areas of London, it was from here that the military operation of the United Kingdom commanded its force in defense of the free world. It was here that Churchill's chair still remains, with the marks of his fingernails scratched into the arms of the chair from which he conducted the most important wartime meetings. It was here that generals slept on makeshift cots. It was here that buckets had to function as toilets. It was here that Churchill had a sign painted, reading "Please understand there is no depression in this house and we are not interested in the possibilities of defeat. They do not exist."

I returned to my studio, and the February sky was a characteristic London, leaden gray. My sons were sitting on and beneath the window, quietly reading. My wife sat with a cup of tea, thinking. I wasn't thinking at all about my artwork, I was really thinking only about my family. The future was so uncertain, the sky was so bleak. I picked up a pad and began to sketch. There was no depression in this house. I began to paint. There was no possibility of defeat.

I painted sometimes for 10 hours a day, over the month. We took occasional trips to hike in the English countryside, to stroll in parks along the Thames, to visit 221B Baker Street. I painted furiously at every moment in between, rising early, working through the day, sometimes staying up late through the night. Only in contemplating the idea of courage did I understand the iconic sculptures and works depicting London's own heroes. Saint-Gaudens's solemn statue of Abraham Lincoln was in Westminster Square, silently clutching his coat, head bowed. Rodin's *Burghers of Calais* were beside the Thames, nooses around their necks. The Roman copy of the Hellenistic sculpture, *The Dying Gaul*, was in Syon House, holding himself up while blood rushed from his mortal wound; Lysippus's *Silenus* was also in Syon House, clutching his son Dionysus and contemplating the gravity of his role as father and protector. Lord Leighton worked in the Royal Borough of Chelsea, painting enormous frescoes depicting the Arts of Industry as Applied to War and Peace, while the city of London witnessed cholera outbreaks and threats of war.

We booked our flight home to New York, and on the final day before our flight, I put my brush down. With the specter of quarantine looming, and with the uncertainty of international shipping, I chose to leave the painting in the studio, in the care of my friend. The painting is still in London. We are all now quarantined to our house in New York. I am sitting at my drawing desk, the birds are outside of my window, frenetic with spring fervor, and the boys are setting the dinner table. The newspapers are announcing one of the greatest losses in stocks in the history of the American economy. New York City has been shut down. Thousands of people are contracting COVID-19. Some are dying.

Pinned to the wall beside me is a poem by another individual who found inspiration in London, Rudyard Kipling. "If you can meet with triumph or disaster, and treat those two imposters just the same..." What do you do when you meet with disaster? You wake up in the morning; you continue to raise your children; you lead the Union army in the Civil War; you pour the coffee; you load the truck; you plant the victory garden. You paint. You carry on. There is no possibility of defeat.

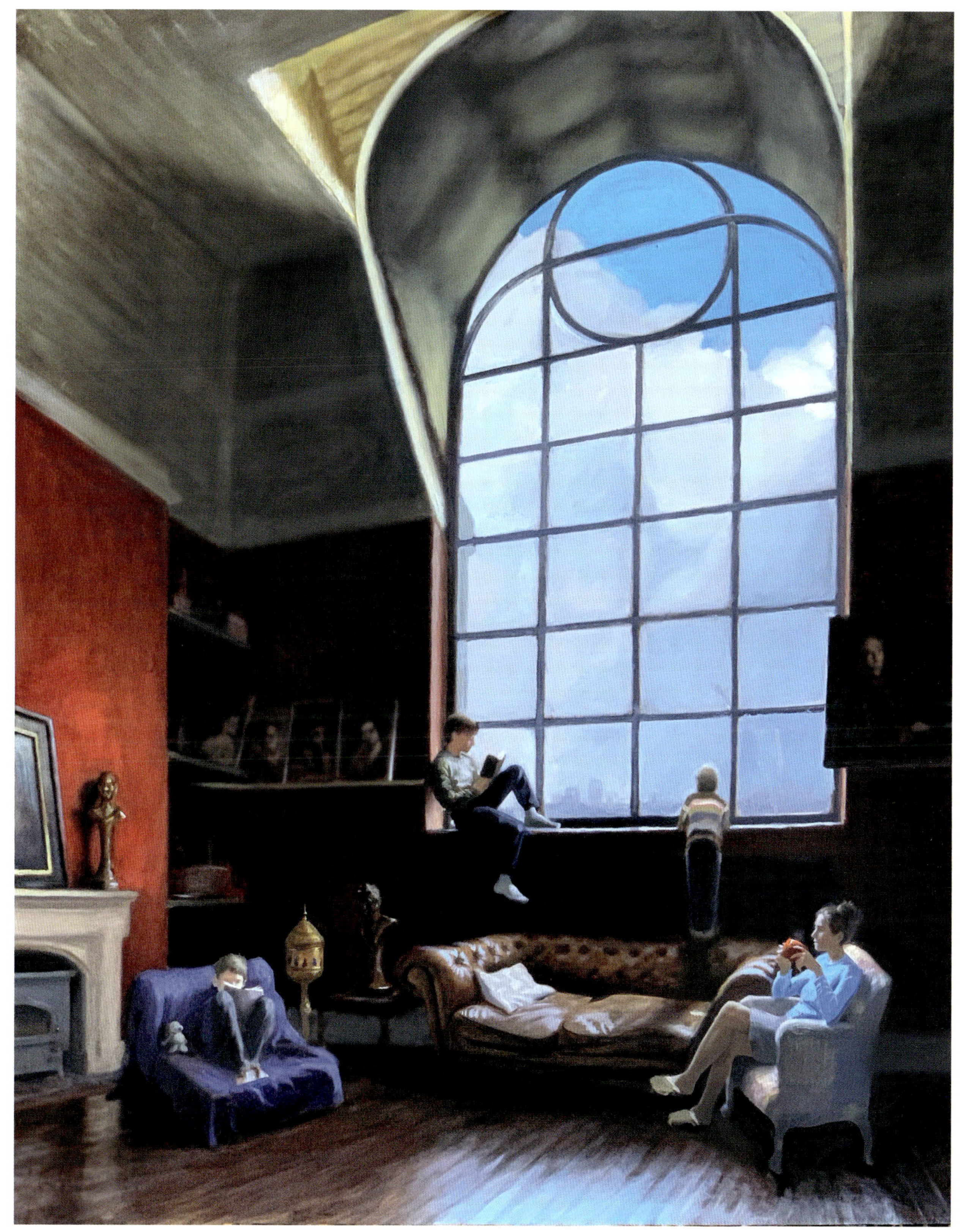

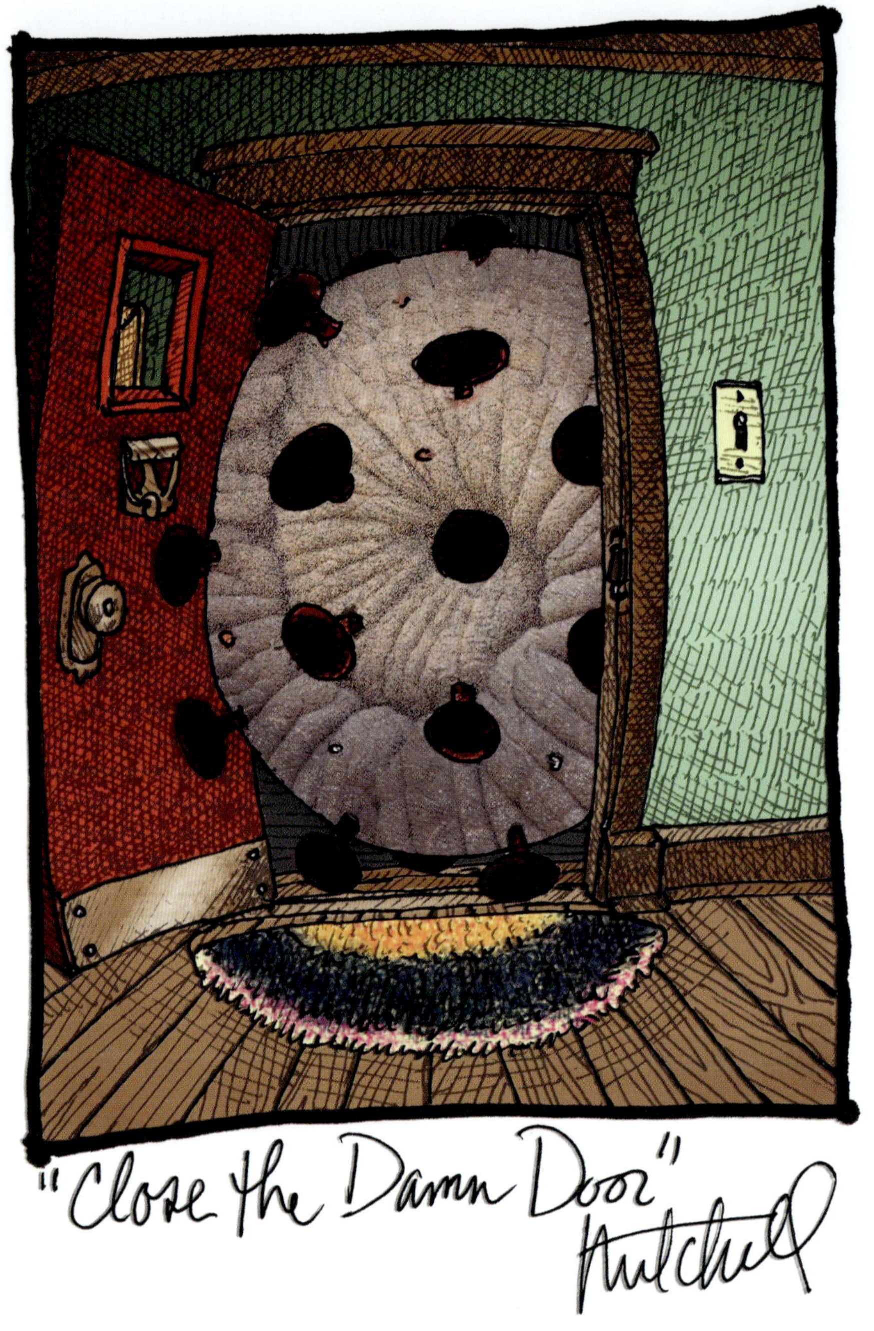

Kurt Mitchell, Illinois

CLOSE THE DAMN DOOR

Close the Damn Door is from a series of 81 pen and ink illustrations Kurt made in response to the COVID-19 pandemic. He drew these almost daily from March 16 (when Illinois "shut down") through June 24, 2020. Most of the illustrations (though not this one) feature 17th-century plague doctors thrust into the world of the 21st-century pandemic. He knew that he had something with *Close the Damn Door* as he colorized it in preparation for a poster for future art displays.

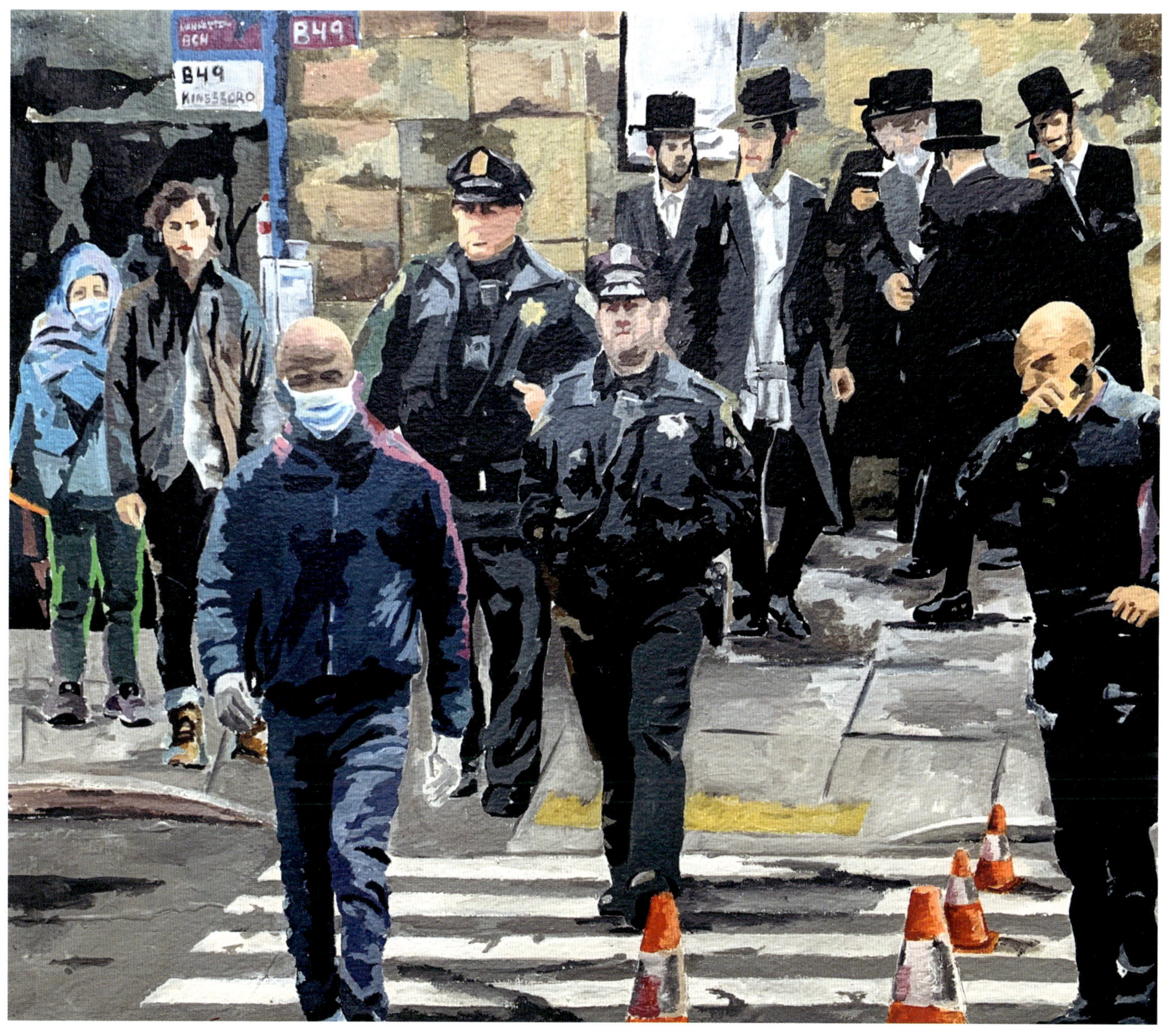

Paul Morado, California
10-66 (SUSPICIOUS PERSONS)

During the inception of COVID-19, many Americans were removed from logic and turned to fear. In this act of despair, the finger was pointed at whoever was believed to be the culprit behind this vicious virus. In my experience as a Black American, I've watched our race become a scapegoat for almost every component that was attached to the spread of COVID-19. Even in the act of taking full precautions, many Americans look to us as what police would call a 10-66: suspicious persons.

Tom Sadler, Florida

GULF STREAM PANDEMIC

The emotions that arose during this pandemic have been feelings of isolation, but also survival. The painting of *The Gulf Stream* by Winslow Homer came to mind, depicting a man not only isolated but also faced with an unknown future and at the total mercy of nature herself. It's the feeling of being "out of control" of the situation that gnaws at you. Some other force is steering the ship where you once had the wheel. This man drifts in his dismasted, rudderless boat, surrounded by sharks and with a waterspout approaching, which in this case represents the pandemic on the horizon. I added a coronavirus in the waters to add to the impending doom. But amidst it all, he and we, have not given up hope. He scans the horizon and unbeknownst to his gaze a distant ship symbolizes his rescue. For me, it now represents a vaccine or some other positive indication that we will be rescued as well and that this too will one day be over.

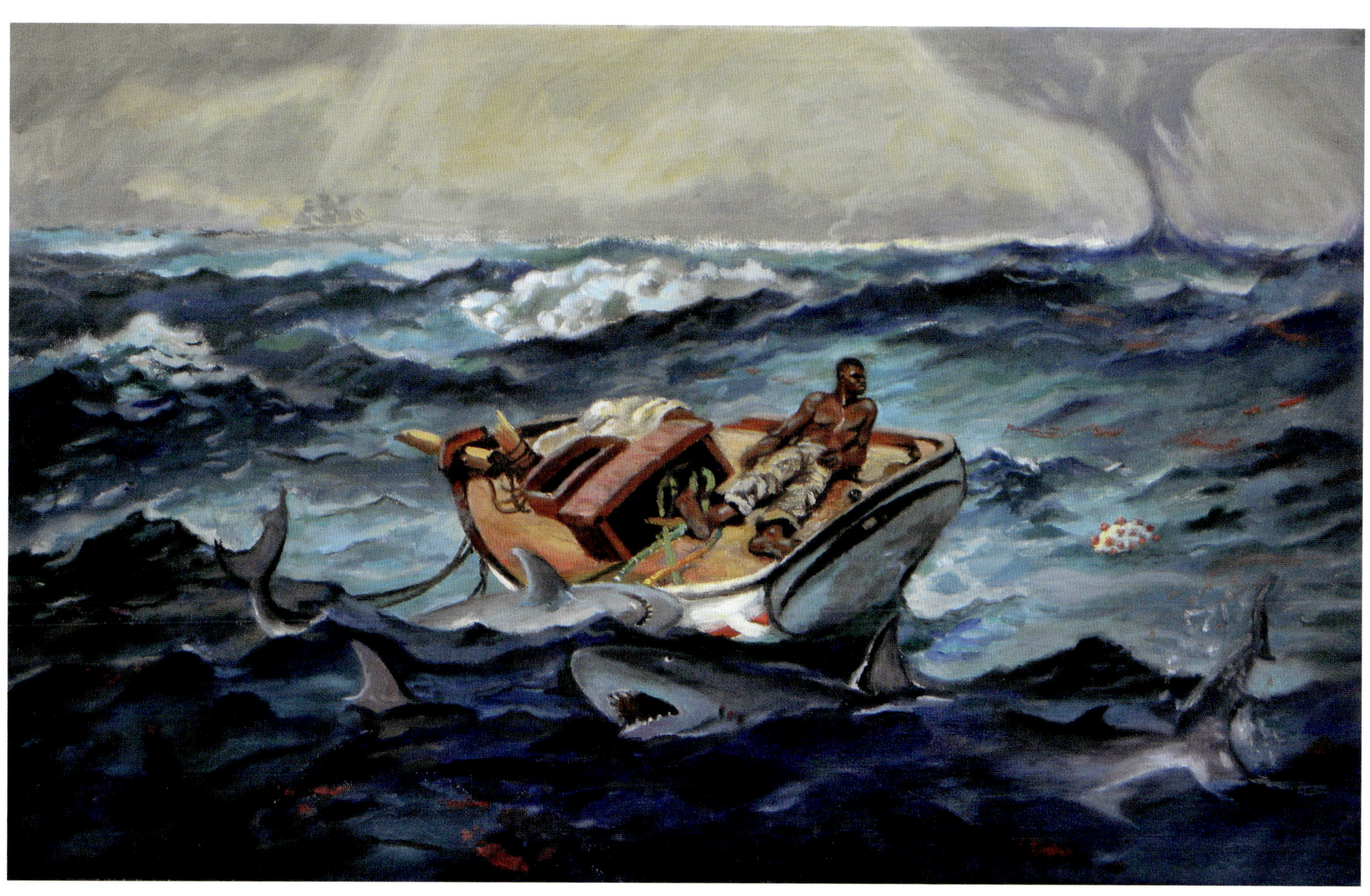

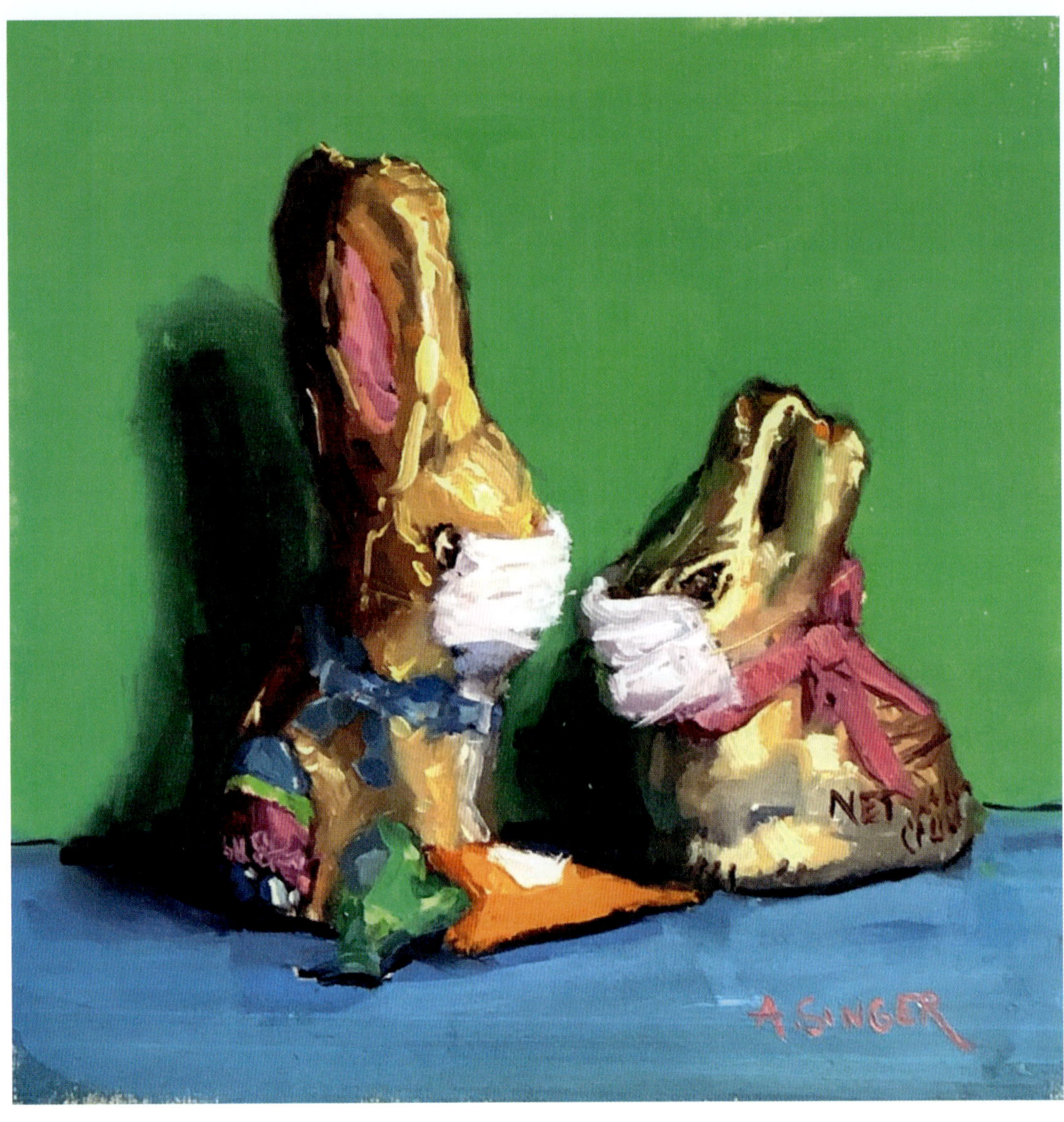

Anne Singer, Maryland

LOVE IN A TIME OF CORONAVIRUS

For the last four springs, I have painted a still life featuring chocolate Easter bunnies. When I did my set up in the second week of March 2020, COVID-19 had burst on the news in the US. I decided to make tiny little masks for my bunnies to wear for the still life. My painting studio is located in the home of my husband's parents. My mother-in-law had been a huge fan of my desire to learn to paint and had purchased a home with a north-light studio with me in mind. She was thrilled with the set up for the 2020 chocolate bunny painting.

Shortly after I finished the painting, my mother-in-law fell ill. After a week in bed, I felt we needed to take her to the local emergency room. She had pneumonia and a critically low oxygen level and had to be admitted. It was the last time I saw her in person. Within three days we had the news that she had tested positive for COVID-19 and was being flown to a hospital with an appropriate ICU. Her husband also tested positive, but thankfully did not become ill. My husband and I isolated with him for the next three weeks. She was on a ventilator for three weeks and then passed away.

Love In A Time Of Coronavirus is her painting.

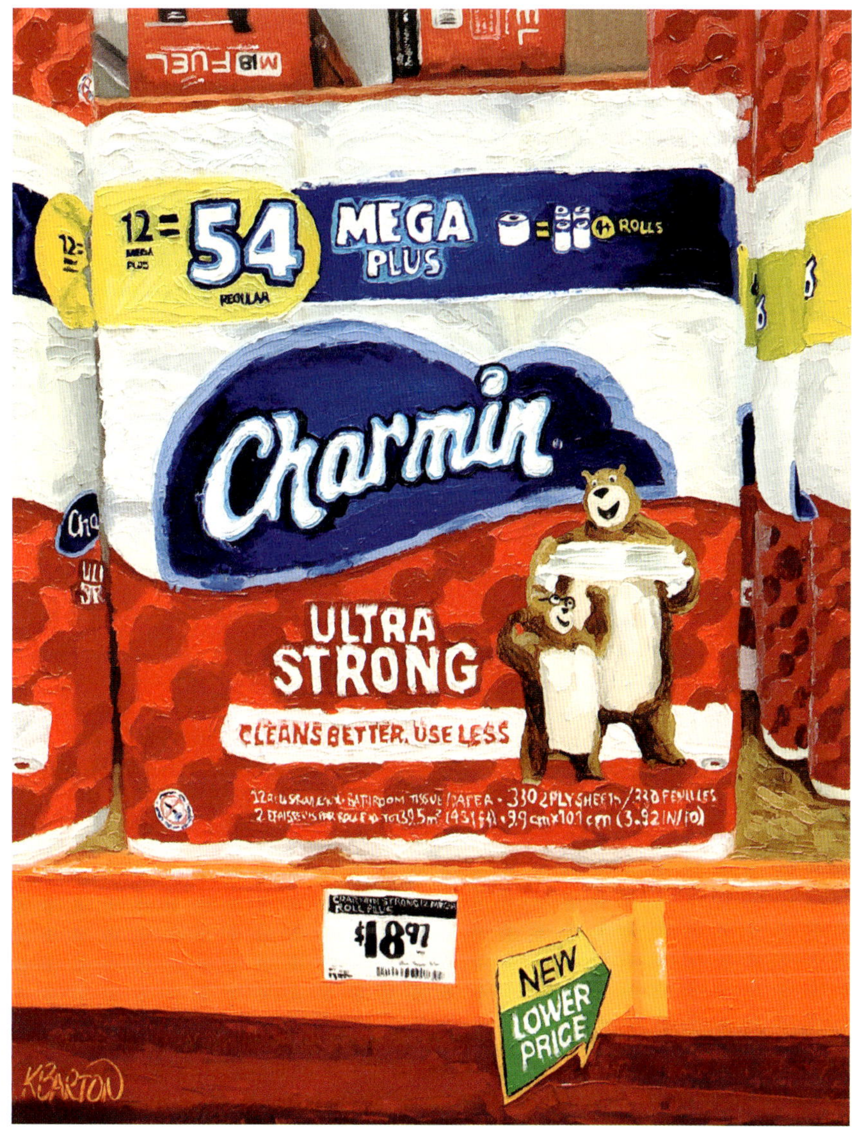

Karen Barton, Washington

DO YOU NEED SOME

My paintings usually represent popular food items that are associated with the era we live in. However, this painting, *Do You Need Some?*, was created based on events that occurred in March 2020.

I could not have guessed what was to unfold, but this painting represents a story to be told in many households across the nation. It all began as a typical day of shopping. My husband needed some items from Home Depot and I decided to go along. On our way to the cash register, we took a detour to pick up some shop towels and I spotted the Charmin toilet paper. It was wonderfully bright with cute bears on the packaging. Although not my usual subject matter, I couldn't resist and took a photo of it sitting on the vibrant orange shelf.

I asked my husband if we needed to buy a package and told him that I had heard that there "might be a run on toilet paper." We decided it wasn't necessary since we had a big Costco-size package at home. Little did we know! It was as if the very next day the US ran out of toilet paper. There was absolutely none to be found! Needless to say, I caught myself saying that we should have bought it when it was still available. "Should have" seem to be words uttered too many times since March 2020 when America realized it had a COVID-19 pandemic on its hands.

I decided to paint the Charmin toilet paper for its delightful packaging and because of the COVID-19 toilet paper shortage. As I painted this fun subject, I often thought we "should have" bought it that day.

Jacqueline Chanda, Arizona

GIRL WITH A TURQUOISE FACE MASK

This 12x9 inch oil painting entitled *Girl with a Turquoise Face Mask* was painted a few months after a trip to Singapore in January 2020.

I had made plans back in August 2019 to travel to Singapore to visit a friend. A week before leaving, my friend sent me a text to warn me about a virus outbreak that had originated in China and was spreading throughout Southeast Asia. She wasn't sure how serious it was but just wanted me to be cautious. I decided to travel anyway. I took all precautions, bought hand sanitizer, sanitizing wipes, immune-boosting supplements, and purchased a few masks before most people in the US had even started preparing. I wore my mask during the flight in spite of the fact that "experts" were saying, at that time, that masks would not help or that it was useless to wear a mask of any type to protect you from infection unless it was an N-95. I wore mine anyway and I think it really helped, along with the other precautions I took, to protect me from getting infected.

While in Singapore, things got worse around the world and I noticed many more people were wearing masks in public, even little children. This painting was done from a photo that I took in Singapore at a Hawker Center—an open-air complex and food court commonly found near public housing estates or transport hubs in Singapore. At this Hawker Center, there was a Chinese New Year celebration in progress. The little girl in the painting was watching the ceremony and wearing a face mask as a precaution against the virus, a sign of things to come. Now we in the US are also wearing masks to stave off the spread of COVID-19. Who would have thought that it would come to this!

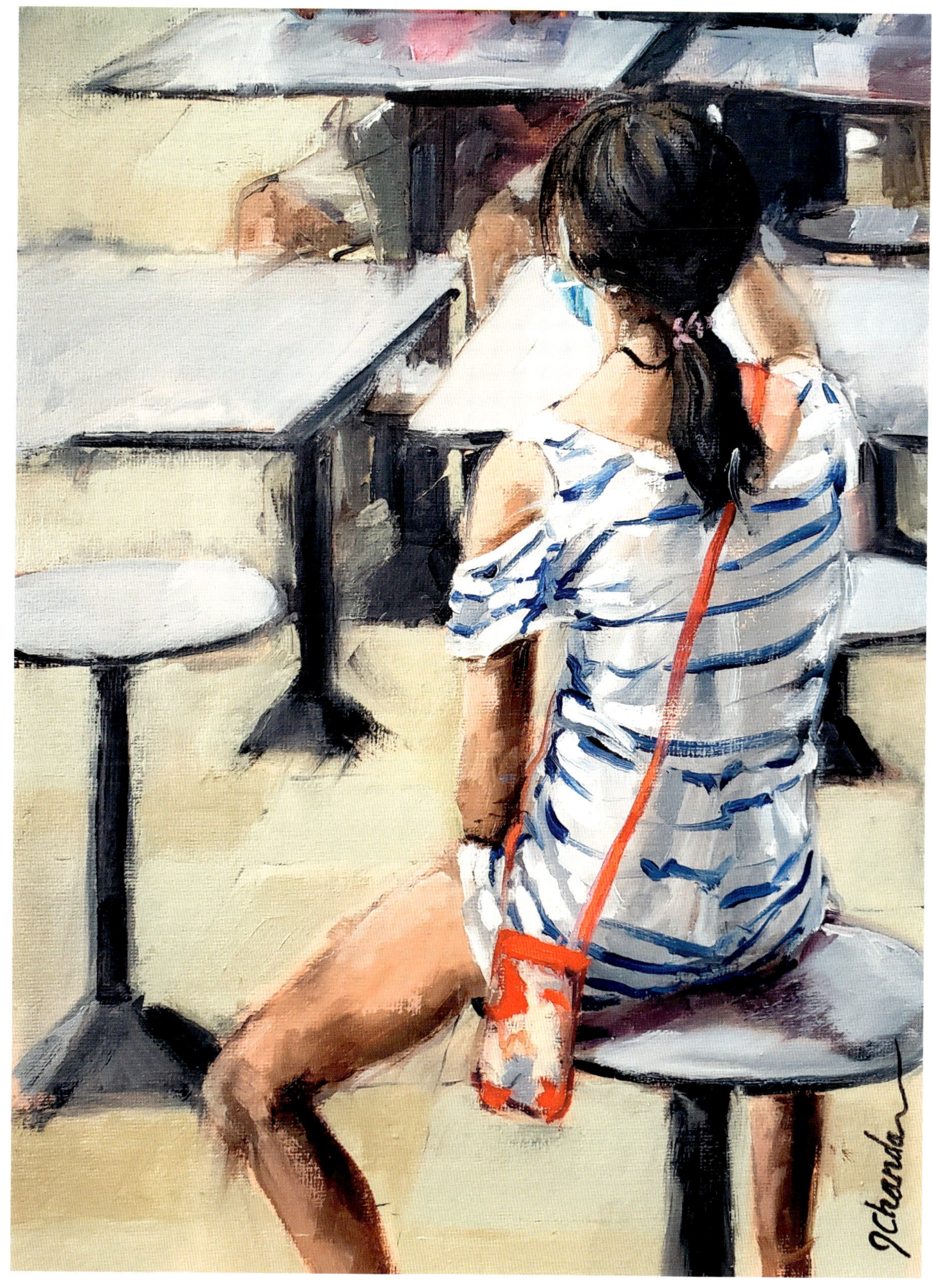

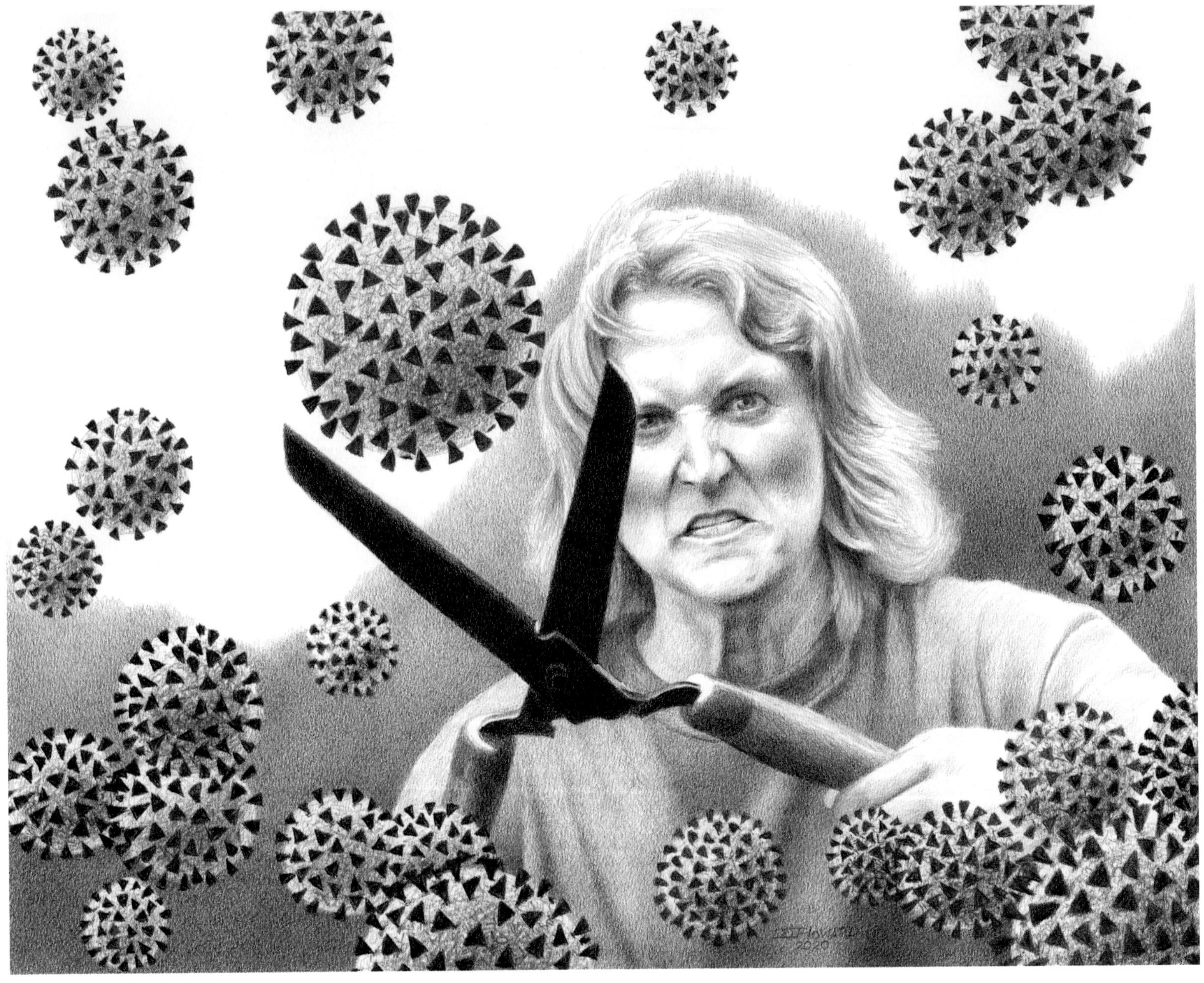

Denise Howard, California

THE ANGRY RESPONSE

This is my response to COVID-19. The shears symbolize the many powerful tools we have, none of which work against this new menace, so our efforts to date are futile and frustrating. It's an unflattering self-portrait because my feelings are not pretty. The backdrop is a graph of the cases. I portrayed it in black and white because the situation has drained all the color from the year.

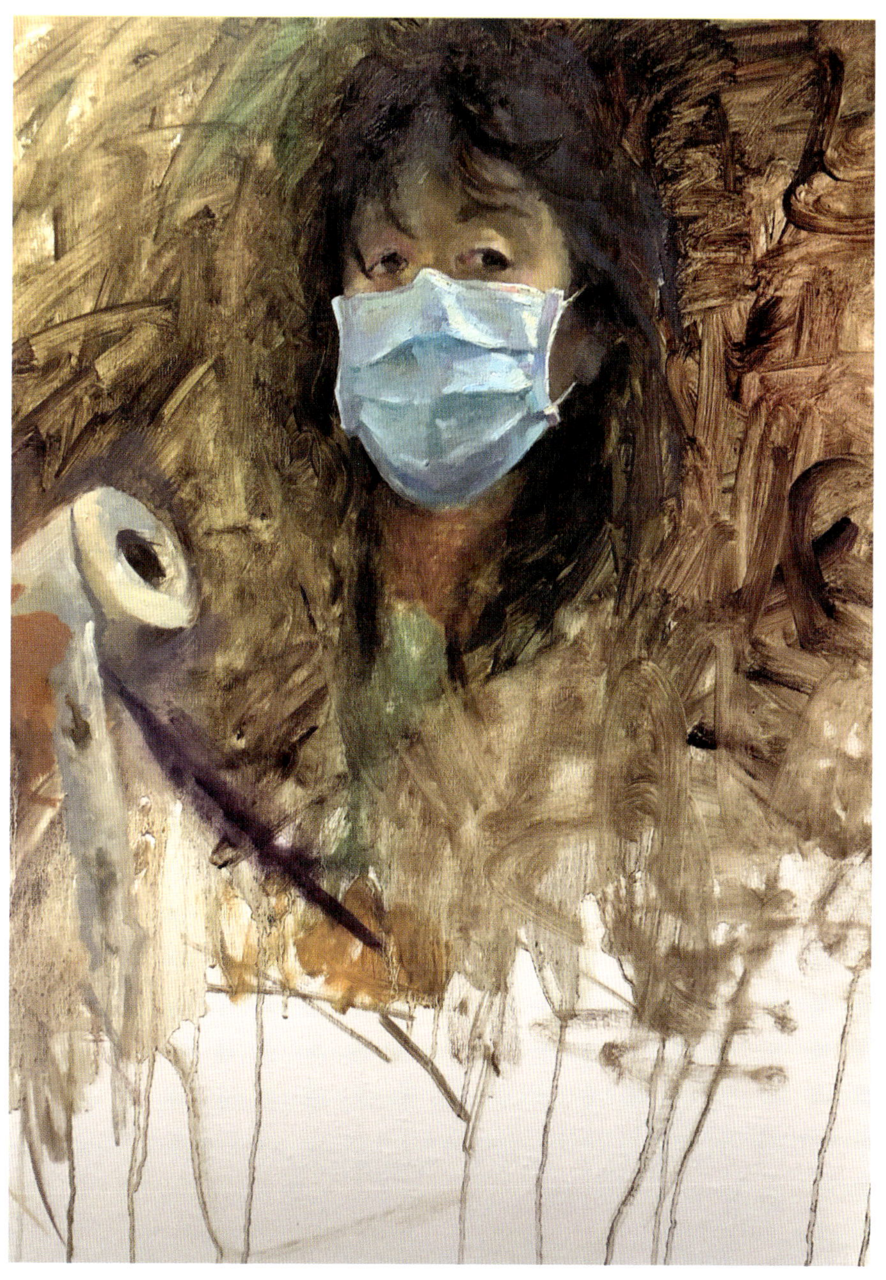

Hai-Ou Hou, Maryland
THE NEW FASHION

When I painted this self-portrait in March, the Coronavirus was spreading and taking hold in the United States. The mad rush for masks, hand sanitizer, and even toilet paper began. The general anxiety over the virus is expressed through the chaotic brushwork of the background while my eyes reflect the troubled emotional state. In *The New Fashion*, masks supplant make-up, and one accessorizes with toilet paper. Like the best fad, everybody wants them, and they fly off the shelves. The new fashion is the new chic.

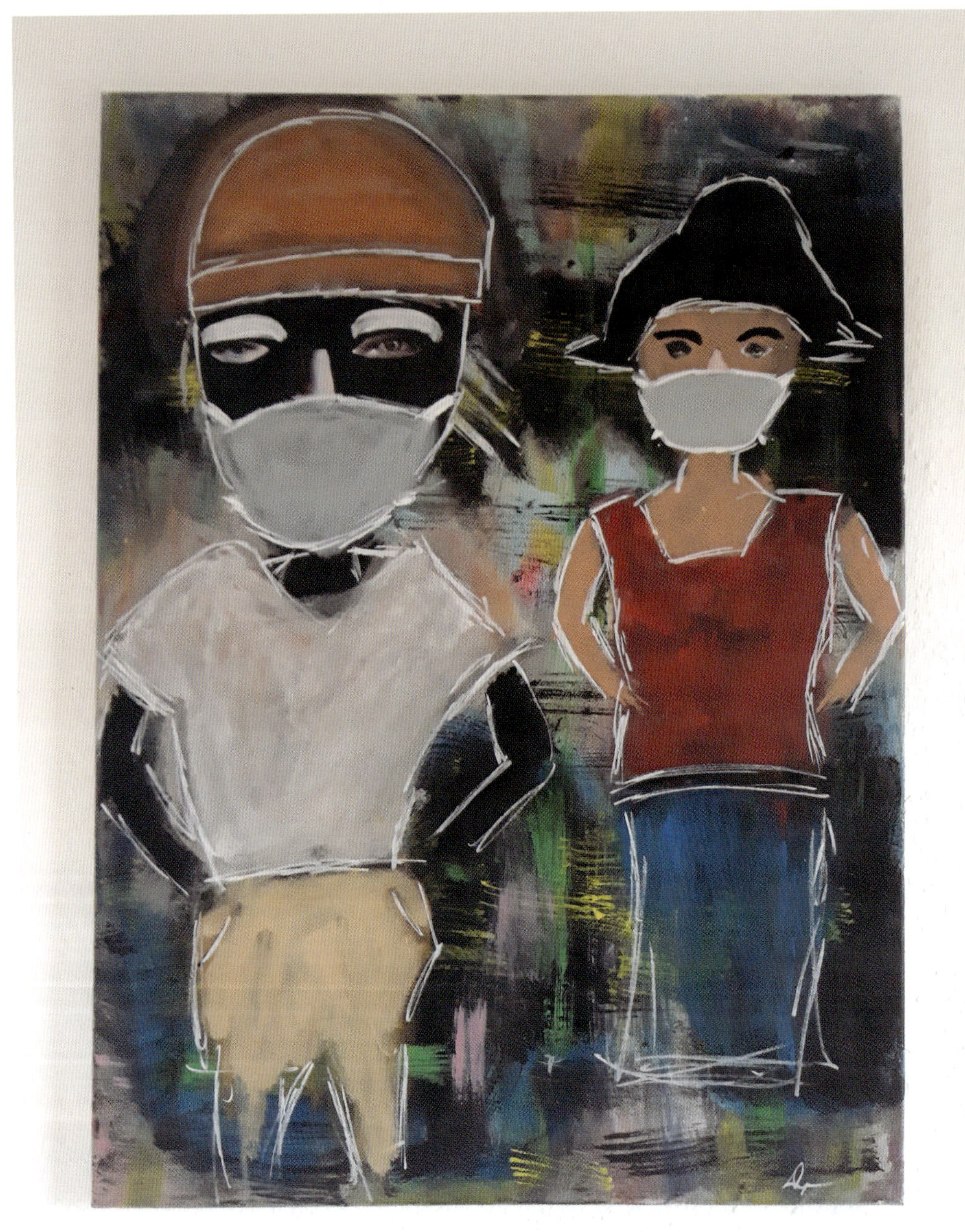

Diyan Antonio Duke, Germany

THE NEW NORM

I created this piece to describe the feeling I had of the unknown that our world was walking into at this time. Information was changing daily about what to do or not to do. However, the singular most polarizing reference point of the whole pandemic has been the mask, as the symbol of our new norm.

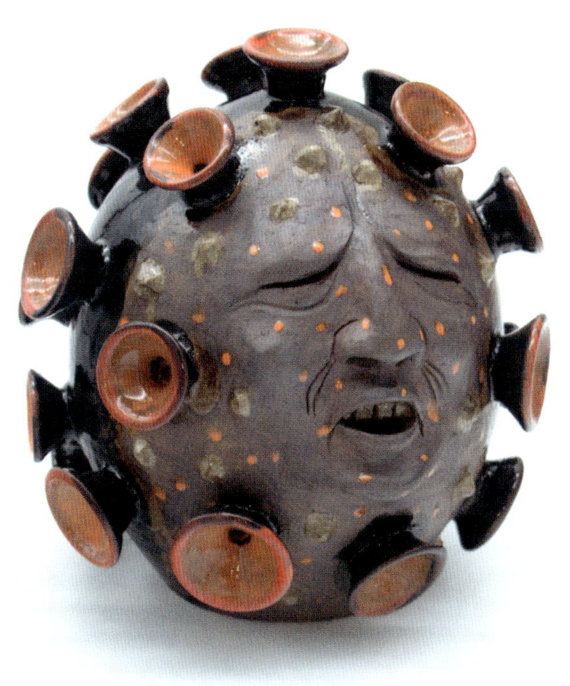

Peter Jones, New York

COVID HEAD

Because my work is done in solitude for the most part, I did not seem to notice a big difference in my day-to-day routine. I wasn't sure if it would affect me. After a while, it became clear that outside and in my community the world was different. I began to sculpt a series of creatures that represented the COVID-19 virus. I had done a series showing indigenous women being harmed by an unseen evil in recent years—a perpetrator that is still at large. At least with this virulent disease, we know what it is and how to fight it. Another series I did was of masked people, after the mask had become ubiquitous with everyday life. Eventually, the virus began to affect people close to my family. The sculpture of the coronavirus head was the latest rendition of the virus causing the pandemic and I was hoping it would be the last.

2 PEOPLE

When I was invited to participate in the Great American Paint In®, I imagined the pandemic would not last long, nor affect me too much. I completed my drawing, *Dreamer*, in the Spring of 2020, with a sense of optimism. At that point, I thought the reflected light in the drawing was an appropriate representation of "the light at the end of the tunnel" (the end of the pandemic). Right now, after a year of living with fear and isolation, I realize that I have used that phrase many, many times, and that "light" sometimes seems very far away. It does, however, shine brightly on the figure in my painting, lighting the way, and reflecting hope.

Barbara Fox
Little Valley, New York

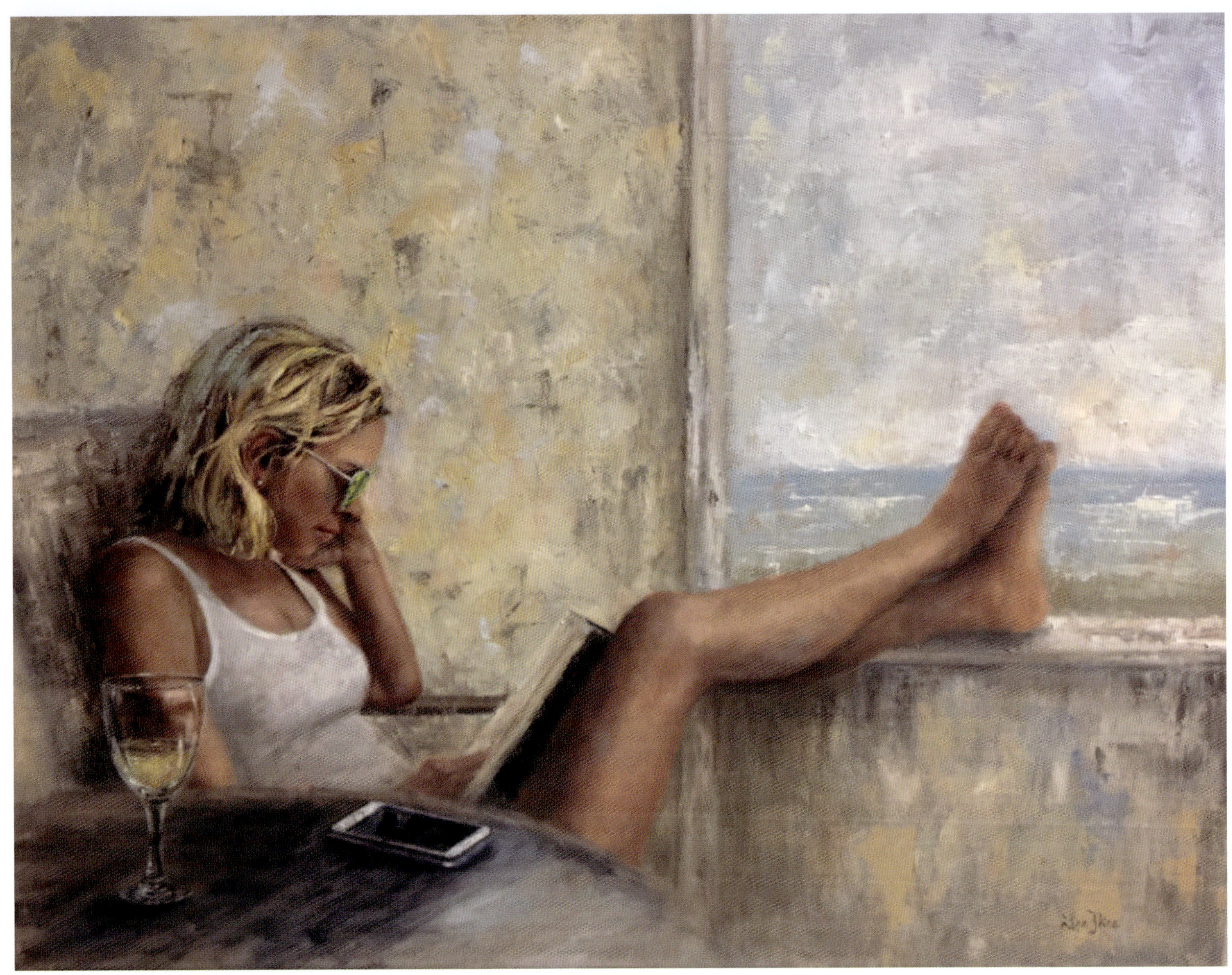

Lisa Price, Alabama

BEACH CHILL

I chose this painting because 2020 has been a difficult year for everyone. This year has provided us with an opportunity to reflect on what we've temporarily lost and to focus on what really matters in life. It has forced me to slow down, be still, and appreciate the beauty in God's creation, and to also enjoy the small, simple pleasures in life...such as a good book and glass of wine while watching the waves roll in on a deserted beach.

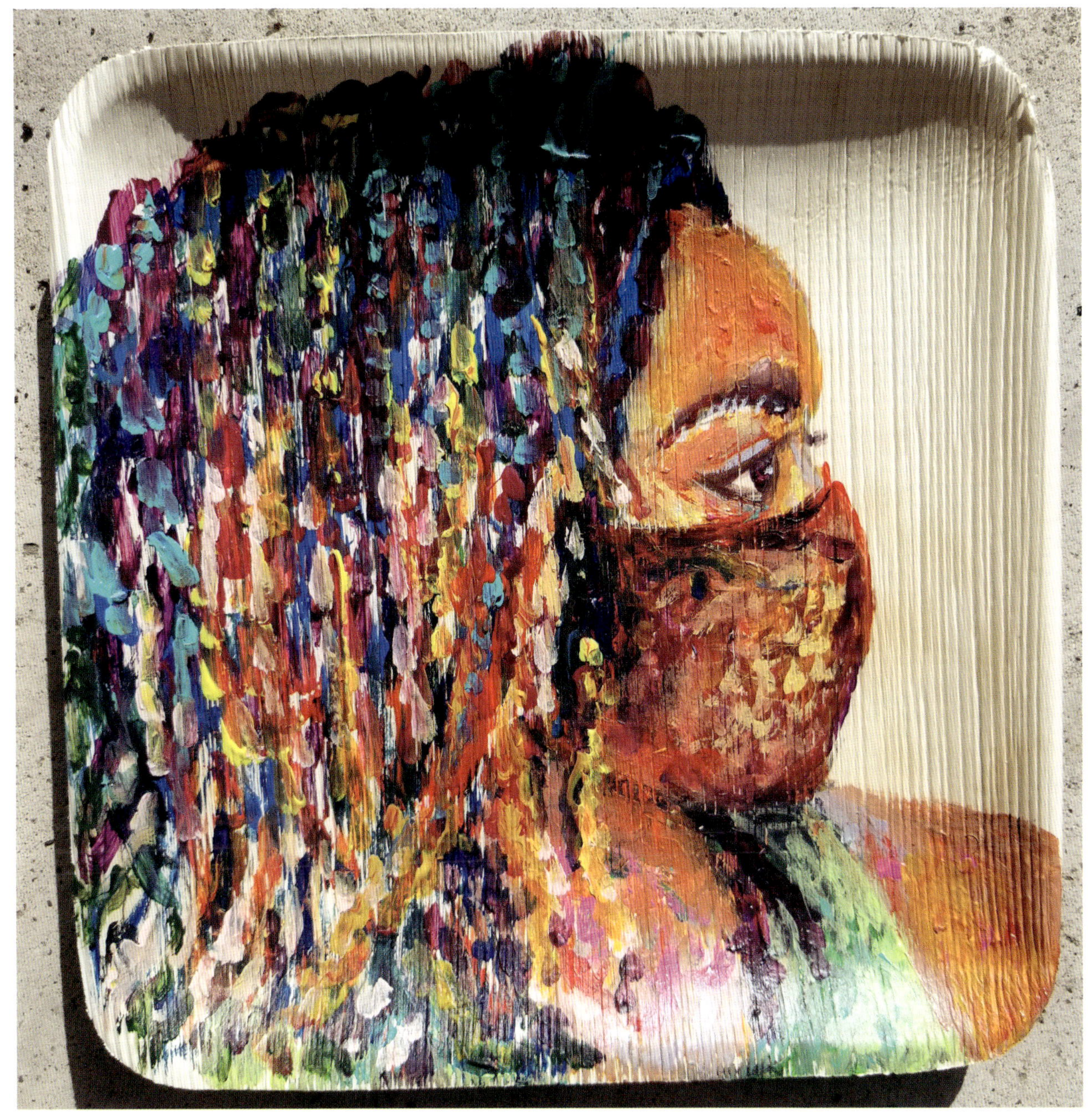

LaShonda Cooks, Texas
SHONDA'S MASK

This image is based on a photo taken Easter 2020, in which I modeled a pair of my friend's custom masks. This painting is part of my "Hair Story" series, but also captures the adaptability and perseverance of the human spirit.

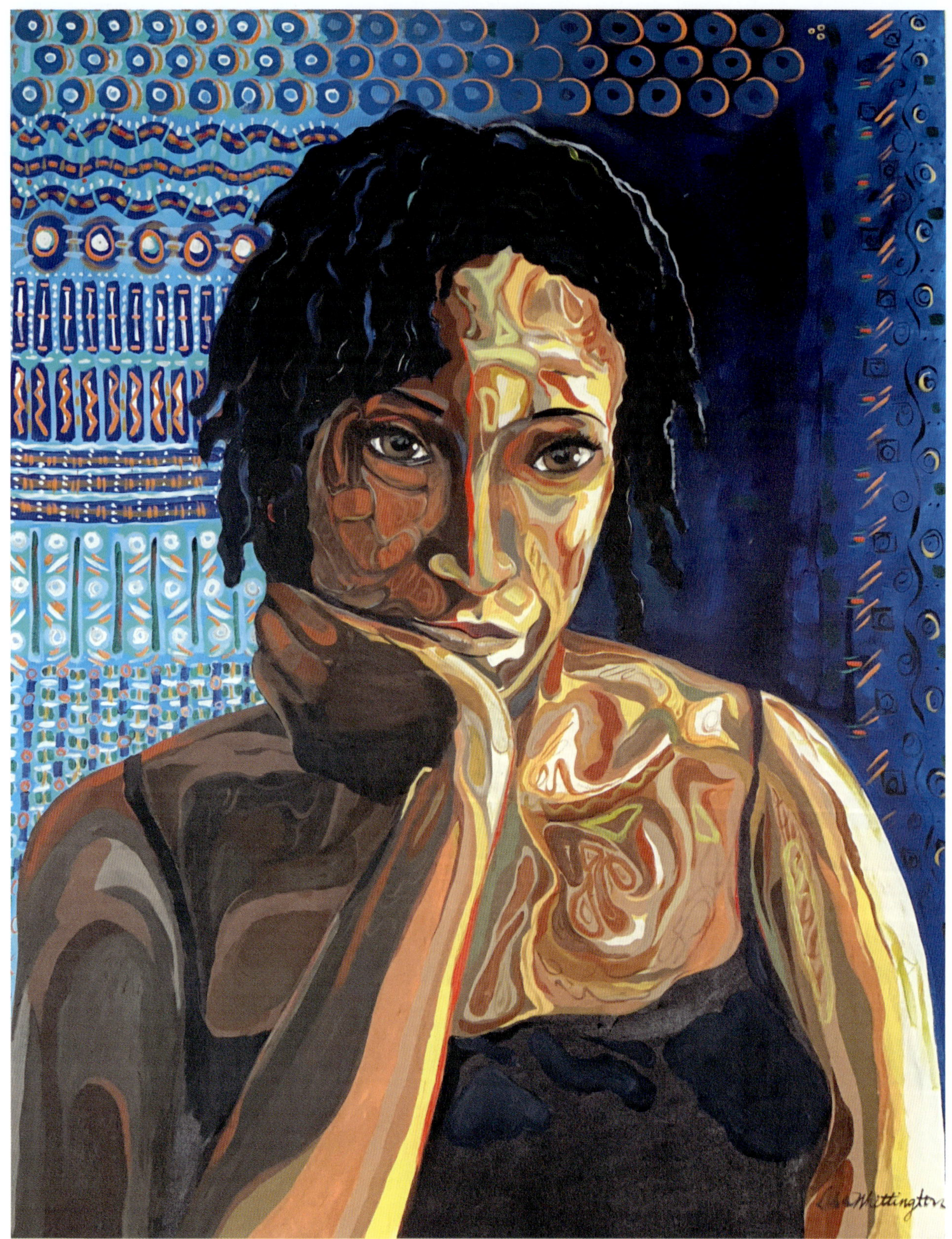

Lisa Whittington, Georgia

WHERE DO YOU GO FROM HERE LISA WHITTINGTON?

Where do I go from here? How do I get there? Where is "there," and how do I know when I arrive? These questions permeate my thoughts as life has definitely taken on new meaning. The pandemic made me examine the world, myself, and my art a little closer. I have been spared to live a little longer and blessed to create some more.

A self-portrait I created just a few years back sits like a queen ruling from her throne, centralized over the fireplace. Her eyes are pensive and demanding and she is postured to continuously question my existence and my purpose every time I see her. I come home—she looks at me. I leave—she watches me go. I cry, yell, sing, and fall asleep on the floor from an exhaustive workday—and she is there in the same position with the same conversation: "Where do you go from here, Lisa Whittington?"

Sometimes she was the only one I would have to talk to, and she reminds me of the importance of touch. Her chin pensively rests in her hand, feeling her face. Even though her flesh is acrylic, I mimic her touch on my face and I thank my art for reminding me that I am human.

For people home alone like me during the pandemic, a touch meant everything. I remember going to the doctor and the nurse touched my arm to take my blood pressure, and I realized that that was the first human touch I had had in a long time. What a difference a pandemic can make.

Sometimes we don't realize the true power of what we paint or why we are painting it. Sometimes, as artists, we paint ahead of our own times. Sometimes the answer is revealed at a later time, like it is now for me as I'm staring back at myself through a portrait. Everything has taken on a new and deeper meaning, intensified by the pandemic. Will I be okay? Will we be okay? My purpose—living and creating and being an artist—escalated during the pandemic. I would sit on my couch and stare back at my acrylic mirror image. My thoughts run through my mind, my ever-racing mind. In a world of time where life is continually being purged from the earth by a pandemic, I appreciate that she reminds me that I am still here.

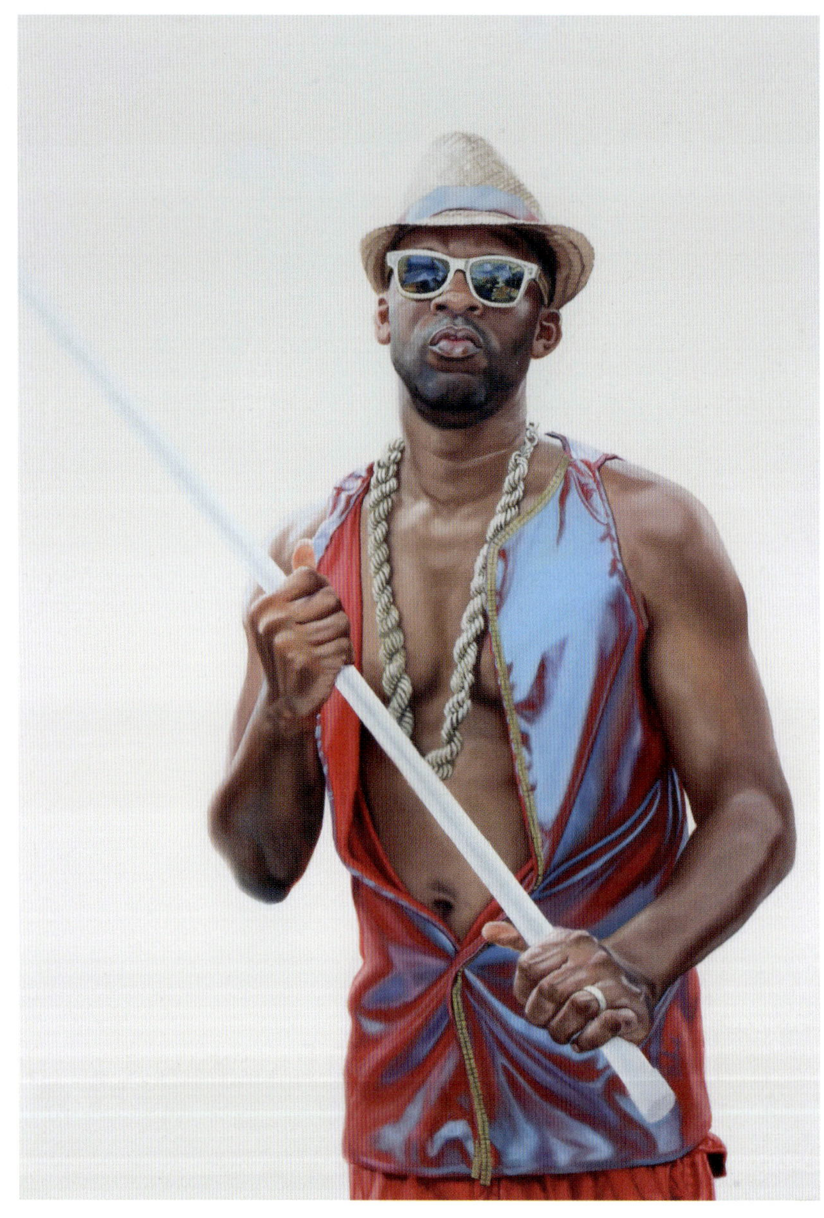

Weldon B. Ryan, Florida
DE FLAG MON

Caribbean people have contributed greatly to America. With the exception of Jean-Michel Basquiat, however, the art world has not been receptive to Caribbean-themed art such as *De Flag Mon*, done in a contemporary realistic style. I paint about the Caribbean Carnival and about the Afro-Caribbean diaspora. *De Flag Mon* was painted to depict Caribbean Carnival with "De Flag Mon" belonging to the Haitian Mas band Ti Chapo as a break-out piece. The history of this Caribbean country is full of pride and determination despite it being the poorest country in this hemisphere. Pride is shown on the face of the male subject in his heroic stance and rendition. My hope is *De Flag Mon* and my many other paintings about our Caribbean fine art culture and community will spur interest in this segment of art.

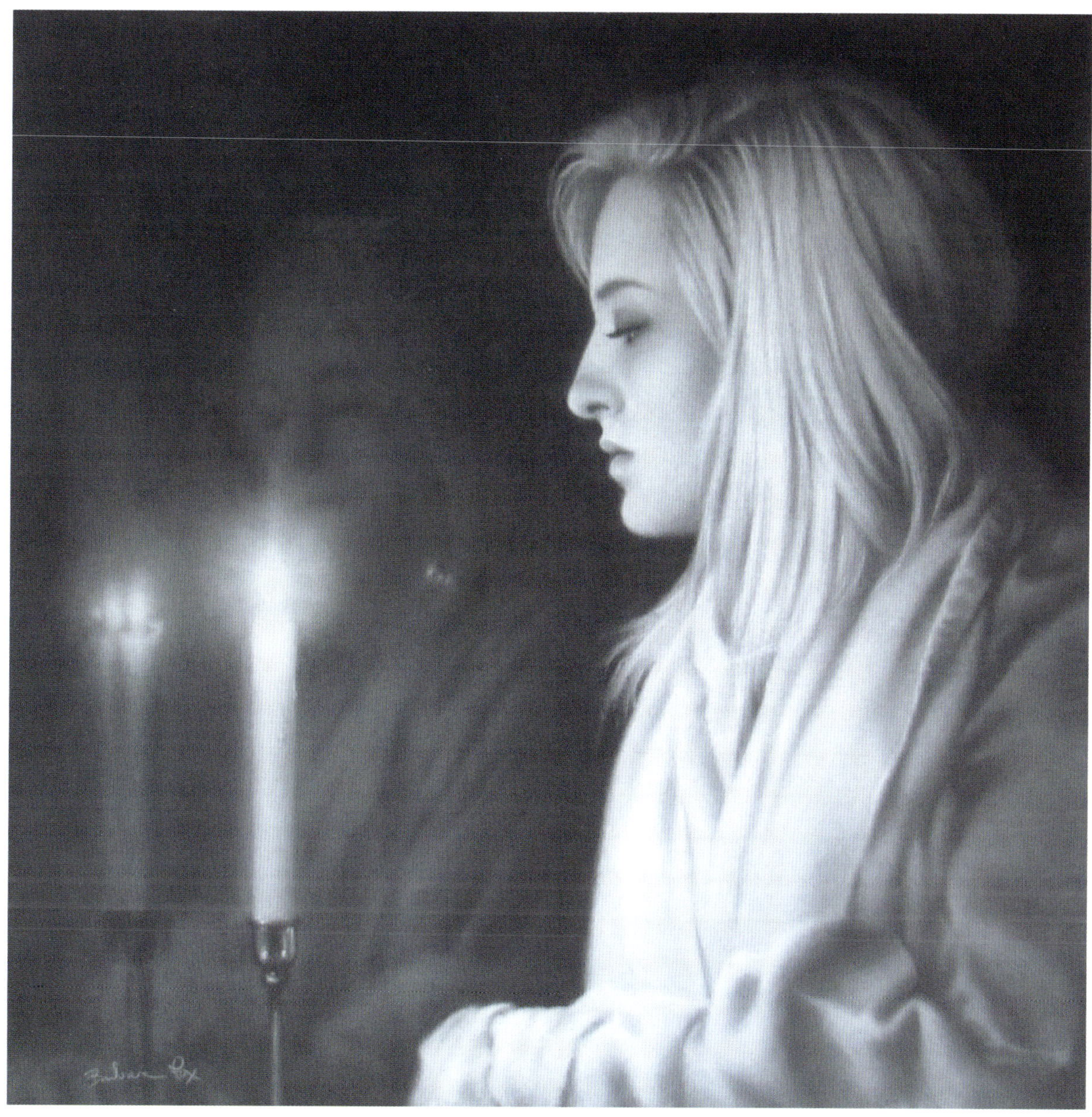

Barbara Fox, New York
DREAMER

This drawing was originally begun in 2018, as a relatively simple image of a young woman with a candle. It had a sleepy, dreamy quality, so I titled it *Dreamer*. At the time, I felt it needed something more, but I couldn't decide what. So, I just lived with it in my studio to see if or when inspiration would strike. As the pandemic loomed, and my state was in lockdown, I felt personally safe, but at the same time felt the fear and heartbreak in my family, friends, community, and planet. Conversely, I also recognize that many of us feel grateful for what we have and imagine a better world when it is safe once again. A few weeks ago, I heard John Lennon's song "Imagine", and the line about not being the only dreamer really struck a nerve. It sounds corny, but creativity works in strange ways. I felt that I could give my drawing *Dreamer* a deeper meaning with the inspiration of the song. I added some reflections to make it complete, with this phrase popping into my head: "A light shines for others, a light that shines in the darkest of times, a light that reflects our hopes."

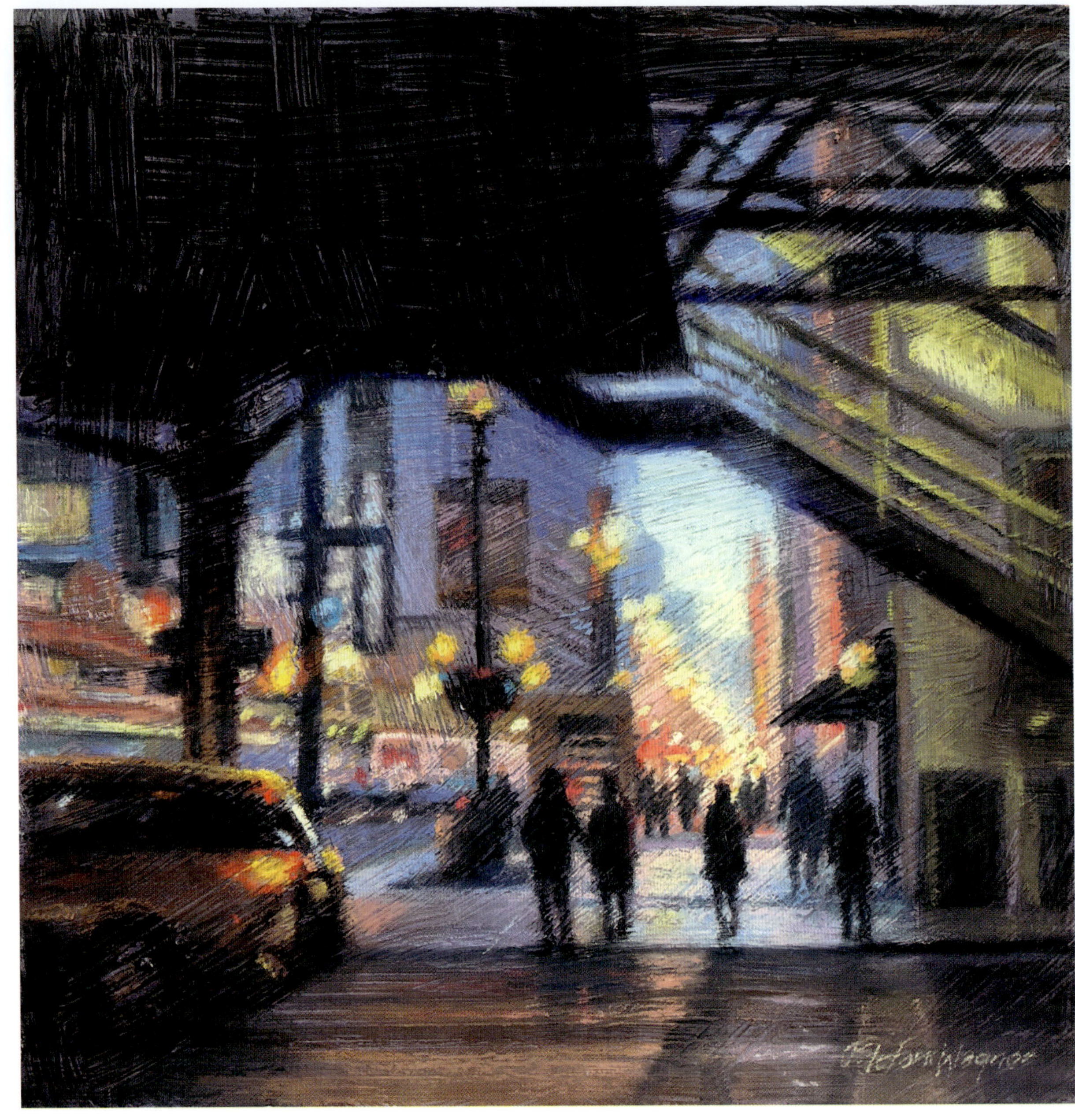

Jill Stefani Wagner, Michigan

JUST BEFORE

Two months into the COVID pandemic, I was completely smothered by the loneliness of our forced isolation. Though safe and well, I missed human interaction but also the sights and sounds of everyday life: the things we have always taken for granted, the things that frame the way we live.

I thought of bustling downtown Chicago, which we had visited the year before, and realized its streets, stores, and trains were now empty and silent. I chose to paint an image of the energetic city as I remembered it, brimming with light, motion, and color...the way it looked "Just Before."

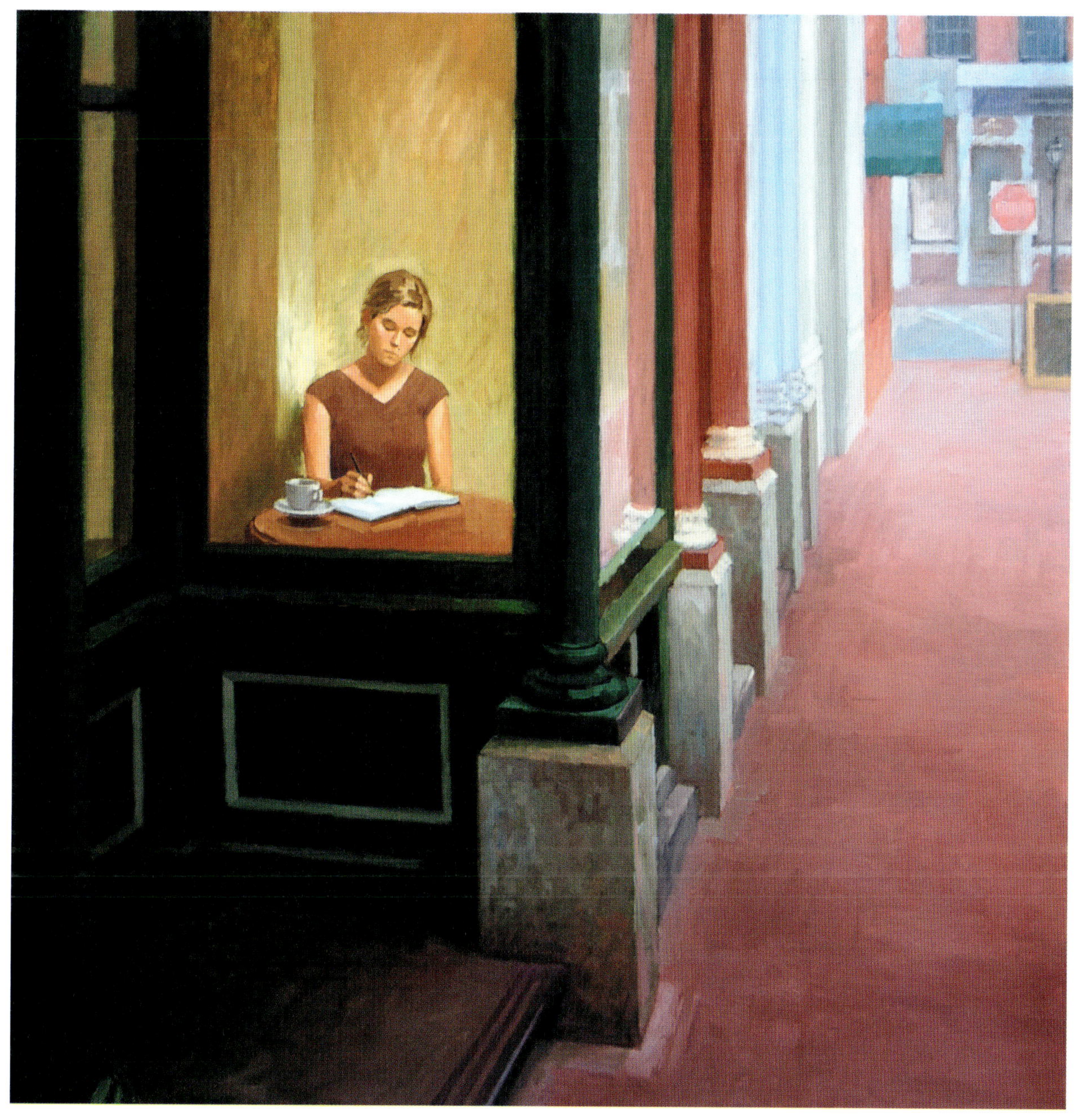

Paul Schulenburg, Massachusetts
NOTEBOOK

In this time of "social distancing," I picked this painting I call *Notebook* to portray the feeling of isolation many people are currently feeling. The painting portrays a woman in a café window in Portland, Maine, but it could be in any older town in America. She is alone, behind glass windows, writing in a journal. Perhaps she is working out her hopes and dreams, making plans. Perhaps she is making a list of things to do, or a list of things she wants to talk about with a loved one. From her glass box, she can observe the outside world. But the streets are empty. No one walking. No cars going by. As I am writing this, many people are communicating from behind masks, through glass partitions, over videoconferencing. We are all looking forward to the time when we can once again gather in cafés together, walk down city streets, and meet and greet our neighbors.

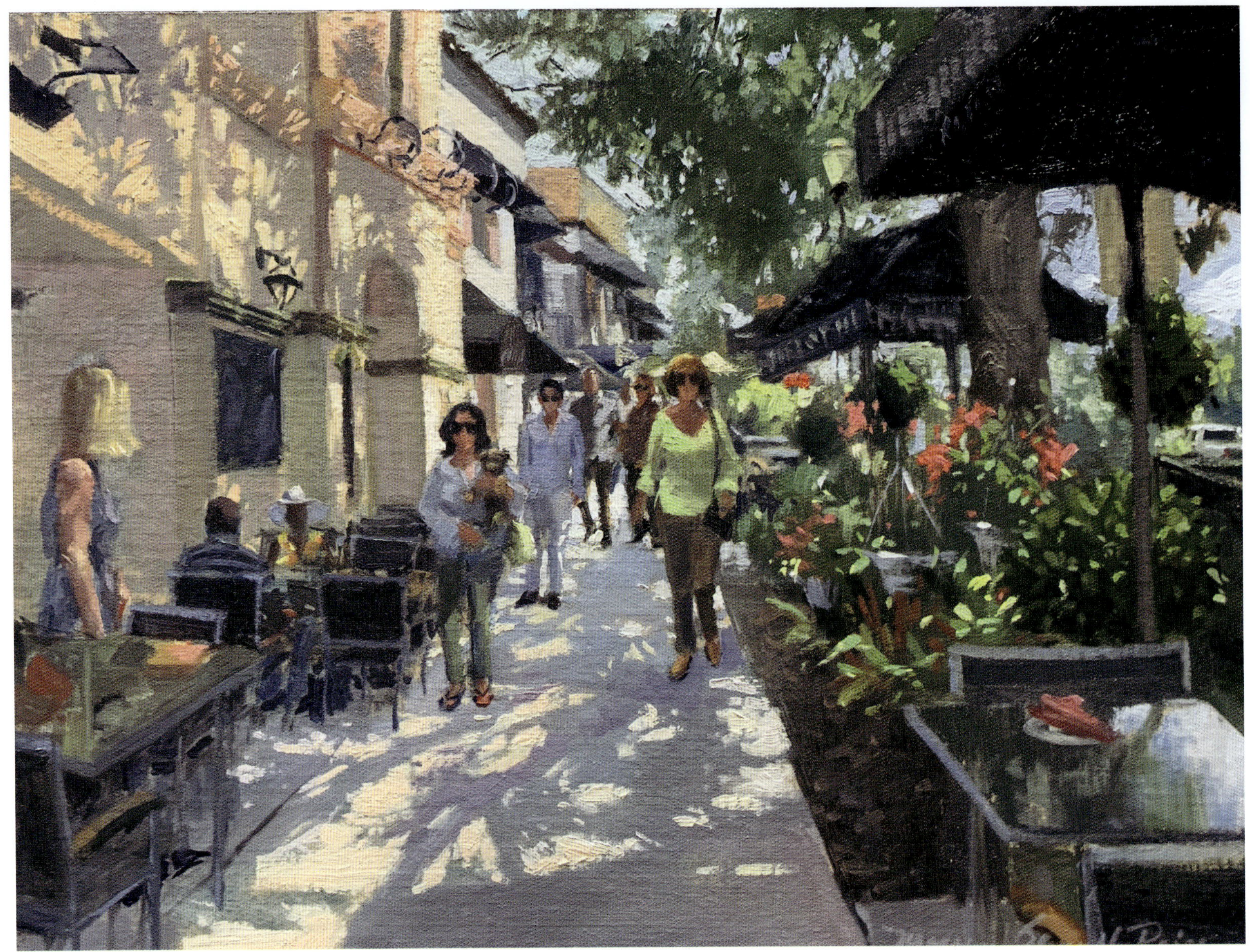

Morgan Samuel Price, Florida
PARK AVENUE STROLL

During this incredible time, I have found that once I recovered from the shock that we would be living like this, I needed to do what kept me centered, emotionally restful, and happy. The serenity produced through living with paintings of Mother Nature relaxes me as if I was outside. What I choose to paint reflects what I want in life: serene moments filled with beauty. This scene of Winter Park is a location that I have always enjoyed. I have walked this charming street my entire life. The stores come and go but the appeal of this street remains the same.

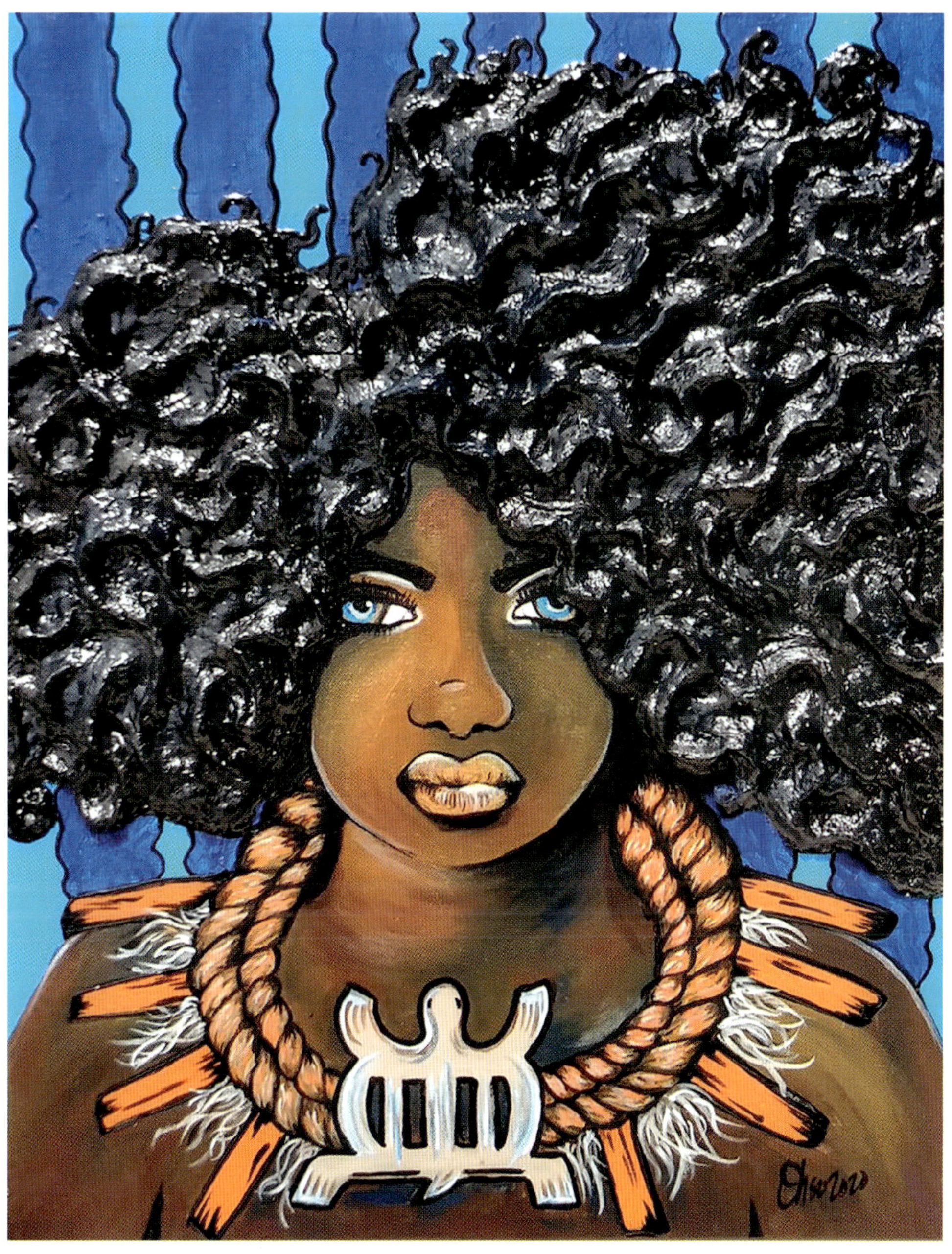

Ohso Fabone, Texas

RESILIENCE YOU CAN'T IMAGINE

Resilience You Can't Imagine is part of my "Law, Order, & Justice" series. Resiliency is the ability to form successful adaptation of coping mechanisms in the face of trauma, obstacles, and adversity throughout our lives. Black people are no strangers to resilience and constantly find ourselves swimming against systemic currents of inequality. With a rise in police shootings of unarmed Black men, women, and children, it is important to recognize and discuss our country's racial past and take steps toward future reconciliation.

Unfortunately, Black people and their contributions are often overlooked, understated, stolen and in some cases, erased. Risk factors such as poverty, lack of jobs, fear and expectation of violence, gender stereotypes, and racist experiences just to name a few all make it difficult for Black people to overcome adversity. "Denkyem" is the Adinkra West African symbol for the crocodile, representing adaptability to those currents.

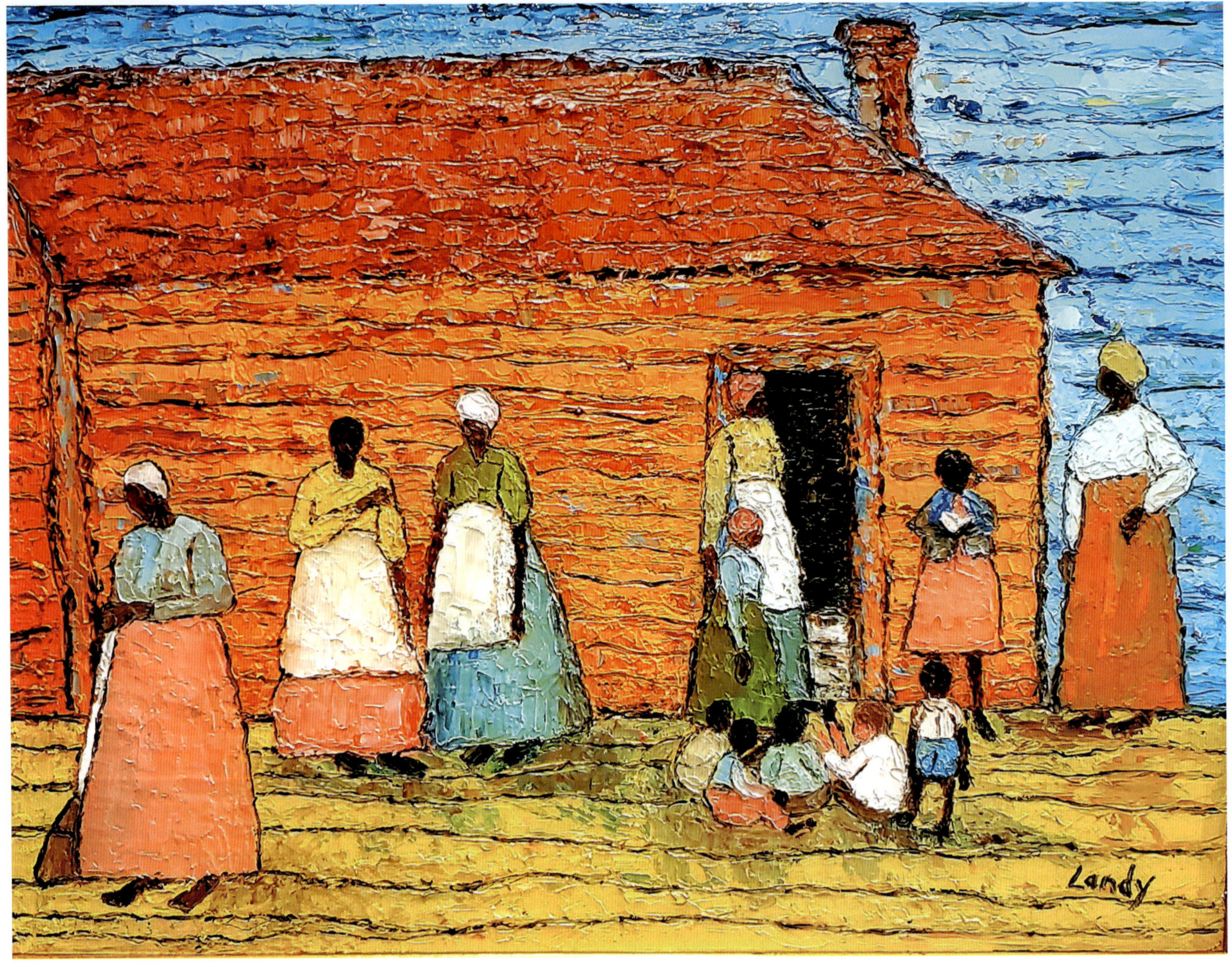

Yolanda Terrell, California
WOMEN OUTSIDE

A lot of my artwork that I've done throughout the pandemic was inspired by the ever-changing events around me. For this painting in particular, *Women Outside*, I was inspired by the schoolteachers who have had to grapple with the responsibility of serving as essential workers in providing education to our children, while also having to come to terms with the challenges that come with our new norm. I love capturing the diversity in the various cultures that I have always been surrounded by throughout my life through my folk art, which many people seem to connect with.

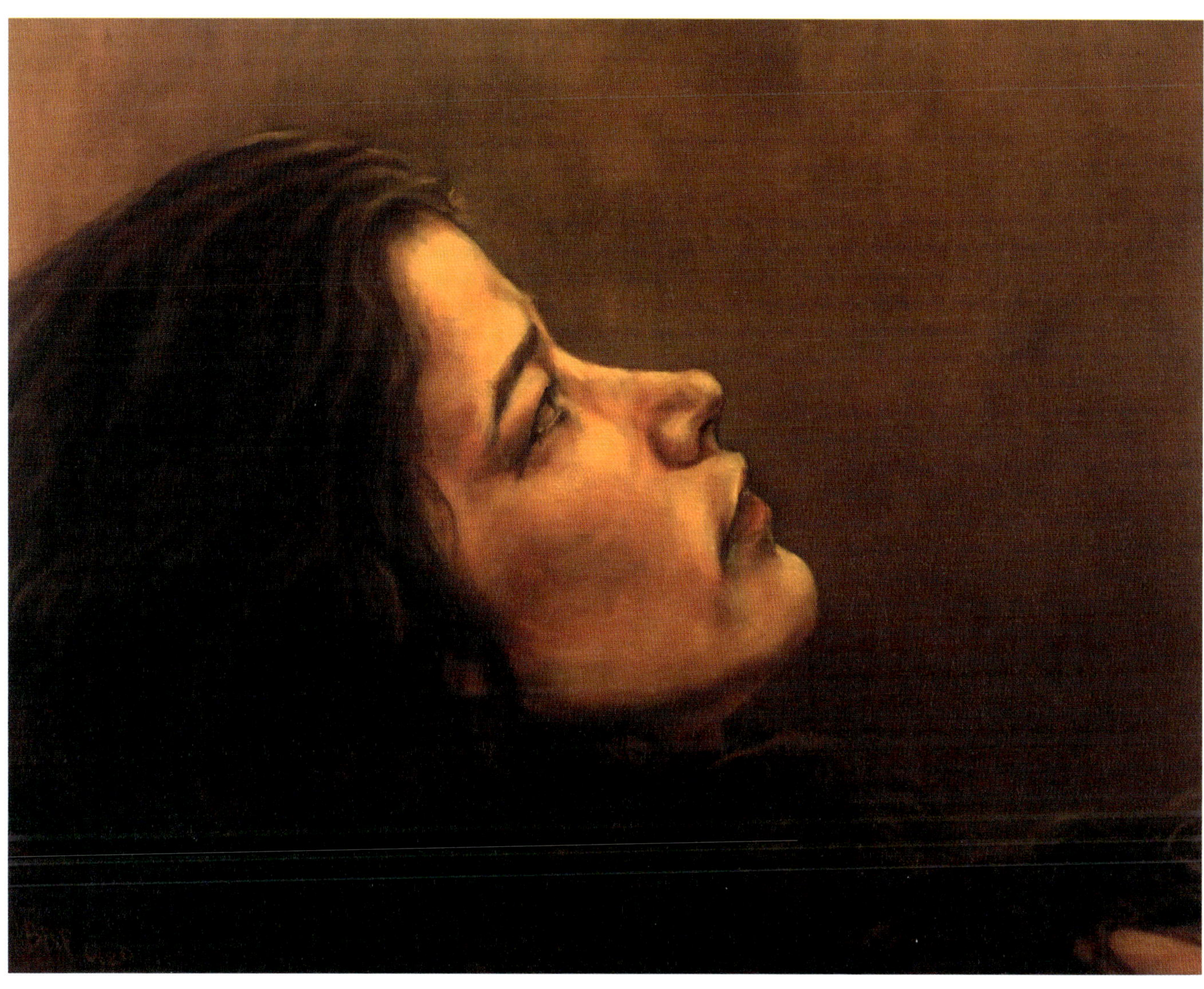

Benji Alexander Palus, Louisiana

LOST

This small work had been patiently waiting to be painted for roughly three years, part of a larger series exploring the effects of different colored light, and how to translate that light into paint. Its references, canvas size, colors, and the title, *Lost*, were all planned out long ago. I knew what it meant to me, knew how I felt about it, and how I wanted to render my model, but then the world stopped, and this little painting became so much more. I suddenly felt lost.

I live alone, and aside from grocery runs every two or three weeks, I had seen no one for months. The future, everyone's future, was suddenly uncertain. And yet, I realized that this wasn't necessarily a bad thing. Despite the vague fear and anxiety, the restlessness, the loss of routine, the loneliness, there was freedom; there was space and time to grow and to simply be. Becoming lost in oneself is scary sometimes, but it is also exciting and illuminating. I poured all of that into this work. The model's expression changed from day to day, and even from one minute to the next—at times with the flick of my brush, and at times without touching her at all. I added light to match those flashes of self-realization. I darkened the shadows when the lack of a simple touch from another human being made me ache, which of course, made the light shine more clearly. When I sat back and realized that this painting was finished, I was not surprised to find that the model's expression was still changing. I posted it on social media and asked whether she looked troubled, or if it seemed like a good kind of lost. The answers were as varied as I had hoped they would be. My conclusion to this work, and its specific theme as it applies to my journey through the changes and upheavals that the entire world has experienced these last few months, is a single thought that popped into my head the day I finished it and has been echoing there since: "Some things that are lost should never have been."

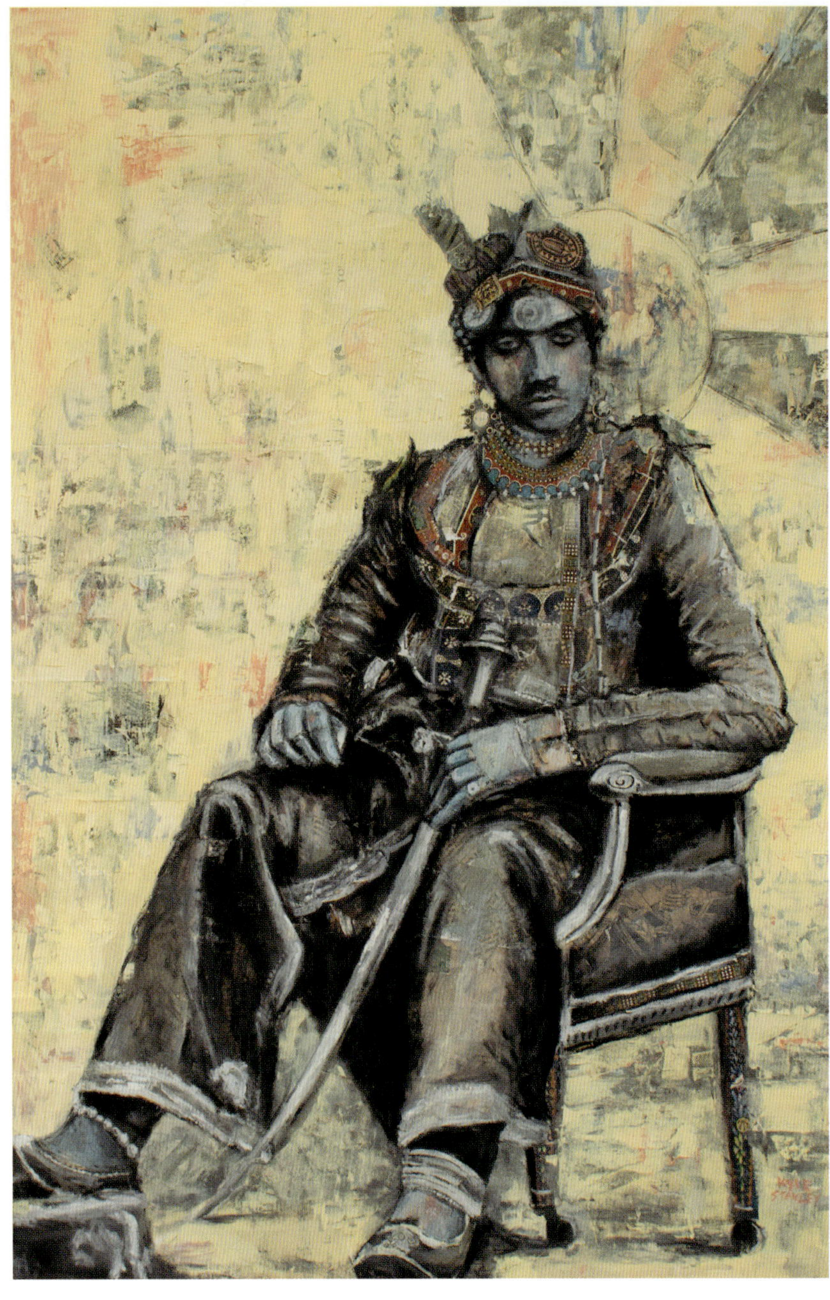

Kyle Stanley, Kansas
THE PRINCE-MAHARAJA

My recent series is an exploration of cultures around the world through the late 1800s. Art is about new experiences; this collection is a transcendental expedition into world cultures throughout the ages. These works are embedded with antique maps, photographs, and postcards, adding patina and lived experience to celestial veneers. Mixed media collage features antique postcards, maps and photographs, and oil paint on canvas and wood panel. History, world cultures, and a stir-crazy wanderlust inspired these pieces; many of which were created while in self-isolation during the 2020 pandemic. Serenity is a definite theme; however, it can come in many varieties: calm serenity, serene confidence, serene intensity, blissful serenity, and even serene desperation.

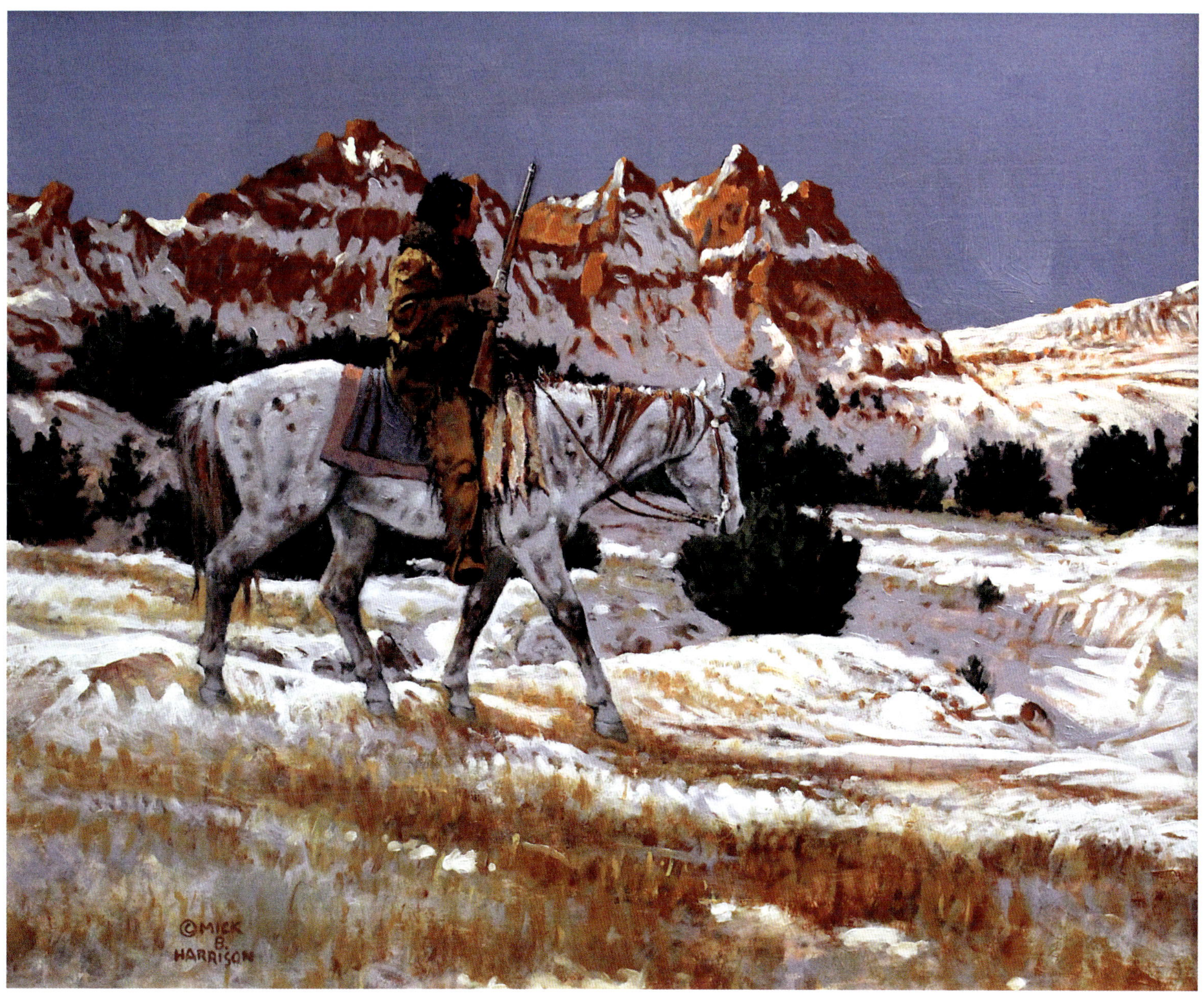

Mick B. Harrison, South Dakota
BOUNTY OF THE BADLANDS

While my state of South Dakota wasn't locked down as severely as some, I thought of how isolation has been endured by many during the COVID-19 pandemic in correlation to the isolation and loneliness in the Old West. Most often, although under different circumstances, this isolation is and was dealt with as life carries on. My painting of a lone Sioux plains Native American hunting for small game in the Badlands of Dakota Territory (now South Dakota) is my example of dealing with isolation along with the need to survive.

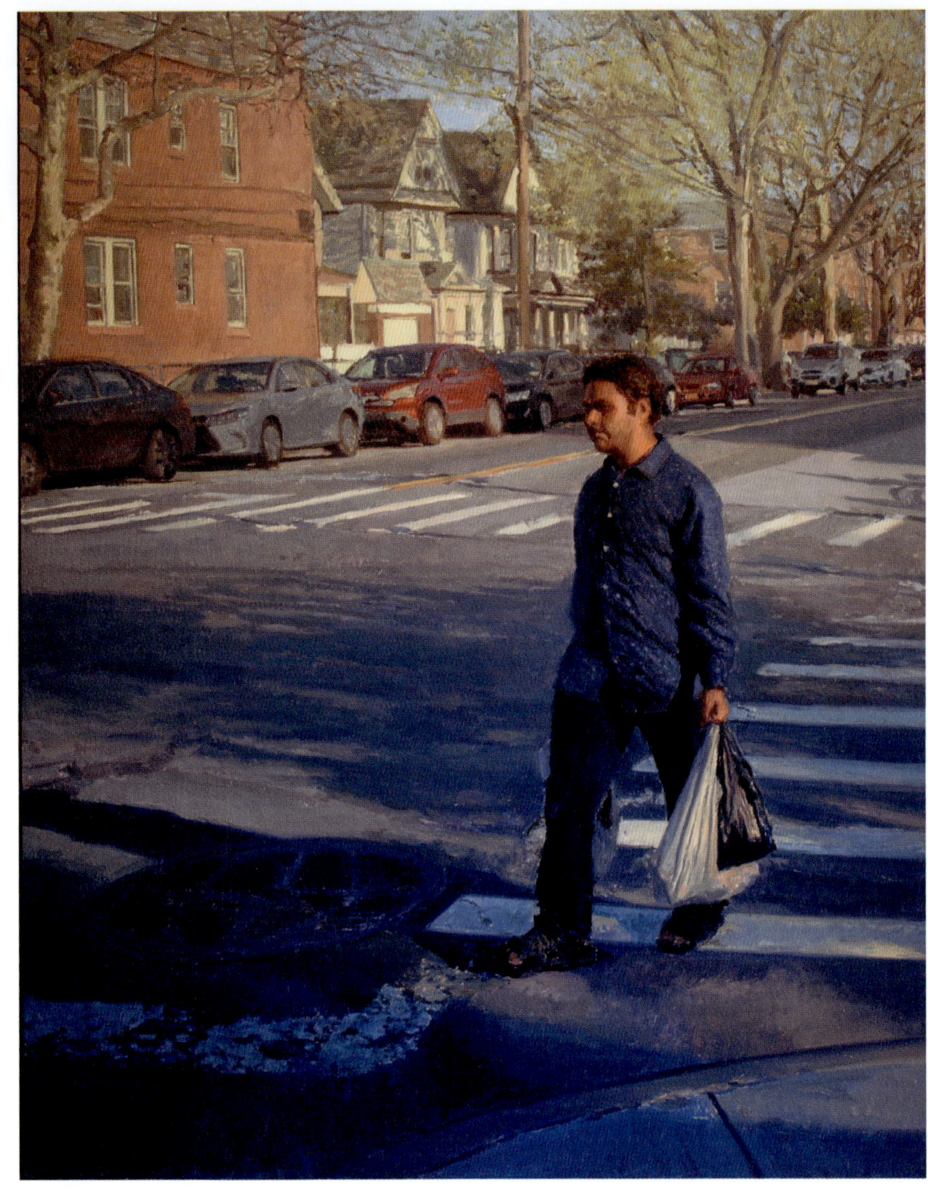

Raymond Bonilla, New York
LEFFERTS AND 95TH

The neighborhood in Queens where I grew up is home to communities of people from Trinidad and Tobago, Guyana, the Dominican Republic, Puerto Rico, the largest population of Sikh Indians outside of India, and many others. The combination of all of these cultures meant I grew up around families from different cultures and religions. As populated as it was, my neighborhood had a very small-town feel where most people knew each other and held onto the importance of looking out for your fellow neighbor, especially in times of need. Everything in the painting, from the way the cars are parked, the shirt, sandals, and plastic bags, is enigmatic of my hometown and gives me hope that one day it and all other hometowns will return to normalcy.

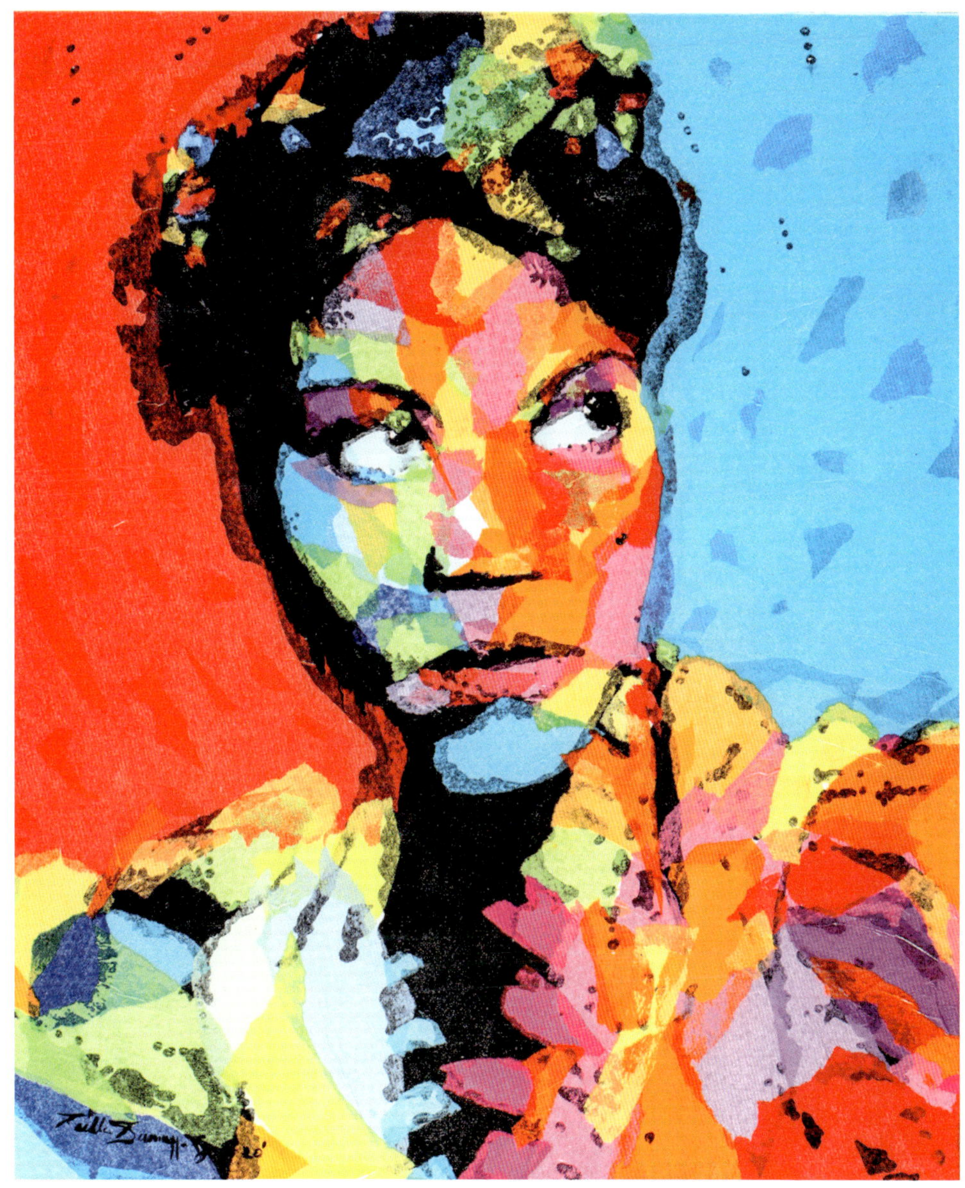

Richlin Burnett-Ryan, Florida
SISTER ROSETTA

Rosetta Tharpe was a popular gospel singer in the '30s and '40s. She had the first gospel record to crossover, becoming a hit on the "race records" chart. She was also known as "the original soul sister" and the "Godmother of Rock and Roll." Her unique guitar playing used heavy distortion, giving rise to electric blues and rock. Little Richard, Elvis Presley, Johnny Cash, and Tina Turner all said they were influenced by her revolutionary style.

This painting is part of a series: "Noted in Red White & Blues—The Kings, Queens, Godmothers and Godfathers, Sisters and Brothers of American Music." These pioneers influenced generations of singers and musicians. In these paintings, I wanted to capture their essence, strength, and beauty.

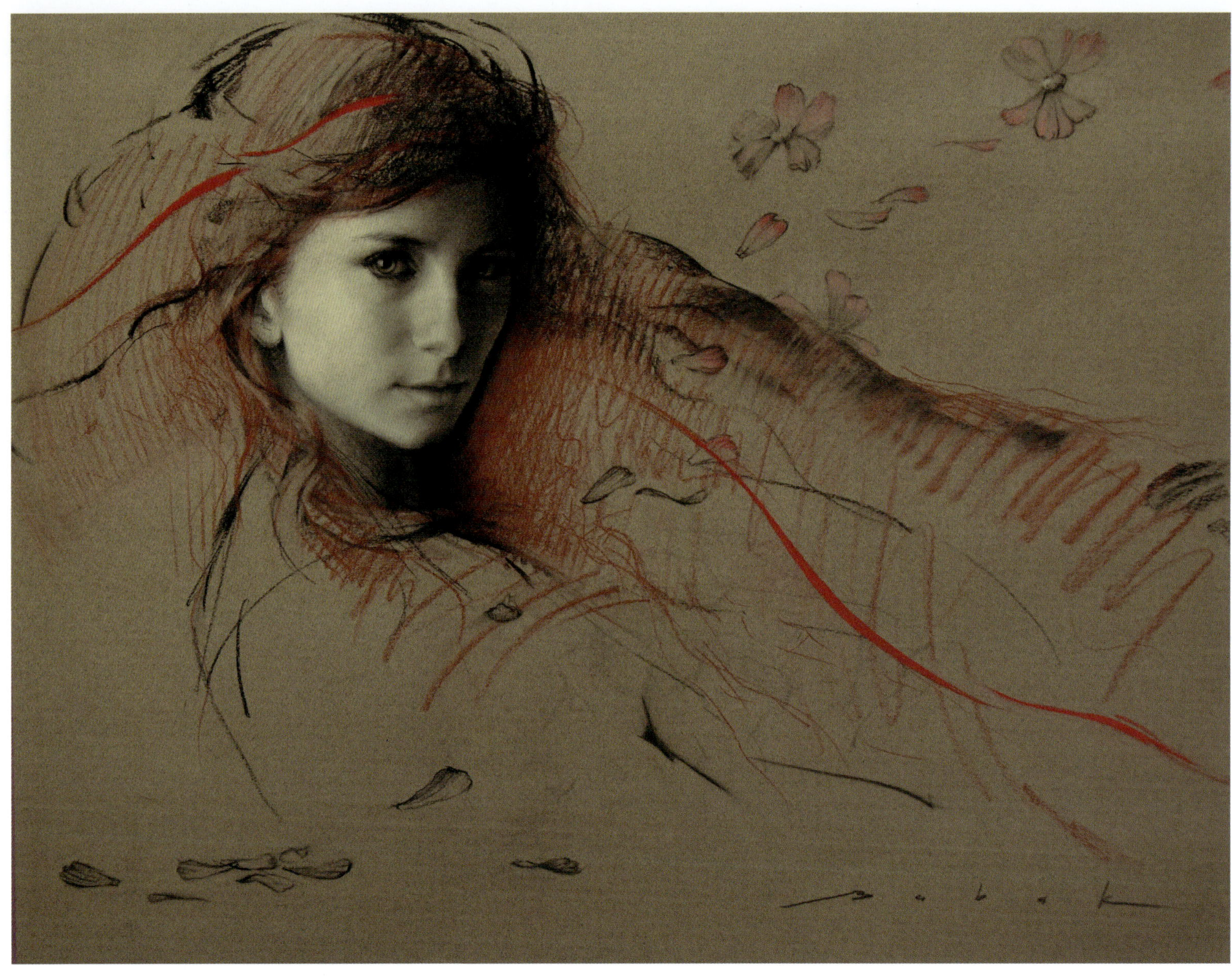

Olena Babak, Maine

RED LINE

This drawing was created in the first couple of weeks of the 2020 quarantine. There was an inescapable intensity to watching the world as we knew it change almost overnight. With every day, the numbers of lives impacted and taken by this new invisible threat were growing. The news had the power of paralyzing almost everyone, screening what seemed to be the absurdity of a sci-fi movie directly onto the walls of our "shelter in place" reality-show homes.

As a child, I remember picking colorful cosmos flowers in my grandmother's flower bed and plucking one petal at a time, playing with them before they landed on the ground. Now it felt as if the whole earth became my grandmother's beloved garden with flowers for picking. They were all together in one beautiful flower bed and very separate with their own destiny, waiting for their inexplicably random fate. The winds of change, the invisible enemy, were taking them petal by petal at random and stripping each of their colors before laying them on the ground. There was a line that, when crossed, was a point of no return, but that line had an ever-changing contour, twisting, interrupting, and ruled by the unknown.

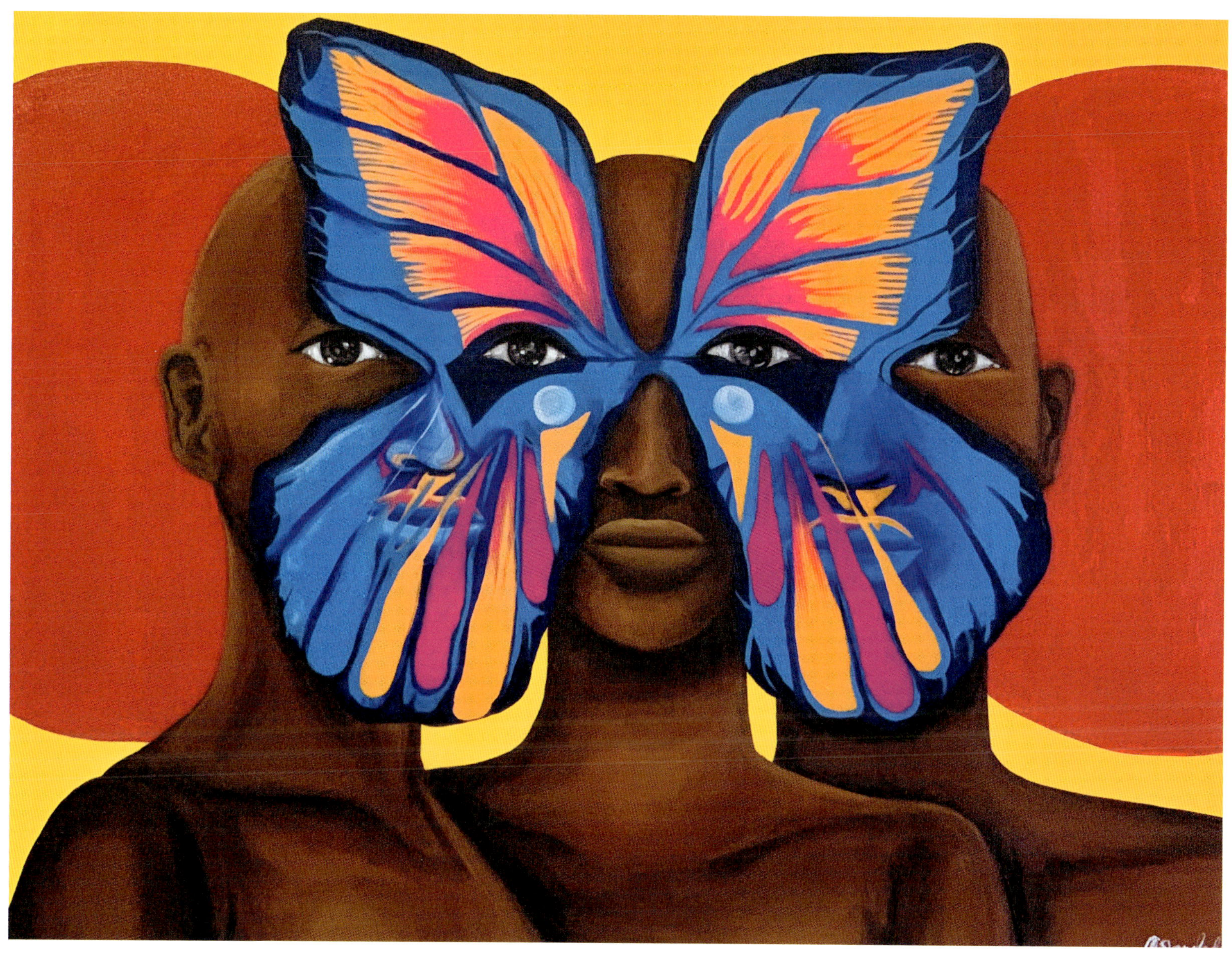

Ashli Ognelodh, Georgia
WE ARE NOT OBLIGATED TO WELCOME YOU

There are three versions of ourselves: the one we show the world, the one we show our close friends and family, and the one only God sees. I realized that all of these versions of ourselves play an intricate part in creating our entirety. We are a privilege, and we are under no obligation to welcome anyone into our personal sanctuaries.

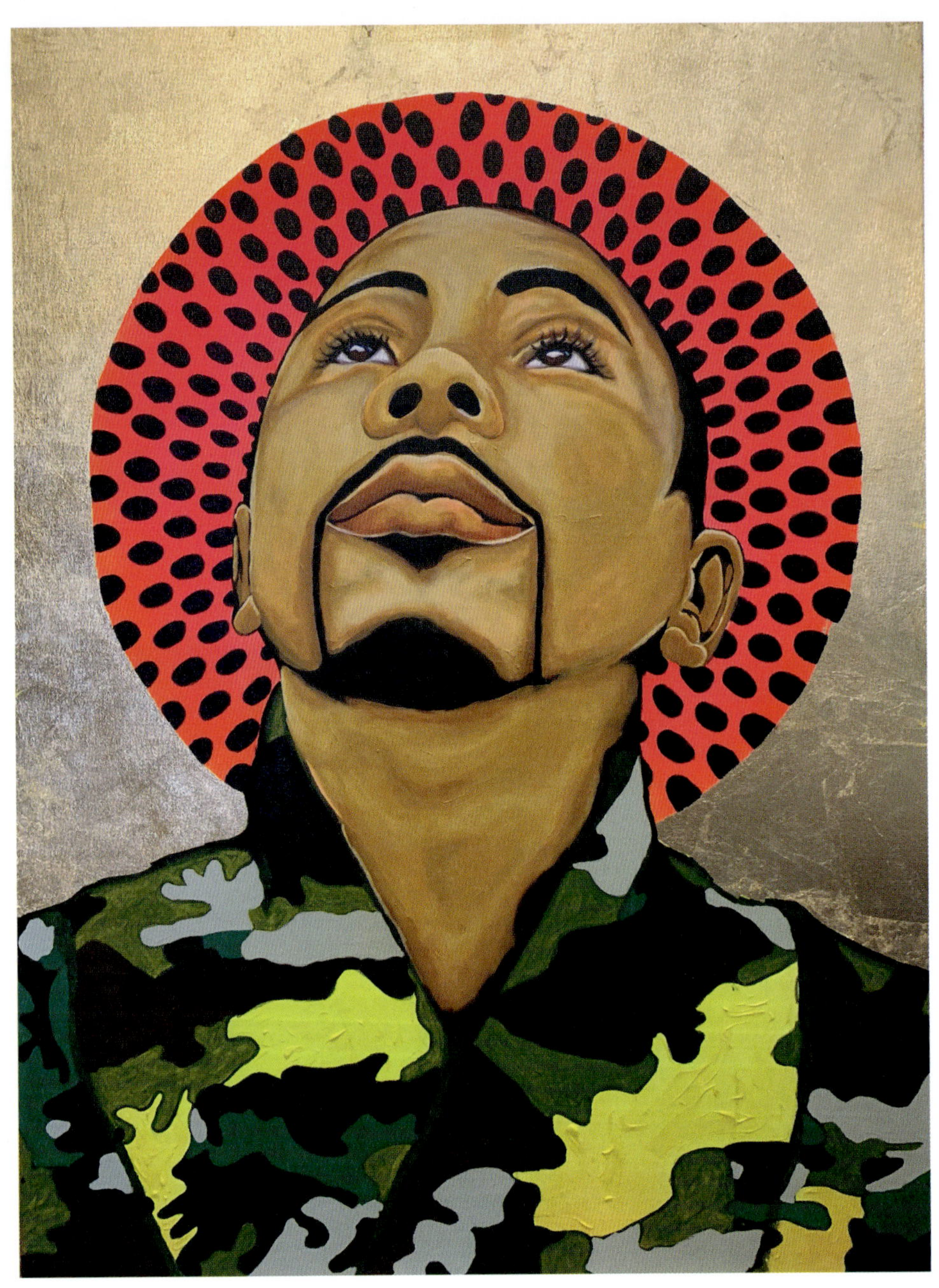

Demarcus McGaughey, New York
WHEN YOU BELIEVE, 2020

Created during the pandemic while thinking how things are uncertain, this painting is inspired by the emotions of hope, faith, and believing. The subject is looking up and onward in hopes of possibilities. My intention was to create a piece using patterns and colors that could spark emotions through motivation and inspiration.

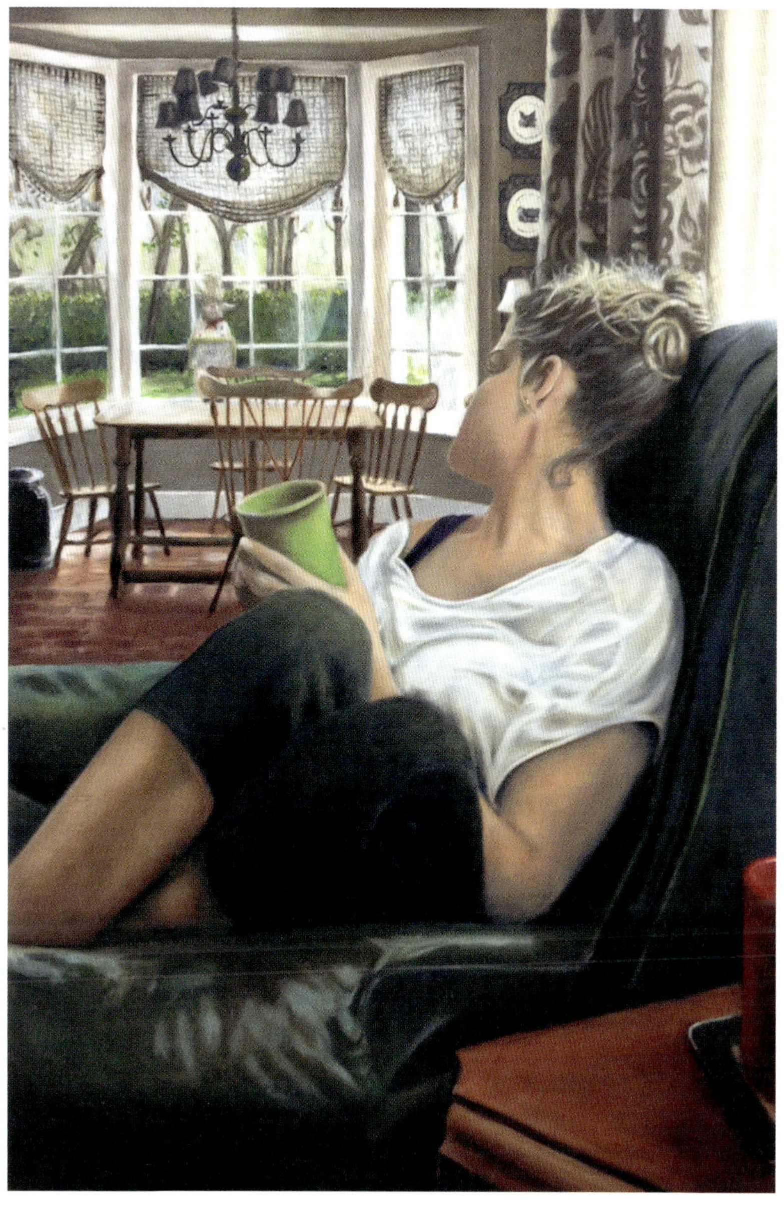

Greg Freeman, Florida

MORNING DAY DREAMER

This painting, entitled *Morning Day Dreamer*, depicts a young woman who could be facing yet another day in lockdown. Perhaps she is dreaming about what life would have been like had the pandemic not occurred, or she may be trying to decide what, if anything, she will do today while stuck at home. I think the gravity of these days has given all of us the opportunity to evaluate ourselves and our lives. We realize there is a lot to be grateful for. Sometimes you don't know what you have until you lose it.

Our nation is blessed and, by the time this is published, the crisis will be over. We will have gotten back to our "normal" lives. This artist believes we should learn from this not to take for granted all we have. So, perhaps the young lady in the painting is thinking just that. Maybe she is meditating on how good it is to be alive. How good it is to have a home to be locked down in. So many are not as fortunate. Maybe, just maybe, she is teaching us something. Be content and grateful for what you have been blessed with: Friends, a home, a family, or whatever. And above all, I think she is telling us to never give up on our dreams.

John Deckert, California

SALLY'S KITCHEN

Though our community had been hit hard by wildfires these last few years, people were coming back together, and this young woman standing at Sally's table seemed to be the thoughtful personification of resilience. "Stay," I said and took a few photographs. The painting that developed from that brief moment hung on a well-lit far wall in the exhibition—my best presentation to date. I was so pleased with it.

Then we heard from the governor to wear masks, wash hands, stay in, and shut down. Painters wearing masks, spaced apart by timed arrivals, retrieved their work from the walls, and the gallery quietly closed to the public. My painting is now about friends who can't gather, galleries that can't open, and paintings that can't be seen in person. The figure portrayed in *Sally's Kitchen* now waits patiently, and the hint of isolation is long gone. She waits for openings, friendly gatherings, and renewed courage to go forward. Granted, it's hardly the degree of sacrifice that has been demanded of many. It is, in fact, quite small. Nonetheless, I feel it acutely, and when I looked at this painting on my studio wall, it seemed somehow appropriate for this virtual exhibition.

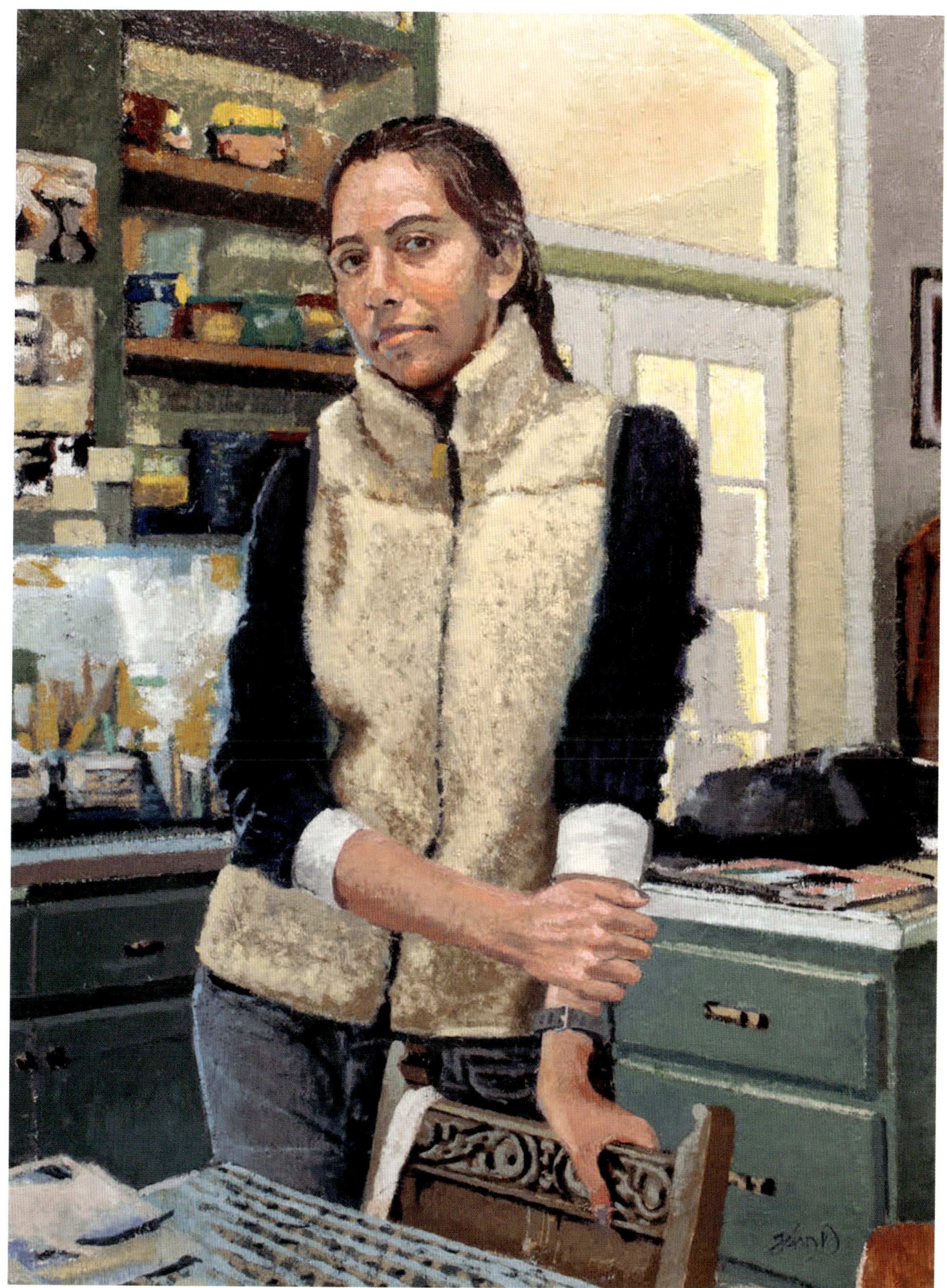

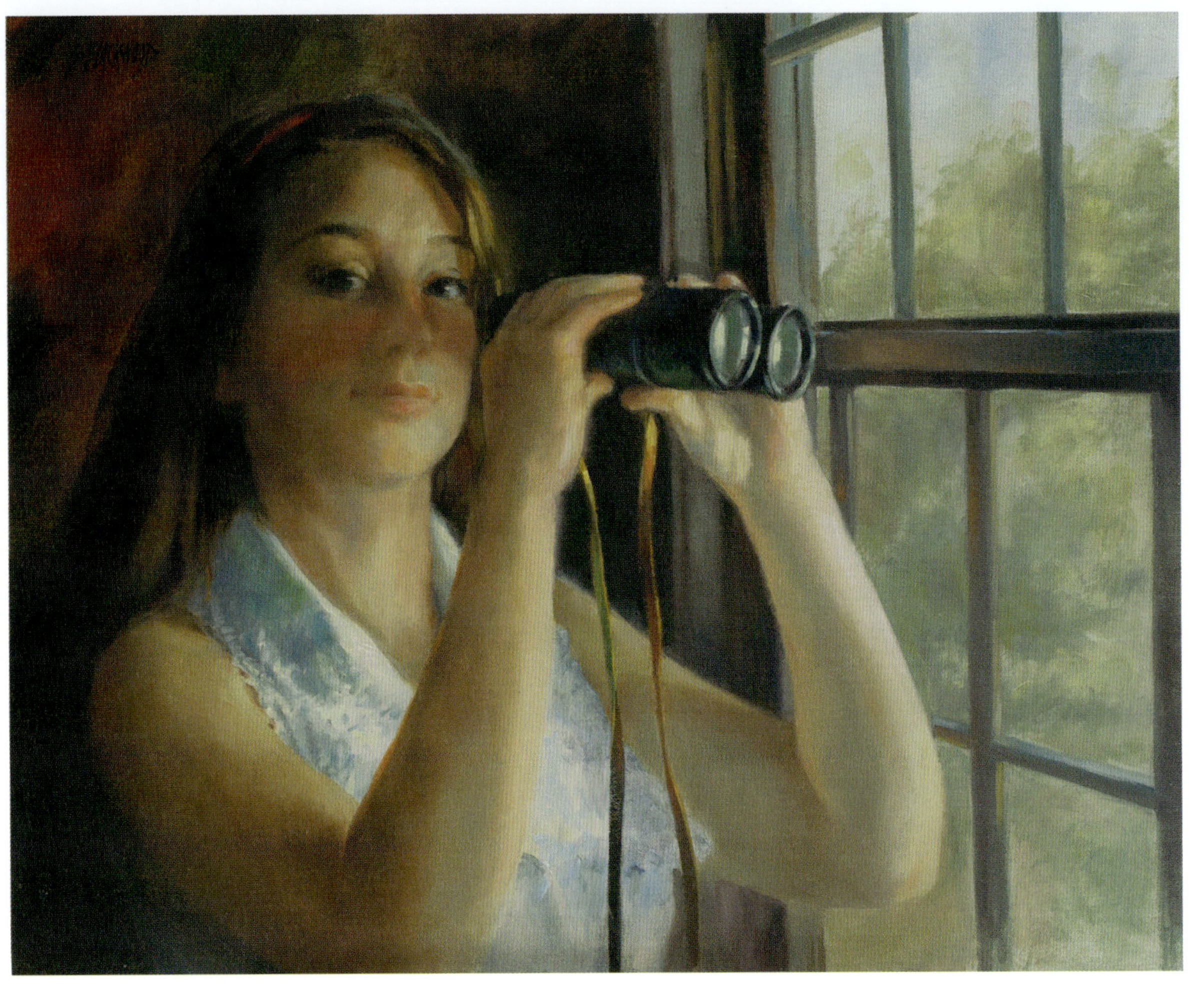

Susan Blackwood, Arkansas

WHAT'S HAPPENING

For many years I have been aware, as an artist, "I" don't find my subject to paint, it finds "me." As I paint, I am always painting for someone I don't yet know, or may never know. As I make each stroke, I am painting for myself, but I am also aware that I am painting for someone else in the world. Someone in the future, when this painting is hanging somewhere or is seen online, will feel the passionate feelings I have painted and know it is "theirs."

In 2012, I felt compelled to paint this image. I positioned my model with this questioning, startled look as she stood at the window. She is caught off guard, maybe seeing something that she didn't expect. In my mind she was standing at the window; looking outside, maybe her gaze was on the birds or squirrels...but was it? I passionately painted this young lady, yet all the while that I was creating it, this image felt uncomfortable to me. When I paint, I always express my feelings in my images, but this painting does not seem about me. Somehow, it felt like I was expressing someone else's feelings. Flash forward eight years—I have kept this painting in my own collection, but I have never found a title that fits. To my surprise, I now understand this painting. I wasn't expressing myself in 2012; I was somehow expressing my future self and my feelings in 2020, living through this awful worldwide pandemic.

As I have gone through the various stages of this pandemic, the overwhelming feelings that I have experienced are exactly the emotions I feel when I look at this painting. I am finally identifying with my painting. It feels as if I was inspired to create this painting in 2012 for my future self: my future self who was experiencing this pandemic in 2020. This painting was painted, not for me then, but for me now. Now, I understand and relate to this painting. We have all been through quarantine and watched the numbers climb; many have been hospitalized and many have lost loved ones. We have stayed inside our homes. We have had so many unanswered questions, not sure what to believe or trust, feeling locked inside like prisoners behind bars (symbolized here by the bars on the window), all the time searching and searching (symbolized by the binoculars) the internet and TV for news of what is happening to our friends, family, and our world. Our worlds have come to a startling halt. We feel incredibly isolated, alone, terrified of coming in contact with the germs of this virus. We have so many questions and behind all of our questions is fear. In our innocence (symbolized by the young woman in the white dress), we stand at the windows of the world and feel helpless. Our lives are changed forever.

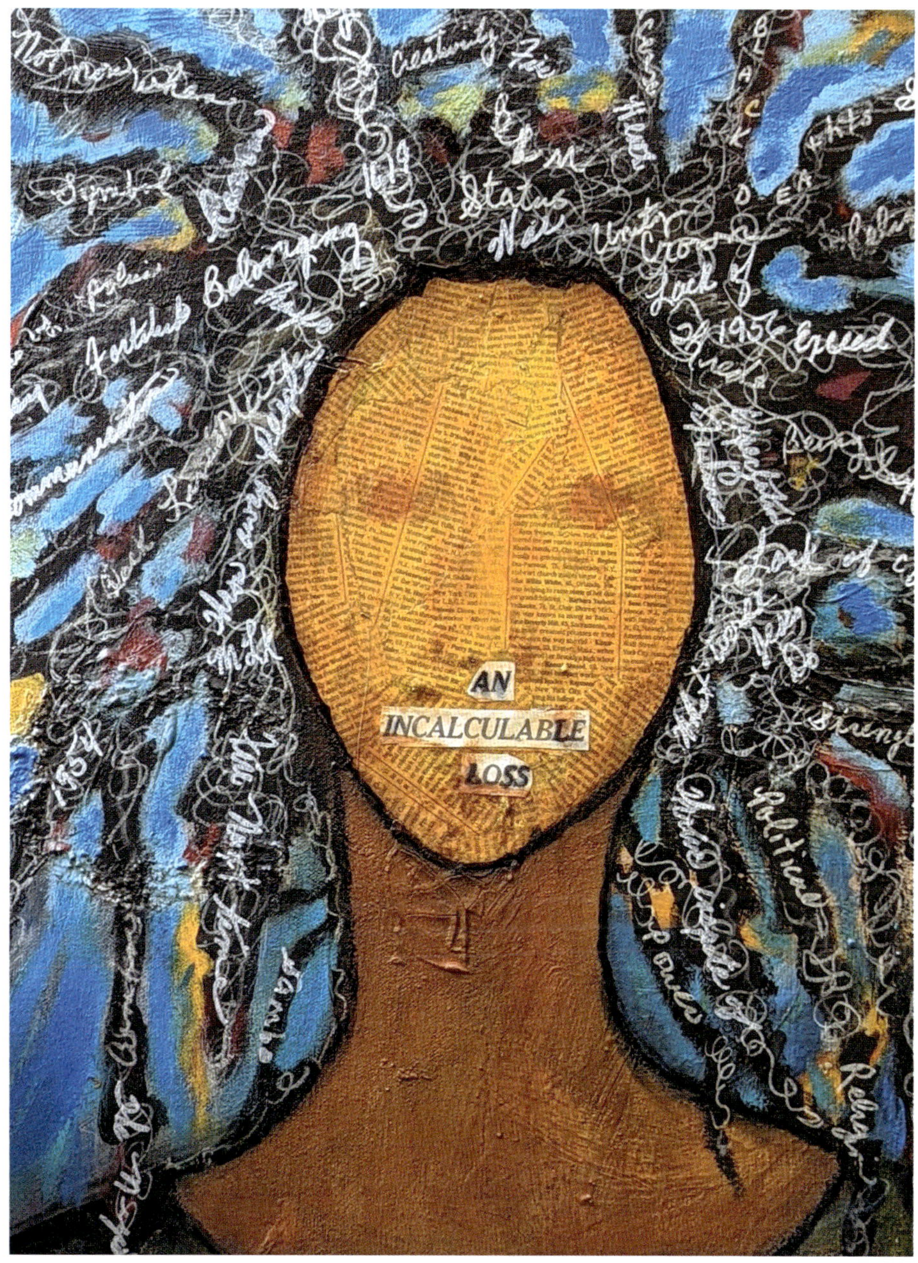

Brenda Robinson, Florida
AN INCALCULABLE LOSS

INCALCULABLE: too great to be calculated or estimated.

2020 was not a very good year. *The New York Times* printed a front-page grim statistic of Coronavirus deaths in the United States. Its stated purpose was to turn this death rate into a more humanistic representation of the scale of human loss. Certain human losses. The lack of concern and nonchalance of the effect of this virus towards the poor and people of color.

There are deep scars that are festering.

This painting is from a series I am doing about scars in and on our bodies. The scars of the ancestors. The scars of not caring. The scars of just being "throwaway people." I believe that these scars will become again like pure gold. The scars in the bones remember.

3 ANIMALS

As we continue to yearn for a "new normal," we find ourselves immersed in habits and routines, longing for comfort in things that brought happiness before life with the pandemic. Animals have long been a source of comfort for many a tired soul—not only do they bring joy, but they also bring solace to lonely, hurt, or saddened individuals.

Even before the pandemic, I found that animals helped explain the pain I felt when I had experienced a serious injury. I hope you enjoy the beautiful array of my fellow colleagues' work, showcasing their relationships with creatures large and small.

Linda Harrison-Parsons
Scottsdale, Arizona

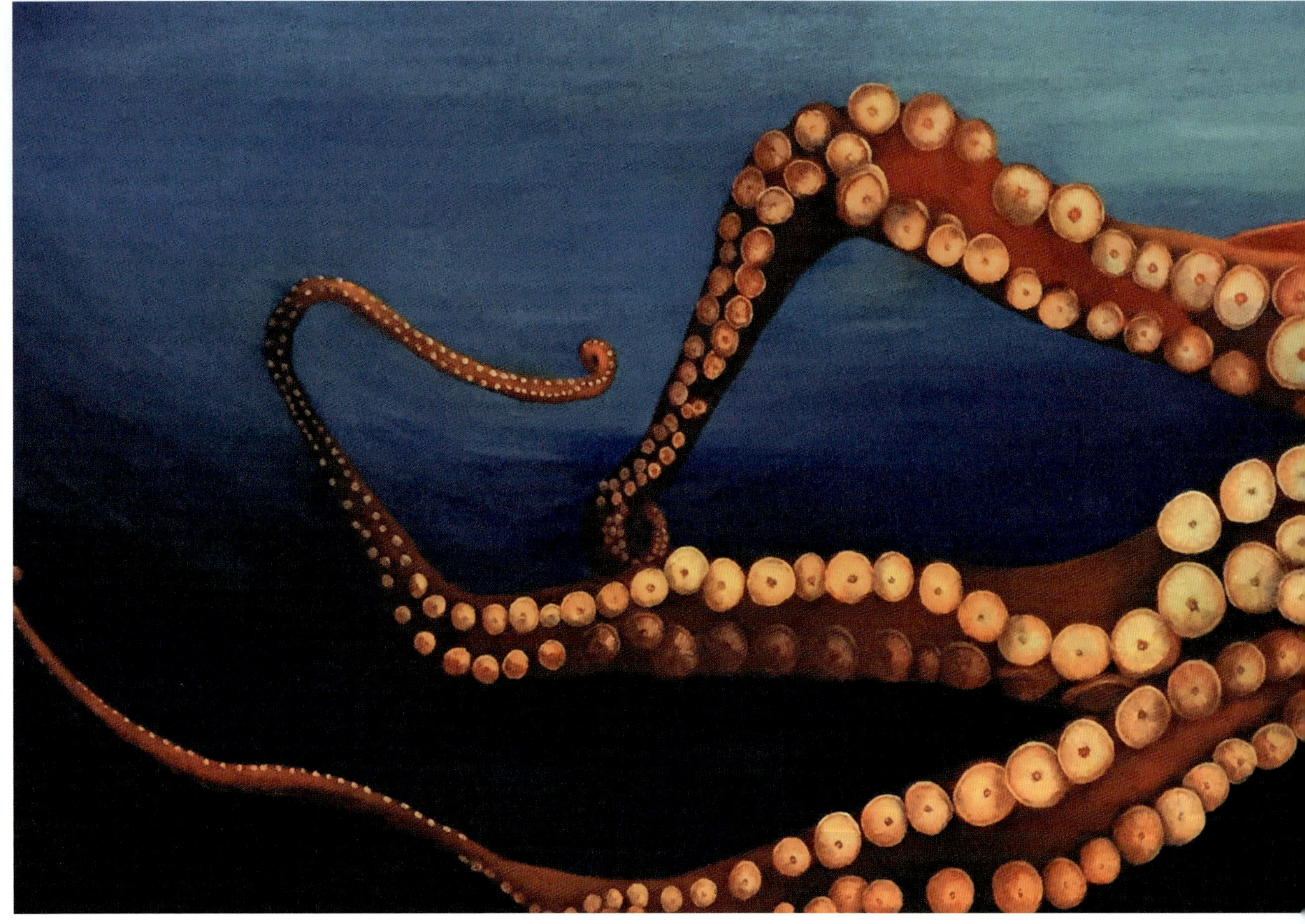

Linda Harrison-Parsons, Arizona

REACHING OUT

I generally do wildlife and nature images, but this year has become the year of the octopus. *Reaching Out* is the second in a series of works depicting these unique and amazingly intelligent creatures. Many years ago, I had a head/neck injury and began to paint octopuses to describe the flow of the pain. When working with a physical therapist, I was asked to explain how the pain moved in my head. As I was thinking about this, I saw this movement of reaching out and guiding the flow of the pain. I realized it was kind of like an octopus, and it was my guide in helping me tell the doctors and therapist the path the nerve pain was traveling.

How does this apply to 2020? I kept having images, artwork, stories come to me about octopuses over the years, but in 2019 going into 2020, the images became a daily event. I felt like it was time, and I had the time, so no excuses—I needed to paint this image that had been in my head for so many years.

Reaching Out became, in addition to my guide, my thoughts of missing contact with friends and family. I was finding new ways to make connections, to see people via technology; to extend through this painting the need to reach out and find the touch. This painting has been my way of maintaining my sanity. With so much craziness in the world, within our country, working on a detail-oriented painting kept me focused. This painting for me was like meditation, and I had to let go of the outside world for that time I was at the easel and enjoying the process.

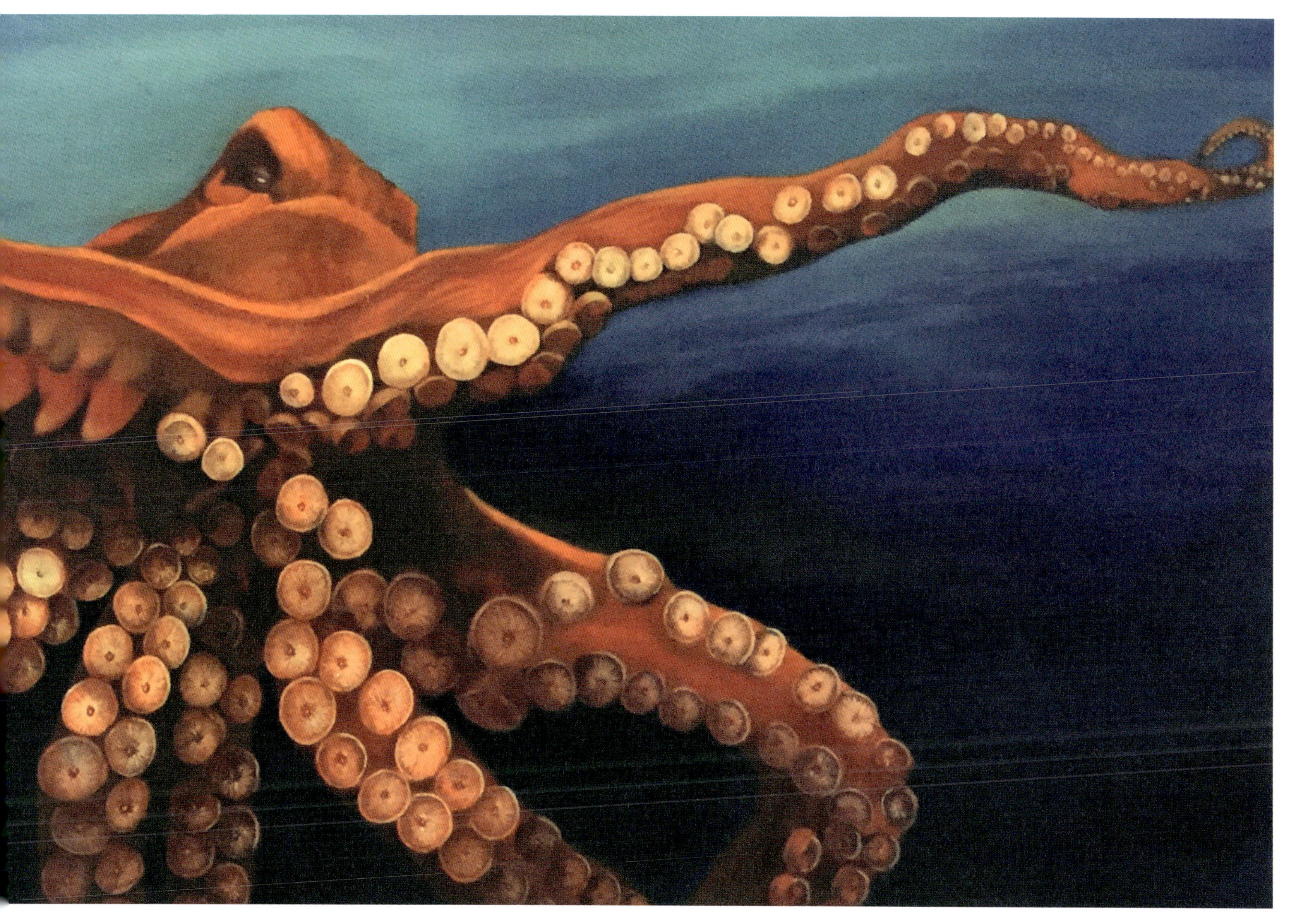

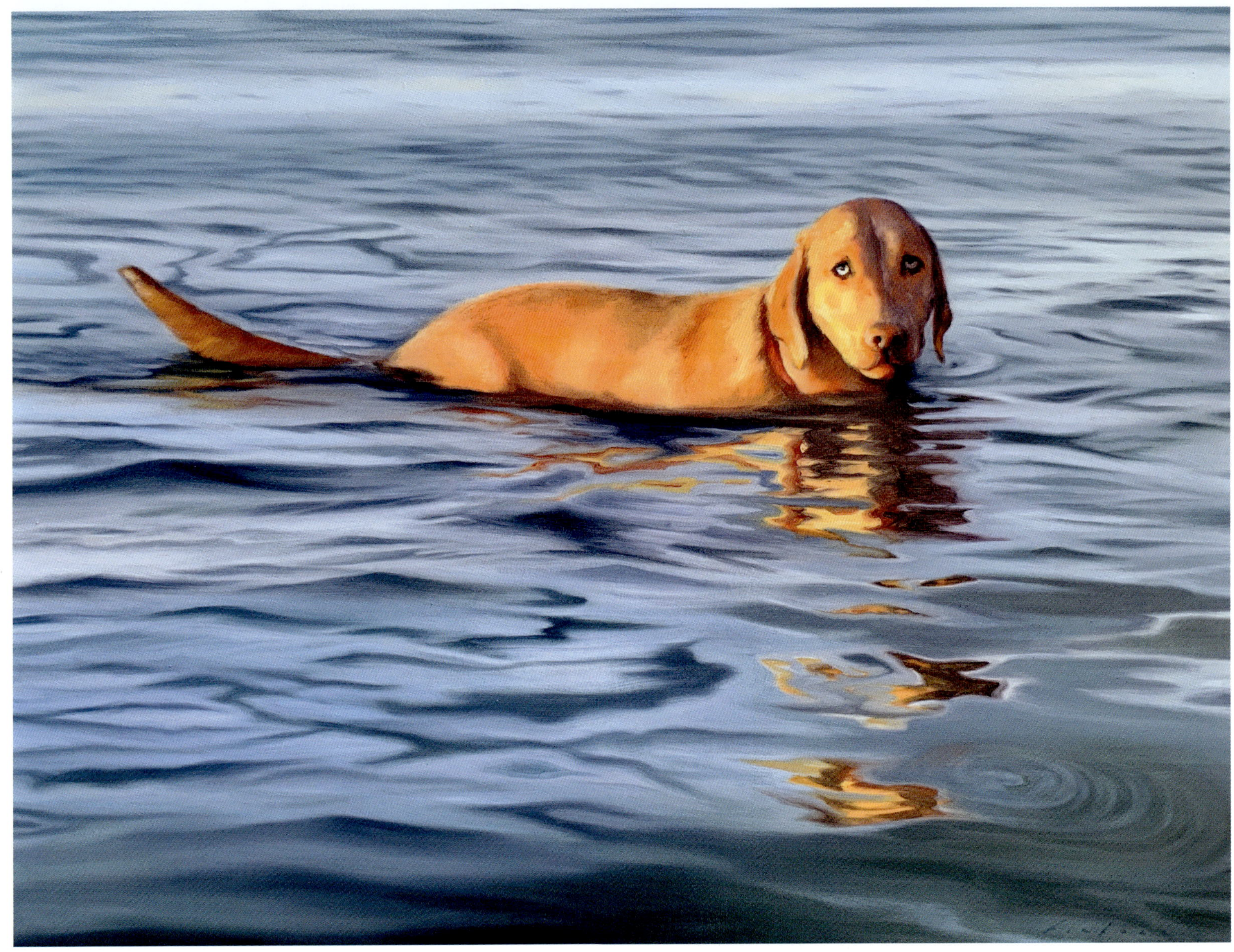

Gabriella Fiabane, Florida
A MOMENT'S PEACE

Walking with dogs, both mine and others, is one of the joys in my life. With anxiety brought on by COVID-19, the walks have become a big part of my meditation practice. Observing them and feeding off their energy daily has helped me gain clarity to keep going. This painting captures a moment, the present moment at that time.

That's where dogs, and animals in general, are our teachers. They are present in the moment.

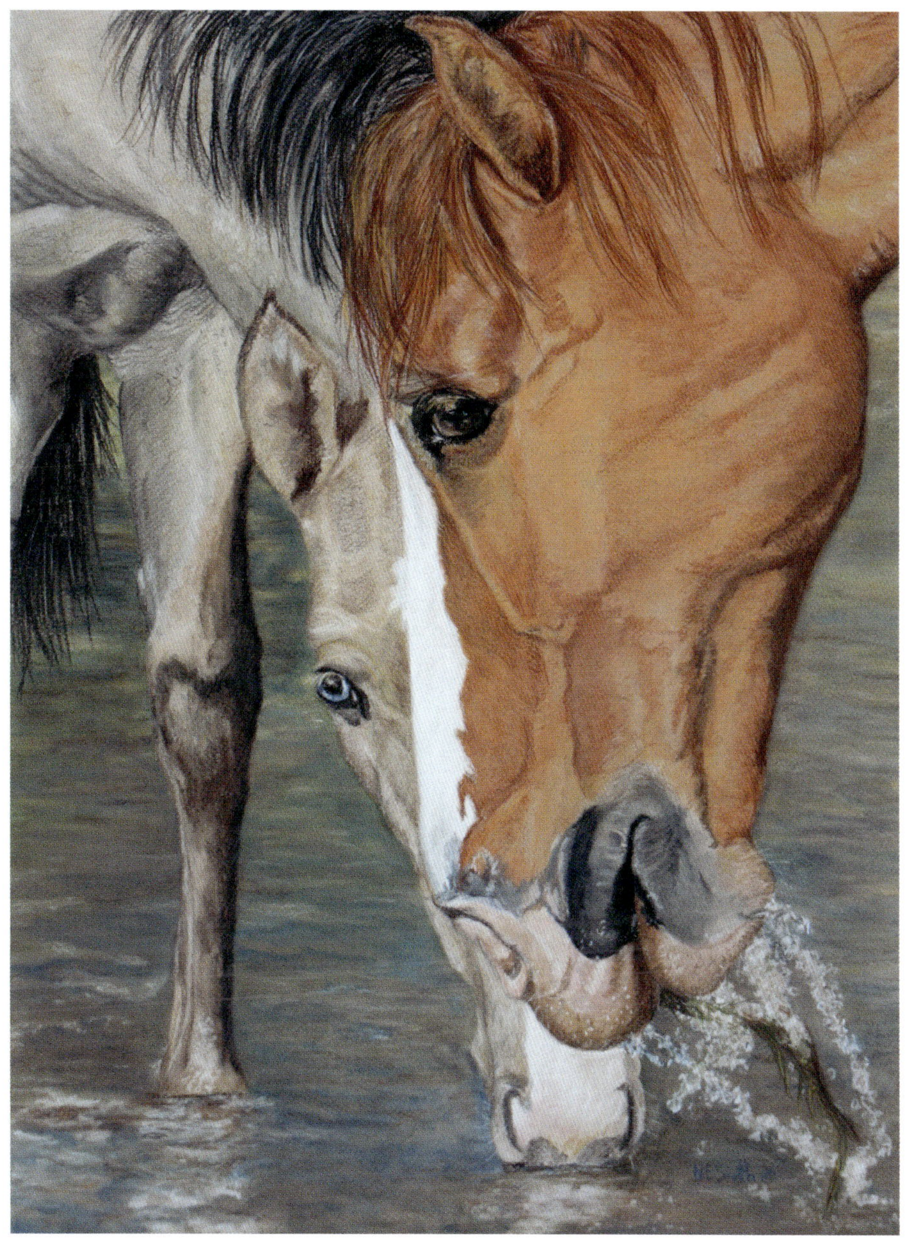

Nancy Smyth, Florida
SALT RIVER GRAZING

My passions have always been creating artwork and riding horses. As an artist, I work mainly from my home studio and occasionally on location, so working indoors is very normal for me. But COVID-19 has restricted me from enjoying my horse and being at the stable. In order to fill the void of not being able to be at the stable with my horse and my like-minded friends, I created this watercolor of two wild horses of the Salt River Basin in Arizona. This painting depicts one of their favorite things to do, grazing on the grasses that grow on the bottom of the river. The creation of *Salt River Grazing* helped me to once again connect my love of the horse to my love of creating art during a difficult time in our lives.

Addren Doss, North Carolina

LITTLE KING

I have always loved and been fascinated by animals of all kinds, and these feelings are very evident in the series of cow paintings I have been working on for many years. This time of being confined to my home studio, or my art residency as I call it, has been a gift to me. It has enabled me to devote all my energy to painting what I love. During my art residency, I have made several additions to the series of paintings I call "Bodacious Bovines." I am drawn to cows that show attitude when they see me coming with my camera. That attitude may be simple curiosity or a slight challenge from them. I often treat their paintings as portraits with them looking you right in the eye.

This very young Brahma Bull has a sense of dignity about him as he quietly looks at you. The late afternoon light is glowing across his ears and creates a beautiful shadow pattern on his neck and upper chest. Some cows are so special to me that I create a number of paintings of them in different sizes and mediums. *Little King* is definitely one of those.

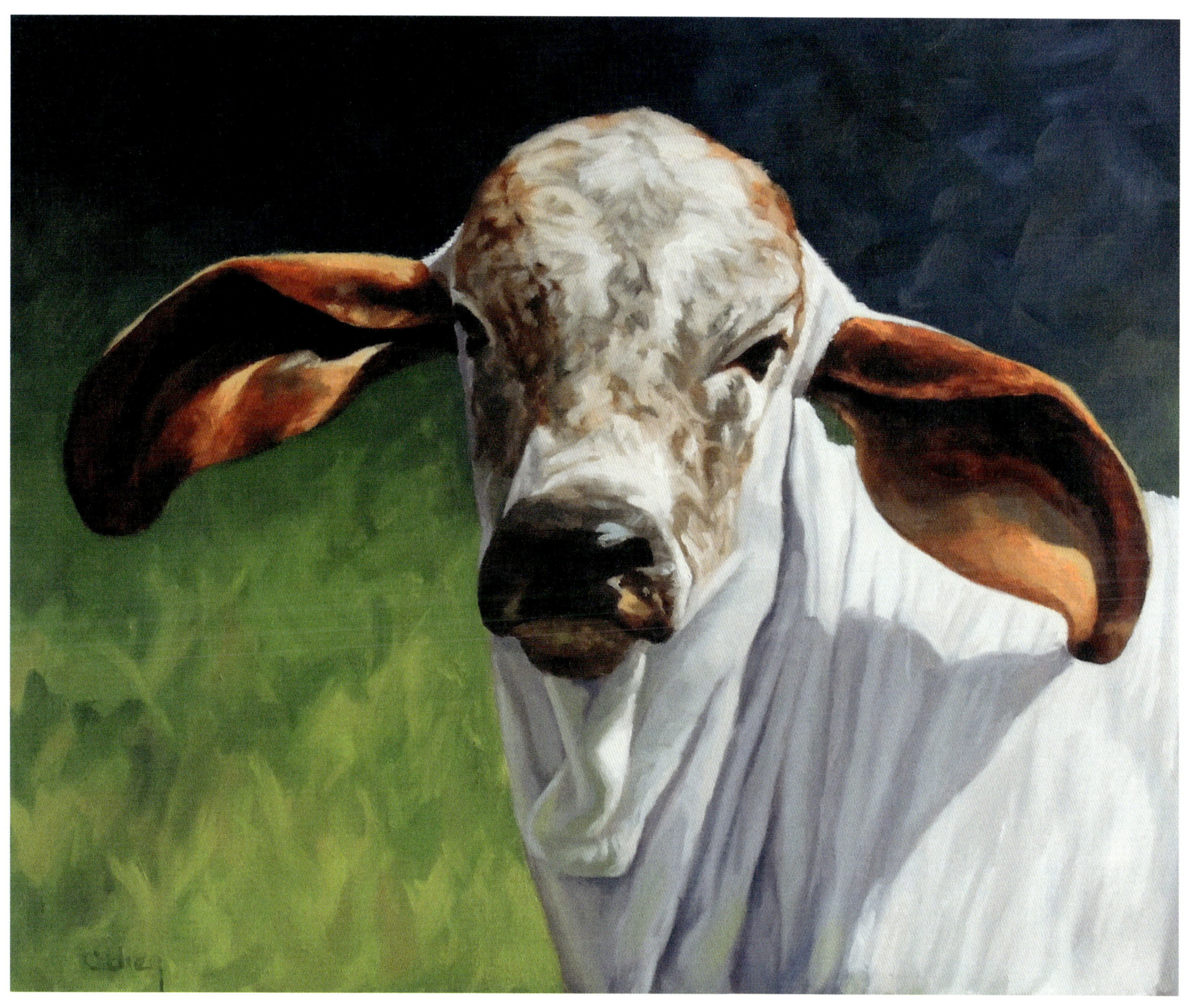

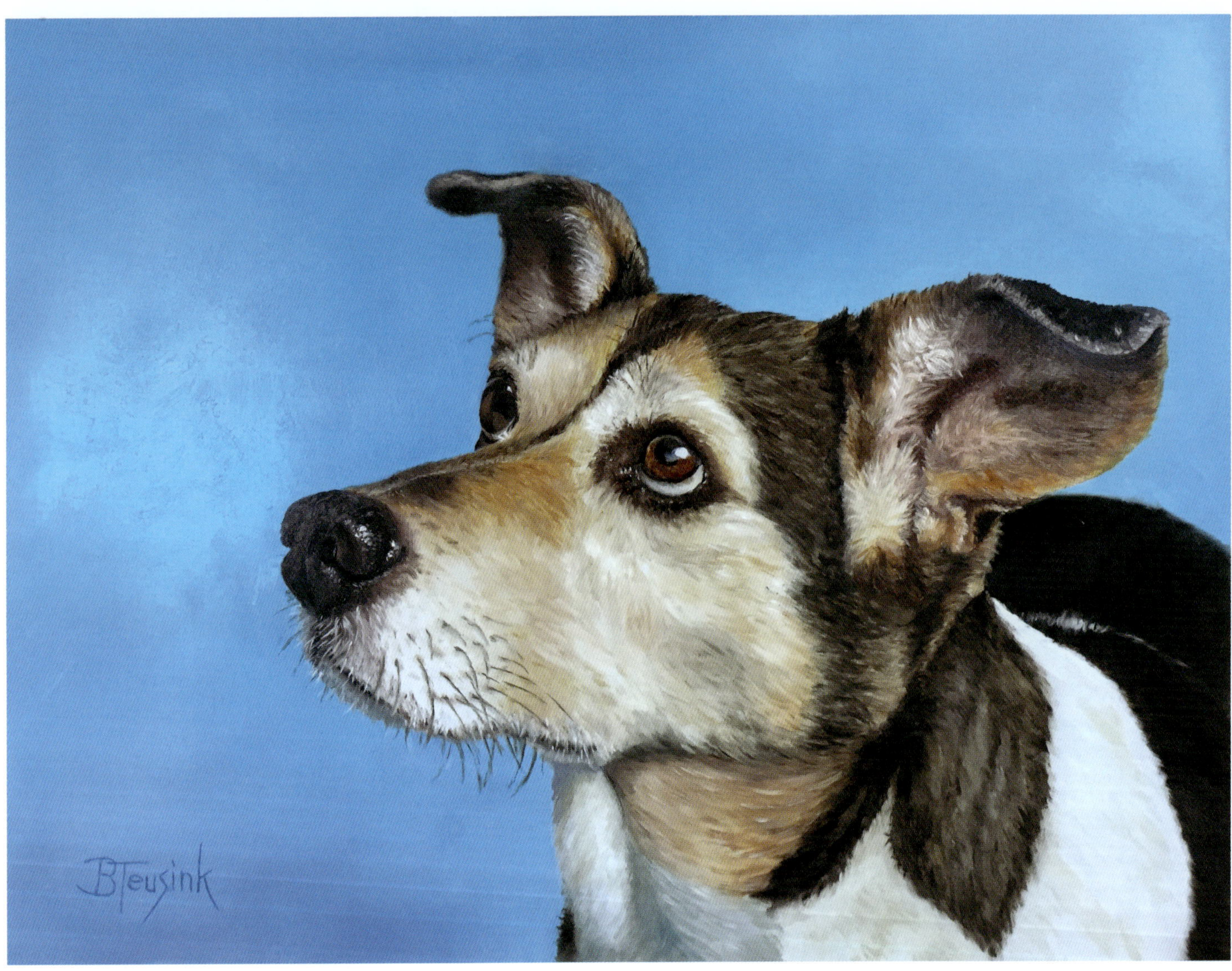

Barbara Teusink, South Carolina
HOPE

I love the intensity in this dog's hopeful gaze. Hanging onto hope has certainly felt challenging this year, but I believe hope is essential. It helps us all to have a positive outlook. Wikipedia says, "Hope is an optimistic state of mind that is based on an expectation of positive outcomes with respect to events and circumstances in one's life or the world at large." As a verb, its definitions include: "expect with confidence" and "to cherish a desire with anticipation." For me, this definitely rings true. I think there is little better to represent the concept of hope than a dog. Dogs are eternally hopeful, and I love them for that. My dogs have always been hopeful they will get to go along for the next adventure: every time I stand up, put a coat on, pick up car keys, or look outside, they are on their feet and at the door. They never get resentful or disappointed when their hopes don't come true; they just wait until the next reason to be hopeful again. They hope they will get a treat, they hope they will go for a ride, they hope it is feeding time, or time to chase a ball. They hope to be scratched or petted; they hope to go for a walk. They hope to have something to bark at. They are always hoping for something and are never disappointed or angry when they don't get what they hoped for, which happens much of the time. I love dogs and I love the hopefulness of dogs, and I try to integrate this wonderful trait into my own worldview. I am hopeful too, every day. When I look at the news, I always try to not lament our world, I hope for a better one. When I am sick, I hope to be well, when I hurt, I hope to be free of pain. When I see bad news, I hope for better news. As with many tough times faced before, we will get through these rough times too. I am hopeful it will be soon.

* This piece is a derivation based on an original photo by Karen Broemmelsick. The unrestricted license was granted to use the image for reference to create this original copyrighted artwork.

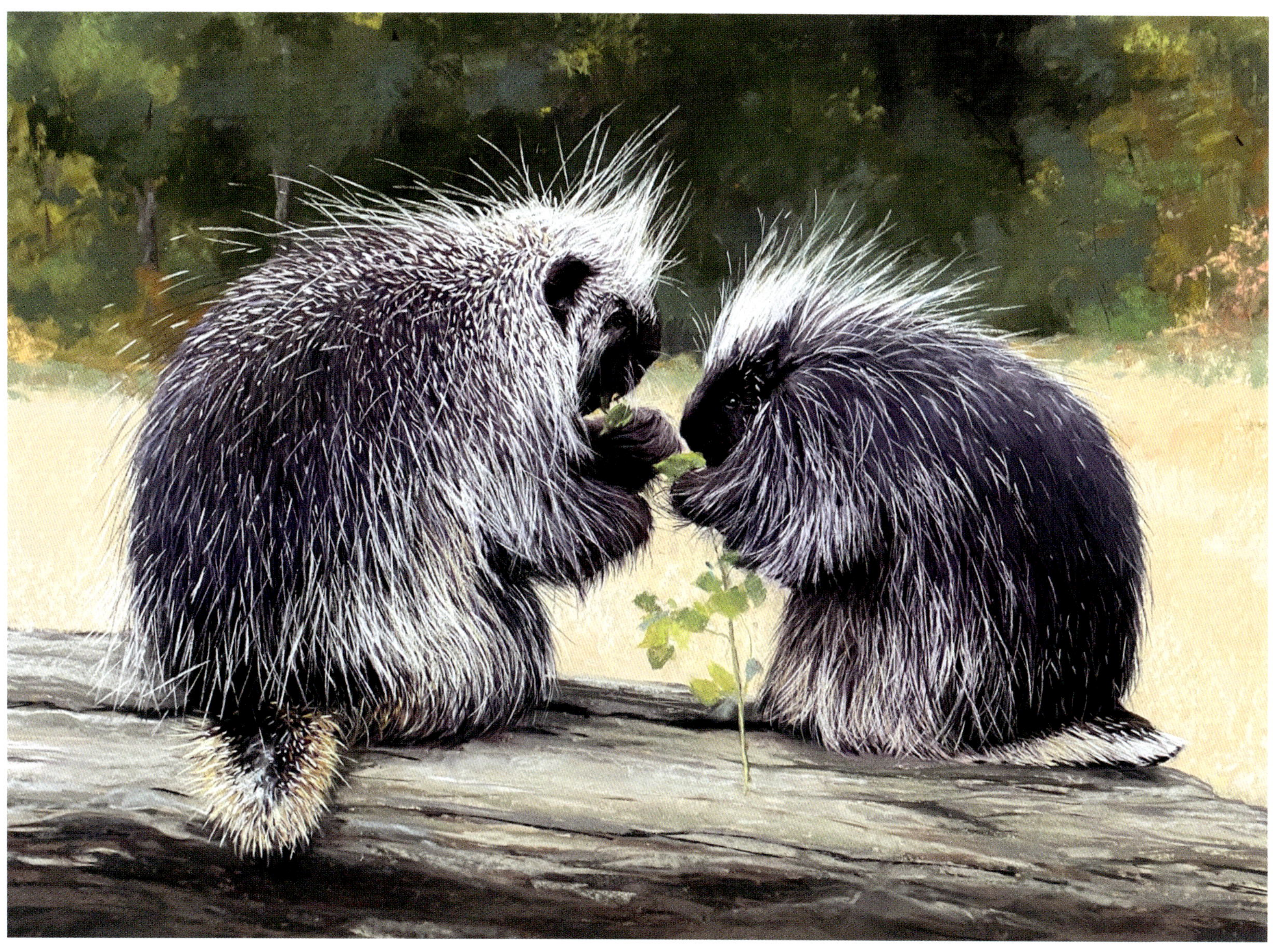

Lisa Gleim, Georgia
LOVE HURTS

I have begun painting more wildlife and was lucky to photograph these two porcupines named Elvis and Presley. During the photoshoot, it was so much fun to listen to them banter back and forth and often share the same twig as they snacked.

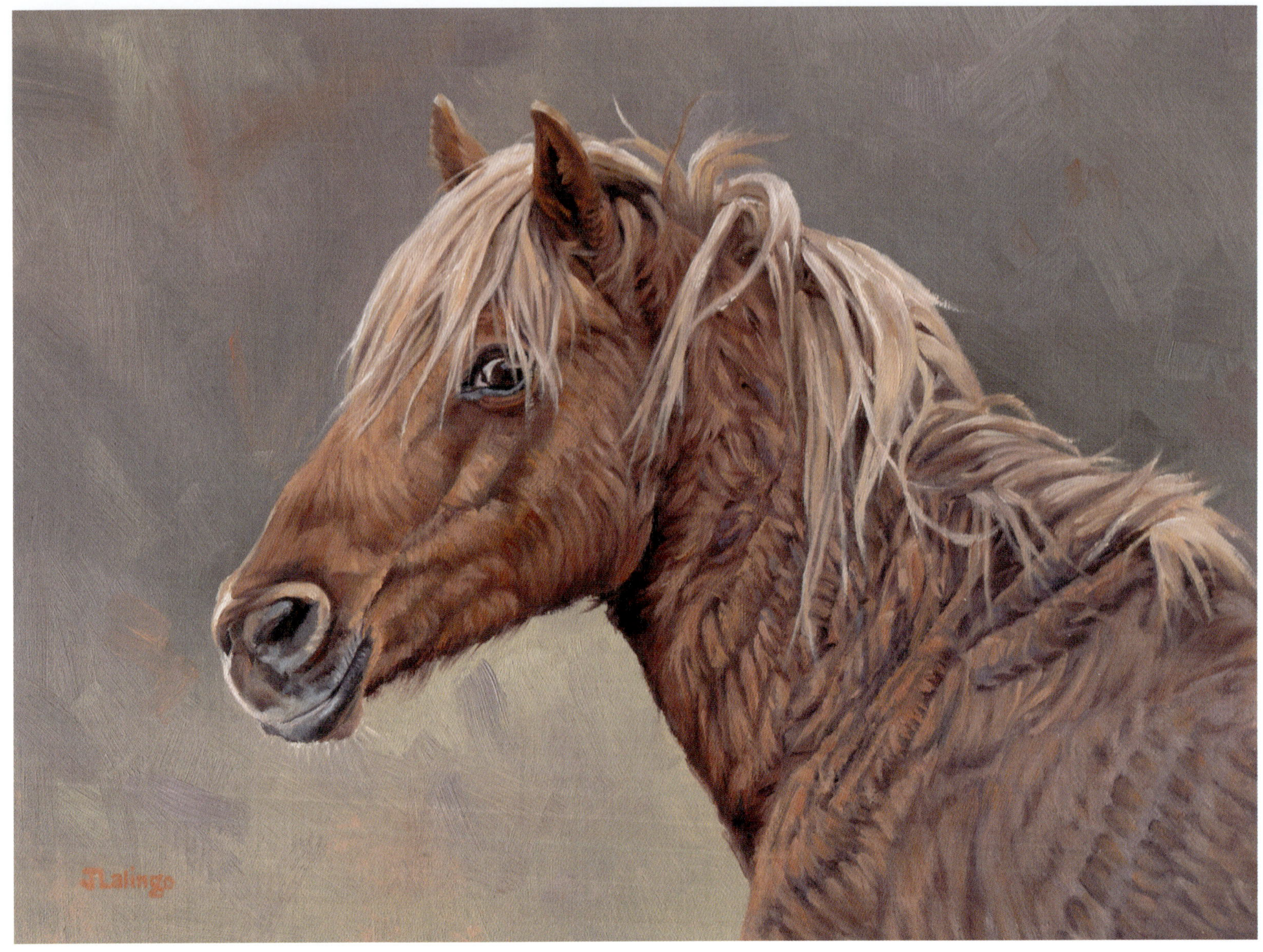

Judy Lalingo, Maryland
STINK EYE!

During these months of the shutdown, I find myself doing a lot of walking through fields and ponds, visiting my equine friends, and going through photos. As I excavate through thousands of memories via reference photos, I'm always trying to decide what to work on... vacillating from horses to wildlife to birds to landscapes, never quite making up my mind, but doing a lot of gathering and remembering. And then, I came across some of my Assateague Island files. The wild horses of Assateague Island have held a special place in my heart since I first discovered them as a young reader through Marguerite Henry's books; visiting the island through the past few years has only deepened that connection. And so it was that I found a memory of a stallion known as Corky—a series of photos of him in April 2019 on a rainy day in Assateague Island National Seashore, Maryland. The weather was cold and wet, but I remember spending the time observing and photographing this stallion watching over a couple of mares. His look said so much that I felt it was worthy of attempting to capture both his attitude and his spirit—reminding me of the wild freedom of nature. I find that comforting.

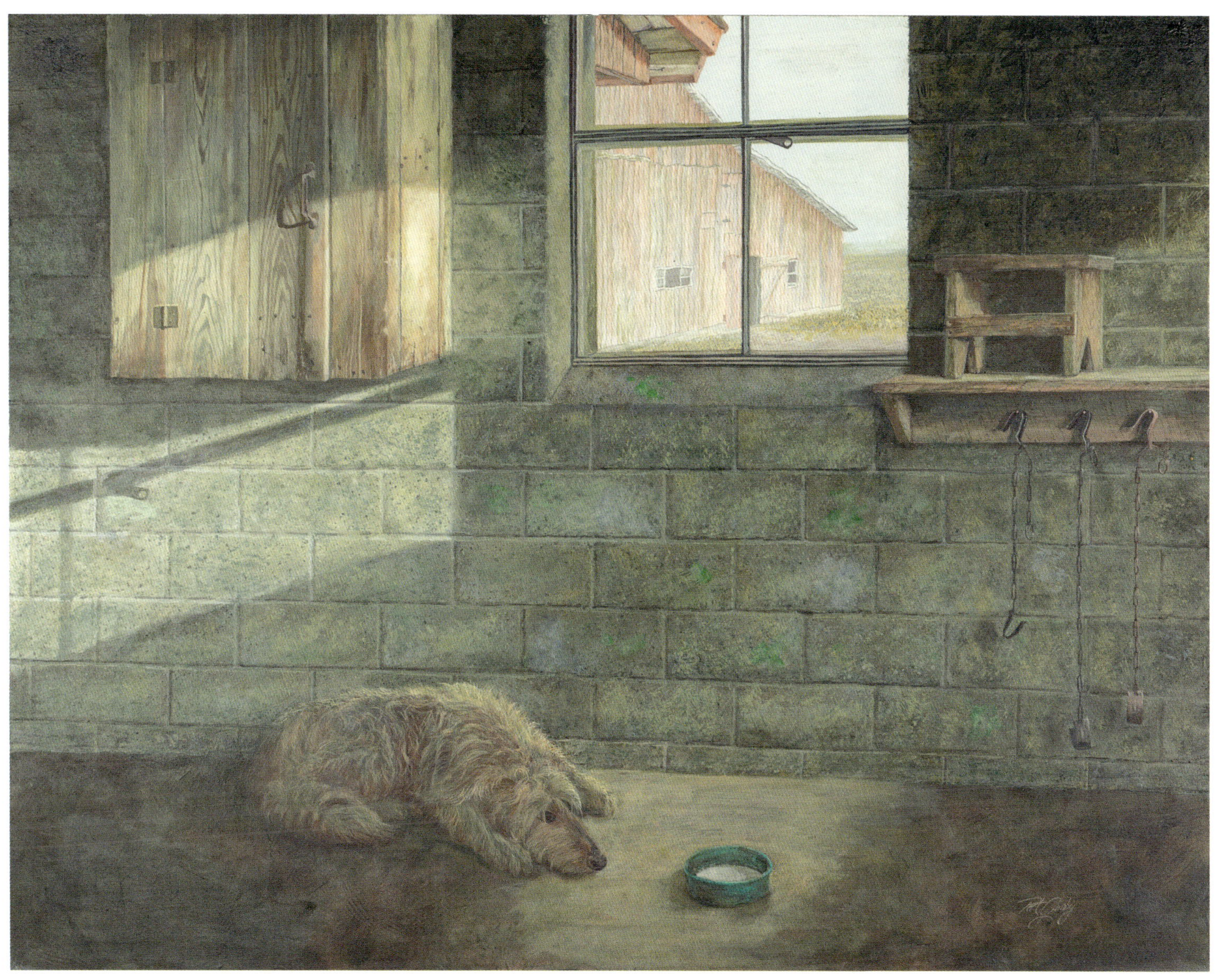

Pat Gamby, Ohio

SEIZE THE DAY

The memory of the stillness and solitude of the walls of our barn kept creeping back and forth during the stay-at-home order from our Ohio governor. The monogamous relationship of hanging our milkers in the milk parlor holds the emotion of our confinement behind cement block walls, which can instructively seize the security of our daily routine. The title of my egg tempera painting, *Seize The Day*, expresses my revelation of never knowing what the next day may bring.

4 BIRDS

For many, birds became the silver lining to the COVID-19 restrictions. Across the country, all turned their eyes to the skies in search of our feathered friends. For some, this new interest meant investing in bird feeders and an exploration of backyard birds; others went in search of species in natural areas close to home or farther afield. In a time when so many of us remained apart, the birds kept us together.

Birds need us, too. We must protect their habitat, restore the ecosystems they need to survive, and reduce impediments to their migration. Climate change is the biggest threat facing birds—and us!—and we must work together to reduce emissions and keep global temperatures from rising. Already birds face greater challenges as a result of sea-level rise, more intense storms and surges, fire, and drought.

At Audubon, we work to protect birds and the places they need, today and tomorrow. Audubon works throughout the Americas using science, advocacy, education, and on-the-ground conservation.

The collection of avian paintings featured here showcases birds as an inspiration, a reminder that resilience takes many forms, including ones with feathers.

Julie Wraithmell
VP, National Audubon Society
Executive Director, Audubon Florida

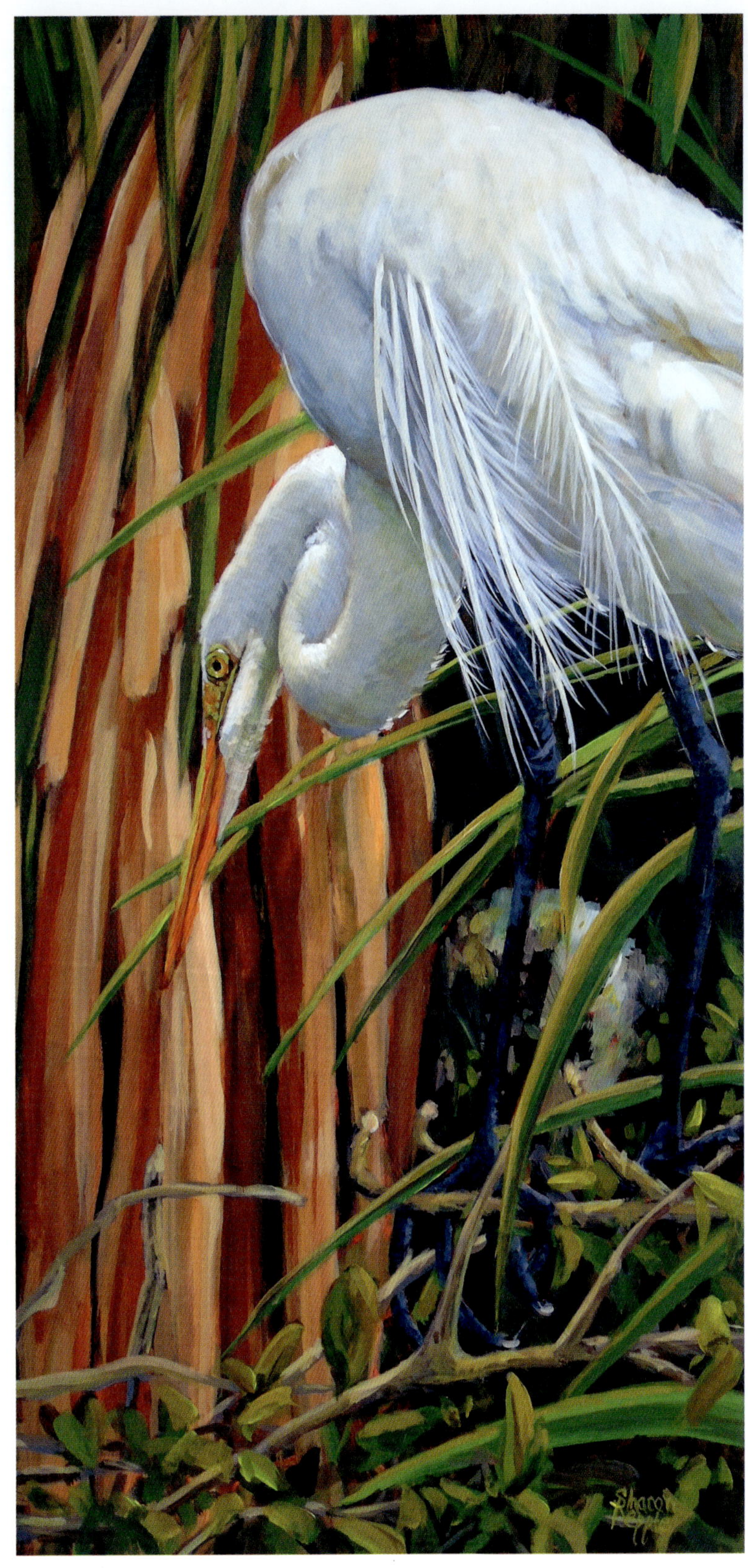

Sharon Repple, Florida

GREAT WHITE EGRET—ALLIGATOR FARM

Painting has been very healing during this time of isolation and social distancing. It has allowed me to focus on the beauty and intricacy of God's creation. As I painted *Great White Egret—Alligator Farm*, I decided to take photos of the whole process. Since I knew others were also isolated, I wanted to offer a step-by-step blog on my website so that they could paint along with me and view my process. Learning while isolated has helped me and others. I entered this painting into an important online exhibition, and I am excited to tell you that not only was it juried into the show, but it received a Merit Award.

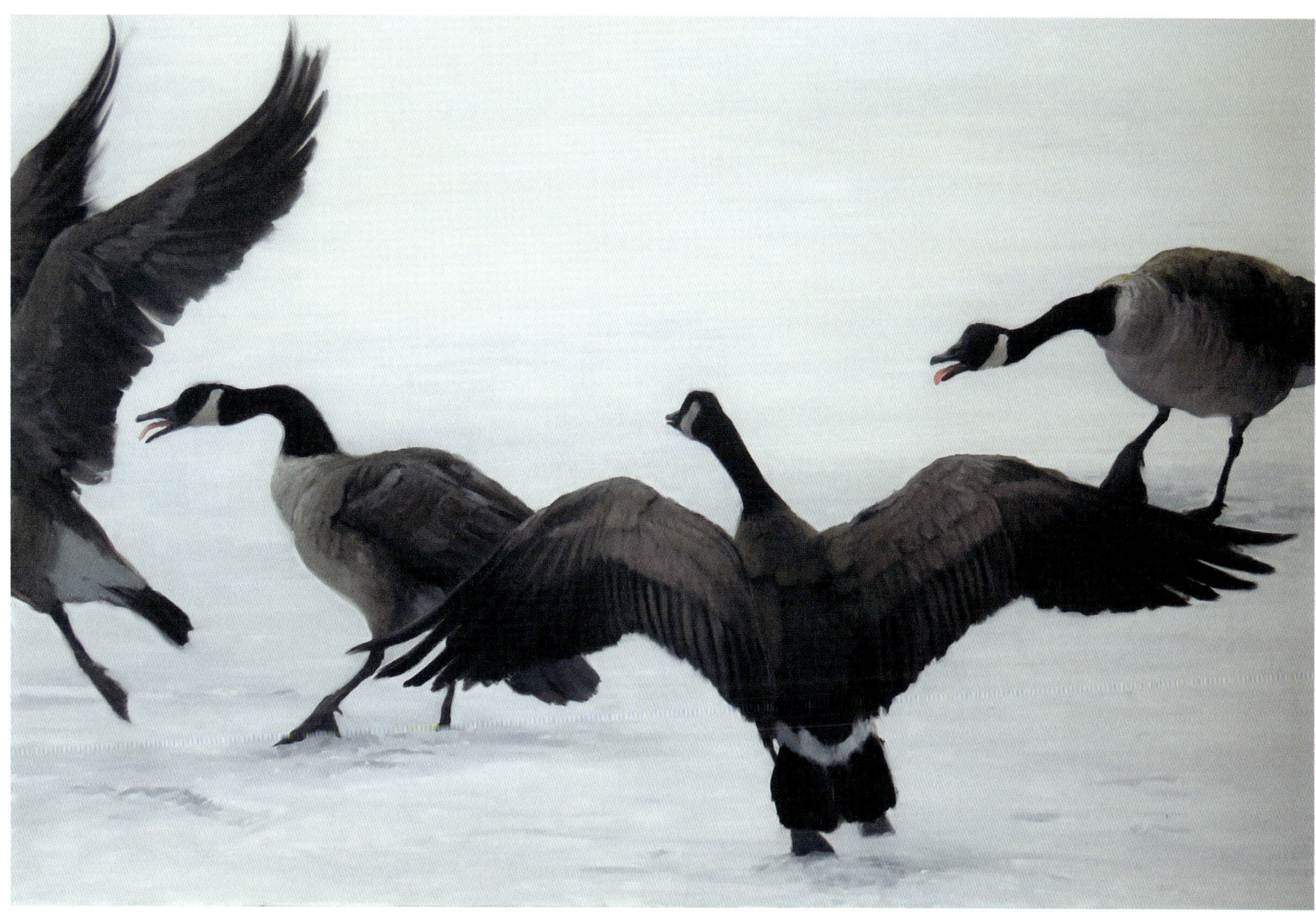

Kathleen Dunphy, California
SCRAM!

This painting evolved into a symbol of my feelings about the COVID-19 pandemic. As the virus spread, it seemed as though all the color had been leached from the world and we were all teaming up to fight the enemy. These Canadian geese hissing and flapping and chasing the badness away summed up our universal struggle against the virus.

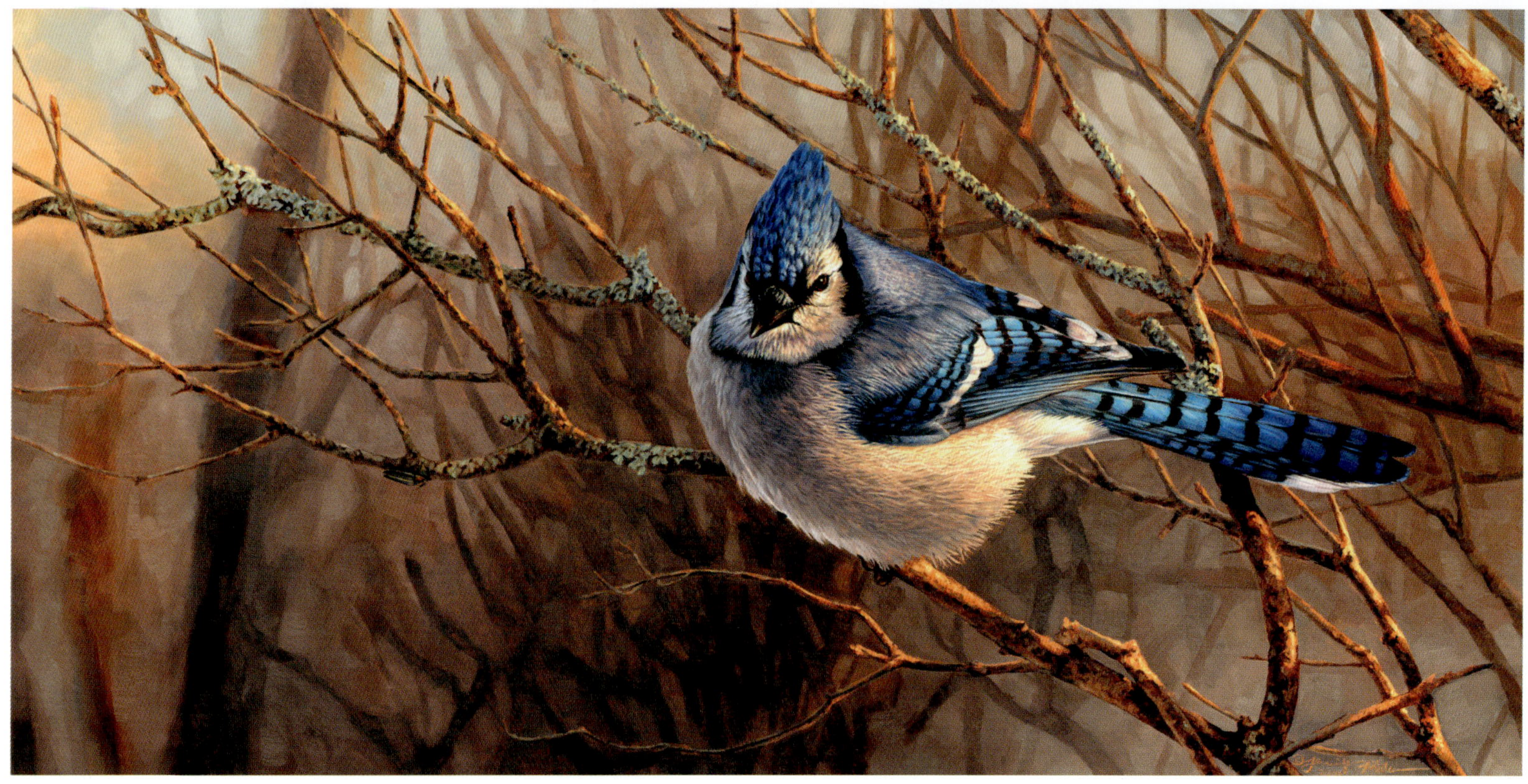

Jennifer Miller, New York
FADING LIGHT

When I started planning this painting, I had intended to experiment with a looser style. Quickly, however, things changed as the COVID-19 pandemic loomed on the horizon, and of course, broke as a crashing wave in my home state of NY. I am an immense nerd at heart and had previously done some study on viral diseases, which gave some foresight on what the looming pandemic might mean for our society. On top of the growing anxiety from the pandemic, the unfolding exposure of human rights injustices, and personal woes, I discovered that I needed to work on a painting where I could lose myself in working on the details of the bird, even if that was a direction I wanted to move away from only months before. *Fading Light* is, in a way, a manifestation of the complex emotions and anxiety weighing on me. I added a firefly, *Ellychnia corrusca*, which is a lantern-less (no glow) firefly active in late winter and early spring, hiding under the branch that the jay is perched on.

Linda J. Schroeter, California

THE PROTECTOR

I am the swan, struggling with the overwhelming fear of entrapment, terrified and helpless, trying to protect my family from threatening fires, rising water, and disease. We live in rural Sonoma County in California. In the last two years, we have been evacuated from bushfires twice, stranded for several days by flooded roads, and have been placed under strict quarantine after our son contracted COVID-19. Women all over the world are struggling with the impact of the pandemic with its devastating social and economic impacts, but I believe women are also the backbone of our nation's recovery. This project has given me both renewed determination and hope. *The Protector* is inspired by *The Threatened Swan* by Jan Asselijn, painted in 1650-52.

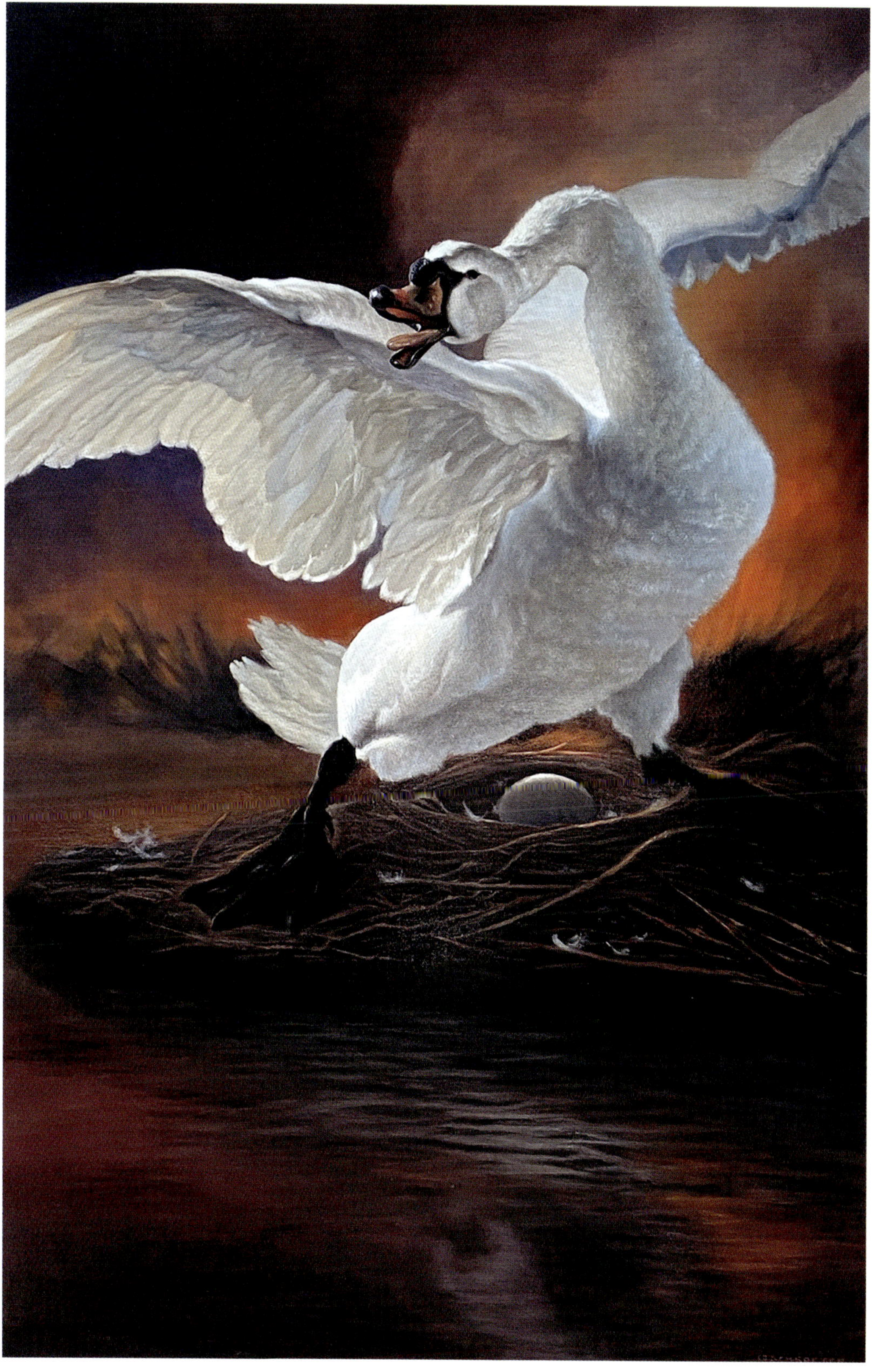

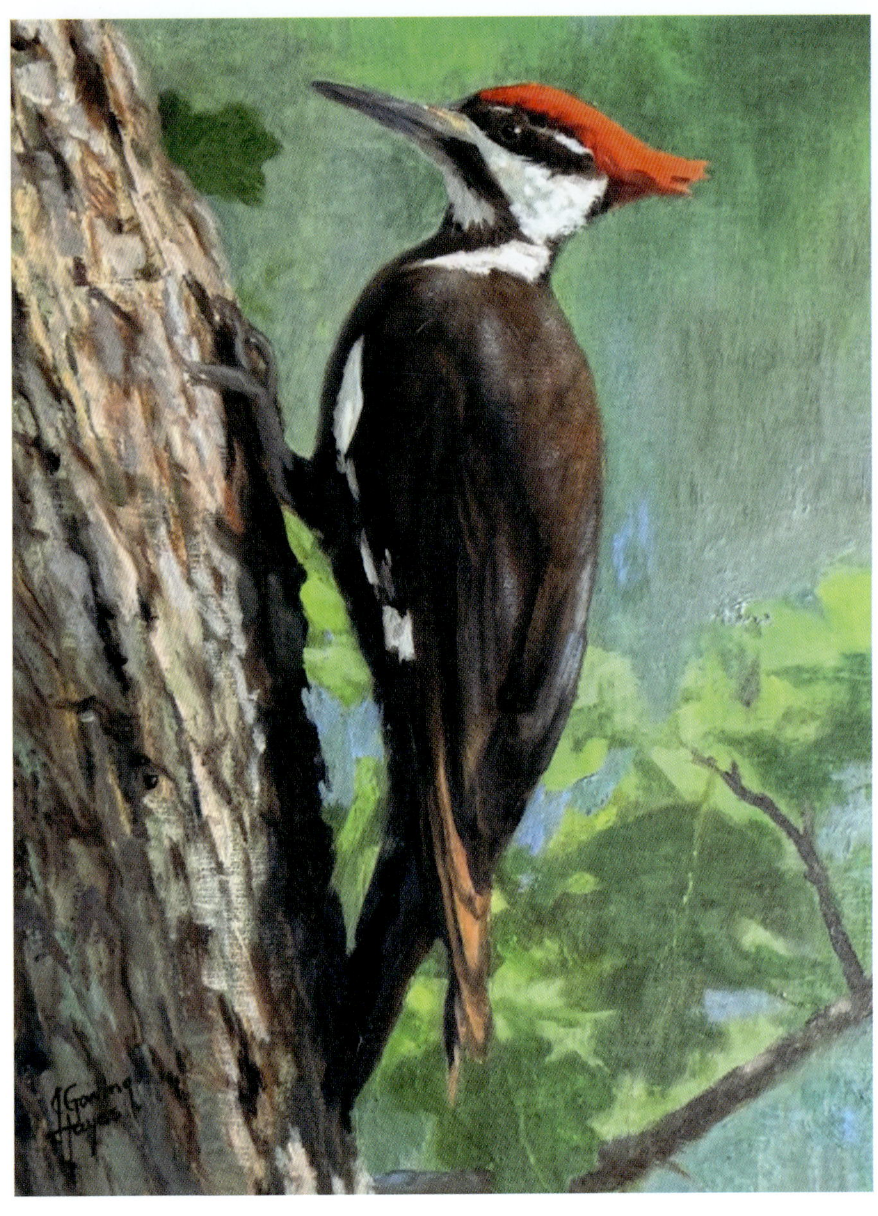

Julie Gowing Hayes, Arkansas
WOODLAND REDHEAD

I have always been an avid birdwatcher, but as COVID-19 began shutting the world down, it seemed the birds stepped up to the challenge of offering amazing backyard entertainment to provide a much-needed diversion from the negativity of news outlets. It was peak migration season and I spent hours watching and photographing, not just the usual visitors. Breeds that only pass through for a brief time usually go unnoticed because of normal everyday busyness. It also gave me a reason to get up and out early as it was a challenge to keep the feeders full every day. Social media provided an outlet to connect with like-minded people to share the beauty by providing photos and exchanging information about the birds—a much-needed break from the negativity of the news.

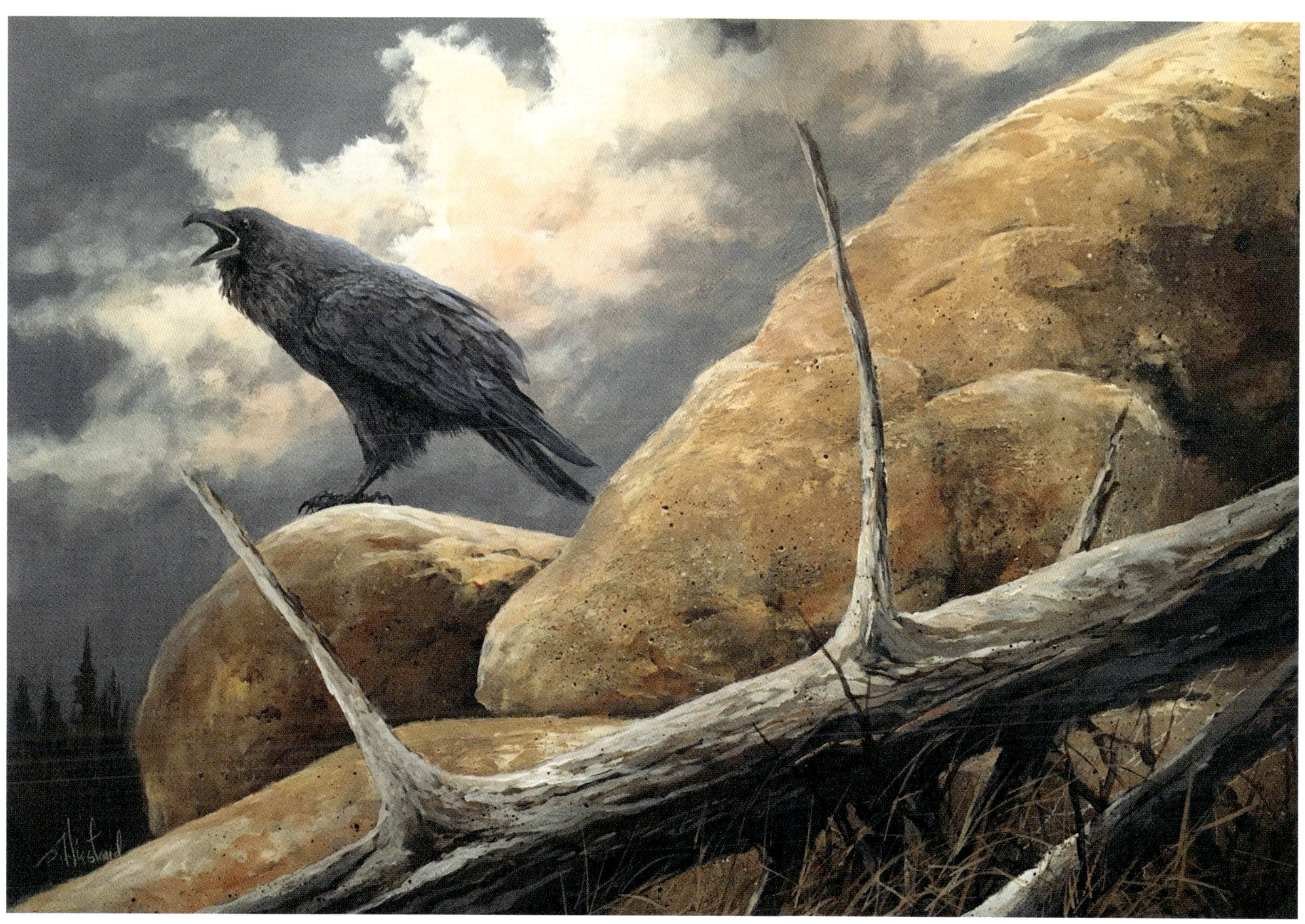

Scott Hiestand
THE OMEN

Ever since I started working inside due to the virus, I have been thinking a lot about my time living in Colorado and my appreciation for its countryside and wildlife. I have added four studio paintings to my repertoire that showcase this area of our country. Recently, I have added four new works, including a bobcat, red fox, and a Canada goose. I am looking forward to our nation's healing and getting back to my love of plein-air painting.

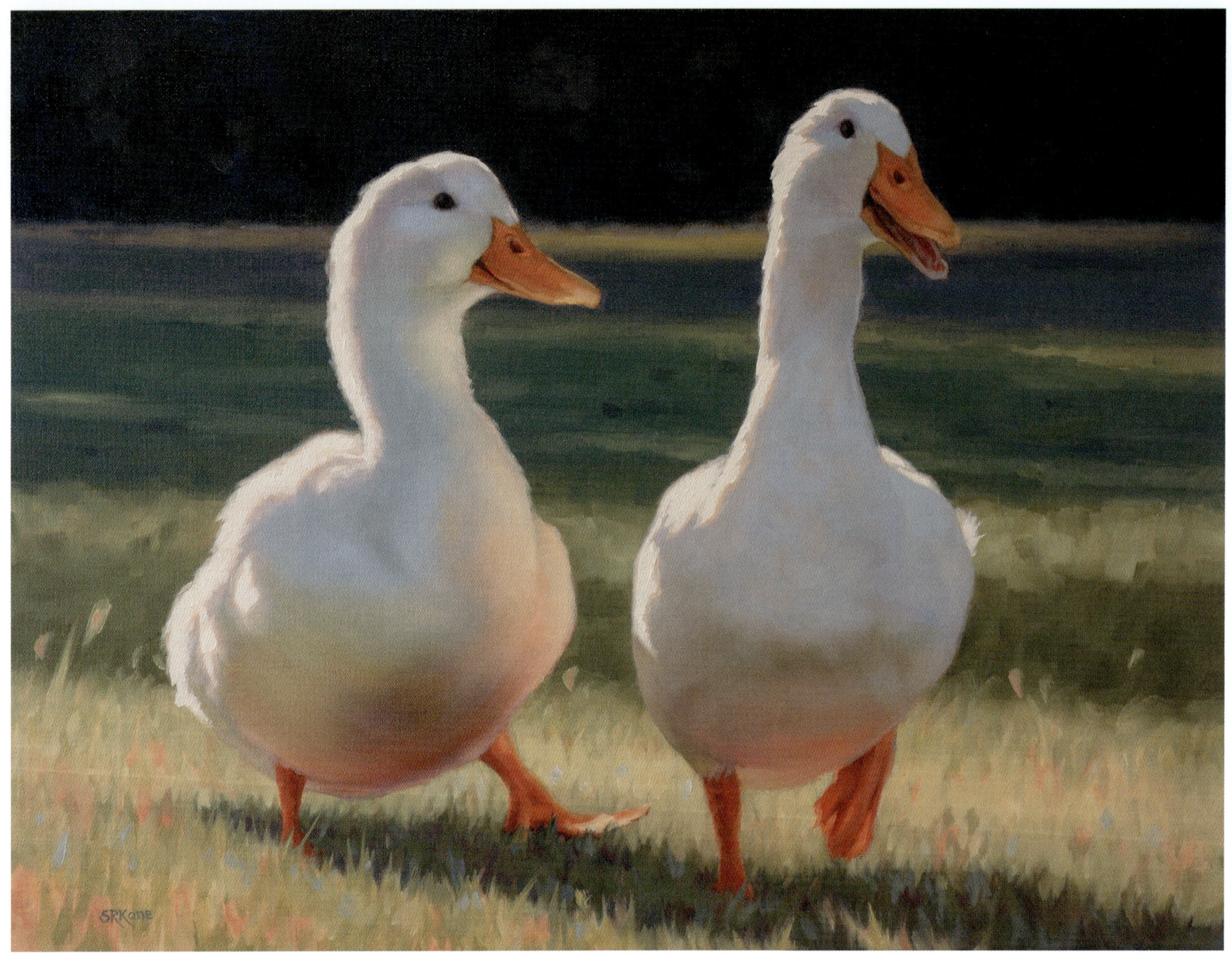

Sonia Kane, North Carolina

LUCKY DUCKS

I often go for walks around one of our nearby duck-filled lakes and, during the pandemic, I've noticed the popularity of these lakes has boomed. Moms and dads pushing strollers, families with kids biking or skating, joggers working up a sweat, people walking dogs of all sizes, couples strolling hand-in-hand...it's a communal "let's go outside and play" mindset. And haven't we all needed that this past year? To me, these happy ducks epitomize that mindset as they play with joyful abandon. Their cheerful personalities make me smile every time I look at them.

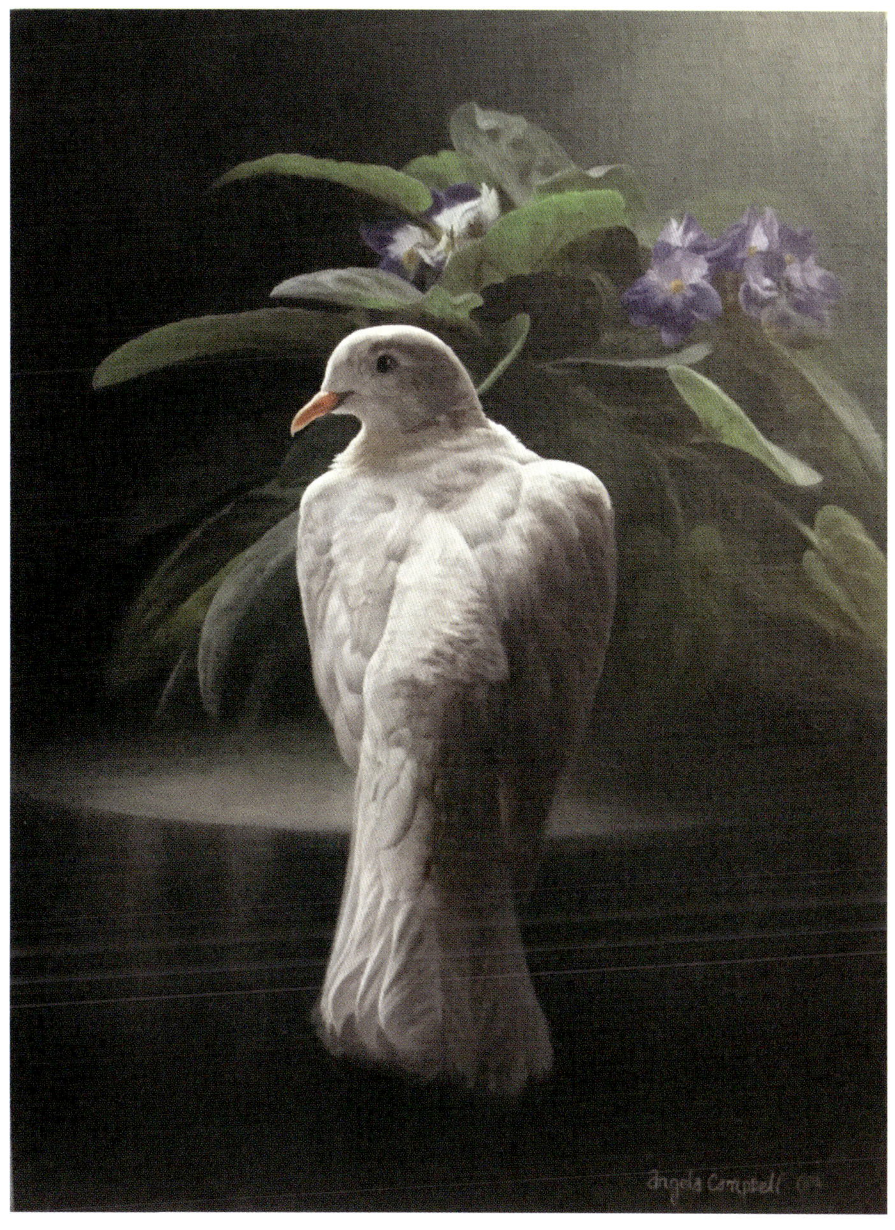

Angela Campbell, Kentucky
PEACEFULLY WAITING

An artist friend wrote on Facebook a few weeks after the pandemic started that artists were well equipped for isolation. While being at home and social distancing was stressful at times, I was happy to be able to focus on painting every day instead of how much I missed being around friends and family. I had thought about doing a painting of our pet dove, Peebers, for years. At this time, I could relate to a bird out of his cage but still trapped inside the house. The African violets behind him remind me that even when it feels like winter, spring will come.

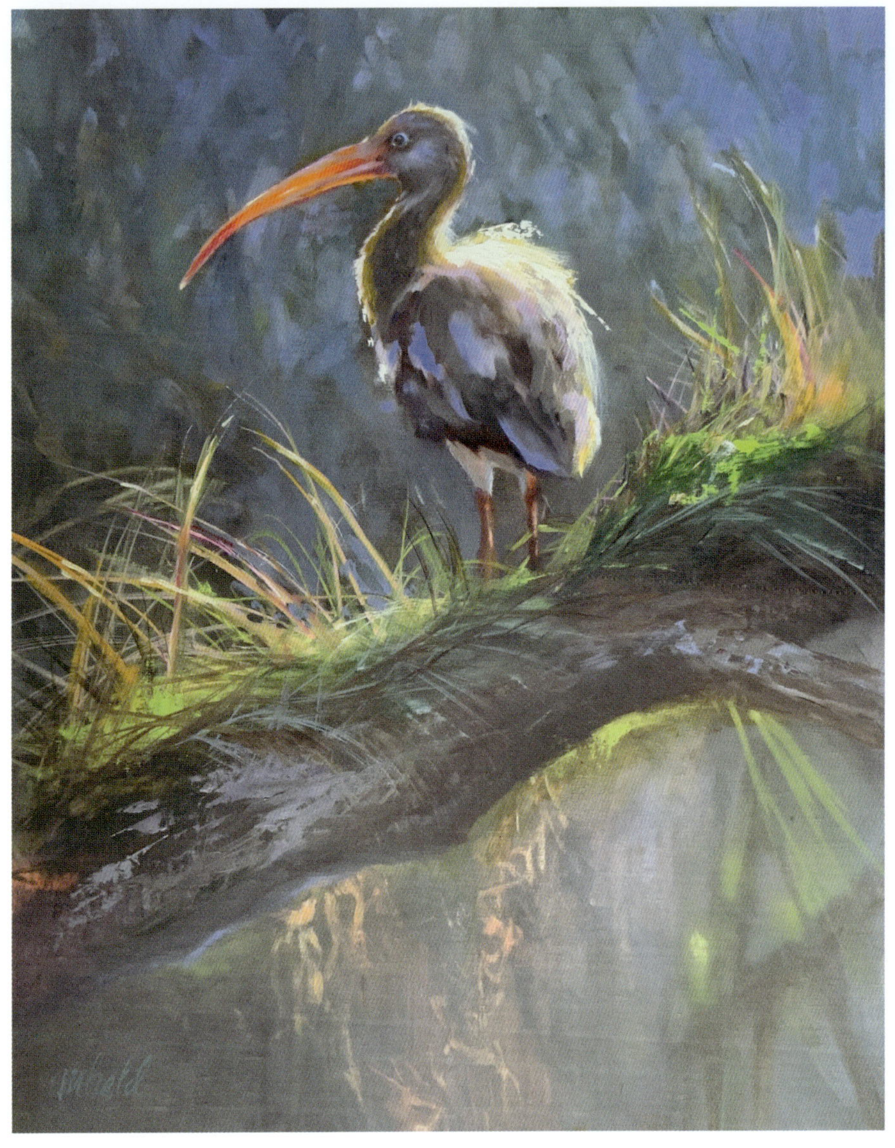

Michelle Held, Florida

MORNING MISTY IBIS ON WEKIVA

What just happened? I found myself in a literal tailspin. I was returning from what is always an amazing painting trip with my closest friends in Wekiva, Florida. Being an artist who does not watch negative movies, TV, or news, it was the most inspiring trip yet. Friends, hugs, art—what could be better?

Fast forward to sitting at home glued to every negative dramatic bit of information as my daughter and son are essential workers. My worst fear hit. It was the possibility that something would happen to my granddaughter and there would be no visitation to a hospital. As you can tell, my intense imagination (that is usually expressed on a canvas) went to a deep, dark place. I was paralyzed!

Meanwhile, the next four jobs were canceled due to the stay-at-home orders. It was then that I was forced to cancel my dream vacation, which was to finally travel overseas...darker and deeper I went. I finally confided in my best friend. Online it seemed everyone was being so lighthearted and dreaming of what they would read or eat that day. My fear was income...how will I survive? My friend, who knows me so well, was compassionate and understanding and she cleverly challenged me to do a painting of a subject we had both photographed. I only had two days to complete the challenge (her rules). I took the bait. I had never felt so happy. I turned the news off and the music on, and this is what came off of my brush. I cried over how emotional this breakthrough was! I can tell you, I have painted many pictures since that day. Take small doses of the news and you will love this painting forever.

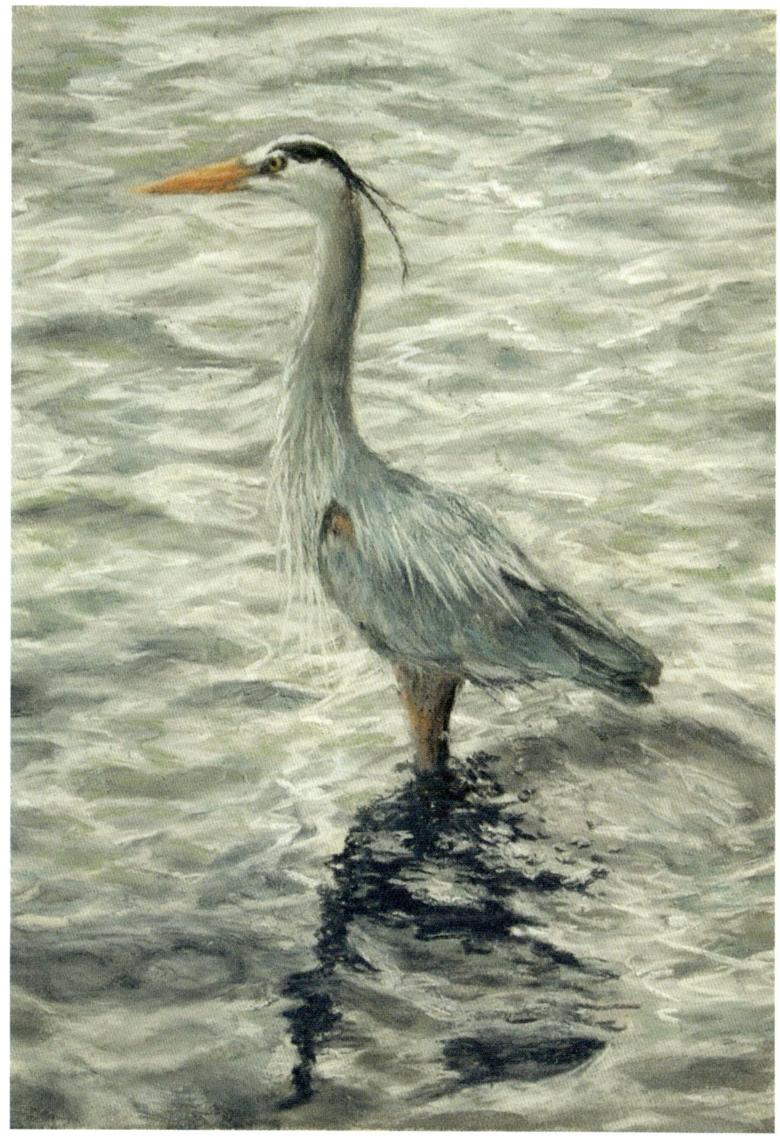

Susan Klabak, Wisconsin

BE STILL

Spending time alone in nature or my studio is a natural way of life for me. When I find myself anxious about the news of the day as COVID-19 cases and the death toll rise, I seek solace outdoors and through painting. Nature frequently rewards me with special moments that bring renewed hope. Through the years, the land has suffered from natural disasters, man-made destruction, and even the harshness of winter, yet each spring brings new growth. Observing the spring awakening of the land has been a soul-lifting reminder of the resilience of nature. Watching this heron brought one of those special moments. He seemed unaware of my presence as I sat quietly watching him, and he stood motionless watching the water. He calmly, peacefully, and patiently waited for just the right moment. The title of my painting, *Be Still*, seemed fitting. While the world was suffering a global pandemic, this heron had not a care in the world other than catching his dinner.

"Look at the birds of the air; they neither sow nor reap nor gather into barns, and yet your heavenly Father feeds them. Are you not of more value than they?"
Matthew 6:26

May we be still as we wait for this invisible enemy to be defeated. If, by chance, art and nature and faith can bring a moment of healing, a sense of peace, a calming of the spirit, let us just be still and accept the gentle reminders that the sun will indeed rise tomorrow.

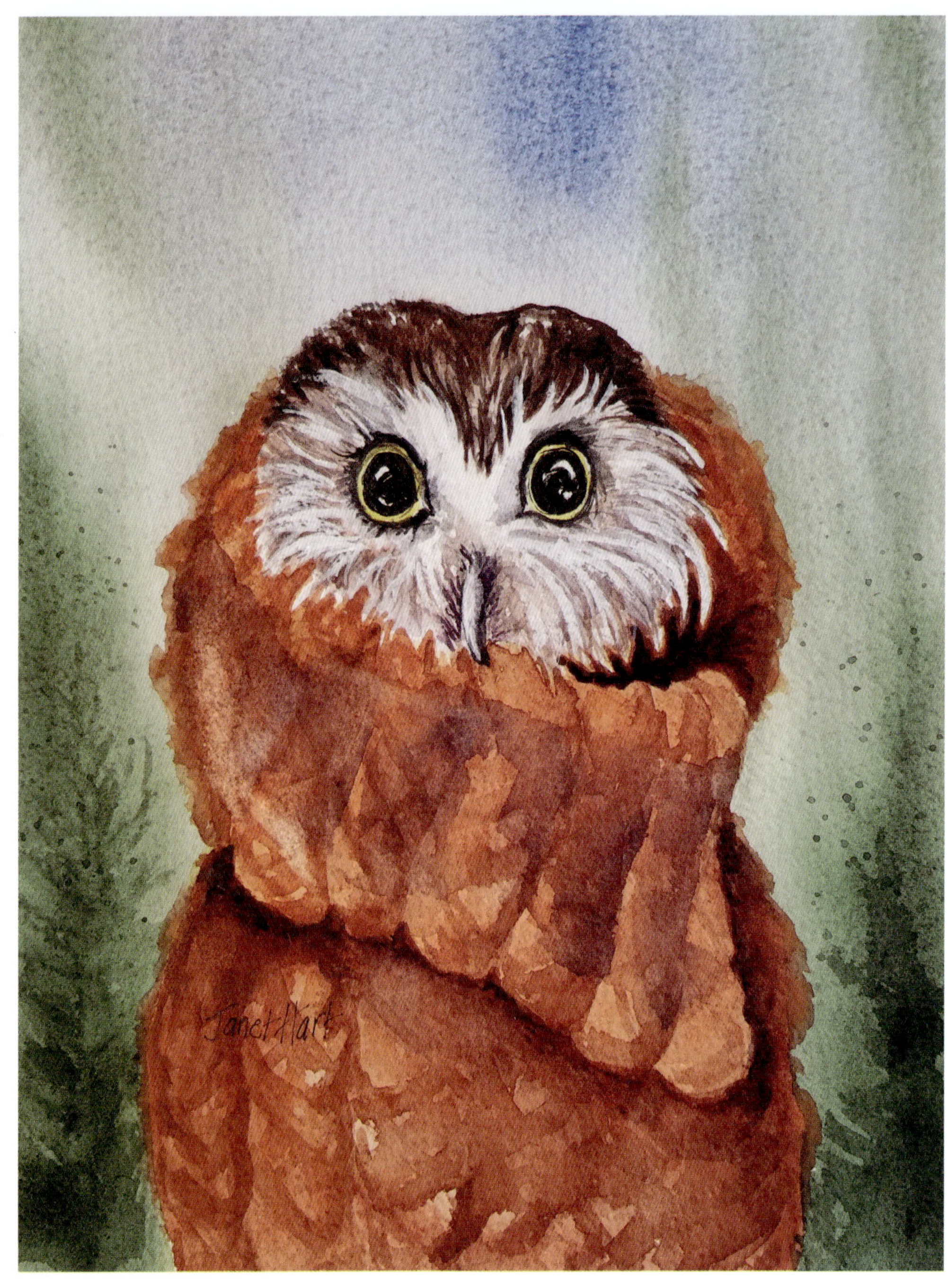

Janet Hart, West Virginia
ROCKEFELLER OWL

During the pandemic, I found myself in my studio every day thinking of new art ideas when I saw the publicity about the Rockefeller owl found in the Christmas tree headed for Rockefeller Center in New York City. I just had to paint that cute little owl!

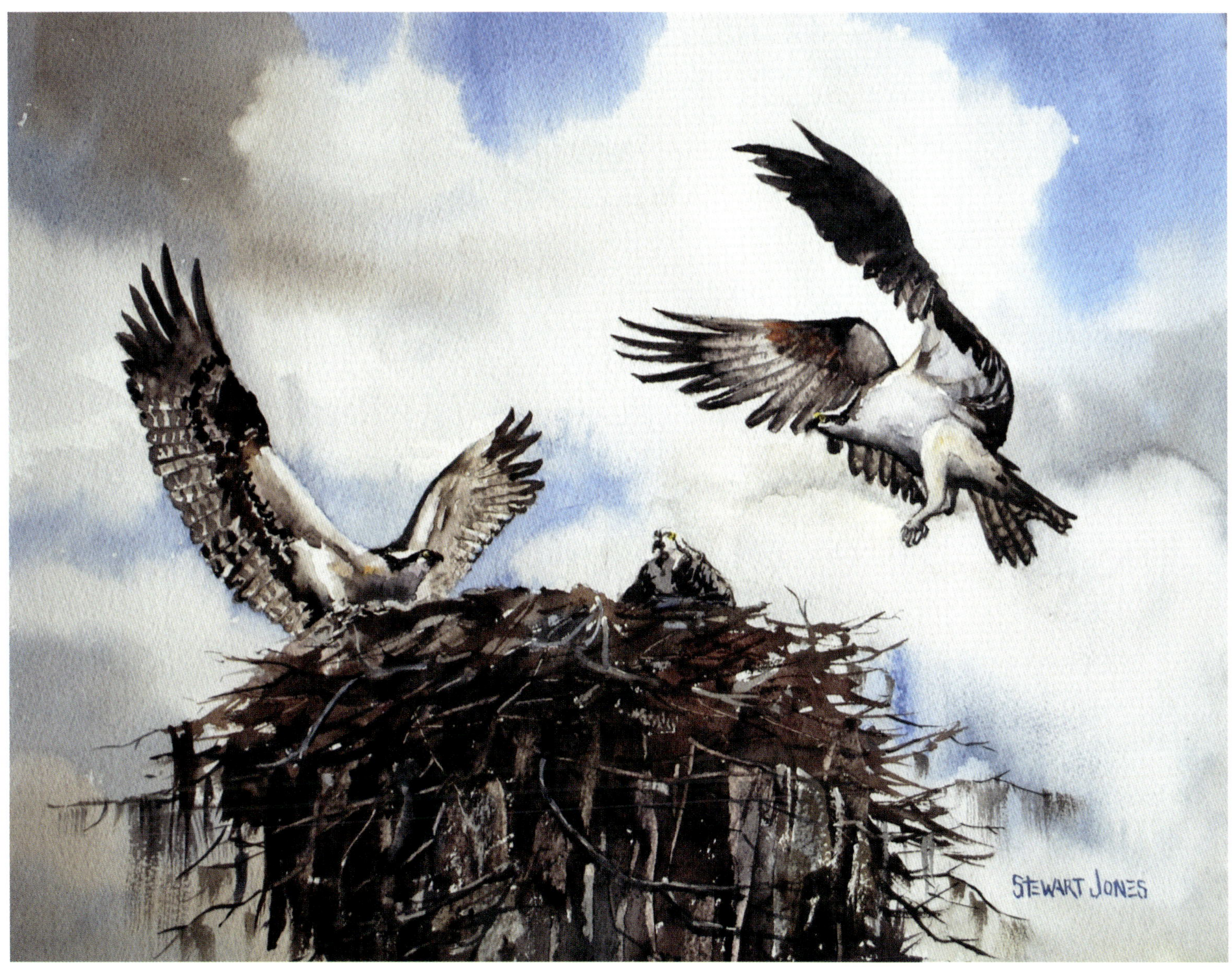

Stewart Jones, Florida

RETURNING HOME

I have been painting for many years, but never before during the challenges and isolation wrought by a global pandemic. I have tried to stay positive and not regret any lost possibilities. Instead, I used the time to work on my art and welcomed more opportunities to paint en plein air.

Before the pandemic, I worked out of my studio/gallery in Sanford, Florida, along with 12 other artists. When we had to close the studio, I painted at home, sometimes enjoying the compositions of the garden in my backyard. Once our studio doors reopened, we followed restrictions and kept six feet apart, and wore masks. As time went on, guests were allowed back into our gallery. I started my painting classes again, working with people who also longed to escape from their isolation.

I have explored new areas to paint and found new inspiration while thinking about family and friends I could not be with. My painting of ospreys in the nest reminded me of how life goes on despite everything that is happening in the world. The birds do what they need to survive, as do we. I am grateful for the time I spent enjoying nature, learning about wildlife, and painting subjects that I have longed to portray.

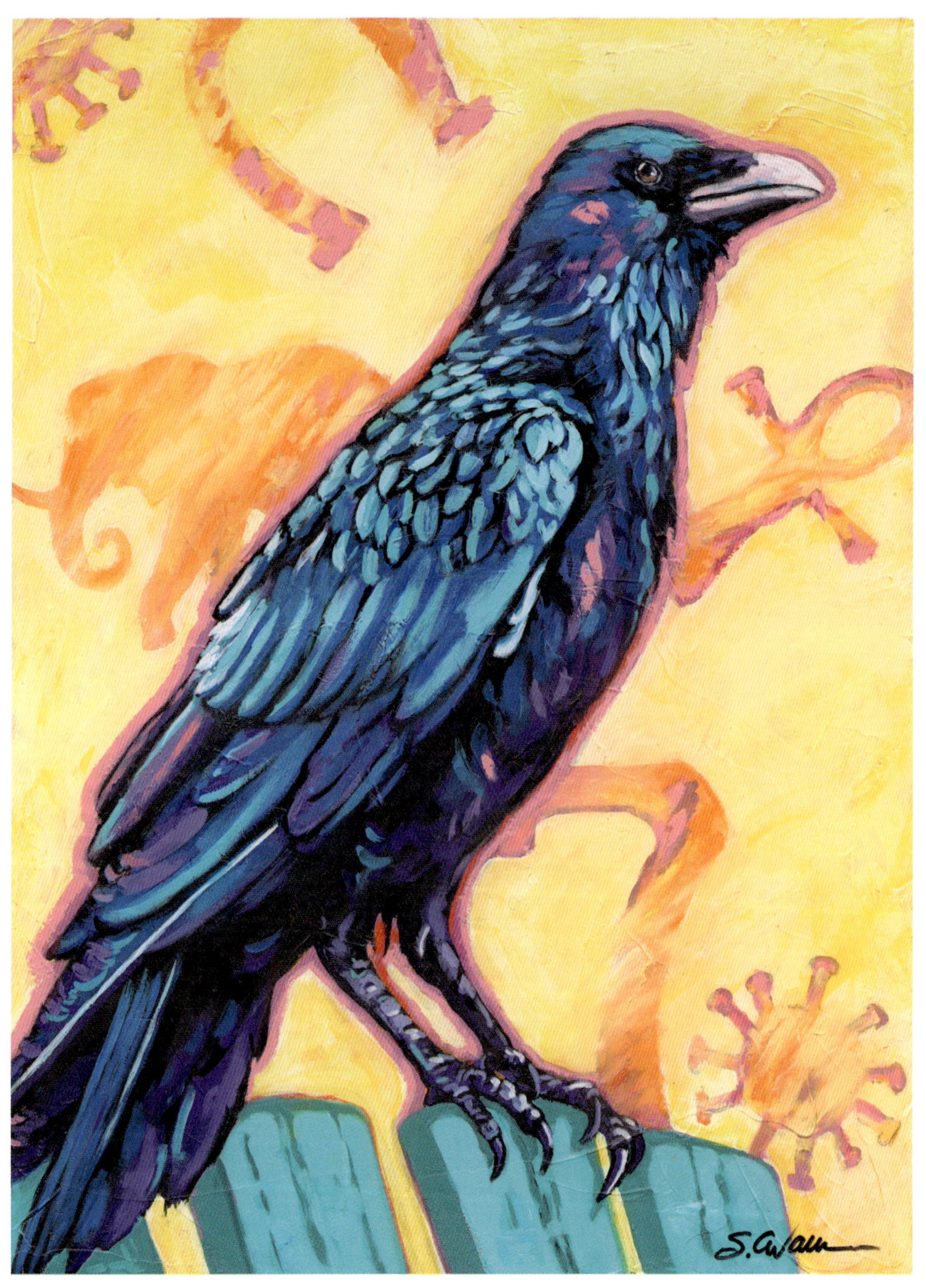

Sally C. Evans, Florida

THE SOOTHSAYER OF THE PANDEMIC

I had just spent the previous week, before the shutdown, out in the Wekiva Forest with my husband Tom Sadler creating work for the Wekiva Paint Out 2020. It was total bliss, being in nature around all of our art friends and painting.

The first Monday of the COVID-19 shut down, I woke up and opened our front curtains to find a crow staring at me, perched on the back of our Adirondack chair and not flying off. It really freaked me out because they are associated with bad luck and we have never had any in our neighborhood, much less on our front porch. It was staring me right in the eyes and stayed there for a bit. I ran and got Tom to see it but by the time he got to the window, it was gone. We had quite a few crows in the neighborhood that March that hung around.

The rest of the week was crazy trying to shop for regular house goods, since I hadn't bought food or toilet paper for over a week, having attended the Paint Out. I thought the world had gone mad! I couldn't stop thinking about the crow, so I looked up what they symbolize. They are a superstitious type of bird. In some cultures, they bring good luck! They are also very intelligent creatures.

As the pandemic and shutdown wore on, art was selling! Things were selling like before the 2008 crash. People were hungry for art and wanted things that made them feel good. Bill and Mary Sue Weinaug called and asked us to create a painting about our feelings about the pandemic. I knew I wanted my piece to be about my contact with the crow, but I couldn't visualize what I wanted to say until this past summer.

The crow was bringing the good news that everything was going to be okay, so I created the painting with him or her on the back of our chair with good luck symbols behind it. I added an elephant, lucky number seven, a horseshoe, and the Ankh (an Egyptian lucky symbol). I hope I'm conveying something more positive during this negative time that I've had about the pandemic. It's been a very trying time for the world!

5 BEACHES

The worldwide pandemic has brought uncertainty in normal everyday routines of life and great sadness for so many. It has also provided a time of reflection in many ways to bring about change. As humans, we turn to what provides solace, being thankful for our own life's scenes while we continue to yearn for a brighter day.

These selected beaches holistically provide a sense of optimism—some depict darkness and uncertainty, some leave you longing for the carefree days of yesterday, while others capture the light in just a way that leaves you feeling that the best may be yet to come.

Tony D'Amico
Madison, Connecticut

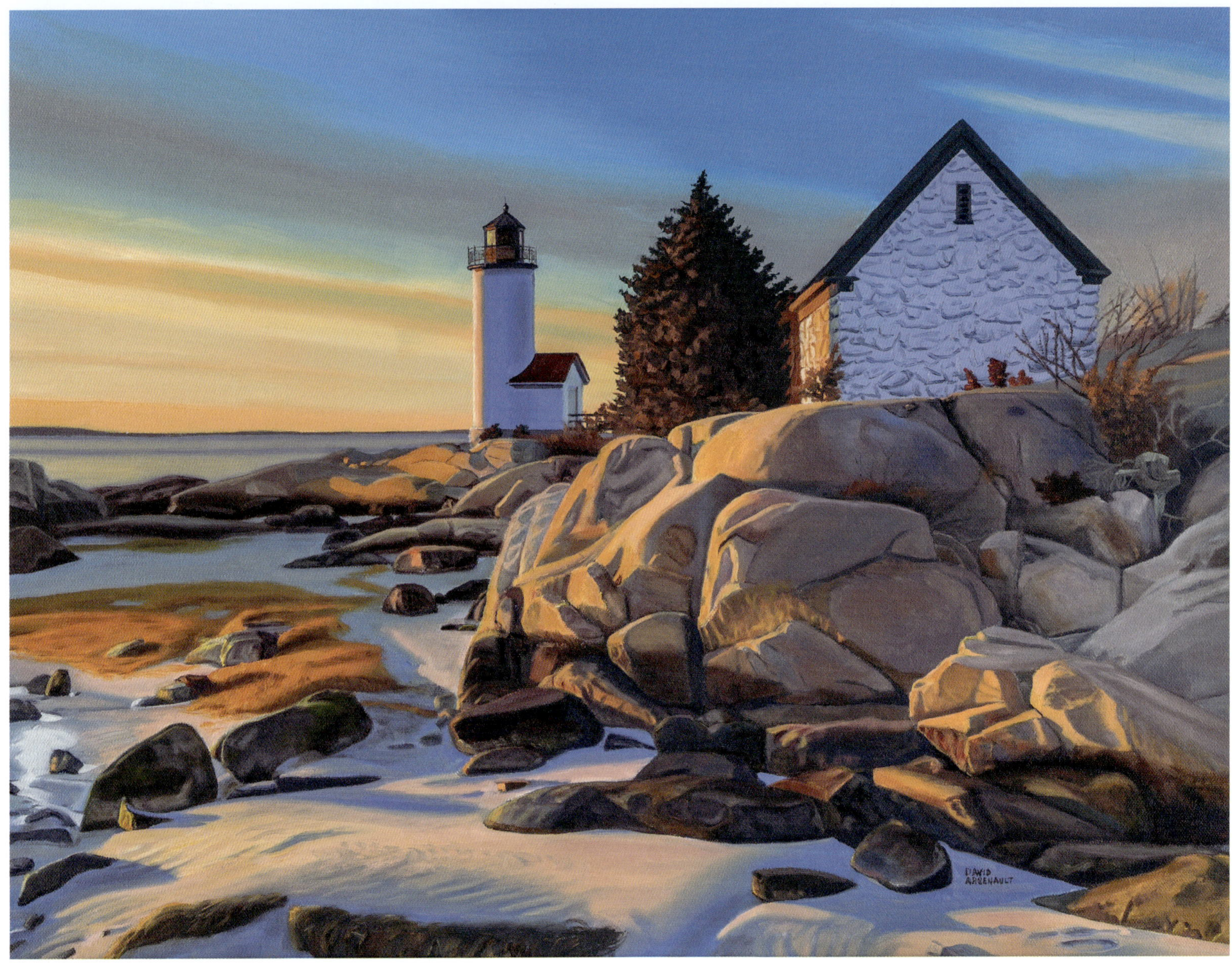

David Arsenault, Massachusetts

GOING TOWARDS THE LIGHT

It's late in the day, the shadows are long, and your workday is over. It's more vital than ever to get outside, to breathe some fresh air, and to experience the sense of freedom you crave. It helps to have a beautiful neighborhood to enjoy and special places to visit—as long as you share what you see. As an artist, that's what I'm called to do.

And when we go out, what do we see? Nature, in all of its life-sustaining beauty and diversity, is blessed with a respite allowing for its return to a more robust state of health across earth, sea, and sky. Nature: something of which we are an undeniable part, offering rest and renewal to people forced to stay at home who are desperate for the gifts of the outdoors. Nature: a source of inspiration for generation after generation of artists, presenting us with endless opportunities to internalize, understand, and express what we feel in her presence. And when bathed in the magic of light, it invites us to do exactly that. And we do... because we must.

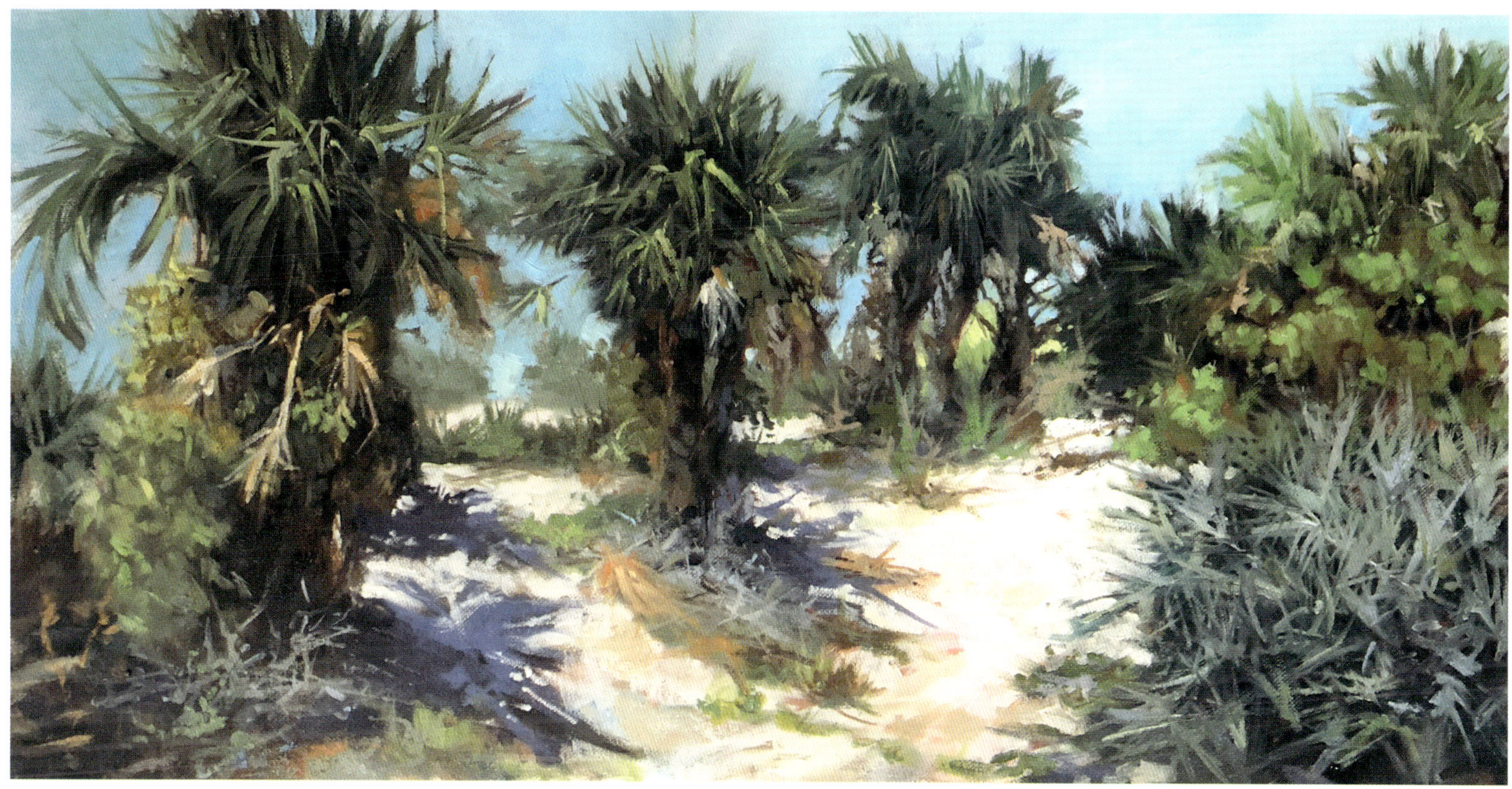

Lynne Polley, Florida
DUNE PALMS

I have always found solace in quiet places.

So, when news of a possible pandemic began, and extreme projections of martial law, I took my chance to drive an hour north to visit one of my favorite quiet spots: Smyrna Dunes Park, in New Smyrna Beach, FL. Since social distancing had begun, and the beaches were closing one by one, I was unsure if I would even get into the parking lot.

Thankfully, they were open. These are my social distancing palms. I loved the contrast of the white sand and the complexity of the palm trees, all choosing their own space. Standing firm. Still beautiful despite the chaos around them. Even though we may all have a "new normal," this spot stays quiet, reminding us to take stock in the places that give us joy.

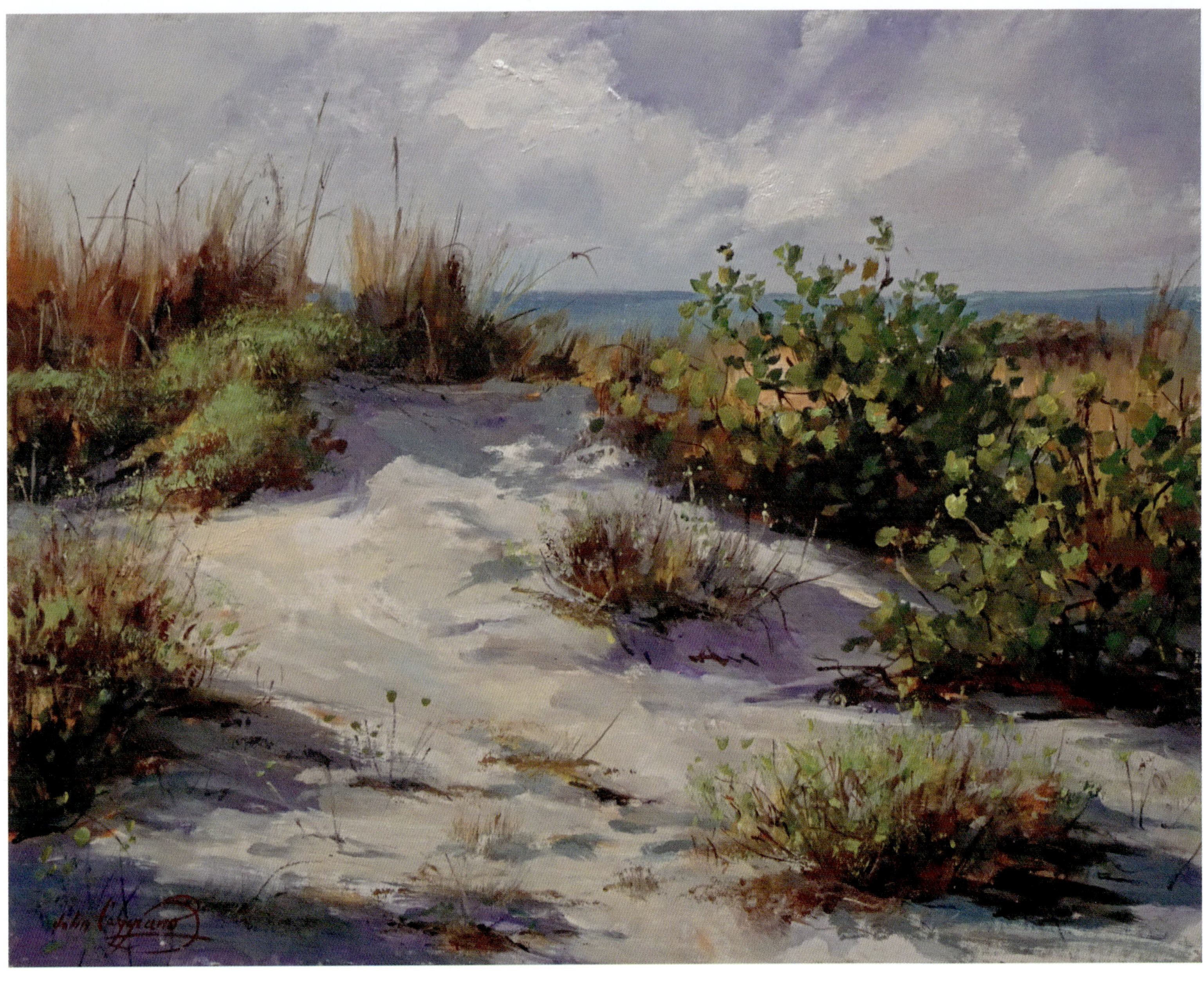

John S. Caggiano, Massachusetts
OVER THE DUNES

This painting has been featured in a *PleinAir* magazine article about me. One of my motivations for painting this subject is its view of the sea. It is right there, just over the dunes. Symbolic freedom. This element always attracts me. At a time such as this, its significance is magnified. How our lives have changed in so short a period of time. Of course, Mother Earth moves right along. She does not care whether we are here or not. In fact, she has used this time to heal herself from the countless injuries inflicted upon her. Hopefully, when this is all over, we will have a different attitude toward our environment.

I am lucky to be an artist. I know that many are feeling isolated. However, an artist tends to lead a solitary existence. So, for me, it is a little easier to adjust to the "new normal." As much as I would like to be out of lockdown, I am happy to be painting. After all, it is my raison d'etre. Likewise, I continue to search for that freedom beyond the dunes.

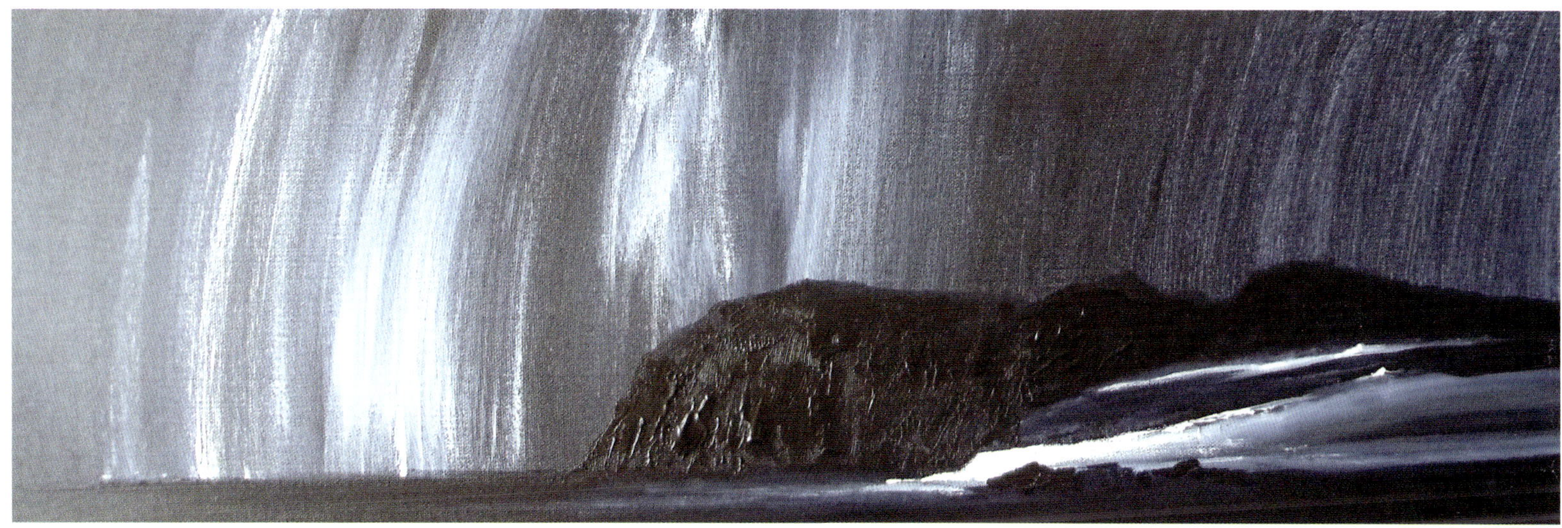

Jos Biviano, Virginia

ISOLATION: WILHELMINA BAY, ANTARCTICA

Newly identified as the Artist In Residence to the One World Polar Team, I was to embark on a Science Expedition to western Antarctica in January 2020. With a year's worth of Antarctic training behind me, I was to accompany marine biological and geological teams, painting in situ, the events of our findings. Never would I have thought that within the span of eight days my trip would vanish before my eyes because of the Coronavirus. The isolation of our expedition's location substituted the isolation I now felt at not being able to travel to the white continent.

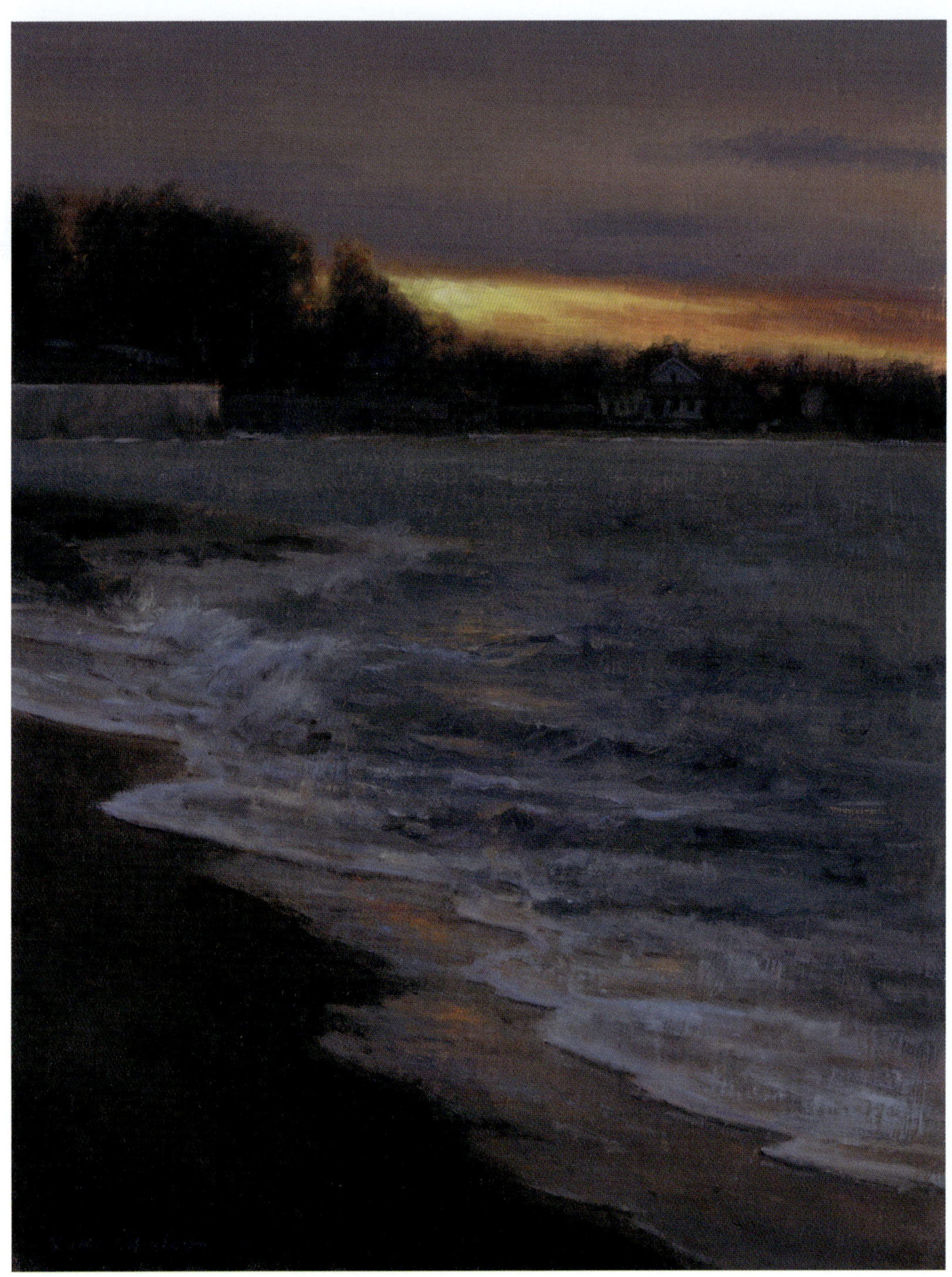

Tony D'Amico, Connecticut

SEAVIEW AT SUNRISE

The premise of this painting was to capture the subtle transition of color just prior to sunrise along the shoreline. I selected this painting for the exhibition because the subject represents hope and optimism. Although the current situation might appear bleak, with faith and perseverance, we look forward to brighter days ahead. A very special thanks to all the dedicated essential workers who risk their lives every day to help us all.

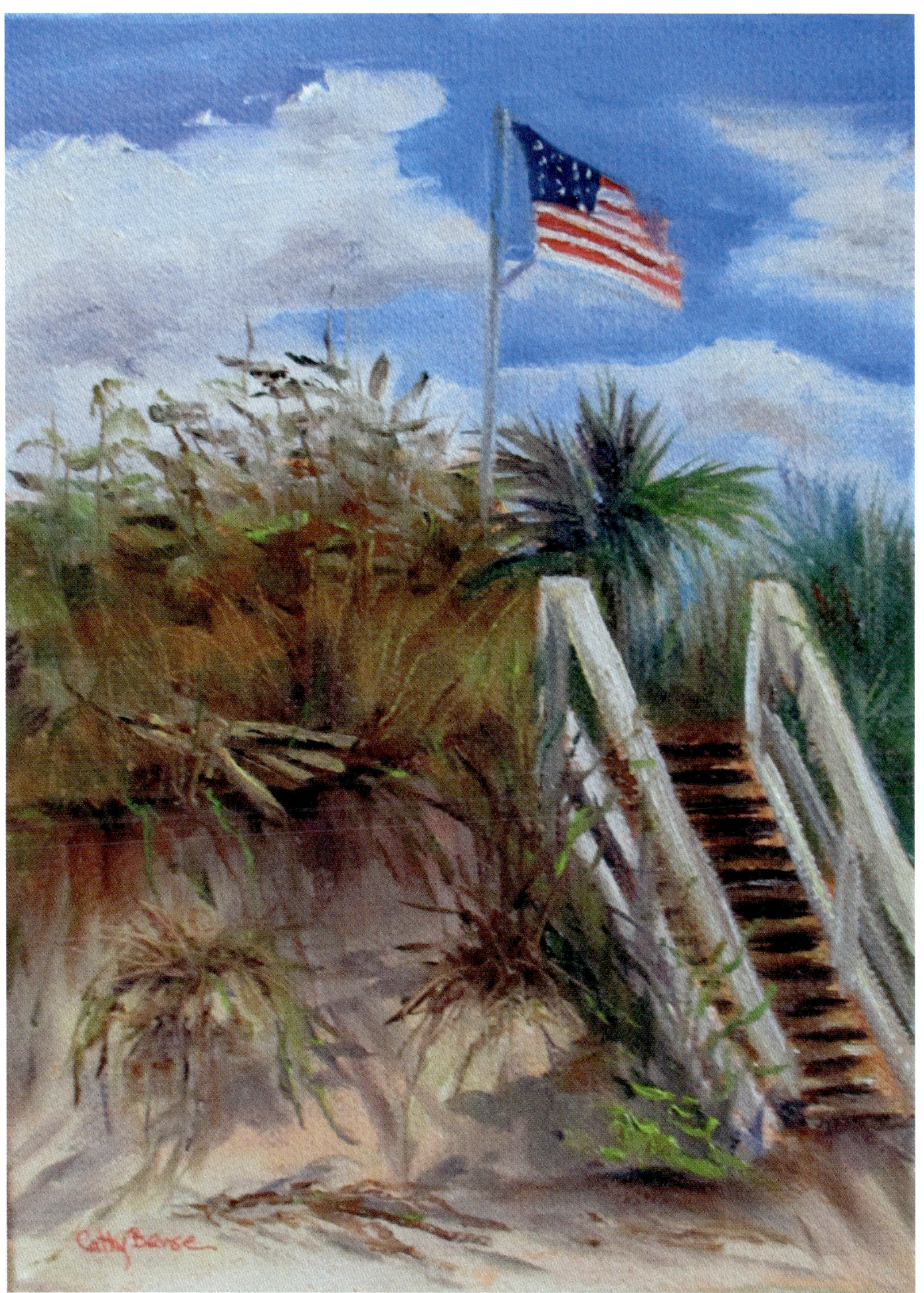

Cathy Berse, Florida

AMERICA A BEAUTIFUL DAY

My friend and I were painting on the beach one gorgeous day. While setting up to paint, we heard that the beaches would be closed down because of the Coronavirus, and so we agreed to paint one piece each day during the pandemic until we were allowed to once again use our wonderful beaches. I turned and saw the American flag flying in the breeze. I knew it would be the best painting to start our project. Now that I look back at 34 days of paintings, I am so proud of our American flag and all it stands for.

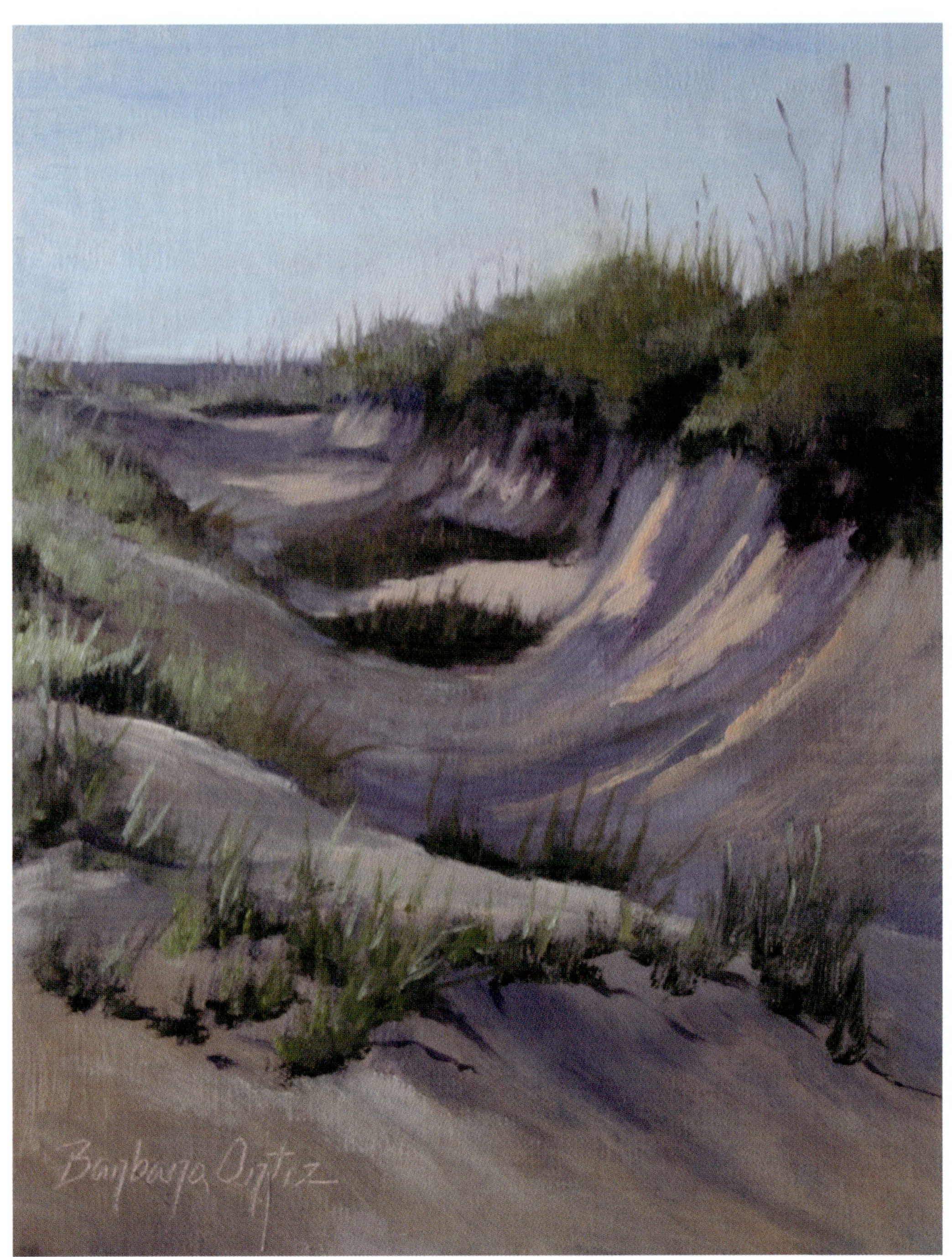

Barbara Ortiz, Florida
ESSENTIAL DUNES

When the stay-at-home order went into effect, I decided that my time spent social distancing needed to be constructive and, if possible, positive. To that end, my dear friend Cathy Berse and I chose to challenge ourselves to create 30 paintings in 30 days. Some paintings were completed indoors from photos, some painted outside of our homes, and some painted in isolated locations that were not off-limits. All of the paintings have a story!

The painting presented here, *Essential Dunes,* was painted on day 23 of the quarantine in Florida. At the time, beaches were open for essential activity only. We were advised that painting was not an essential activity. Thankfully, I was able to paint from the closed drive-on ramp to capture this scene.

Since then, I have spent a lot of time thinking about what is "essential." My essentials include my family and friends, as well as health, food, and shelter, and the means to provide them. It is also essential that I paint. Painting is what grounds me, and also what allows me to soar. It is my way of sharing and communicating with all of you, especially in the days of social distancing and isolation.

The environment is essential. The dunes are essential.

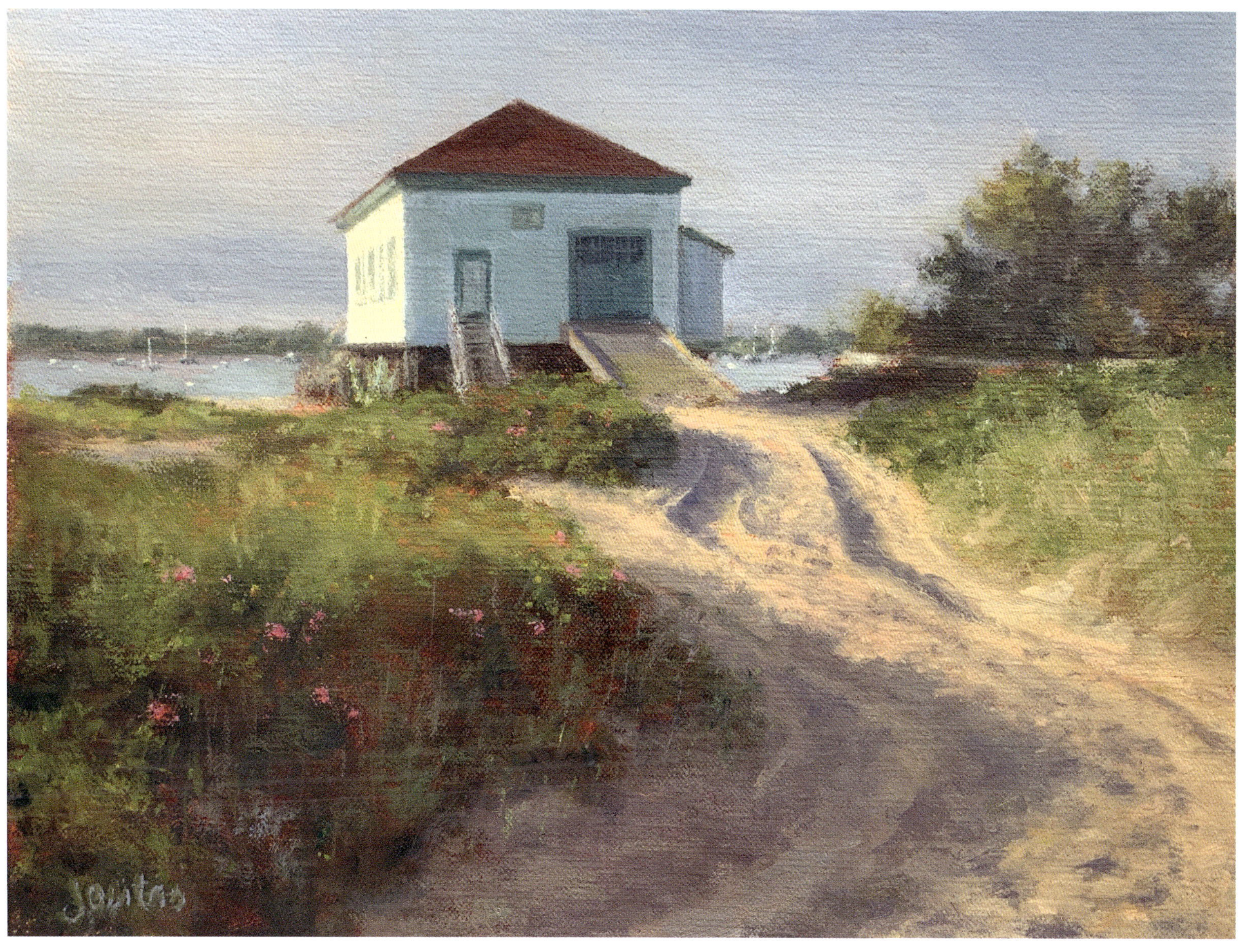

Susan Jositas, Connecticut

THE HATCHERY

Rather than abandoning plans to teach a destination workshop on Nantucket Island during the pandemic, I was grateful that the technology was available via the Zoom platform to teach it online. Years of plein-air painting on the island provided me with an abundance of photo references to use for a "virtual" plein-air experience. The workshop, titled Painting with a Meditative Process, was taught over four sessions, each one "visiting" a different part of the island.

Anyone who knows and loves Nantucket will recognize this location. A former US Coast Guard boathouse at Brant Point, it is now owned and operated by the town as a research facility to spawn and grow oysters, scallops, and quahogs to release into the harbors and augment the wild shellfish population. Illuminated by the early morning sun, the simplicity and beauty of this structure is striking, surrounded by the softness and natural beauty of the landscape.

6 SEASCAPES

I love the ocean and love to paint it, sometimes on-site and often in the studio. On a typical trip to the coast, I take hundreds of photos that I then review and crop. If I find one or two that I can use in a painting, I am happy.

When the pandemic hit, everything closed down, including the beach. I had no upcoming shows to work towards and I was at a bit of a loss. I decided to just have fun and I turned to my reference photos and began experimenting with small pastels. I tried papers and techniques I had not used before. I had no plan to exhibit these, so I was free to try anything, including one I did with my non-dominant hand. I learned so much during this COVID-inflicted study time that it informed and energized my larger work.

Sandra Kavanaugh
Salisbury, Massachusetts

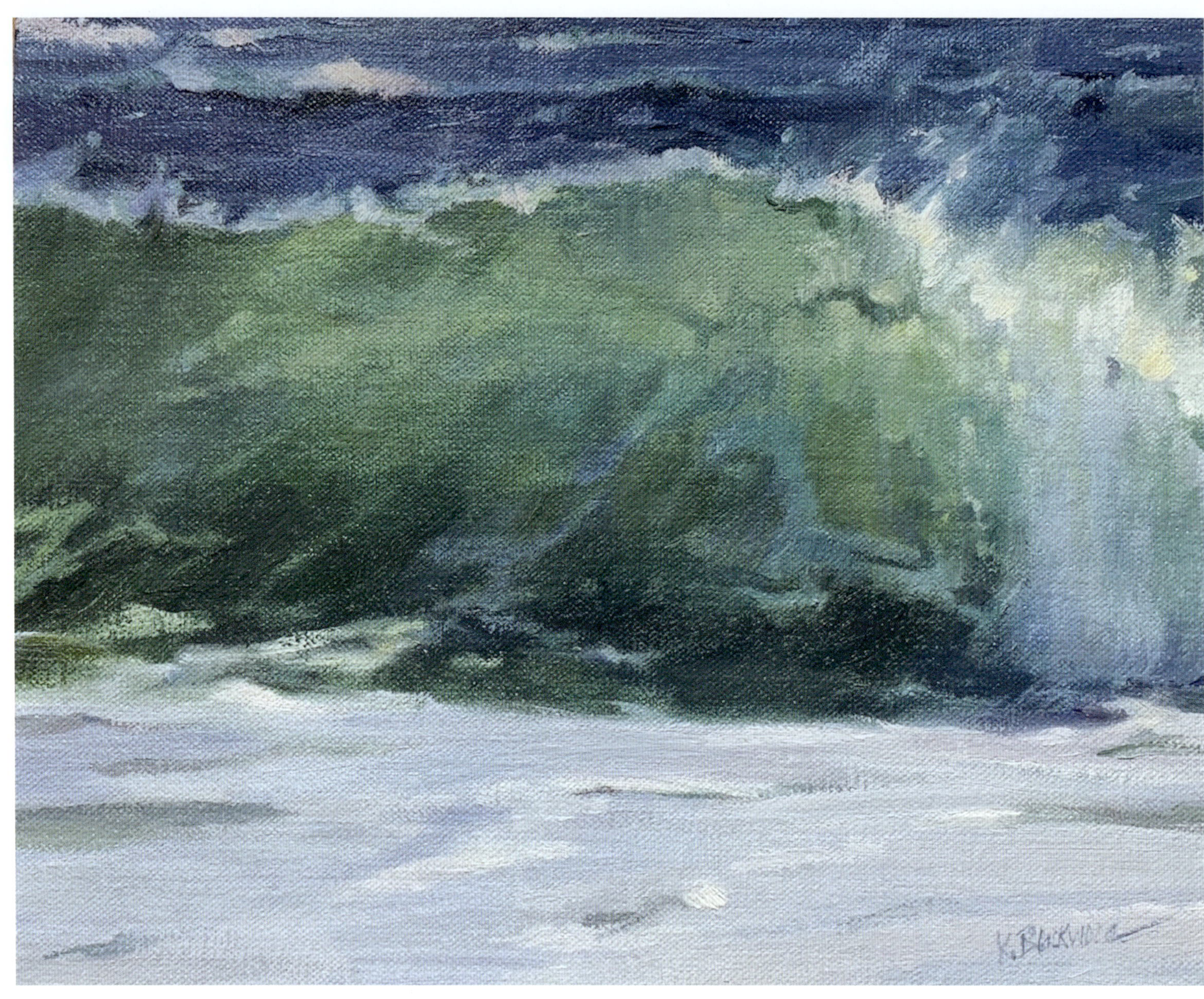

Karen Blackwood, Massachusetts

INNER LIGHT

I have found myself drawn to the light more and more since the chaos of the pandemic.
Who doesn't need a little inner light?

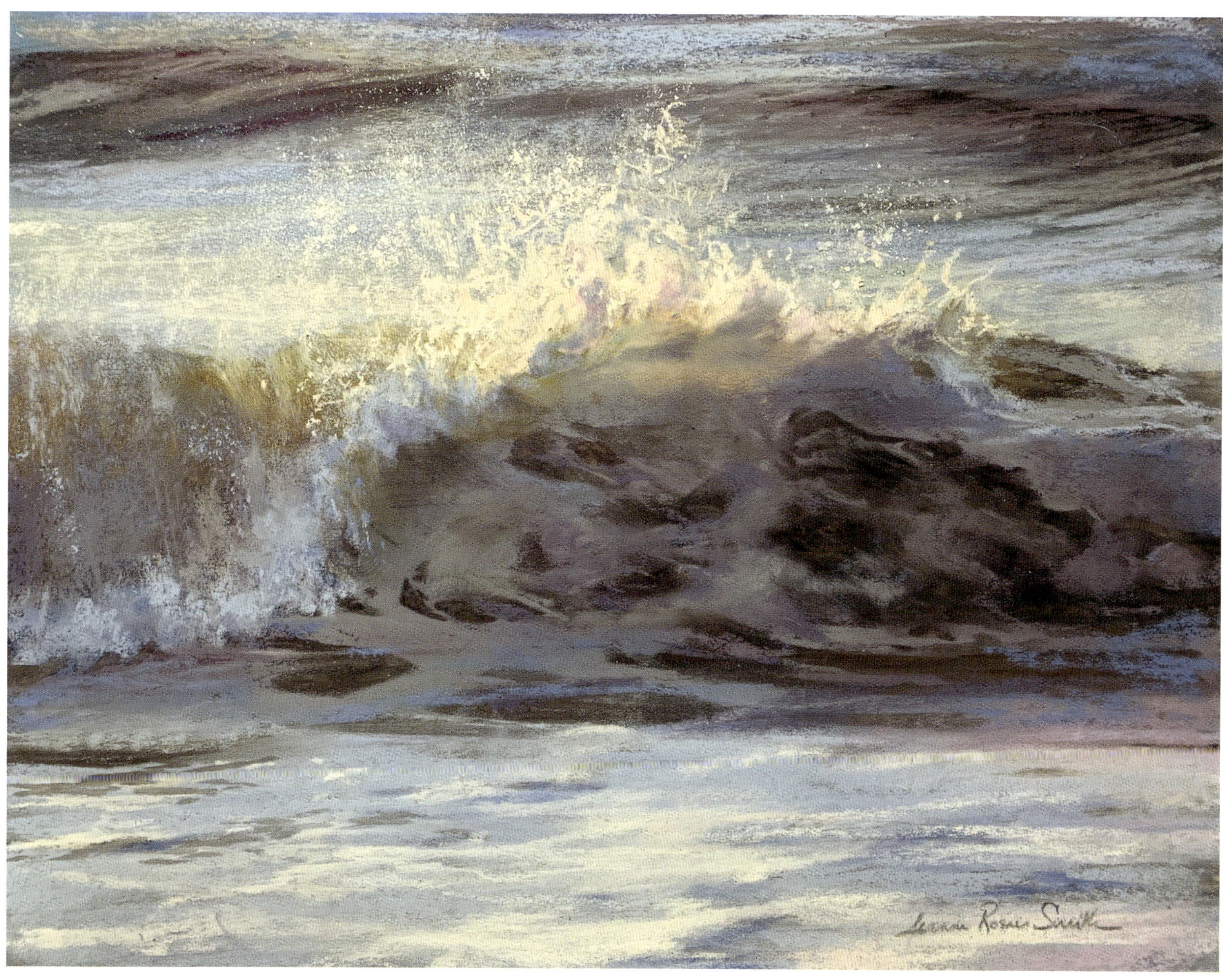

Jeanne Rosier Smith, Massachusetts

A LIGHT NOTE

Now more than ever, my easel is my source of joy and renewal. Last September I spent a month in an art residency on Boston's north shore. This extended studio time has allowed me to dive into my reference materials from that time. The ocean instantly calms me: our human problems seem so small in comparison. *A Light Note* captures both the light and the dark: deep dark shadows still anchor the water, but early morning light dances off the spray and lifts the spirits.

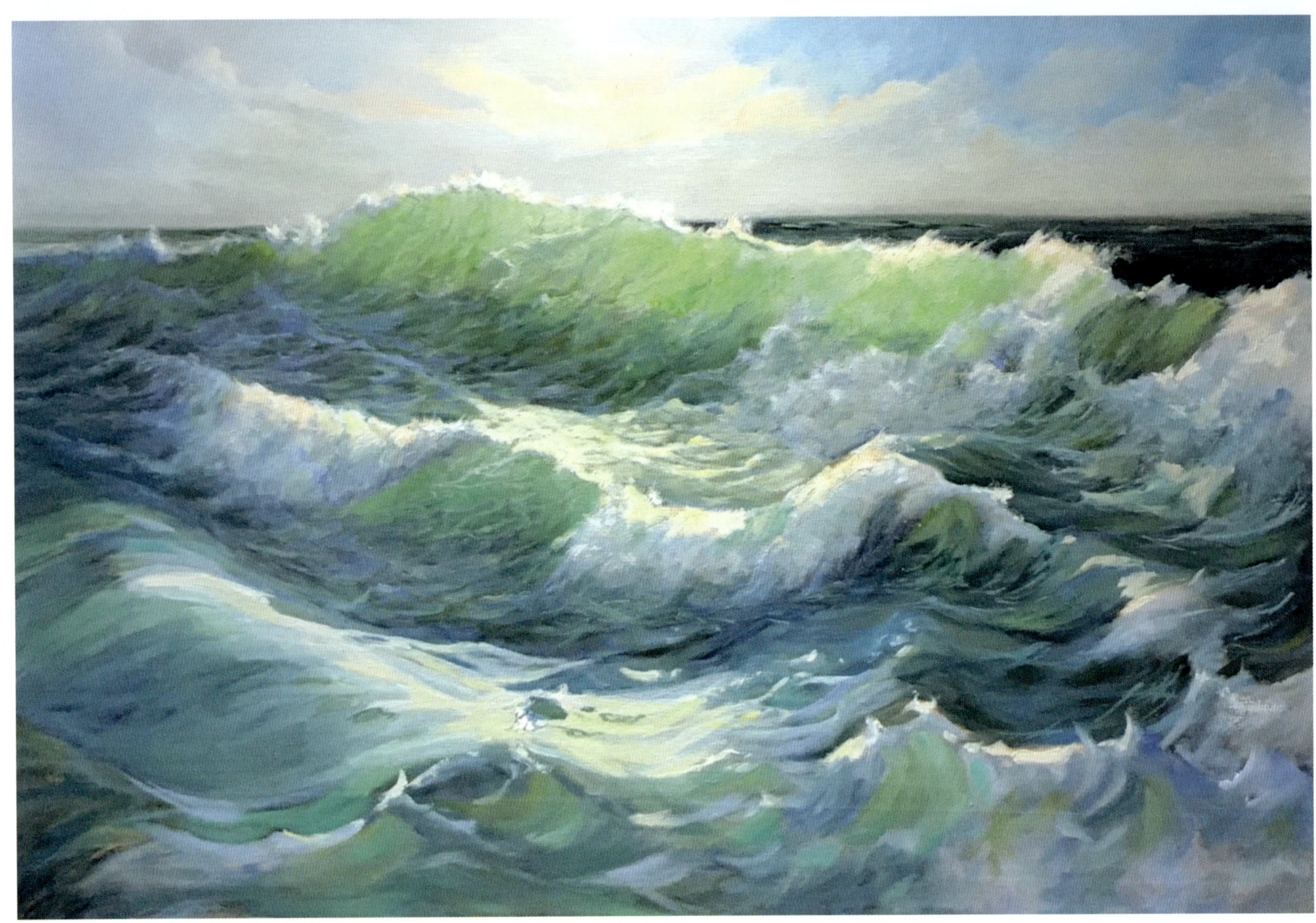

Diane Larson, North Carolina
LET'S DANCE

The ocean is my place of calm in a storm. Right now, during the lockdown, if I could be near the ocean I would feel so much better. Sadly, all I can do to put my nerves at rest is to keep painting my muse. *Let's Dance* is about the joyful feeling of weightlessness when one bounces up and down in the warm waters of the ocean.

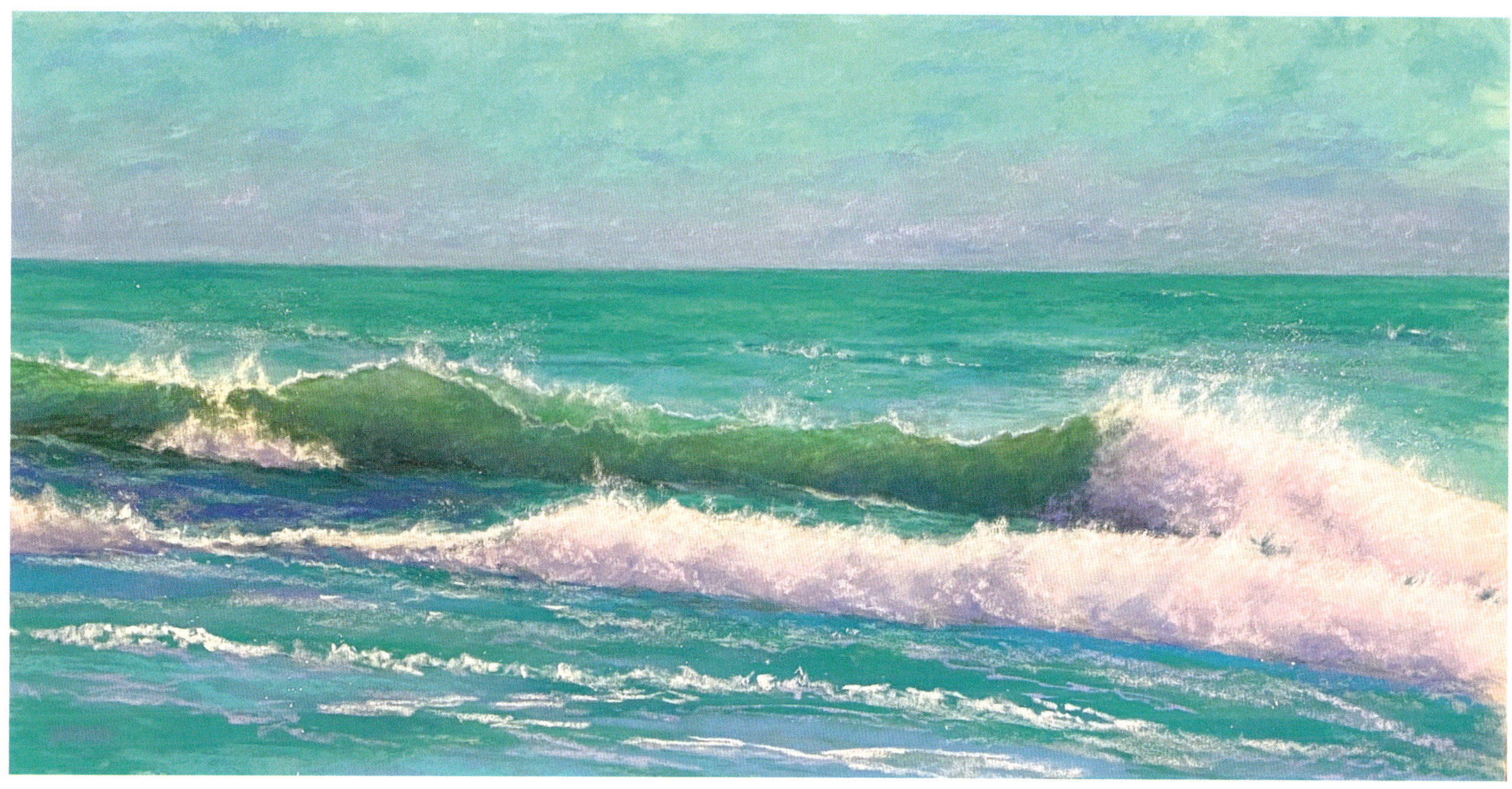

Dina Gardner, Massachusetts

OCEAN'S JEWELS

My happy place is at the ocean, watching the waves roll, crash, saunter, and dance their way to the shore. I love to paint anything and everything to do with the ocean including waves, the shoreline, rocks in the water, and the sky and clouds above the sea. When I'm not traveling, which COVID-19 has certainly squashed, I split my time between Boston, MA, my adoptive city of almost 35 years, and Southern California, where I was born and raised. I grew up near the water, was an avid scuba diver throughout my 20s, and have always loved the ocean.

I began painting about five years ago and, in addition to being passionate about it, it has truly made this time of COVID-19 and quarantining bearable. For lack of a better word, I feel like painting has saved me during this unstable time in our history. I honestly don't know what I would have done with myself if I couldn't paint during this time. I'm so grateful to have found pastels and to have the freedom to paint the beauty I see around me. This painting was from a wave photo reference I took in CA but I painted it with the Caribbean colors in mind. I love how it glows. However, my favorite part is the sky, which is incredibly luminous with its purple and turquoise values. The entire painting looks like a fine piece of jewelry to me.

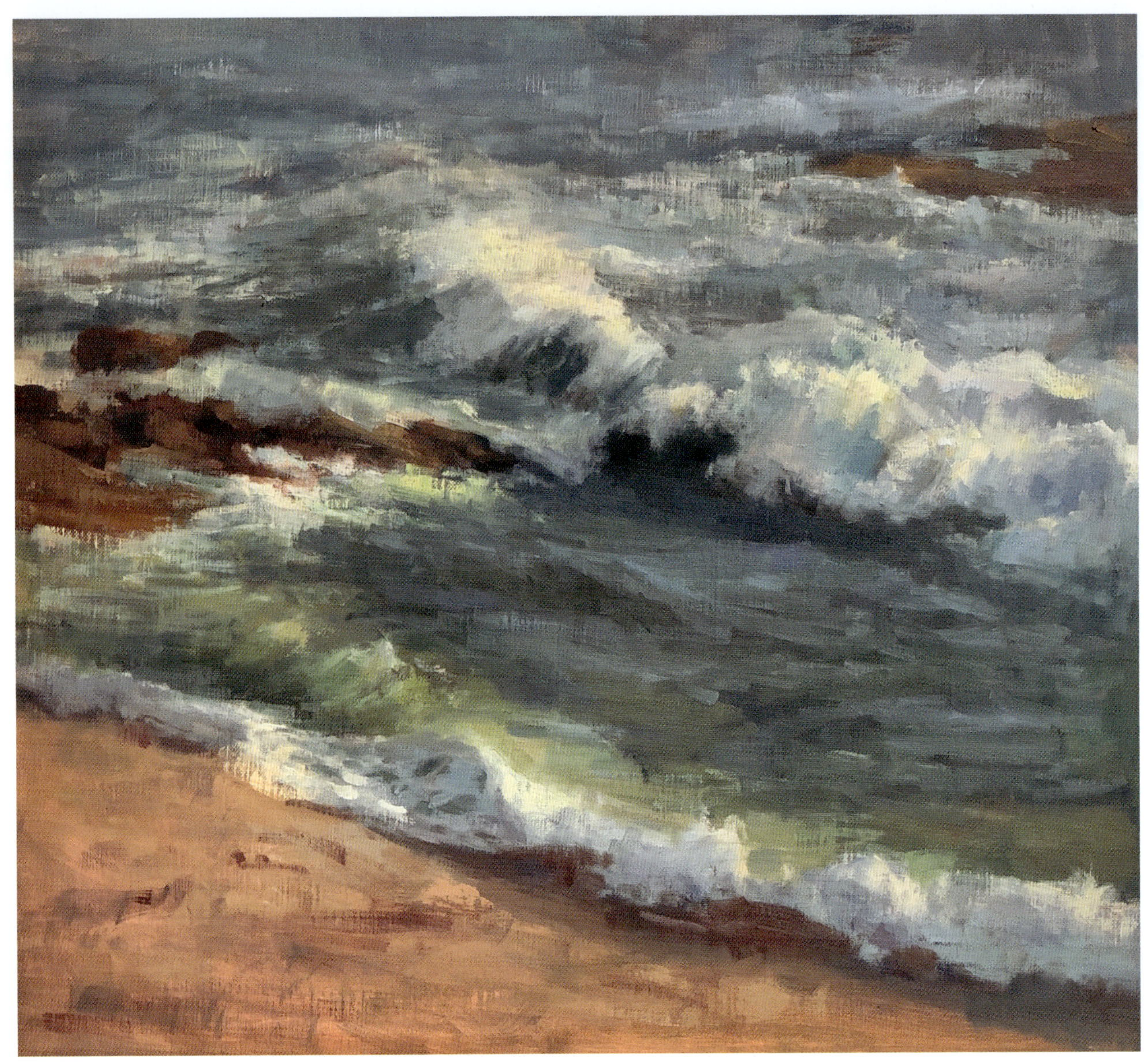

Karen Leoni, California
COASTAL AFTERNOON

I enjoyed spending a quiet hour at this deserted beach last December. It seemed so special because usually it is filled with people but because it was 4 pm on a chilly Wednesday, no one was there. It was just the sound of the waves, the vast ocean, the sand, and me. Sunset was imminent and early due to the short days. Little did I realize that stillness and quiet would be all day and everywhere as the world gradually shut down just a few months later. The pandemic necessitated this action and activity slowed to a crawl everywhere. I decided to start this painting in April to not only remember that particular day back in December but to represent the moments when we can be reflective in the hushed silence...and create.

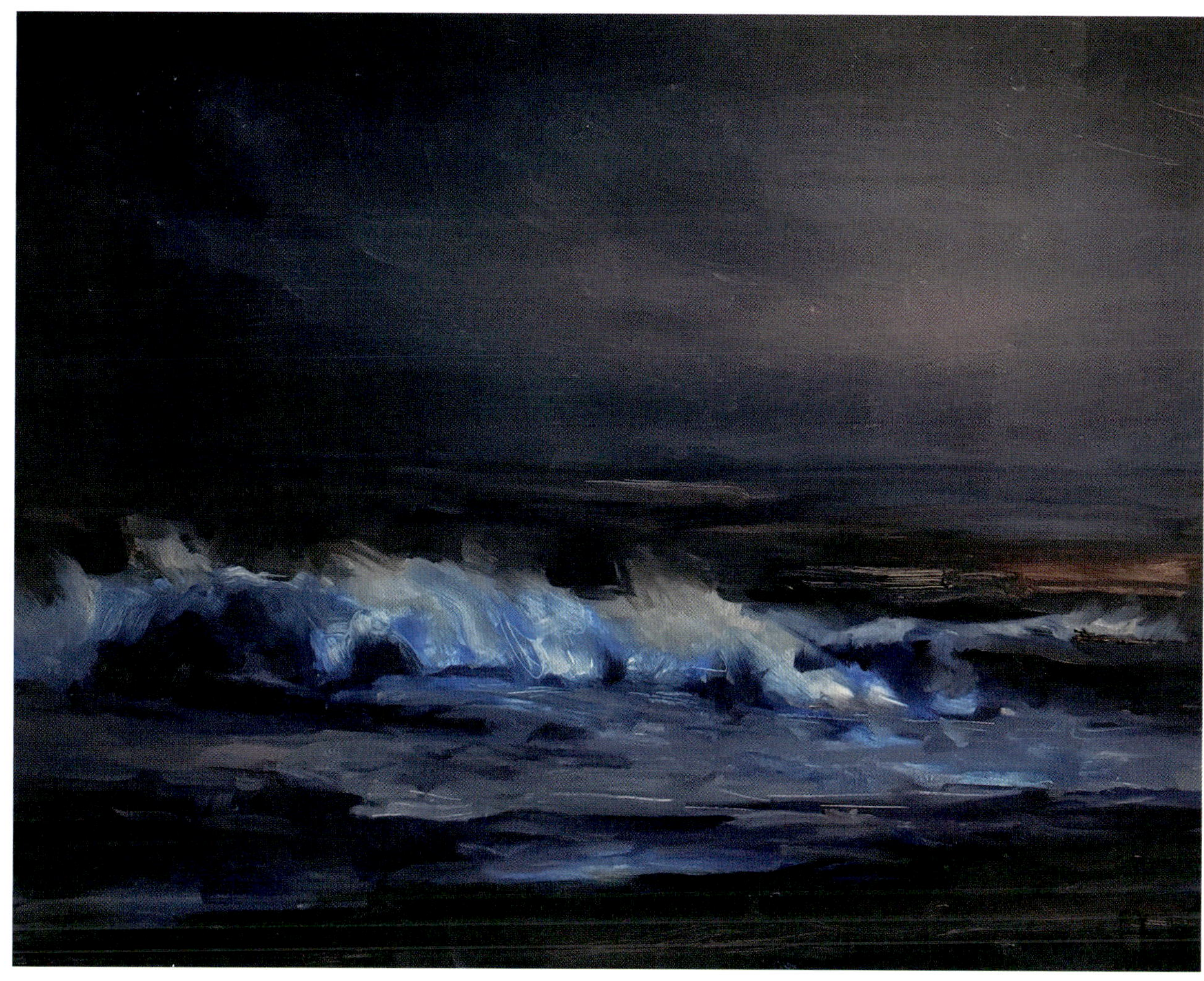

E.E. Jacks, California
RESONANCE

Resonance was wholly inspired by the beautifully evocative bioluminescence found in nature. During these distressing times, I have found myself searching for beauty and metaphors. In this nocturne painting, I have juxtaposed the light and dark, in hopes that it will resonate with someone if they need to find that spark in the night.

I know I need this beautiful thing
that chimes before the morning bells ring
this tempered light
that solemn bright
that thing that sparks
then dims
the night!
for when the daylight fades away
and its clamor recedes to the edge of the clay
I will rise and greet my sacred friend
and begin our nocturnal conversation again.

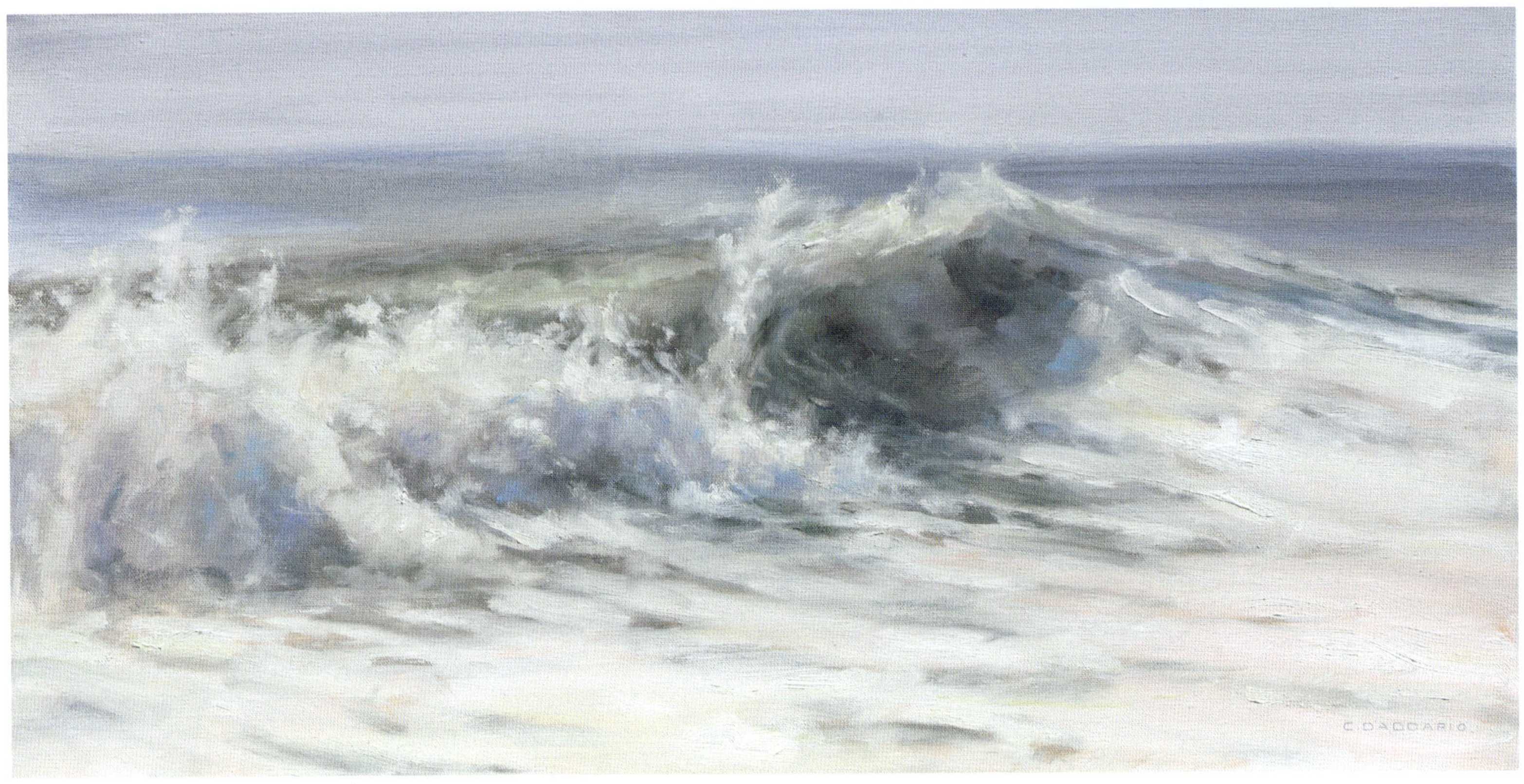

Christine D'Addario, New York
WAVE OF LIGHT

While the rest of the world was fighting COVID-19 and politics in 2020—I was fighting aggressive breast cancer. I began chemo on March 11th, 2020, two days before lockdown, but I knew in my heart that everything would be okay if I went to all my doctor appointments and kept on painting! Now 2020 has passed, and I am grateful to be healthy. I look back on the pandemic days with fondness because it gave me time with my family and my studio.

Being faced with a life-threatening illness motivated me to wake up every day asking... "What can I do that will be the most fun? What can I make that will share joy? How will I make this day matter?" This is a mindset that I wish to hold onto every day.

I chose to share my original oil painting *Wave of Light* with you all because this painting is a symbol of hope. This piece is meant to give the viewer a visual cue to take a moment for inner reflection and to refuel their mind and spirit. To my delight, this piece was selected into an important exhibition in 2020 and received the "Visitor's Choice Award." Since then, more good things have happened! In 2021, my artwork was featured on the covers of *Dan's Papers*, a popular Hamptons publication, and *Newsday Long Island*. I also had the chance to open a pop-up art gallery with my friends in my hometown of Locust Valley. Both were dreams come true.

These accomplishments inspire me to keep dreaming and taking chances. After all, we only get one life to live! Many thanks to my family, friends, doctors, collectors, and fellow artists for providing me with much love and support through this time. I am grateful to the Great American Paint In® for sharing my journey. My goal is to uplift others through my story and art. We are all in this together! Happy painting everyone! Please visit my website, www.cdaddario.com, and follow me on social media!

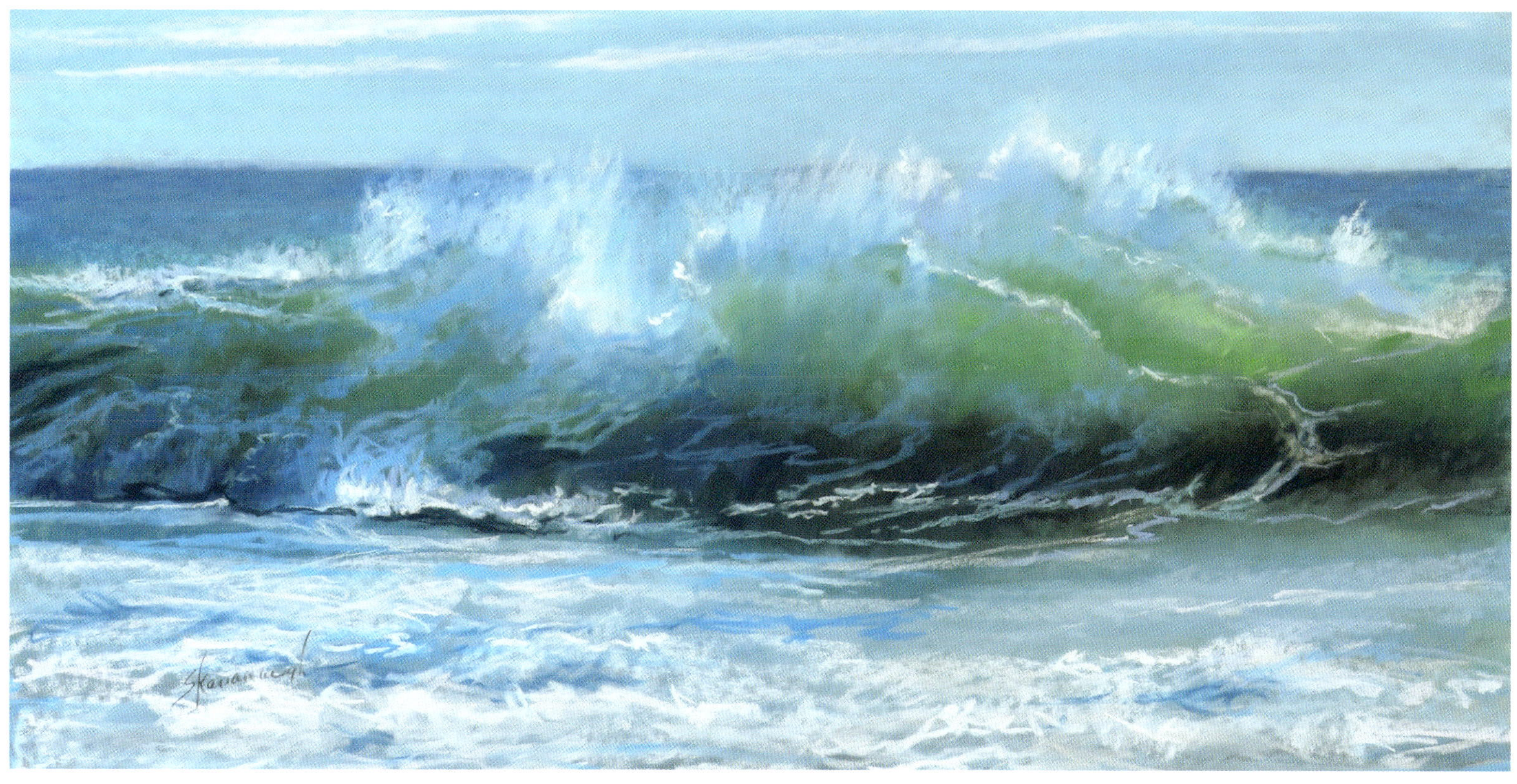

Sandra Kavanaugh, New Hampshire
TOGETHER AGAIN

The ocean is my special place. Its sounds, sights, and scents are soothing. A walk on the beach in all seasons is meditative. When the pandemic hit, not only were my shows and galleries closed, but the beach was too. I turned to my reference photos for my seaside meditation.

The painting I chose to include in this project is named *Together Again*. These two waves will be one again and we will be together again. The scene was captured the day after a storm when the sun was out, but the sea had not quieted.

7 SUNRISES & SUNSETS

Being an outdoor lover, feeling the outside elements, and enjoying nature overall is what drew me to drawing landscapes and plein air. I love the ever-changing environment, the seasons, the weather—everything about it!

When the pandemic hit, it was pretty scary. We didn't know what was to come and, being sheltered, I made a makeshift studio in my son's old room. I even continued to teach students from his room on Zoom! Through it all, I found that art continues to be good for mental health and uplifting attitudes.

The pandemic has inspired change in my paintings as well. While I'm drawn to the sunsets and the warmth of the light, it provides hope, not only to me but hopefully to others.

Ellen Howard
San Francisco, California

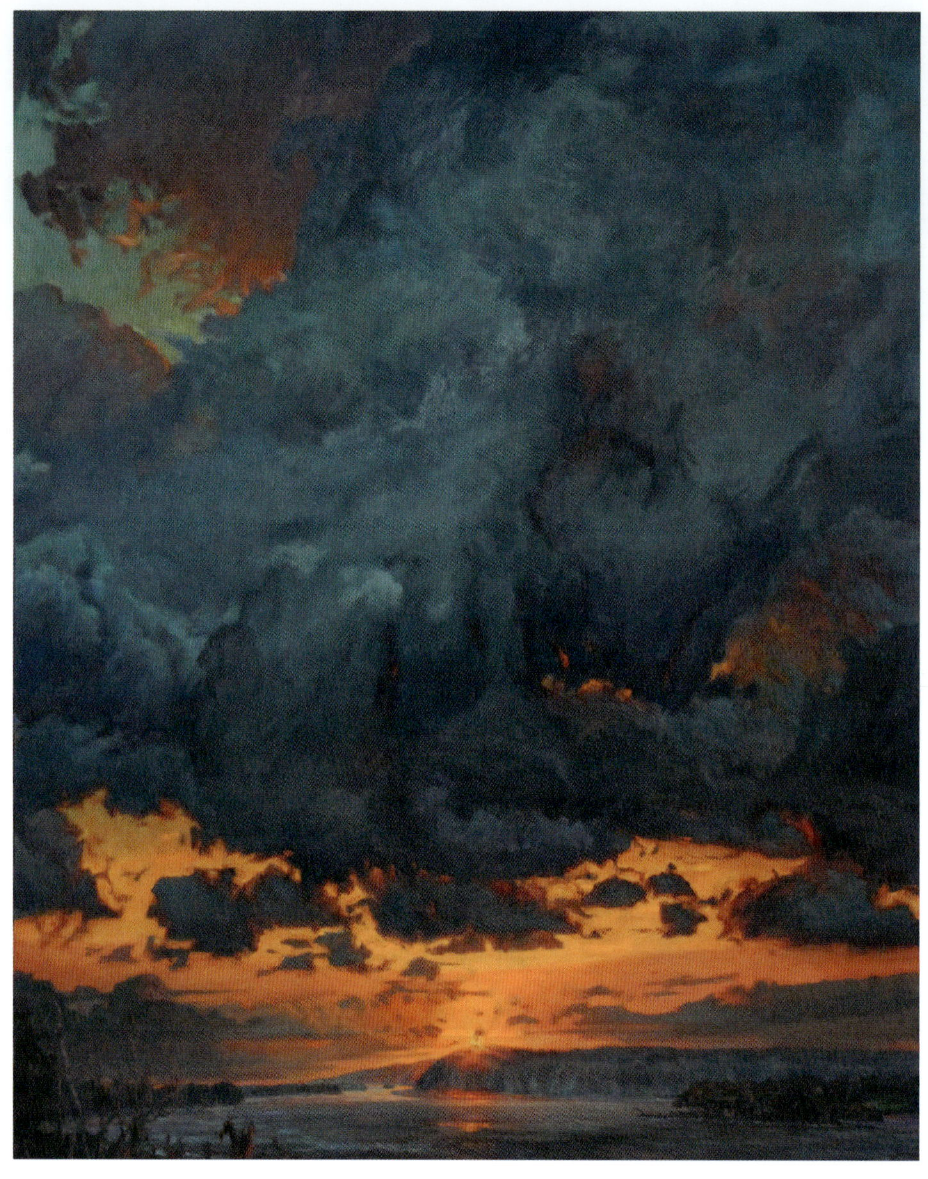

David Coughtry, Illinois
DRONE, RIVER BEND

For the representationally challenged painter, the great Mississippi River flowing past a unique stretch at River Bend, between Alton and Hardin, IL is never less than compelling. It makes an indelible impression, this being one of the quintessentially majestic places of the Midwest. While teaching bluff-side along the Mississippi at Principia College's Center for the Arts, I have rarely left this river alone for very long. The place incites behavior entrusted to painting. *Drone, River Bend* suggests the heat of summer and the great uplift of bursting clouds over the Mississippi in the coming twilight. Its visual vantage point is an impossible setting, comprised of bluffs, islands, and wild shoreline. The significant content is the storm's dynamism—the emotion felt by its immensity and confrontation, caught in a painted sketch to be utilized for a larger arrangement in the studio. There are moments since making this painting when I see it as a kind of a visual metaphor for the current state of the country and our world, as days grow dark amidst the problem of a pandemic. I trust that, as in this image, the storm will pass, and pray that the coming dawn has its beam.

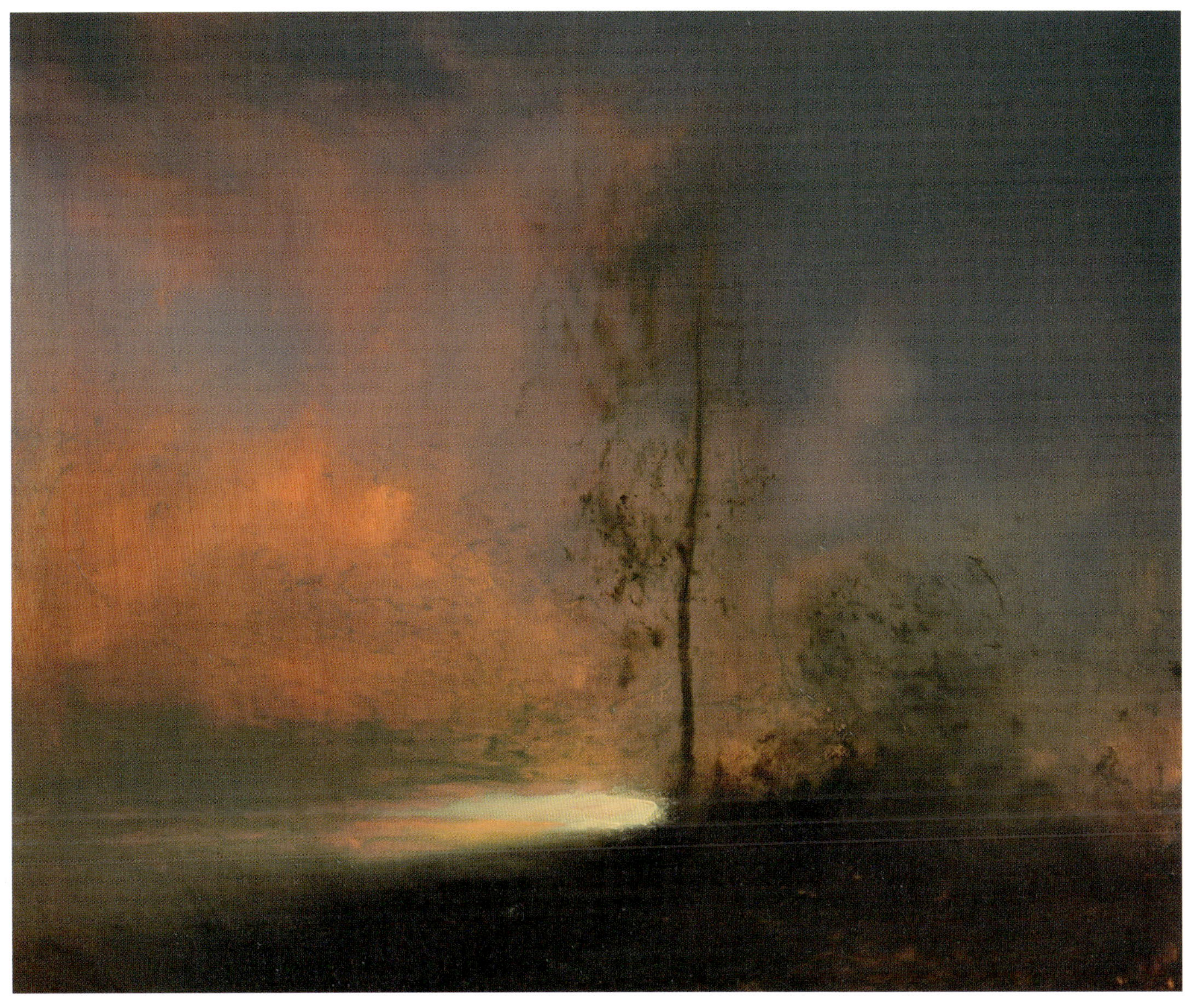

Justin T. Worrell, Virginia

FERMATA II

The title of this piece, *Fermata*, refers to a musical notation that indicates a note (or rest) should be prolonged beyond normal duration. As a Tonalist, I paint moments of compromise between the temporal and eternal to arrive at a heightened sense of spirituality. I want to find the light which serves as a causeway between realms and prolong my exposure to it in the hope that I will find meaning. Quarantine has, in its own way, served this purpose. It's been both an adversary and a conduit not only for my everyday life but certainly in my art as well. Tonalism, I feel, is an optimistic art form and I believe we will prevail in these trying times and come out the other side all the better. At its core, I suppose this is what my art is about: finding peace and a place warmed with belief.

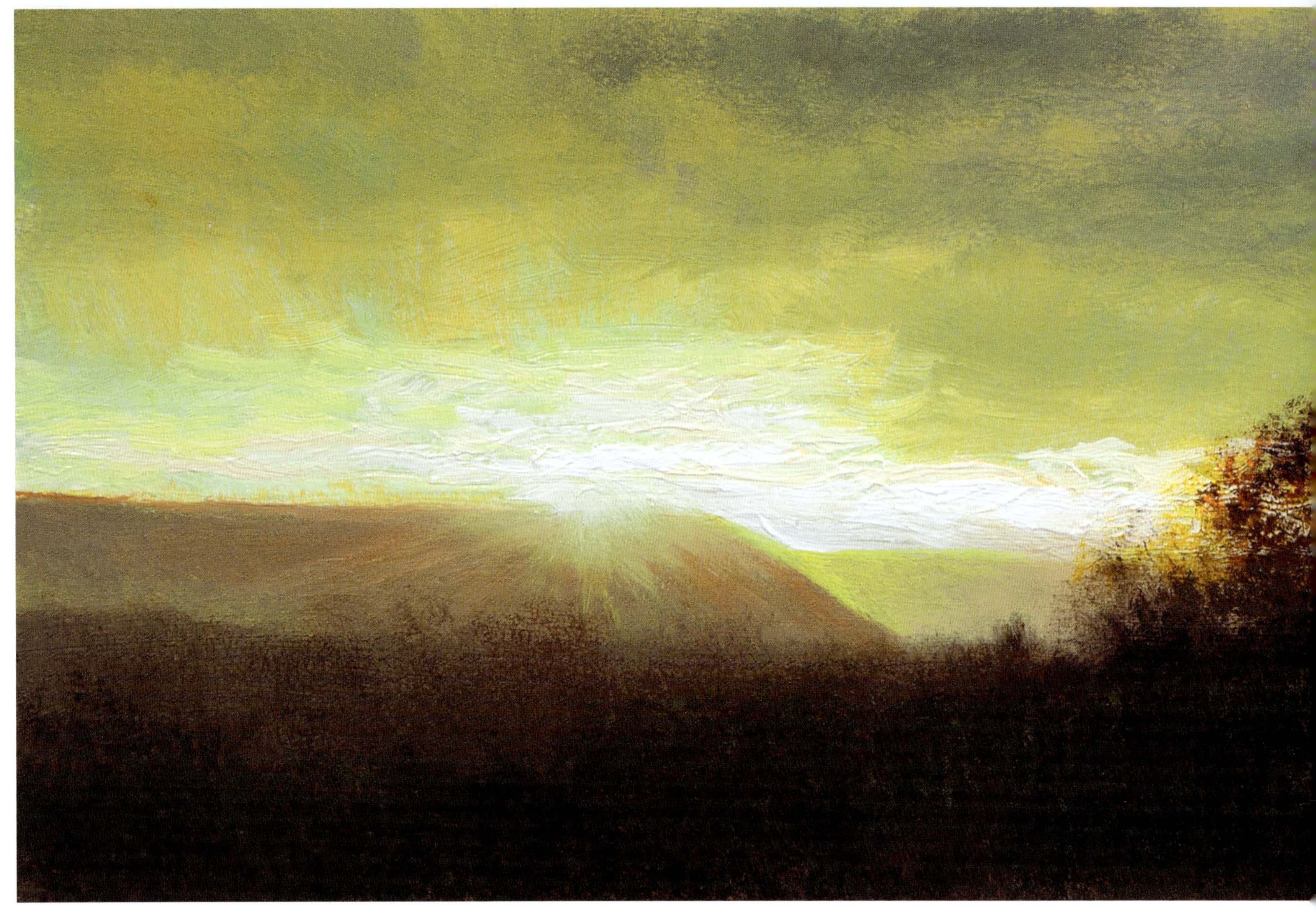

Thomas Kegler, New York
NEW DAWN, PSALM 63:5-6

Some of the blessings of the current situation are time with family, a respite from agendas and schedules, and the opportunity to work on paintings that have been in my head for years. This painting is one such scene. A few years back I was driving to NYC to the opening of the American Masters Show at the Salmagundi Club with a good friend. We were driving through one of my favorite scenic areas in Central New York as the sun rose and gifted us a warm yellow infusion over the valley. I think of the canvas as visual music and attempt to harmonize not only the color relationships but also the cadence of the shapes and movement/flow of the eye. I love exploring these experiences after the view has had time to settle in my soul and resonate with me.

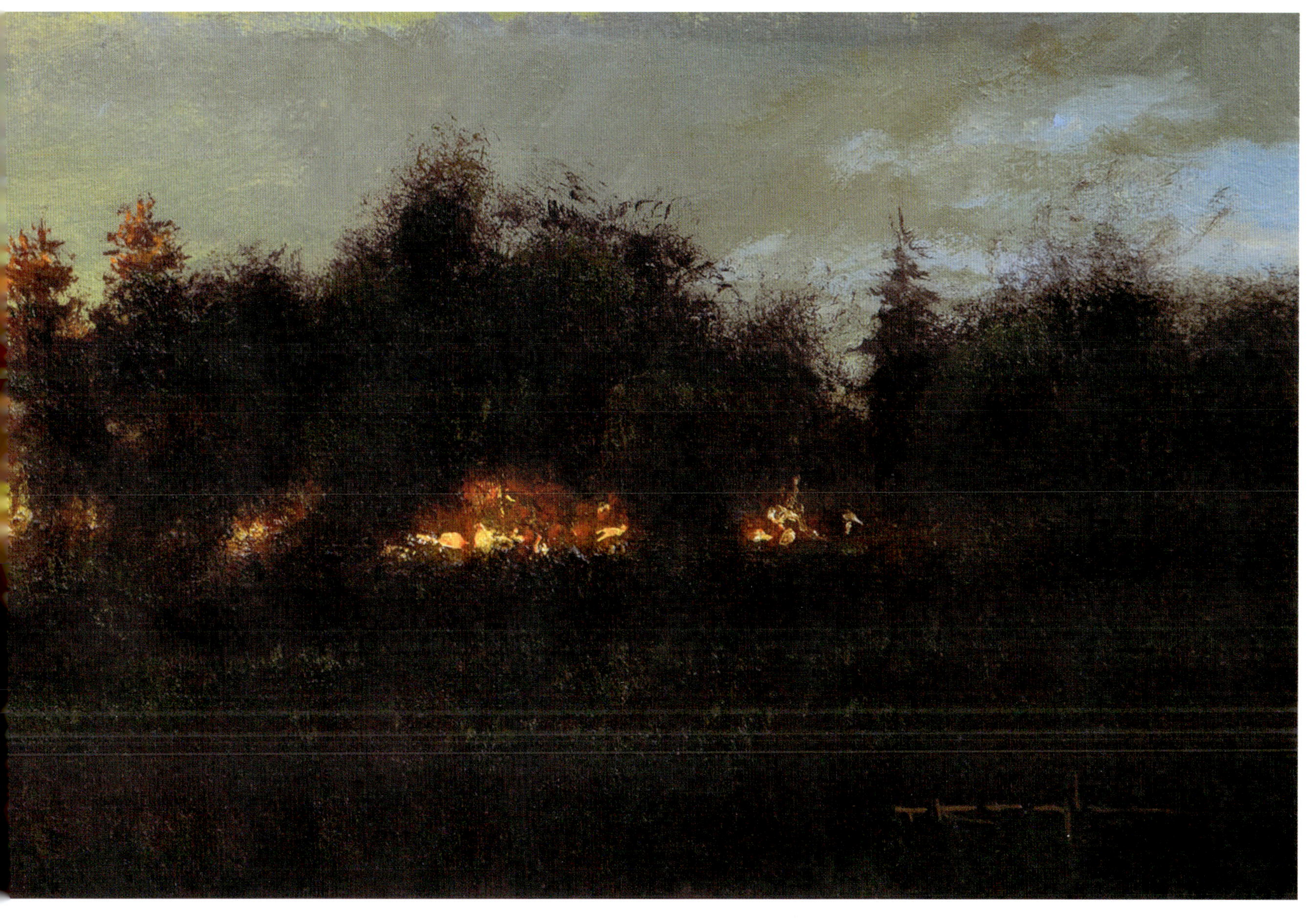

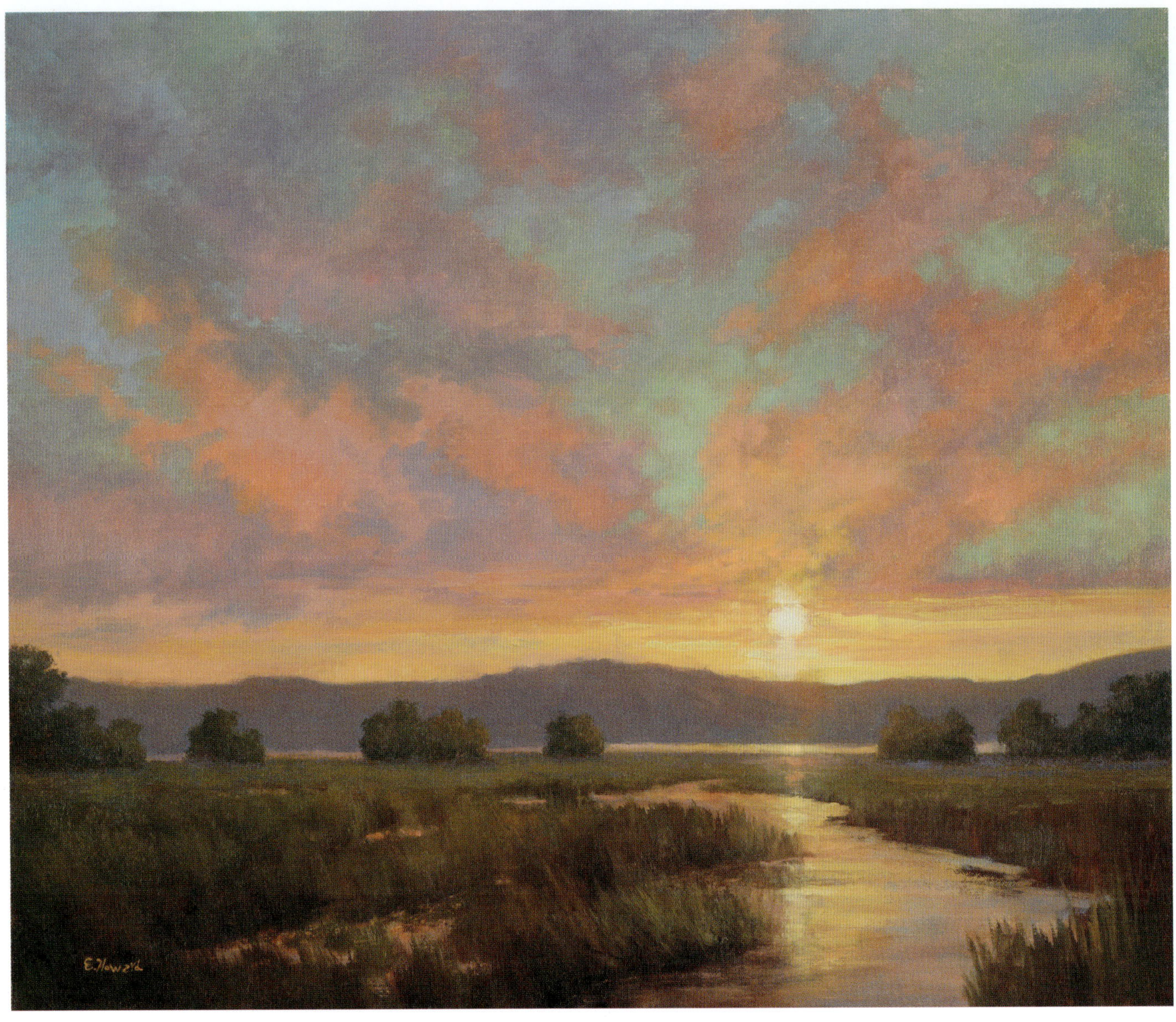

Ellen Howard, California
BEYOND THE LIGHT

At the start of sheltering in place, I had anxiety about what COVID-19 was and how people in our local and global communities would be affected. There was so much information being presented, from so many sources, which often contradicted each other—it was hard to know what was true. It was difficult to get a handle on the current situation and our situation seemed to change every day. I was disheartened as I watched all my commitments to gallery shows, art events, and competitions get canceled. I made the conscious decision to take some time to center myself by taking hikes, listening to music, meditating, and of course, painting.

I realized at a much deeper level that I could only control myself and my thoughts and that I could choose how I looked at our changing world. I choose to look for the "light" or positive hope in every situation and to accept the changing environment around me. I started to be drawn to painting sunsets. I loved the vibrant, cheerful colors that are seen in sunsets. Every sunset is spectacular, and viewers feel a sense of peace and happiness having seen one. I was also drawn to the sense that sunsets represent the last ray of light at the end of the day—a ray of hope that one day has ended with anticipation that another day full of promise is on the horizon. My painting *Beyond the Light* is my expression of this beautiful ray of light signifying our hope for a better tomorrow with a greater understanding of ourselves and our fellow human beings.

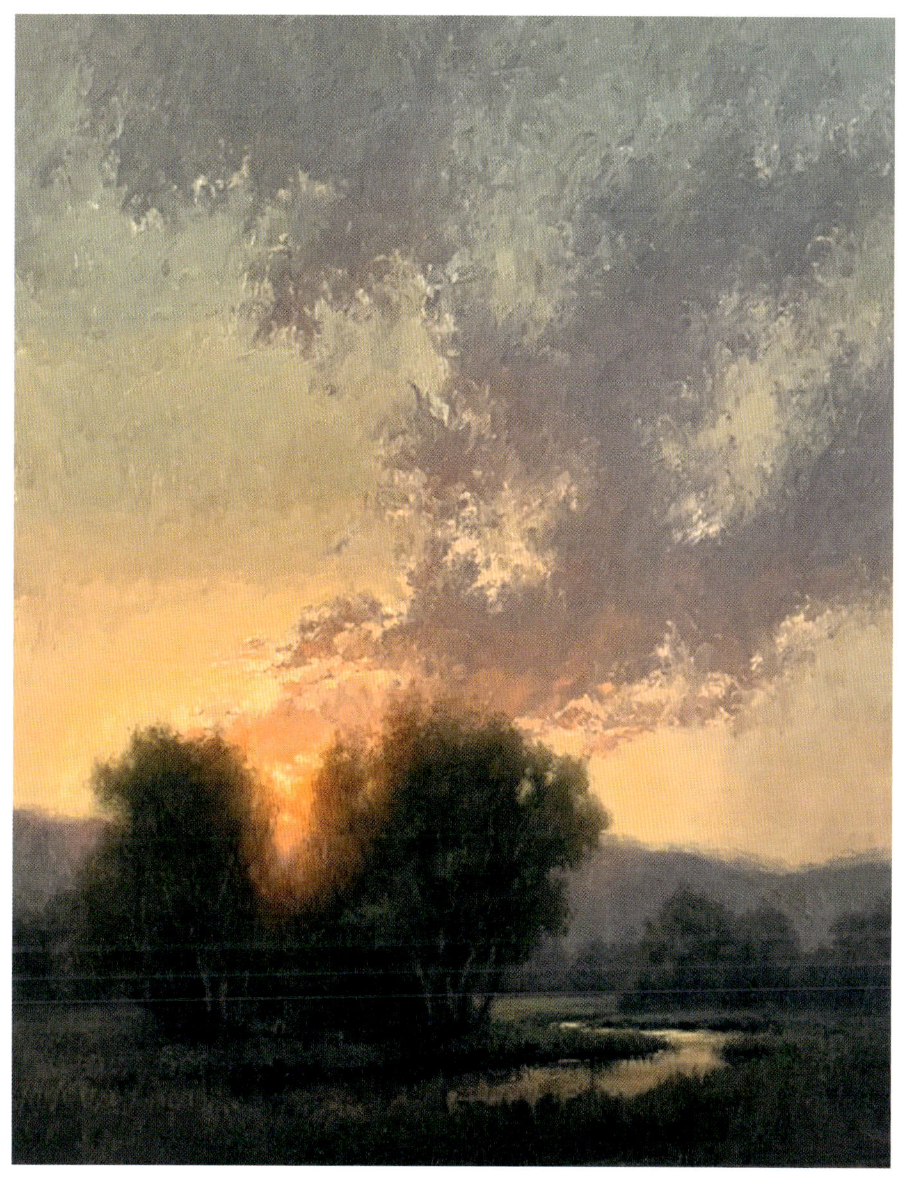

Jane Hunt, Colorado
EVENING'S PROMISE

The Olmsted Plein Air event would have been held a couple of weeks ago if not for COVID-19. The event has moved completely online and we can each paint one competition piece. I wanted to create a painting that could offer serenity to its viewers. So, I pulled together my most peaceful plein-air studies and reference photos and this painting is an amalgam of those. I've always found sunsets to be a symbol of hope so I named this piece *Evening's Promise* as a reminder that there will be better days ahead.

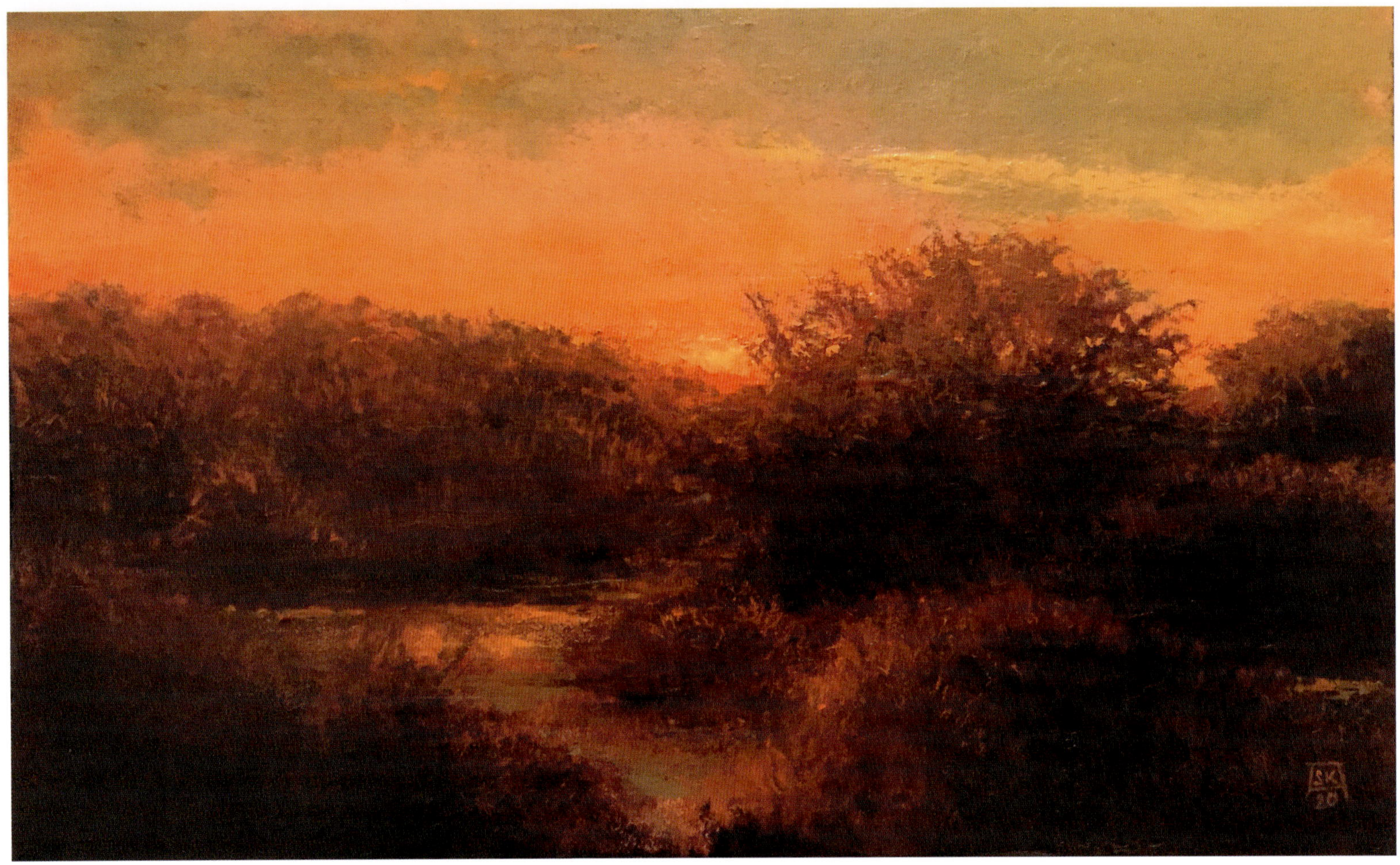

Shawn Krueger, Michigan
EVENING MARSH

Anyone following my career for even a short while will have undoubtedly heard me mention the imaginary 50 acres of property I own. It is near the mountains with plenty of rolling sidehills, rocky erratics, and gentle waterfalls. These eventually flow down towards the lower spots of the property where there is marsh and sedge. There are plenty of pine and birch trees that bend gently for their chance at some morning or evening light. It snows there a bit, but not too often.

Because it doesn't exist, no one can trespass on it. Its imaginary wildlife is safe, and no one leaves their trash behind. I love this place. I didn't need any excuse for staying in and mentally hiking this land for inspiration. While I do appreciate the invaluable lessons that have come from years of experience in plein-air painting, I find now I am able to better focus on a sense of place when I am not in a particular place, and that, ultimately, is what I think I care more about these days.

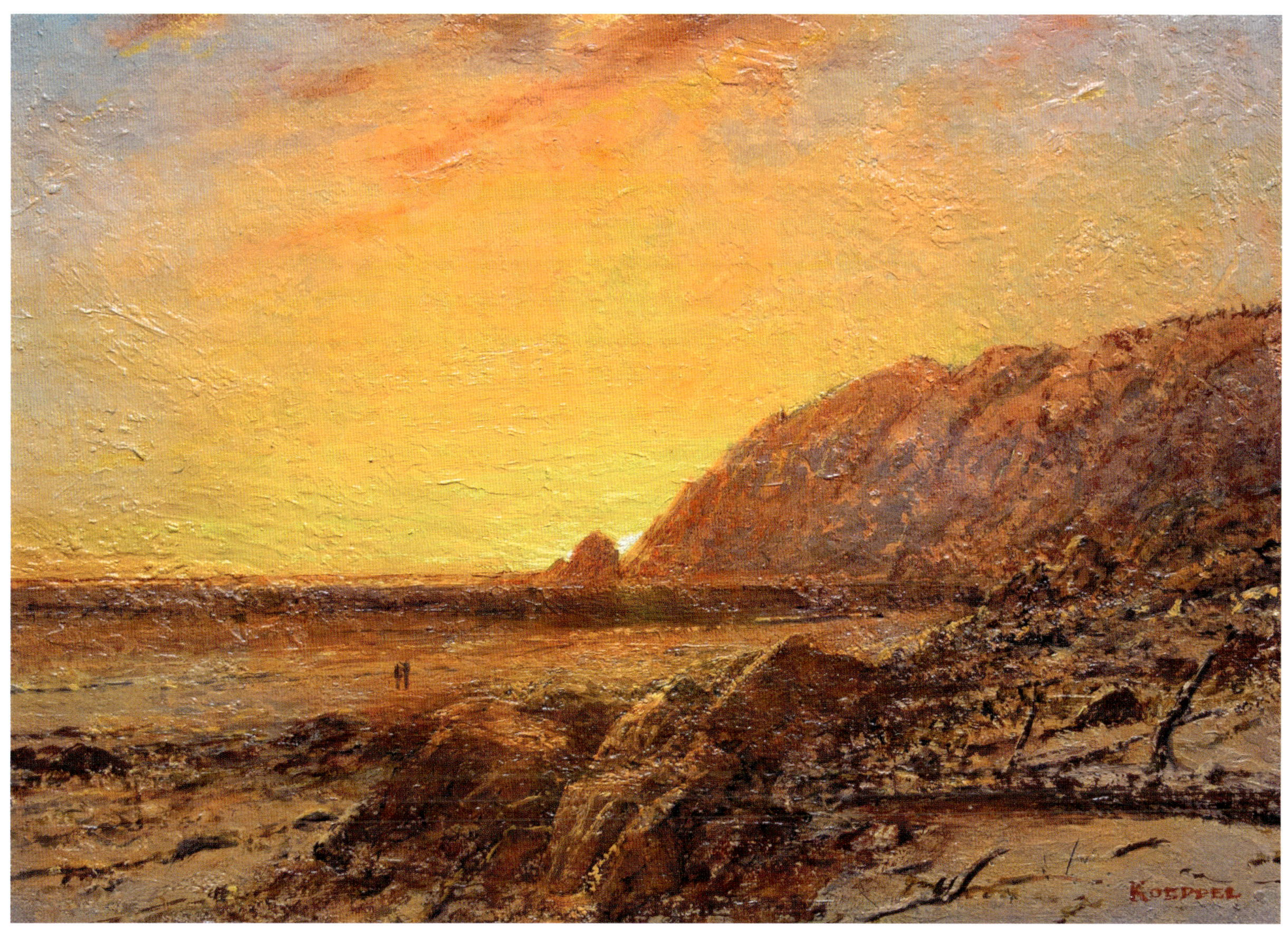

Erik Koeppel, New Hampshire
SUNSET ON THE COAST

A friend gave me this panel several years ago to try out. It sat around my studio for a time before, and I eventually started using it for almost abstract design experiments using the paint that was leftover on my palette. It was dark and moody for a long time but kept changing. Over many layers of this process, the air cleared in the painting, and my imagination brought forth an invented scene of sunset on a coast. It has a lot of texture on the surface as a result. Once the image took hold, and I felt the peace of this warm sunset, I worked to resolve the picture, and it eventually arrived at the image you see today.

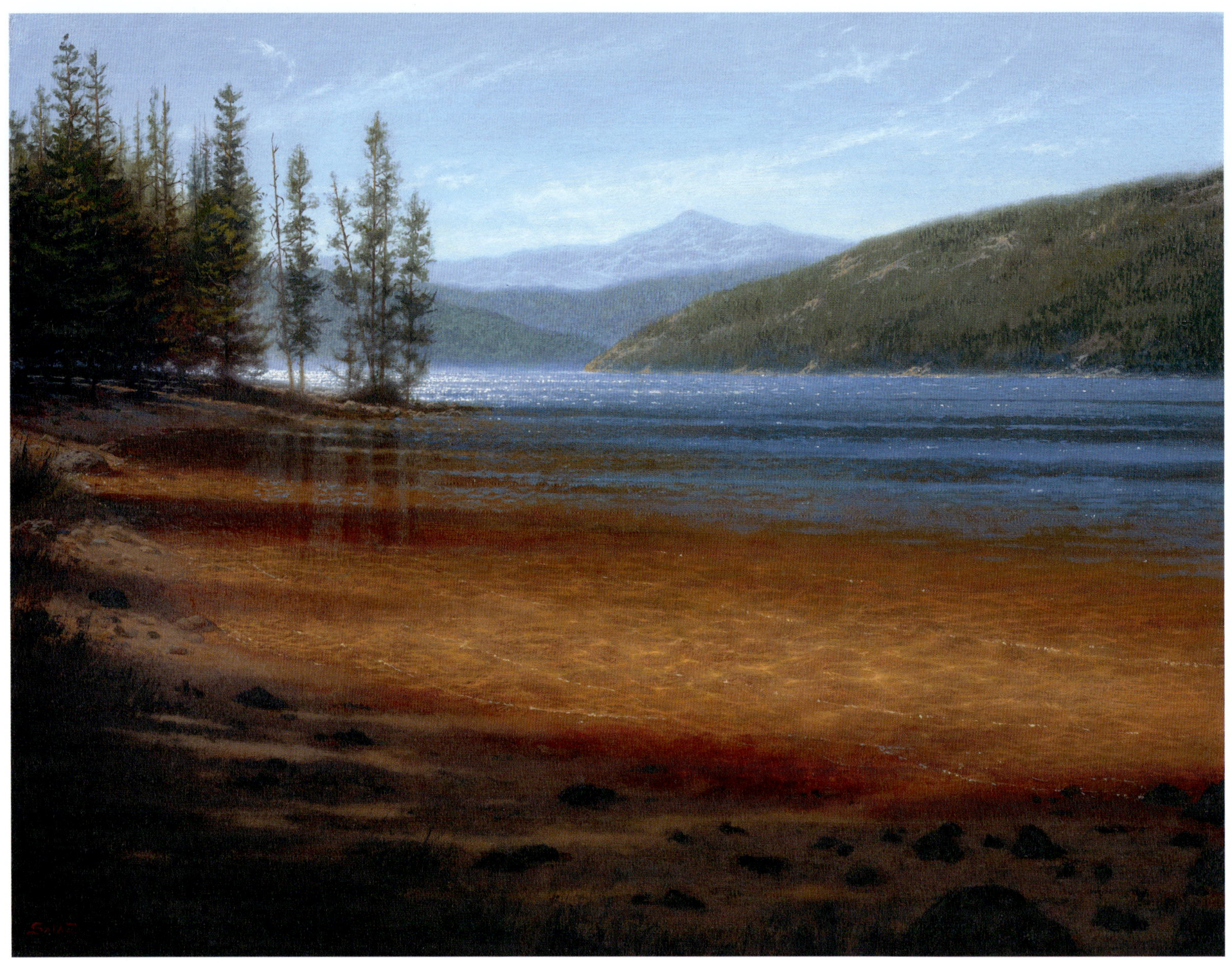

Ken Salaz, New York
FRESHWATER SUNRISE

Several of my friends have died from the virus. It was quite intense here in NY. I am currently spending quite a bit of time with my family. We live in the Hudson Valley and have been taking long weekends up to the Catskills to swim and be in nature. There are very few people we encounter, so we feel like we are doing "isolation" in the best form possible—by being surrounded by nature. This painting is inspired by waking up in the early morning and arriving at the edge of the water, which was waiting to be splashed in and enjoyed. However, the beauty was too astounding; I had to capture it as best I could before getting in.

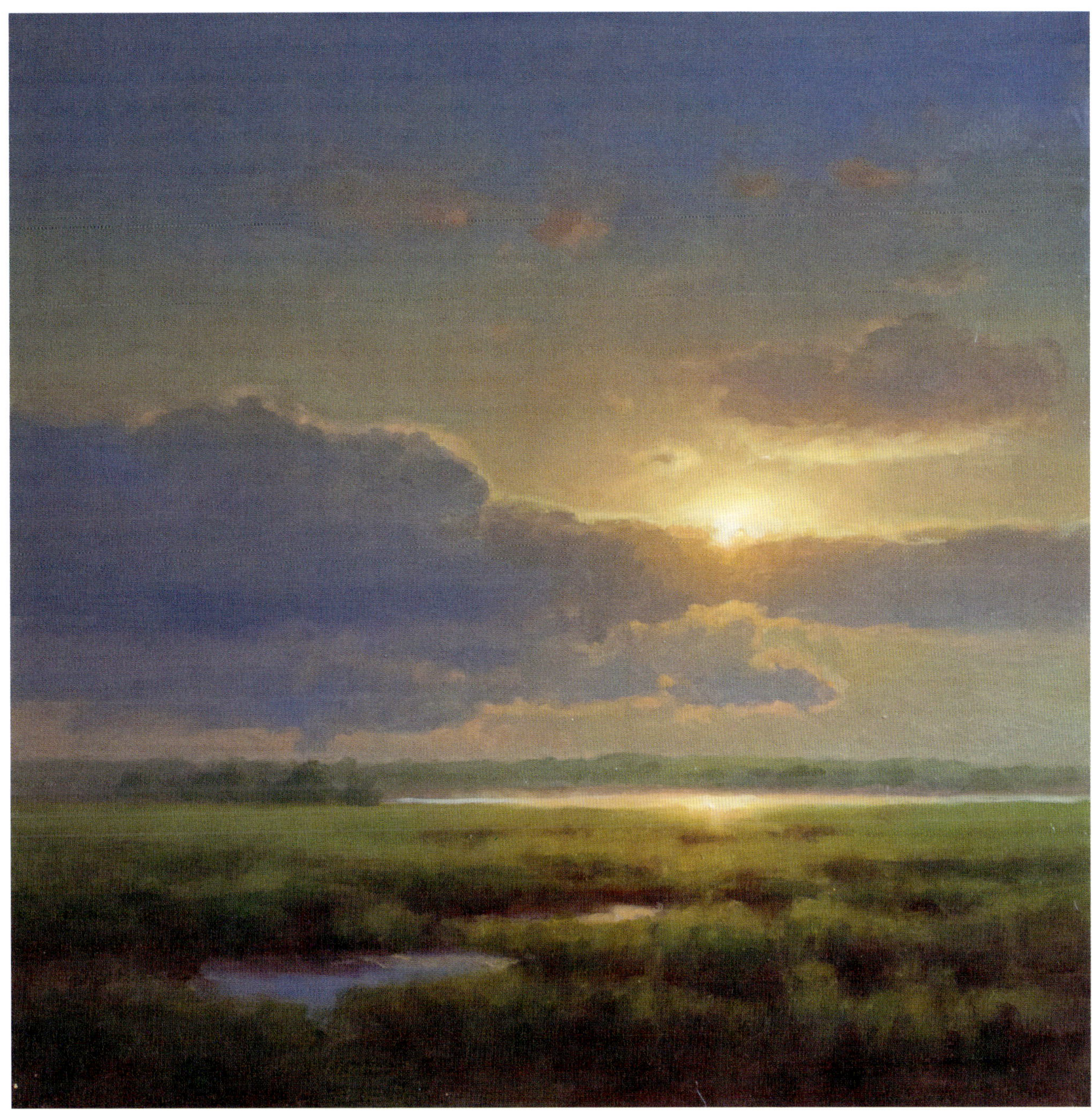

Hillary Scott, Massachusetts

SUMMER HAZE

This painting takes me back to simpler times and features a favorite view of Plum Island. The island is named for the wild beach plum shrubs that grow on its dunes. It's a barrier island located off the northeast coast of Massachusetts. My mother-in-law lives on the basin side of the island, and the sun sets right on the marsh that lies a few feet from her house. It was one of those hot, hazy summer evenings. I was naturally drawn to the magical shimmer on the water as the sunset. Oh, take me back to that summer haze!

8 WATERWAYS

Landscape paintings that feature lakes, rivers, and waterways, are my absolute favorite to paint. I've always been drawn to streams, waterfalls, lakes, springs, rivers, and the wildlife which lives there.

Florida offers some fascinating views from the water. My painting *Emerging from Darkness into Light*, is a scene from North Florida, accessible only by airboat. The dense forest of cypress trees growing out of the water, hanging Spanish moss, and the mass of birds, was so mesmerizing and peaceful that I never wanted to leave. Thankfully, I took a multitude of pictures as, just two months later, the quarantine took effect.

Luckily, as an artist, I'm comfortable with long stretches of isolation and so took advantage of the quarantine time to work on larger, more detailed paintings. I took extra time to build up the layers of paint, creating depth to achieve that special scene that was still fresh in my mind. I picked this particular painting for the collection because of its significance of dark to light.

One thing I love most about painting waterways is the interesting way trees and plants grow near the water; often contorted, overgrown, crowded, and struggling to reach the light to survive. Wildlife is abundant, from alligators to beautiful birds, dragonflies, ducks, and fish. to name just a few. It is so peaceful and, whenever I get the opportunity, I will paint en plein air from life on location. I'm fortunate to live on a small pond and so spend many days on my porch watching the wood ducks go about their day, oblivious to the crazy pandemic going on around them.

For me, water is a soothing meditation. I want my paintings to draw the viewer in, imagine a quieter place to relax, and enjoy the beauty of nature. Even in a pandemic, nature is as beautiful as ever.

Elisabeth C. Ferber
Mt. Dora, Florida

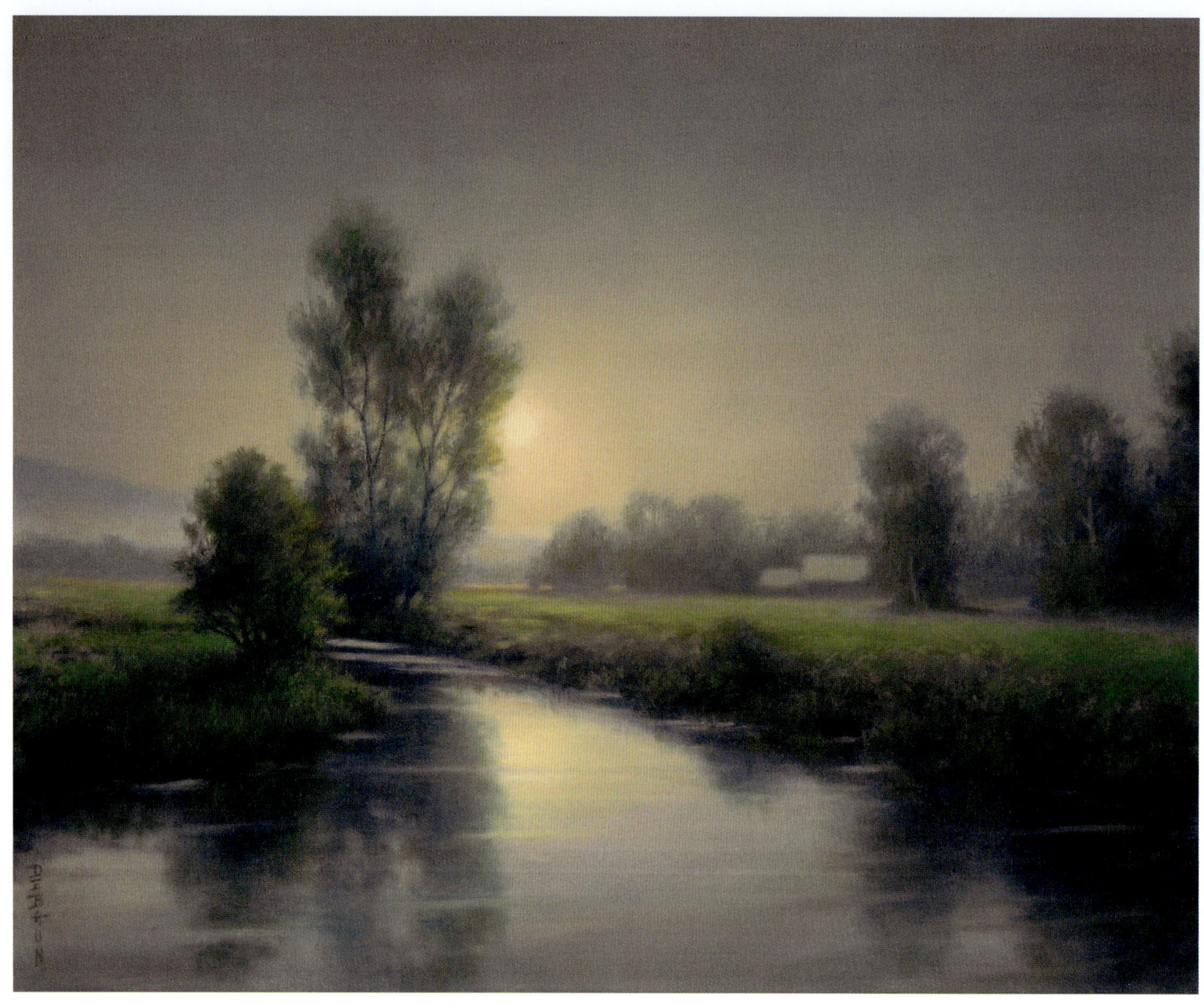

Barry DeBaun, New York
SERENE MORNING

This image depicts the rising morning sun over a pastoral landscape. I painted this imaginary landscape in my studio during the quarantine from a desire to paint a calming scene during these difficult times.

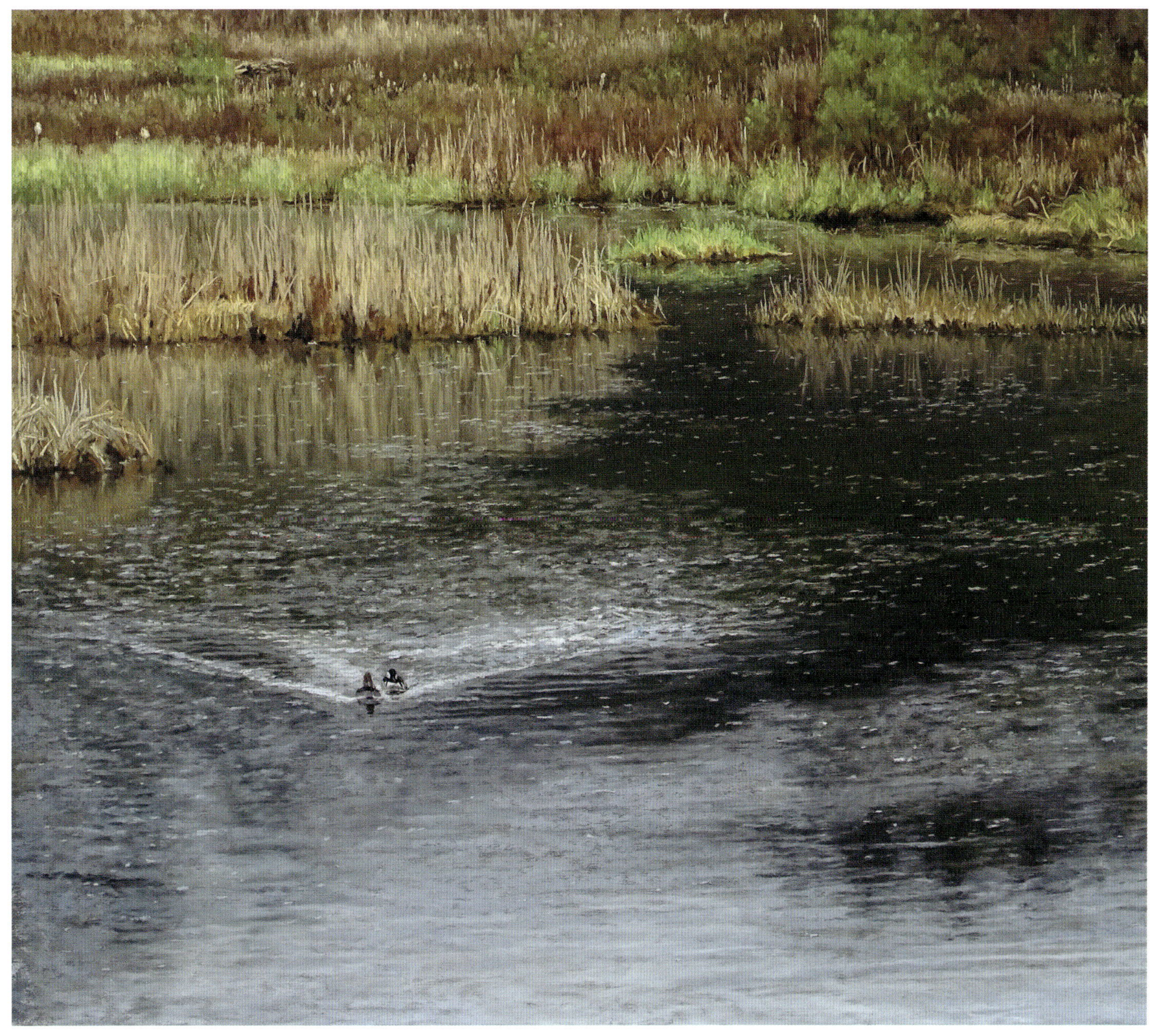

Cindy House

SWIMMING IN THE RAIN

Swimming in the Rain is inspired by one of my favorite nearby marshes that I often visit in spring. I am fortunate to have spent my life enjoying nature. Birds never fail to provide me with a source of subject matter, as well as entertainment. Due to the solitary nature of my career as an artist, I am accustomed to "social distancing," particularly for long periods during winter; there was just never a name for it. This year, people—some perhaps unaccustomed to solitude—have discovered opportunities to go outside to escape the four walls of their surroundings and have found themselves enjoying nature. It is my hope that these moments brought the same solace to them that I find in the natural world, and that the impressions and memories remain with them always. My thanks go out to those working hard in this fight against the pandemic and I hope for healthier days ahead.

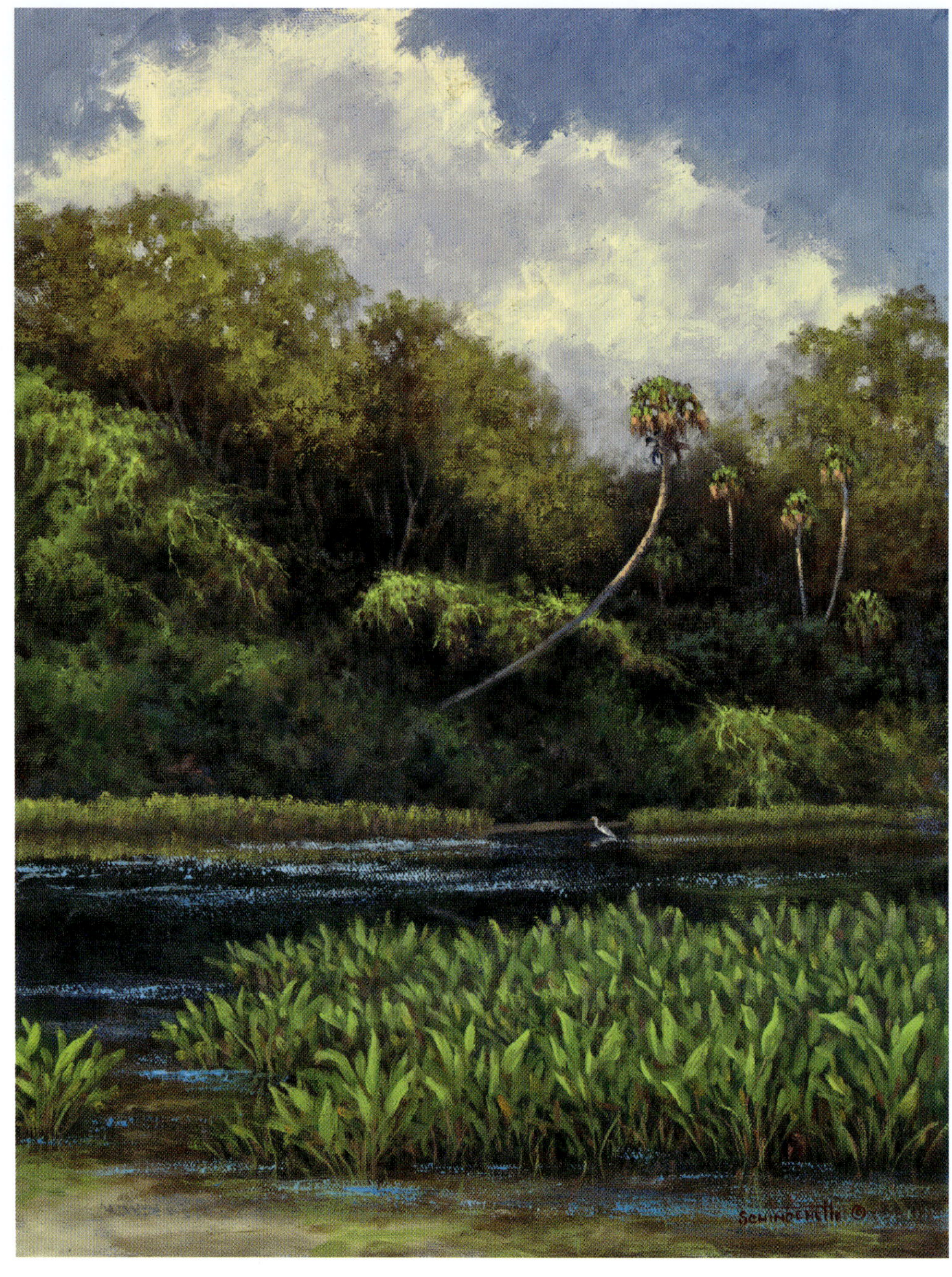

Jacquelyn Schindehette, Florida

A DAY ON THE SILVER RIVER (EDITION 1)

I lived in Ocala, Florida, for a number of years. Silver Springs State Park was just minutes away from my home. While there, I often paddled my kayak up and down the Silver River that is fed by the flow of water from the spring head. I worked on many sketches and studies of the river, finally completing this painting.

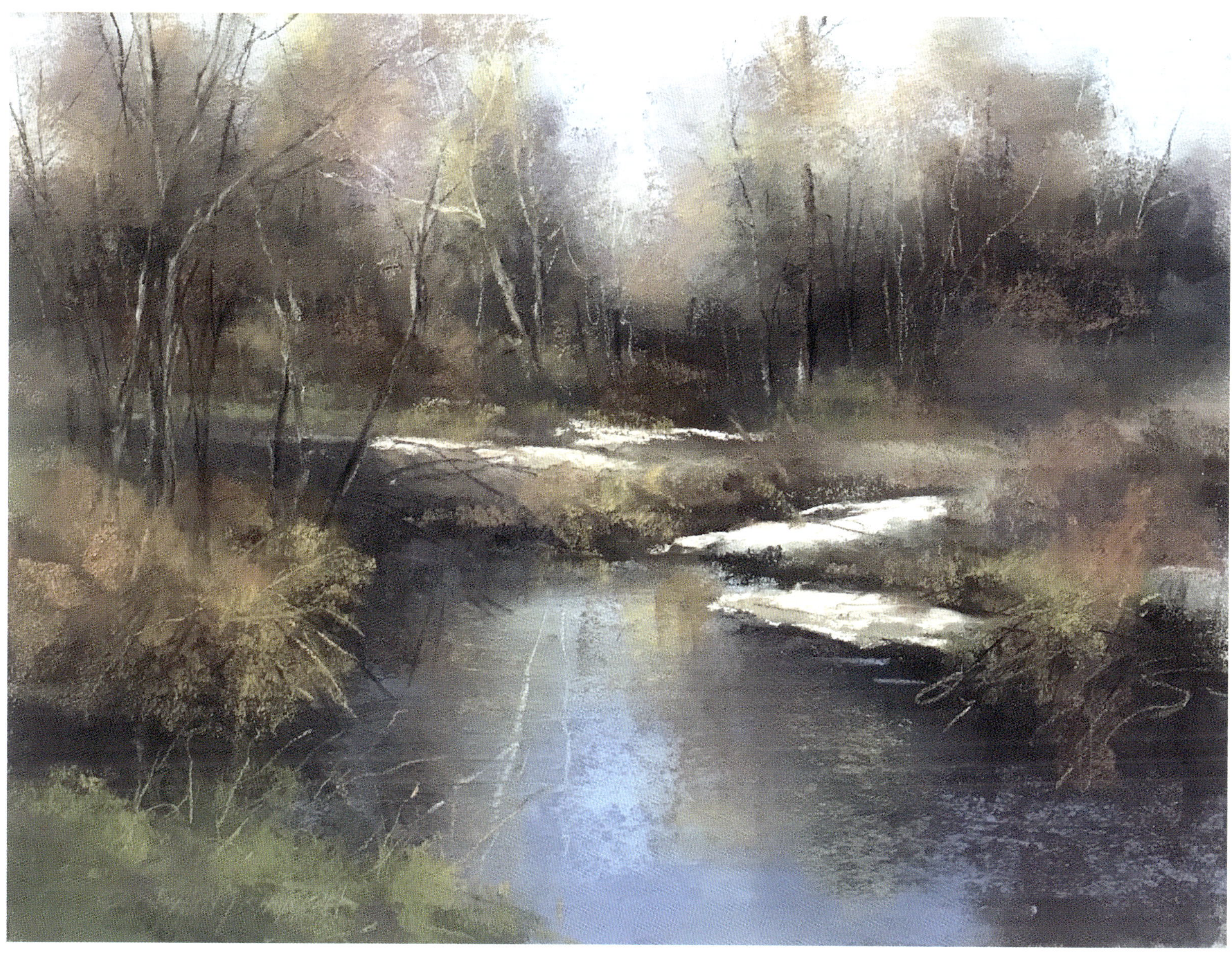

Bonnie Zahn Griffith, Idaho

HARMONY

I am a plein-air painter so I frequently work alone in secluded and some remote areas around the western United States. With the onset of social distancing and isolation during the pandemic, painting solo took on a new feel. One felt really alone as there was very little activity on roads and streets. It was like time sort of stood still.

Painting was my "normal." During lockdown, I painted in the studio but then, early in April, I realized that I could get out to some favorite painting spots and still maintain isolation criteria.

This painting is painted at Eagle Island State Park in Idaho, where the Boise River splits into two forks and creates this large island. Along the northern border is a great view of the river. In early spring, the greens are hardly visible, but there is all this great subtle color in the undergrowth and brush along the river to capture in a painting. Going to this spot gave me an escape from the unknowns of the pandemic; a feeling of normality and a sense of worth in creating a work that shows the promise of spring and that creates a challenge to achieve harmonious color. So, it became *Harmony*.

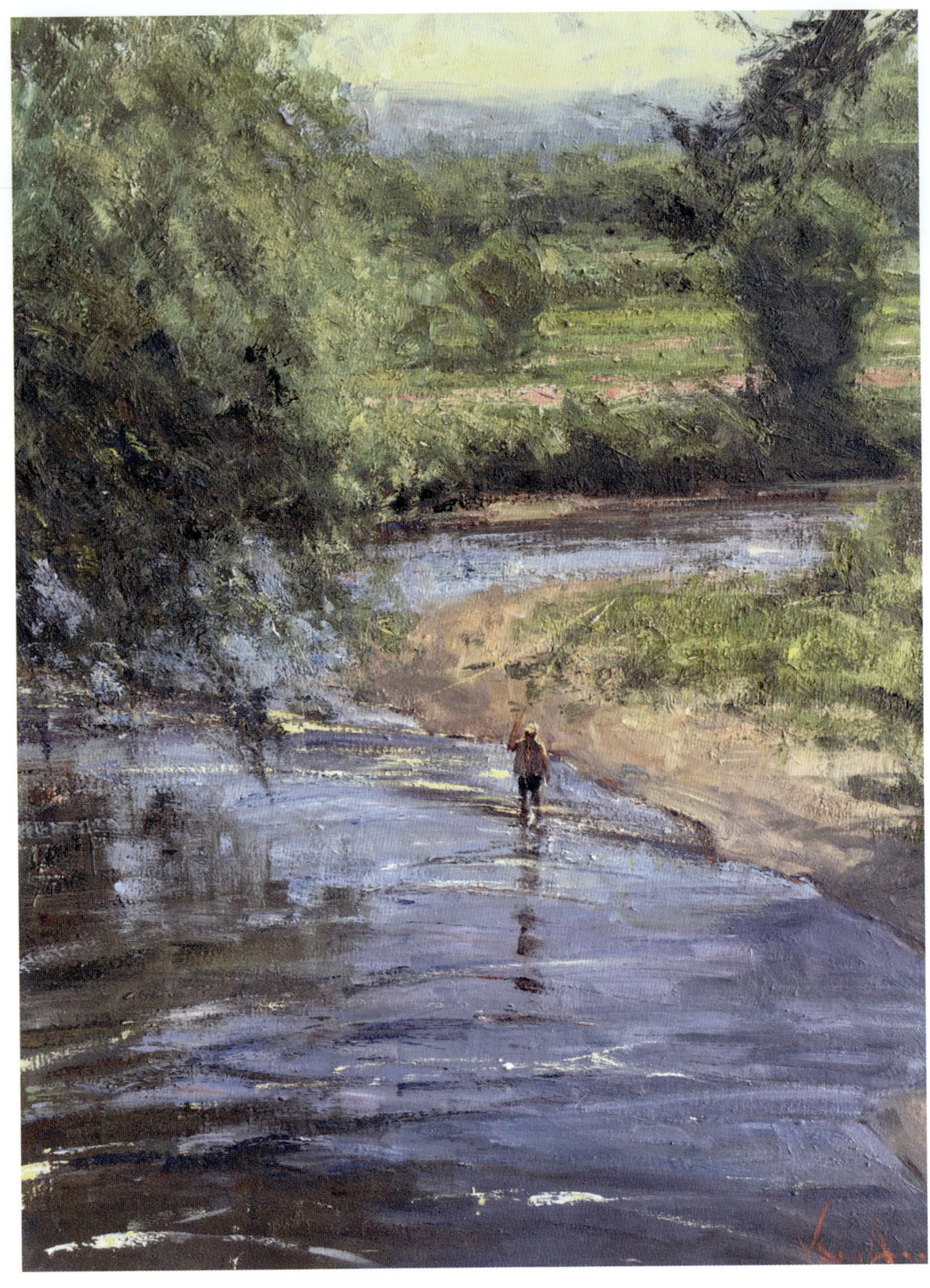

George Van Hook, New York
CASTING AT THE RIVER BEND

I have painted all along the mid stretches of this renowned fly-fishing river over the past 30 years. It provides endless beauty and tranquility, and the occasional fisherman. This scene never grows old for me. I know that it will do the same gracing one of the walls in your home. Many of my river paintings have gone to the American Museum of Fly Fishing in neighboring Manchester, Vermont, for their art auctions.

Sam Paonessa, Canada
PRIMAVERA

The following was written by my student, Irina Oliver, who saw my painting and was inspired to write these fitting and powerful words:

Canada the Voices
Government speaks. Leave the workplace. Lock the schools. Close the borders. Go home. Stay home. Don't go out. Everything will be different. You need to change. The line is climbing upwards. Who is to blame? We will help you. Listen! Public health beseeches. Shelter in place. Socially distance. Physically distance. Wash your hands. Don't touch your face. Remember the elderly. We are in this together. Help bend the curve. Take care of each other. Be kind to each other. Find joy within. Listen! Nature whispers. We have brought spring. We have arrived from beneath the earth and from the south and from Above. Where are you? We are now as we were in the Beginning. We are always the Gift for you. Remember the First Garden in the First Week. Pristine. Shimmering. Joyful. Safe. Pink and orange. Blue and purple. Green and yellow. We gave so much. And then you arrived. You took too much. Where are you this spring? We are now thriving, multiplying, healing, celebrating. One day you will return. It will be different. You must change. Remember the Covenant: protect; respect; love. Soon we will be back together again in the same home. We will welcome you and share all that you have missed. The dazzling colors; the glorious songs; the pure waters. You will find solace. Remember. Take care of us. Be kind to us. Listen. Hear our prayer.
by Irina Oliver, spring 2020

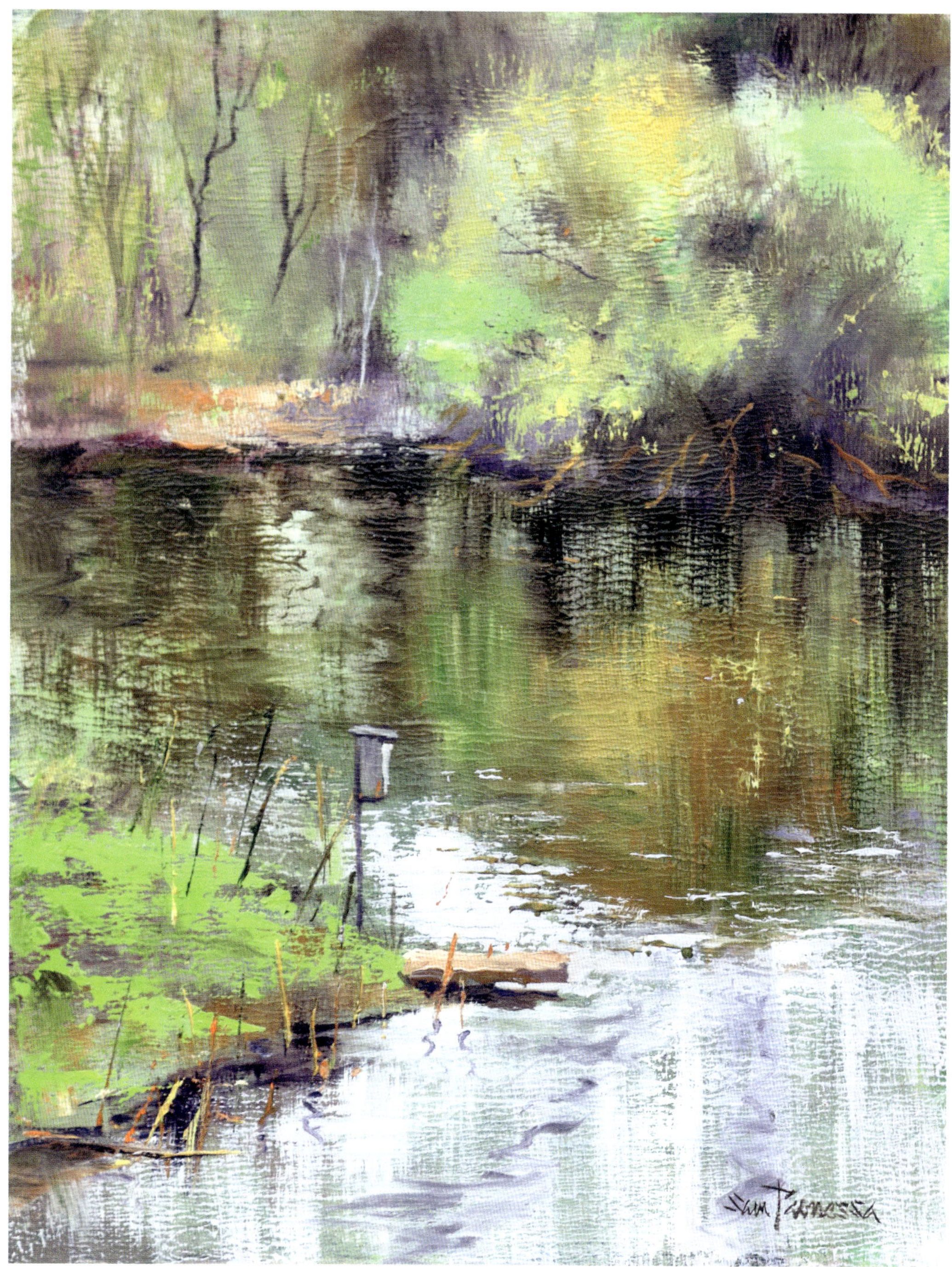

Kim Lordier, California

THE FOREST HAS EARS

I walked into my studio on February 11th...an unease for the last couple weeks sneaking into our community through the news. For the most part, business as usual; schools are still in session but county officials are declaring local health emergencies with seven reported cases of the virus in California and our first death. For the last few months, I had been actively working towards a solo exhibition opening in August 2020 at a gallery in Carmel, California. The show paintings are coastal landscapes full of rich color and luminous light. I couldn't bring myself to paint towards my goal on the 11th. I felt a deep quiet, a very brief contemplation of why I am painting when things around me are in turmoil and unrest. Thoughts are momentary at best, unmemorable for others, but poignant to me at the time.

The painting, *The Forest Has Ears*, was started on February 11th. The color palette is a departure from my usual; the idea quiet, peaceful. A sense of calm, the strength of granite slabs, and pure clean water flowing through a forest in seasonal transition. Around that time, the reports of air pollution clearing up in China were the only upside to this freight train coming our way. No matter where one sits politically, watching the improvement to the air quality around the globe is a beautiful gift to the Earth and its inhabitants, especially those with difficulty breathing during this time.

On February 14th, I realized something was missing in my painting. That is when I placed the observer in the background. Often, when designing/developing a painting, the major shapes and organization of a piece are decided beforehand, and all the elements should support the idea or concept. Rarely, for me, does adding something at the end ever work out. The silent observer here is waiting to hear, still in her stance, what we as humans have to say to the world. She came to me and is patiently waiting to make sure I stand strong like granite, allow the flow of life to run through and around me, and continue to create beauty to share with others. Yes, I have questioned whether standing before my easel is a selfish act or a gift to share. I believe it is a bit of both.

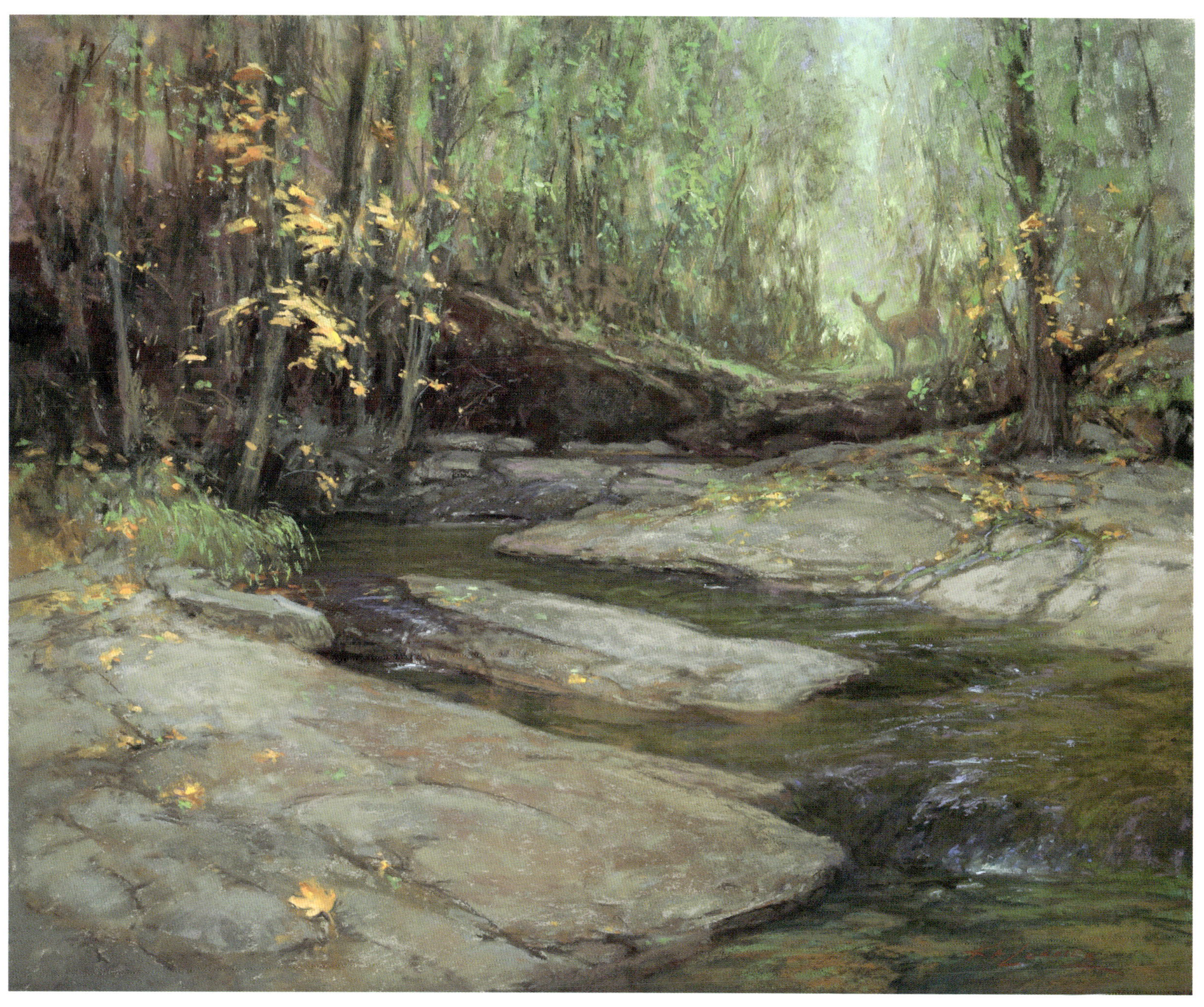

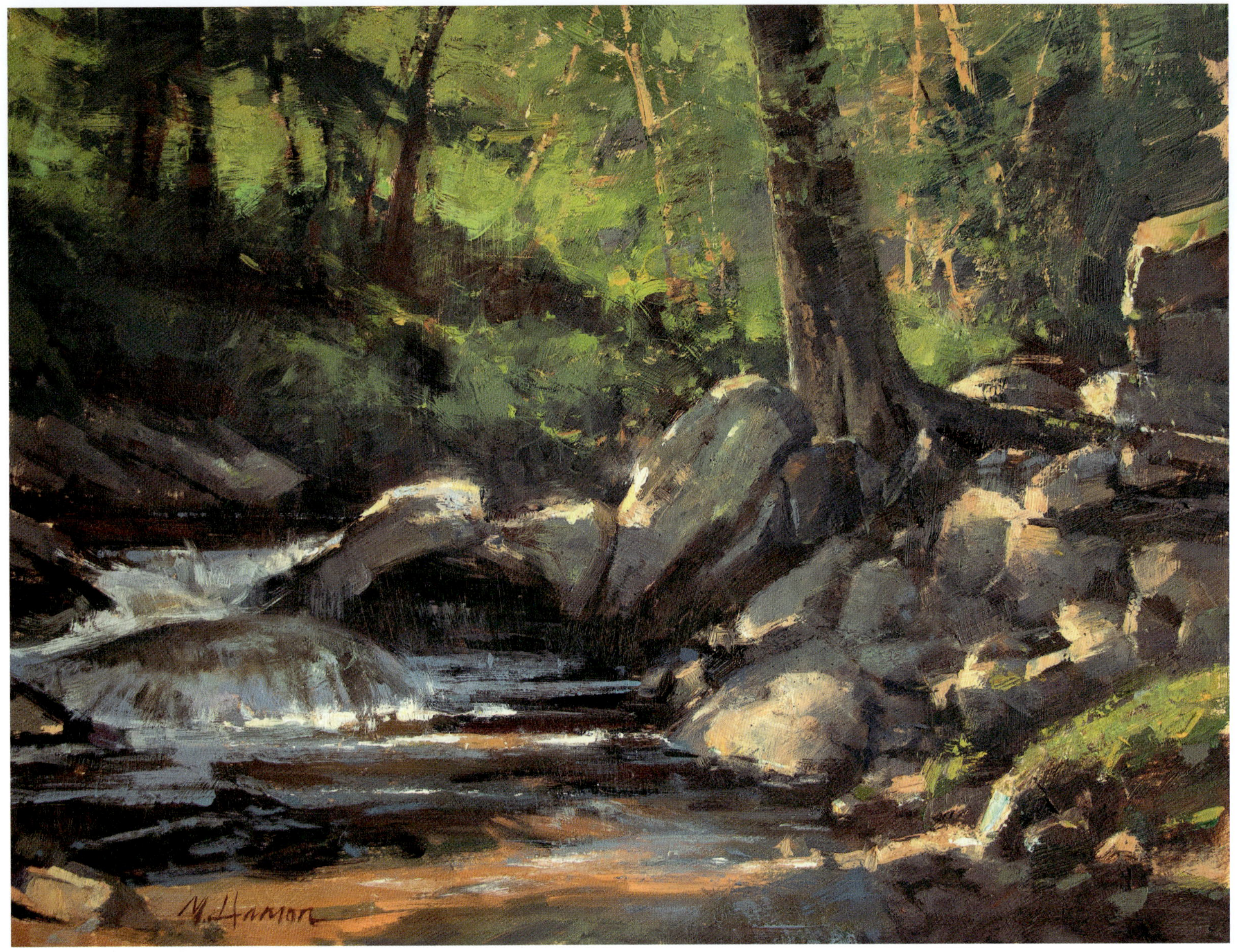

Marc R. Hanson, Georgia
BELOW THE POOL

As a landscape painter, my most fruitful and educational time painting is while standing out in Mother Nature, allowing all that she is to enter my psyche and influence what I want to say about her beauty. Since late March, and the beginning of having to limit our exposure to others, being able to get to some of my regular painting locations has become more difficult. Despite that, one of the wonderfully special things about being an artist, a painter, is the ability to put yourself into places, times, and events that you can't physically be a part of, and create meaningful images, despite not being there. During the time of COVID-19, I've found that I have more time to think about the "why" of paintings that I create, and paint pieces about places, and ideas about those places. The painting that I've submitted for The Great American Paint In® is of one of those places; a quiet little stream in the mountains of North Carolina. *Below The Pool* is where I would like to be right now, maybe painting, maybe casting a fly upstream into the pool to let it drift down towards me, or maybe to just sit and dream. It's comforting to think about being there right now.

Mike Barret Kolasinski, Illinois
GLIDE TO BE HERE

Shortly before the sheltering-in-place orders, I was gliding through a county park in Michigan cross-country skiing when I came upon this small stream. Noting the composition, and particularly the light, I realized this image may create an interesting painting. Once I began staying at home and—for me—coloring "outside the lines" in the studio became the norm, I was "glad to be there," so this winter landscape was an easy one to title.

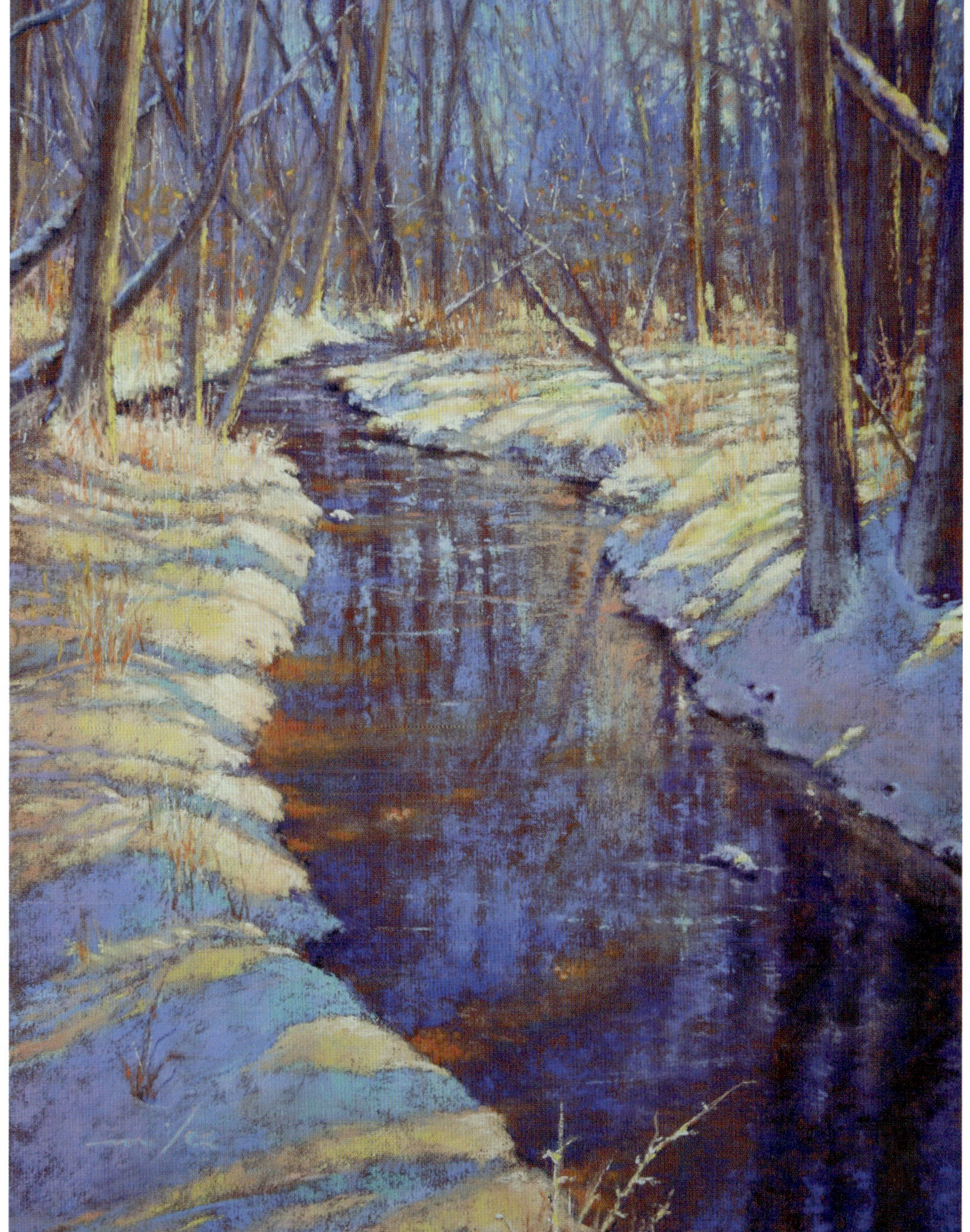

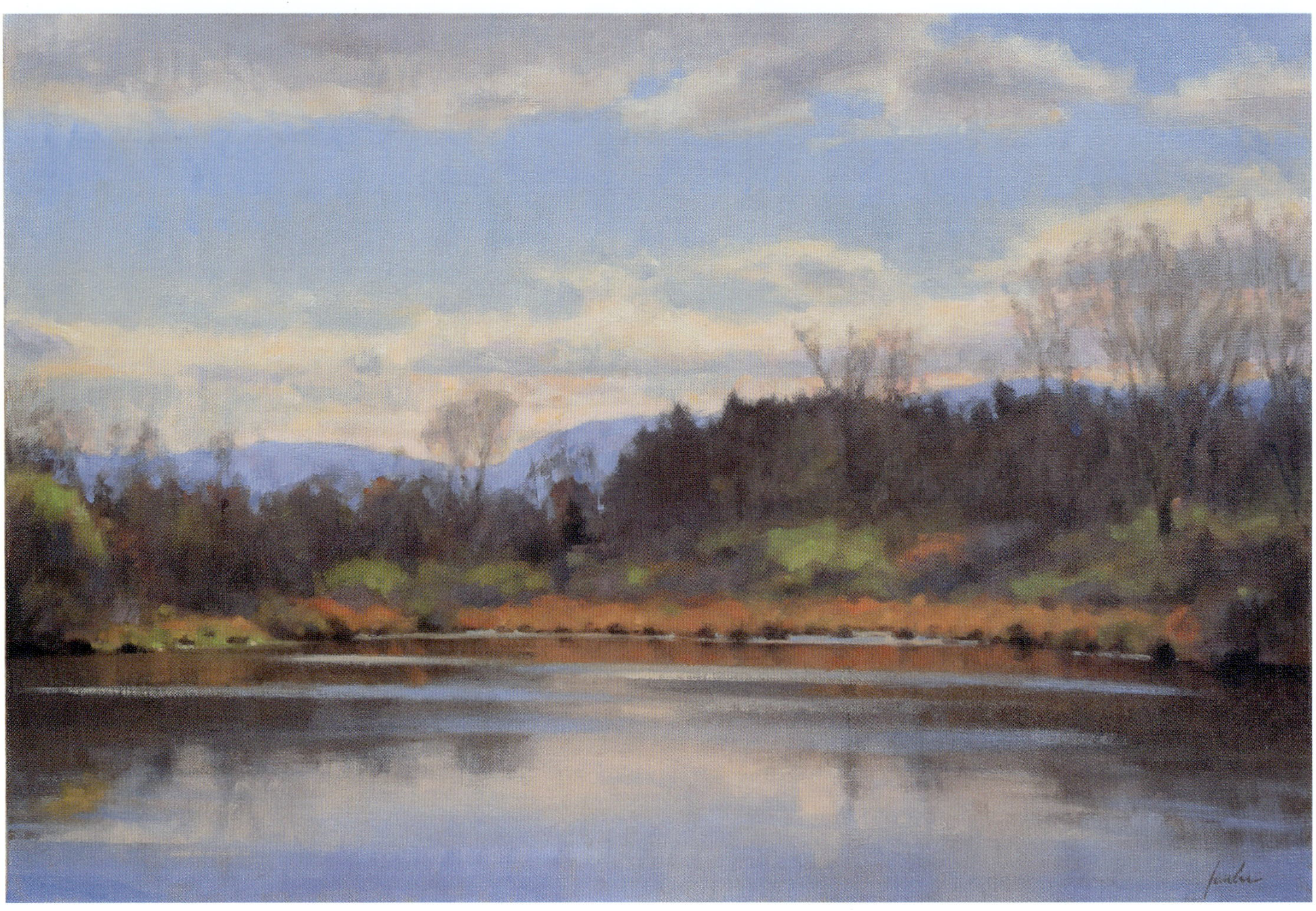

James Coe, New York

POND LIGHT: INTO THE SUN

Completed in my studio this past winter, shortly before the Coronavirus pandemic took hold of our world, *Pond Light; Into the Sun* is the largest and most recent of a series of paintings representing this little hidden pond located in what is currently a park in the Hudson Valley village of Greenville, New York, just a few miles from home. Historically, this was a shallow farm pond, as the park is situated on lands that had been maintained and farmed since before the Revolution by the Vanderbilt family, and which were donated to the community just a few years ago. I have painted this same view looking across the reflective surface of the pond, south towards the northernmost escarpment of the Catskill Mountains, many times—both onsite and in the studio. I have taken groups of students to share the view and paint the scene with me. I know it so well!

Obviously, the nature of the scene can vary with the season and with weather conditions. It can be dark and brooding or blinding with the sun. The water can be still and mirror-clear, or crusted with swirls of bright-green scum, or frozen solid and packed with snow. But the peace and solitude I find in this location is what moves me most. Few visitors to the park or dog-walkers ever bother hiking down into the hollow where the pond is tucked away. During these past weeks of self-isolation and social distancing, my wife and I have found that the park and the trail that leads down to "my" pond have provided a welcome escape on our walks together. The view is always inspiring. The motif calls me to paint it again. And I look forward to setting my easel up there very soon.

Ellen Rice, Delaware
MOORED IN THE MIST

When the pandemic became public knowledge, I was, like many people, having difficulty fathoming the reality. I didn't know what to do, so I did what I do best: paint and write. Strangely, for the first few months I felt calm and remained fairly so. It was time to focus. *Moored in the Mist* is the second painting I created in the early months of the pandemic. It is a commission for a gentleman who brought me a beautiful but very damaged photograph he'd taken 30 years ago of a favorite place that he hoped I could recreate.

The photo spoke to me, and it fit my mood. Light shone through a heavy mist that shrouded almost everything in the scene. Painting slowly, thin glaze after thin glaze, allowing each to dry between coats, I established the trees and weeds and boat in fine detail, and when those were dry, I started bringing in the mist. I shut out thoughts of what was happening around us, to me, my gallery, the world; and as I worked, I became one with a small fish pond in the hills of Pennsylvania. I wanted the painting to glow, to draw your eyes to the light. While I sought to be true to the gentleman's photo and memories, I focused on the sun burning through the mist, lighting the boat's bow and blossoms on the foreground weeds. I found it symbolic of the time. Keeping our eyes on the light, pointing our bows in the right direction, we will come through this.

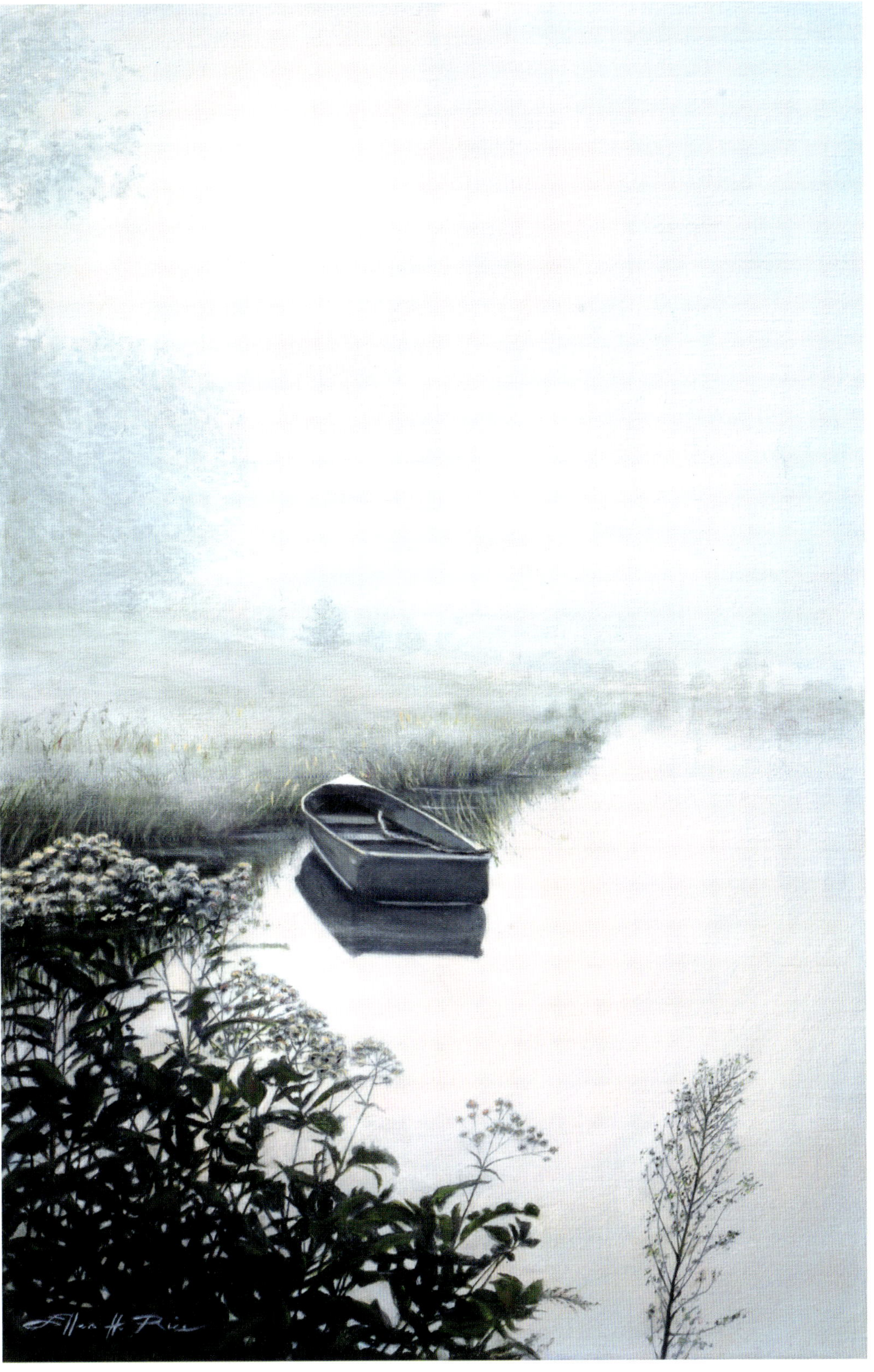

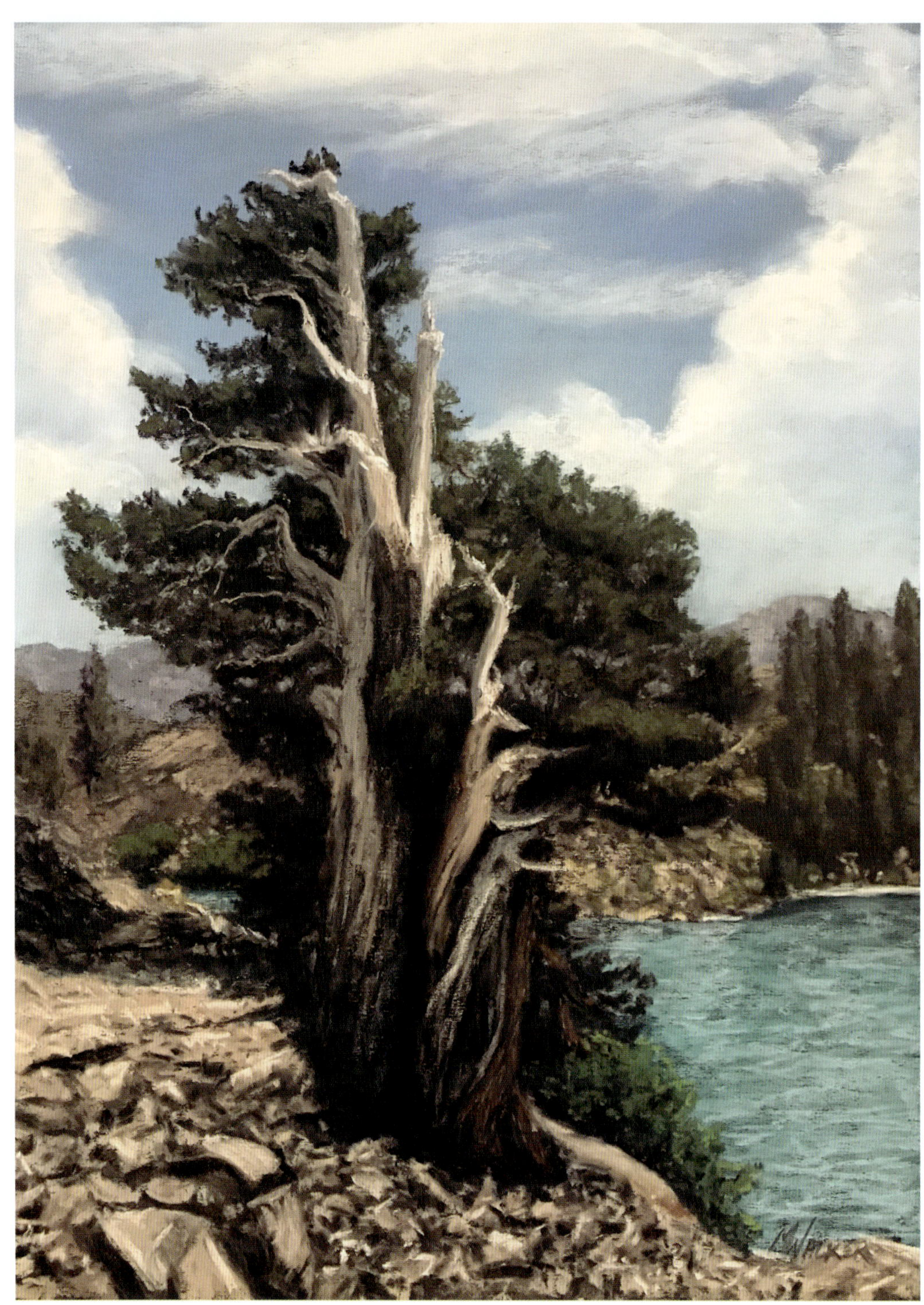

Marti Walker, California

SIERRA SENTINEL

This awesome western juniper resides between Heather Lake and the Pacific Crest Trail in Desolation Wilderness. Every hiker passes by it and most stop for an iconic photo standing beside it!

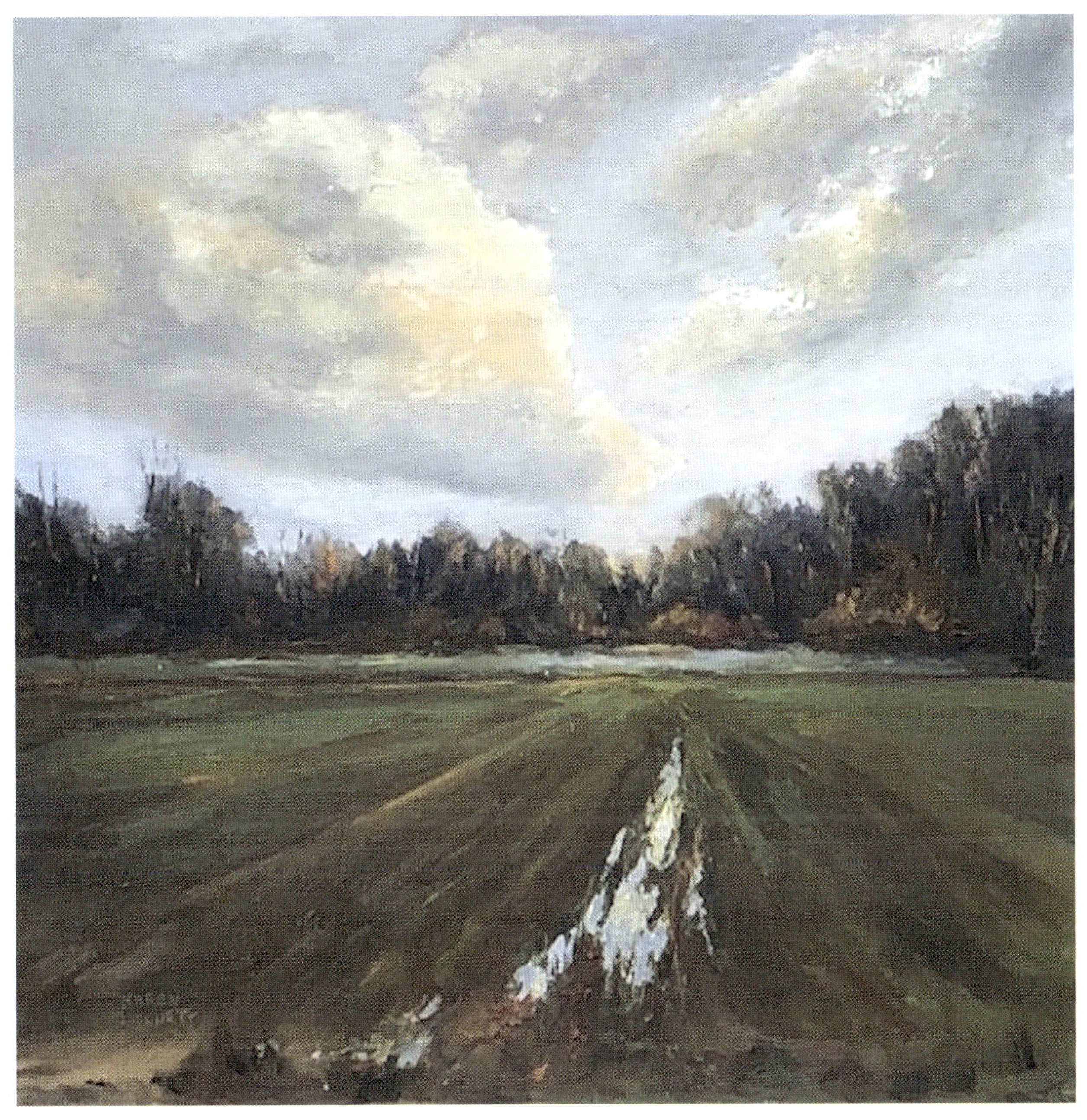

Karen Bennett, Mississippi
AFTER THE RAIN

I created this painting in February, before cases of COVID-19 began escalating. The title, *After the Rain,* lends an element of encouragement, as we travel through the pain, isolation, and quarantine to a new day of hope and promise. To me, this painting expresses the tears of pain, the reflections of what was, and then the process of moving forward to the hope of tomorrow.

Thomas Adkins, Connecticut

HARBOR SUNRISE

During this difficult time, I have not been able to visit one of my favorite locations. The serenity and tranquility of this place remain as an everlasting calm in my thoughts, just a short stroll from Secondary Studio on the coast of Maine. Needless to say, I am longing to return. I have been able to paint this in my studio from memory and numerous plein-air studies I have done over the years.

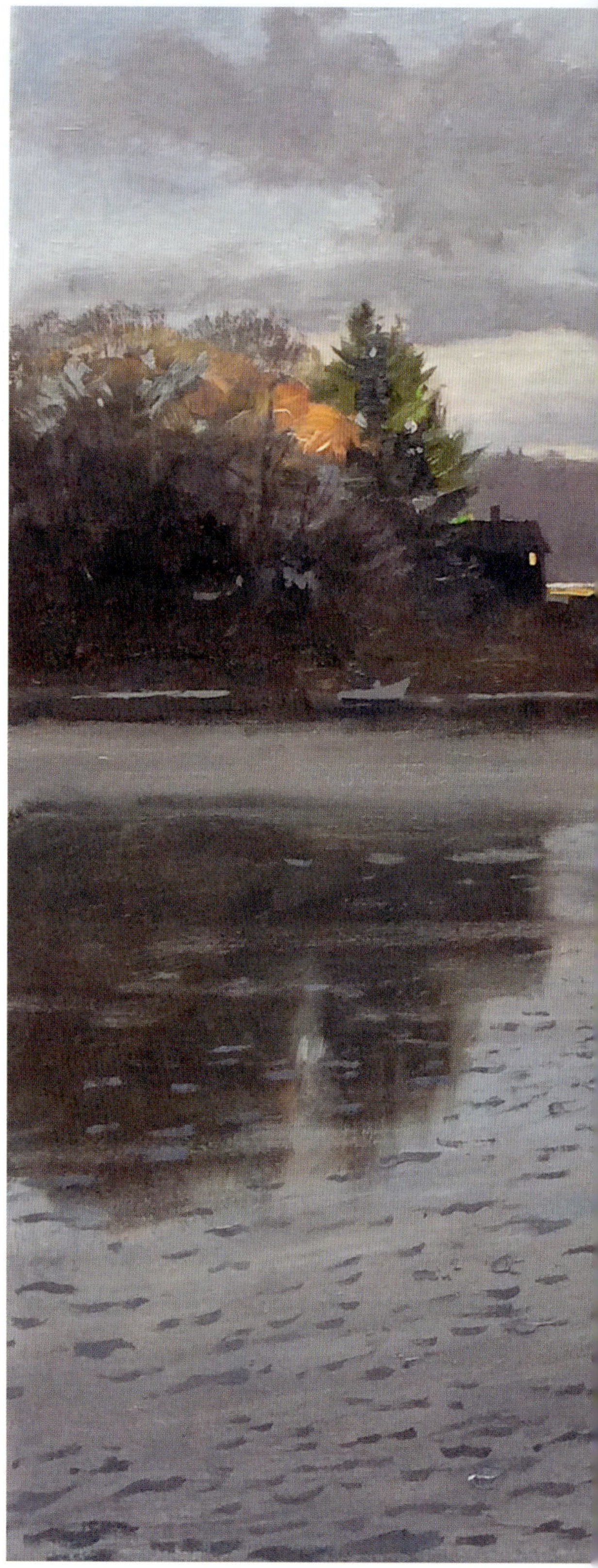

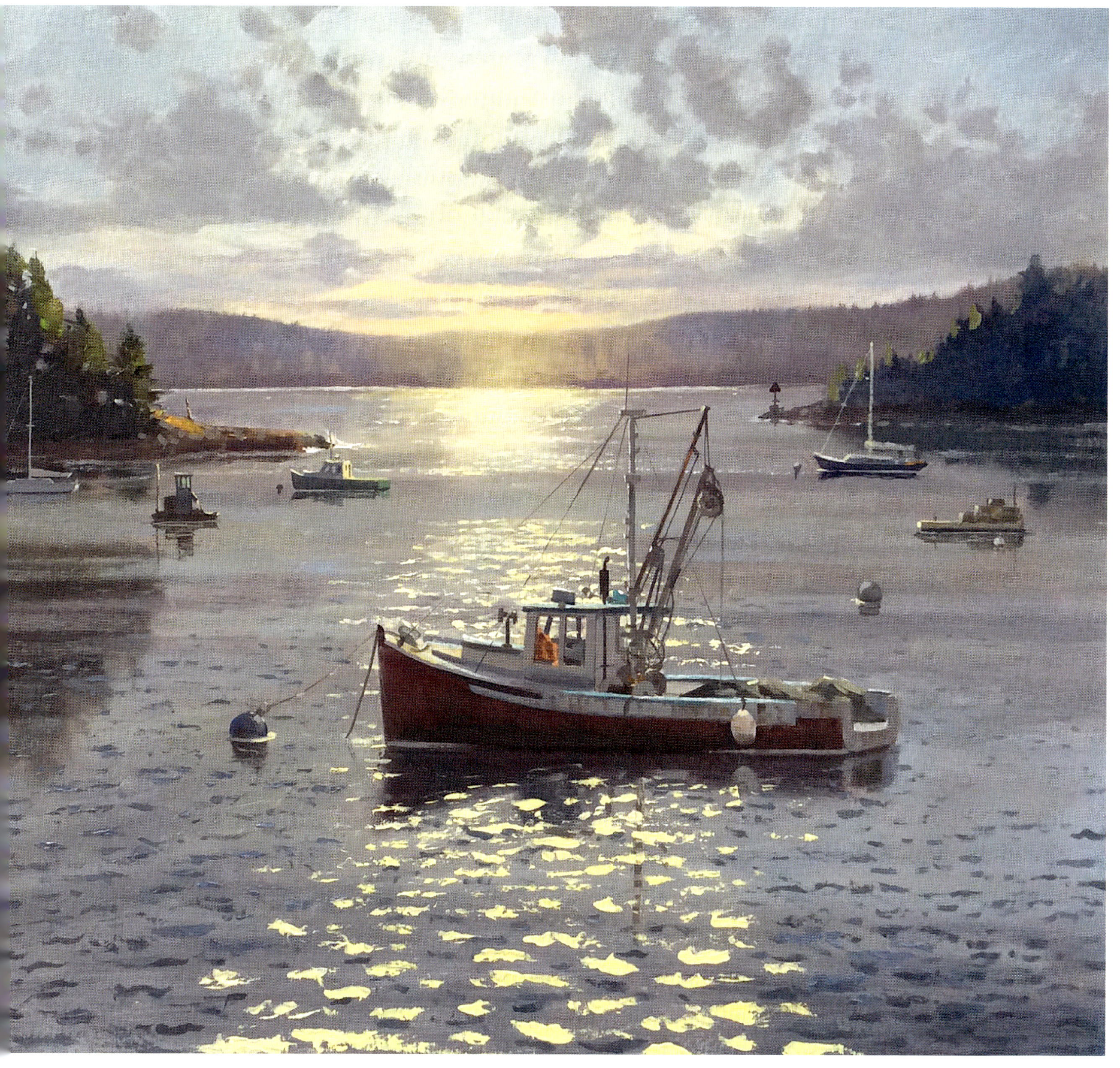

Michael Orwick, Oregon

THY LIGHT

In the last few months in quarantine, I think we have all figured out how important a little sunlight and fresh air can be. My entire goal is just to help people remember how blessed we all are (especially in the magical Pacific Northwest) to be surrounded by such exquisite beauty. We just need to slow down, take a long slow breath, and look. Stuck in the studio, due to a mix of COVID-19 and bad weather, I have been yearning to get back to plein-air painting. During this mandatory hiatus, I have been contemplating why painting in nature affects me so deeply. It must have something to do with taking time for deeper observation and reflection in nature's own settings. For just a little while, I move outside of myself, away from the frenzy of everyday life. When painting outdoors is going well, it is like a meditation or deep prayer, but it can often feel daunting.

Maybe you have felt that paradox, too. Mother Earth does not give up her secrets easily or quickly. Wouldn't it be easier to simply paint in a comfortable studio, where light is controlled, tools are at hand, and the scope of the scene is already selected? No rain, no drifting shadows.

Despite this conundrum, I somehow pluck up the courage to face the test inherent in the task, and I once again pack up my easel, load it into my Honda, and return to nature, undeterred, with my head bowed in reverence, my spirit eager, and happy to learn just a little more from the great and demanding teacher. Once I arrive, unload the car, and set up my easel, paints, and brushes, I survey what nature has to offer. Is this a moment of serenity? No. Nature can fling so much at me that it is difficult to simplify and organize this information overload. As I begin, I ask myself, how can I capture even one small part of the beauty before me? Then I remind myself of Ralph Waldo Emerson's advice: "Adopt the pace of nature: her secret is patience." Slowly, with much effort, and counting on the struggle to be part of its own reward, I am able to find focus and start a visual correspondence with the scene. Gradually, as I start to paint, the process becomes about me, as the artist, and this place, this time together with my subject, the influence of light, the weather conditions, and everything else that is in the air. It not only includes the wind and bugs, but also the sounds and smells.

As Neil Gaiman wrote in *The Graveyard Book*, "Wherever you go, you take yourself with you." Painting in nature forces me to be keenly aware of myself, yet willing to get out of the way, to practice humility, and to clear my ego. It is thus that I may show gratitude while I try in some little way to honor the beauty before me. And it is then that I experience the freedom in nature, the sky, the trees, the grasses, the piercing light, the mysterious shadows—and it is then that nature becomes part of my own nature. Just as Albert Einstein wrote, "Our task must be to free ourselves...by widening our circle of compassion to embrace all living creatures and the whole of nature and its beauty." I hope you and I get to paint together soon and share in the rigor and reward of painting in nature. Like Anne Lamont quipped, "Almost everything will work again if you unplug it for a few minutes, including you."

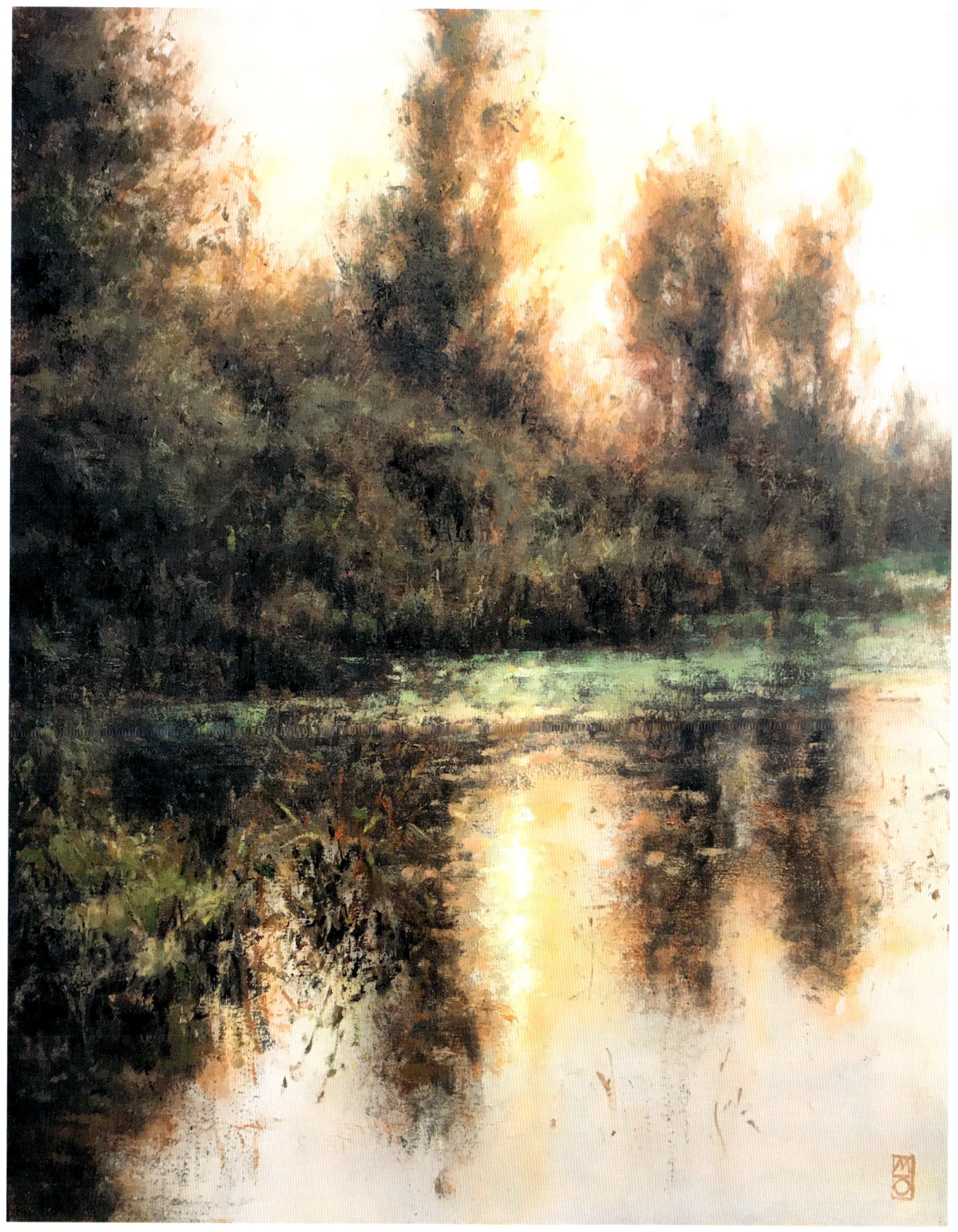

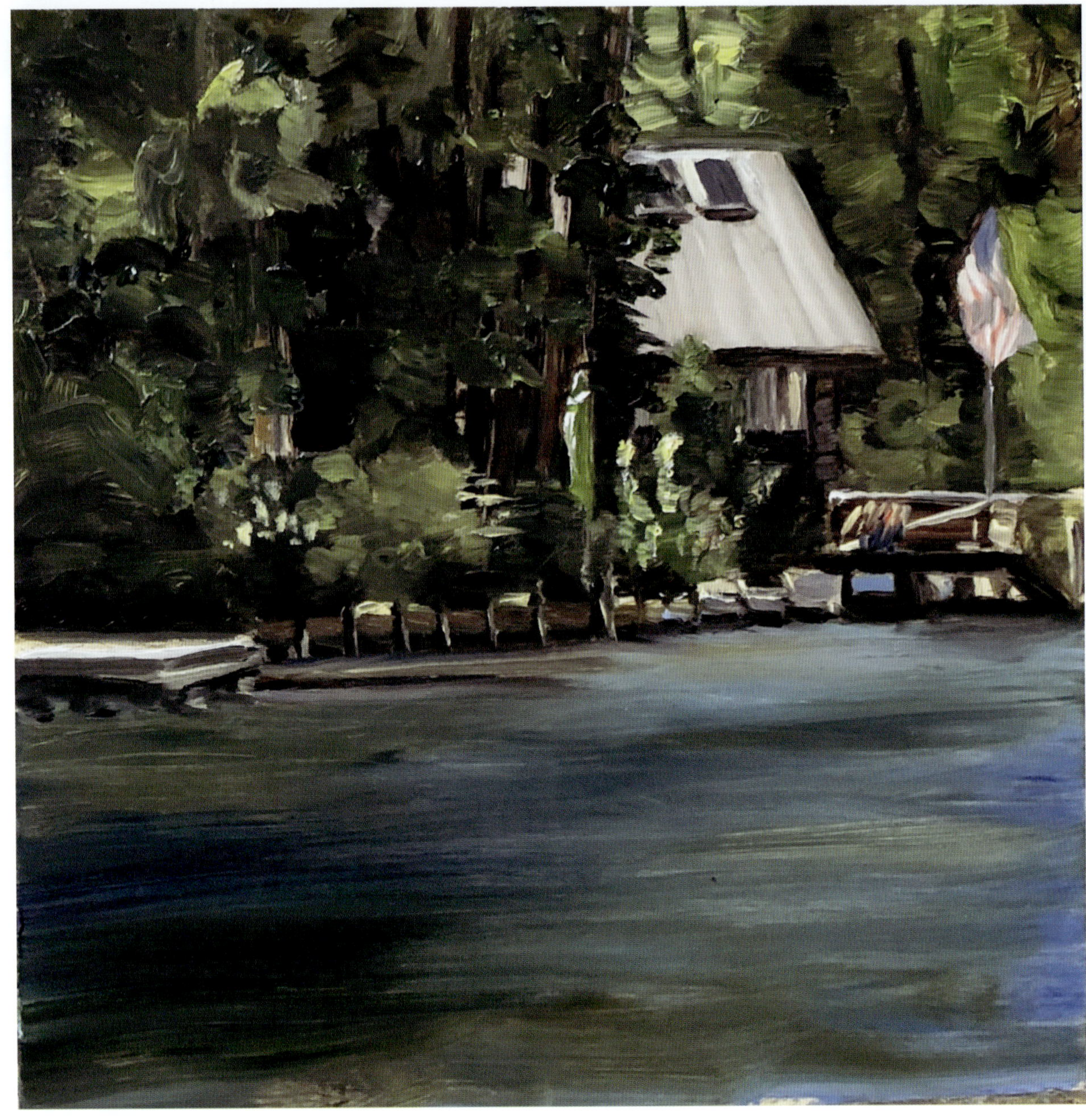

Cathryne Trachok, Florida
DONNER AFTERNOON

I grew up in Reno, spending every summer first in Tahoe until I turned 16, then up at Donner Lake. Since leaving my home at 21, I have lived all over the United States, before settling in Napa, California, 21 years ago. There are worse places to be during this year of the virus, and I can think of only one place that would be better, and that would be Donner Lake. This painting was done last August when I was visiting my sister. I got to stand on the pier and paint the little cove facing where their cabin sits. In these strange times we are living through, I find comfort in knowing this too shall pass, and that the Sierra Nevadas will last forever. Or at least as forever as I can imagine. This little painting, done on a hot August day, is a reminder that Donner Lake is still there, and whether filled with people as in last August or mostly empty like now, it is more than inviting; it is waiting like the rest of us, for when we come back.

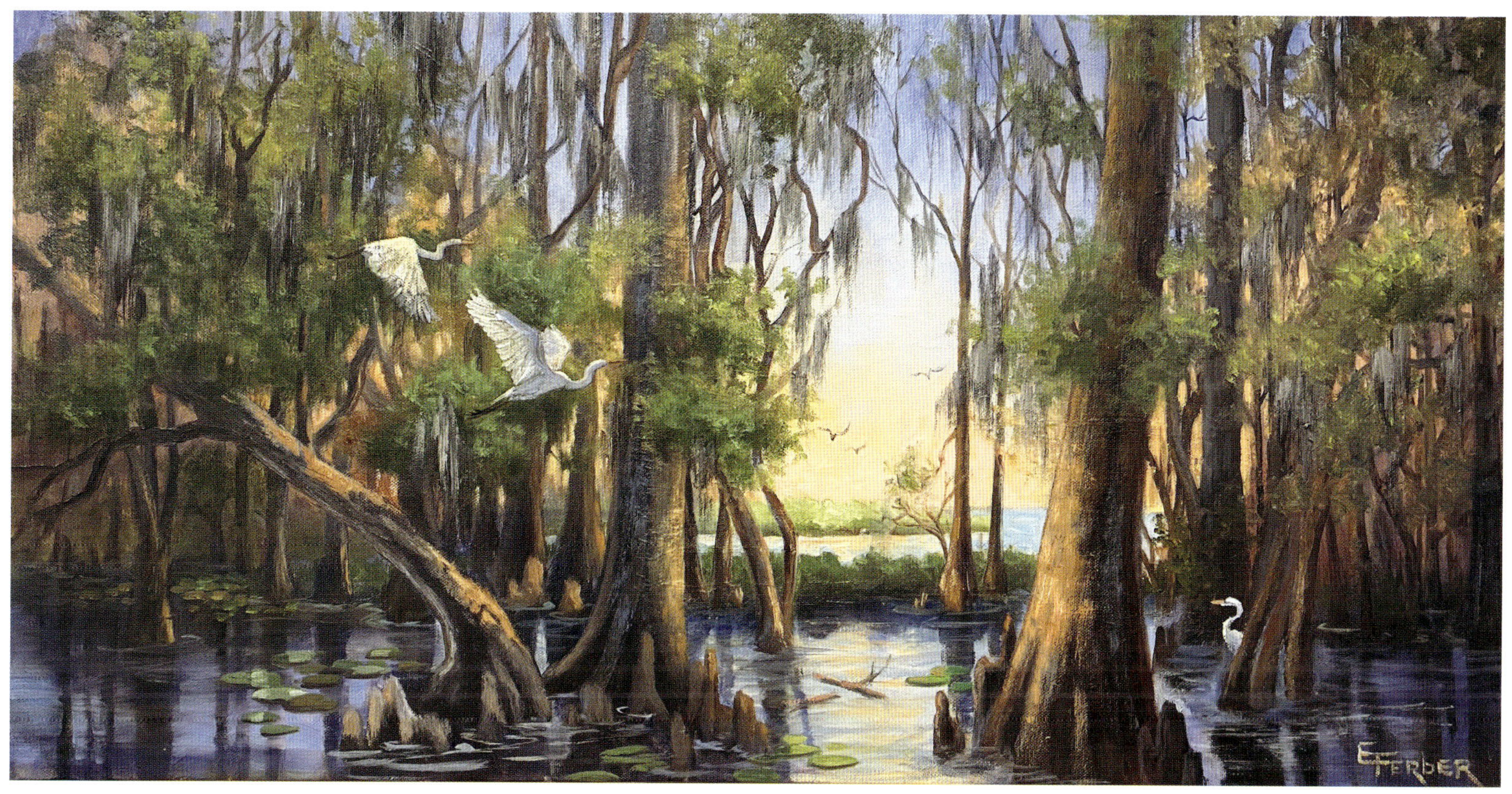

Elisabeth C. Ferber, Florida
EMERGING FROM DARKNESS INTO LIGHT

During this pandemic, I decided to take advantage of "at-home studio time" to paint a larger painting. I selected this subject based on the world's current situation. In January, I took an airboat ride around Appaloosa and took the photo which was my painting inspiration. The viewer is under the shelter of a dense, shadowed tree canopy. Beyond the dark interior is a path. Follow the water path and it opens up into a lighted area suggesting a larger wide-open lake inviting the viewer outside. The birds (humans) are sheltered in the forest (homes), but a few have ventured outside the protective forest. As we humans slowly begin to venture forth from our homes, reopen stores, and return slowly to work, the darkness opens into the light.

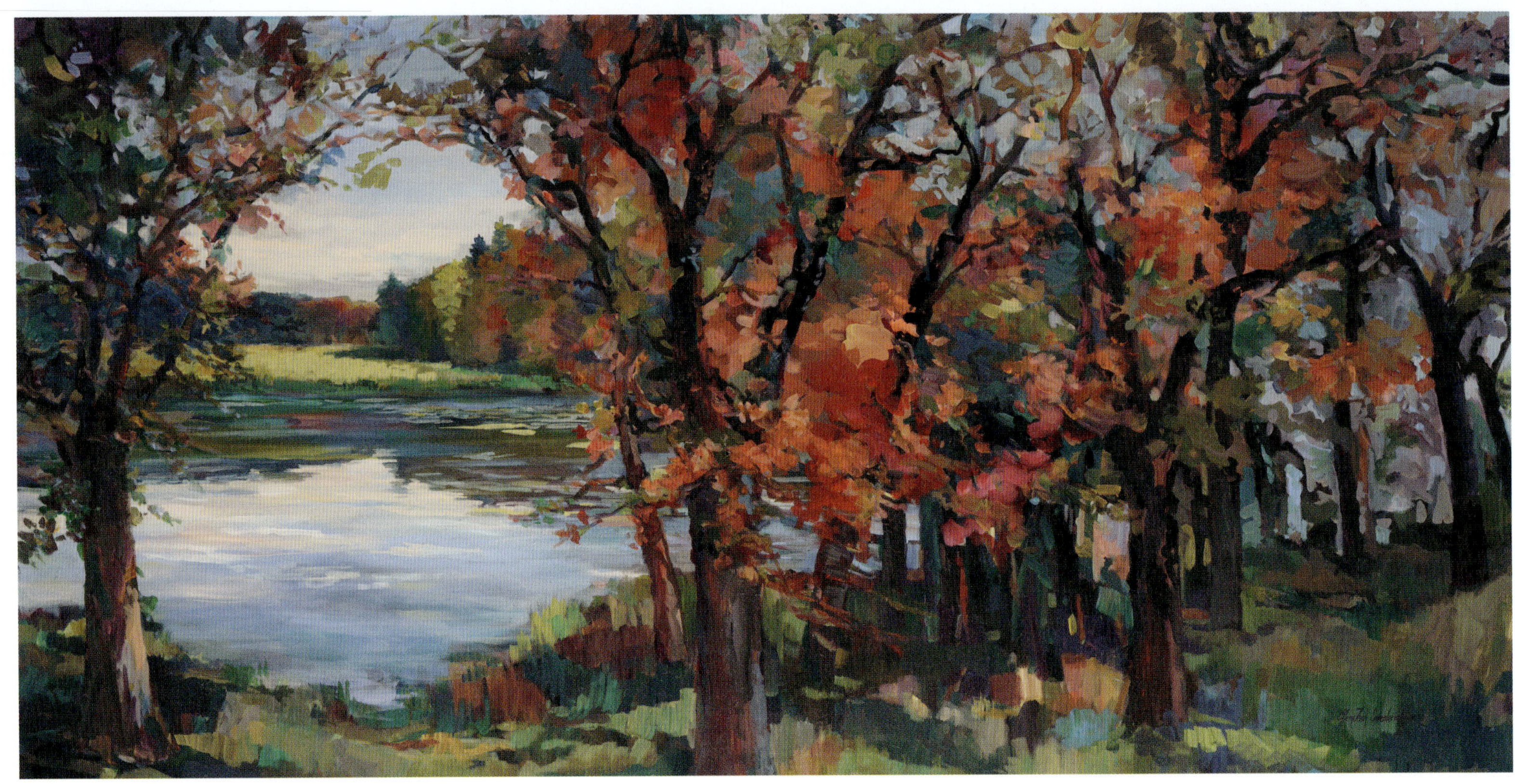

Ellen Jean Diederich, North Dakota

FOREST ARCHWAY

On my summer weekends, I walk up Pelican Point Road to and from the "Magic Hill." I call it that because it's the perfect exercise at the lake in central Minnesota. Last fall after a rain, I noticed that the vines growing on the oak trees had turned red and so I took their picture. They were beautiful! My photographs, however, didn't look as good as my memory and so became merely a reference. After painting the vines, the detail became distracting, so I simplified them into directional brush strokes. The cattails in the background were beautiful, but the water reflected in the pool was inspired by a sunset pontoon ride. When I look at this painting across the room, I feel a calm, refreshing peace. In the painting, this palette was originally planned to be predominantly red, along with turquoise, black, pinks, and greens. By increasing the amount of water shown, it became evident that I needed to infiltrate more blue into the composition and change the balance of the colors. The calligraphic brushstrokes and the color are what define my painting as Neo-Impressionistic. On this original, I hand-painted the sides of the painting, extending the scene. It seems to walk you right into the painting.

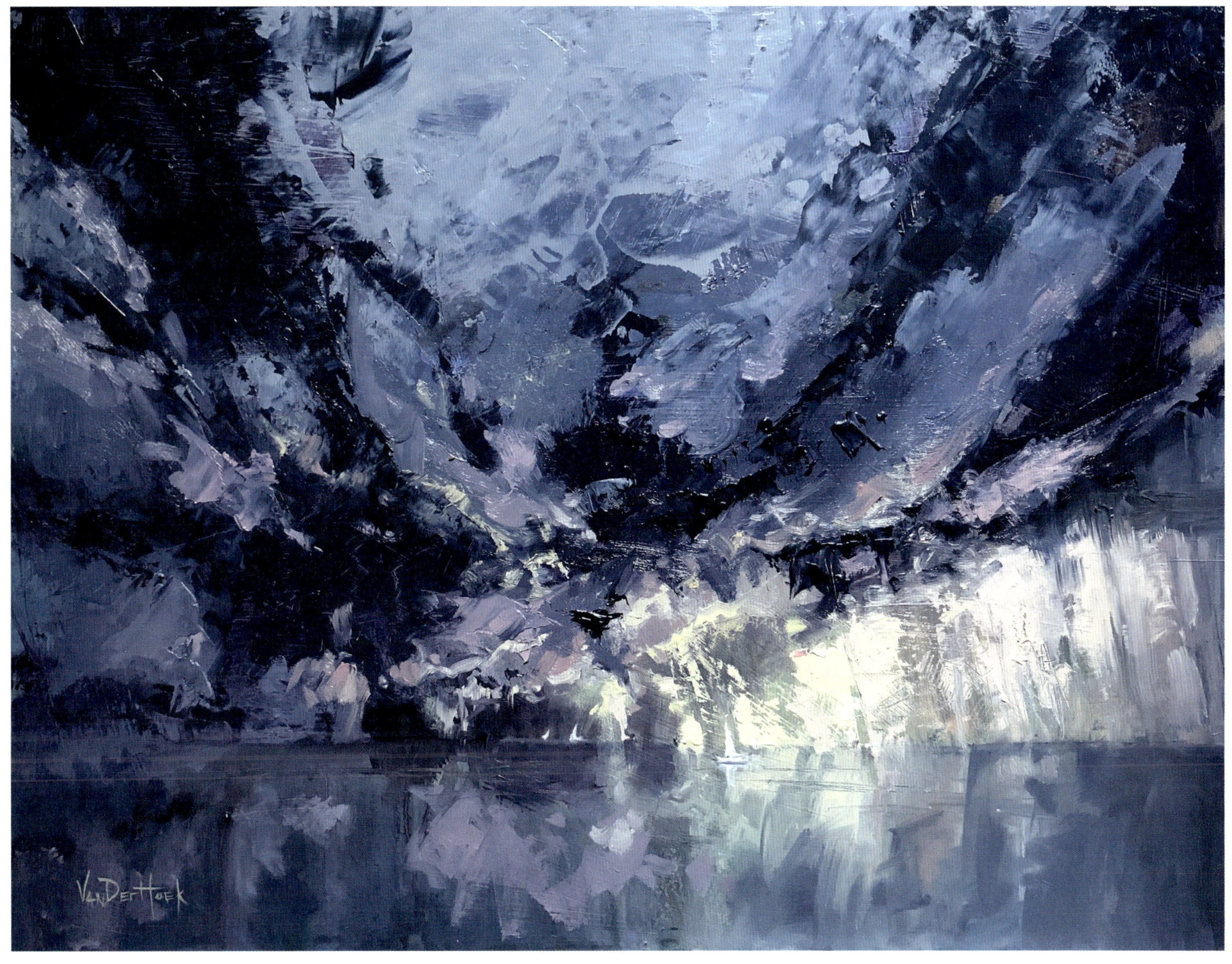

Kim Vanderhoek, California
BREAKING THROUGH

The turbulent feeling in this painting is a direct reflection of my emotions during the pandemic. This one started out as a peaceful harbor scene, but it quickly evolved. The sky filled with dark storm clouds and, much like all of us in lockdown, the tiny boats (look closely to see them), found themselves in uncertain times. Hope was not completely lost though, as bright sunlight along the horizon holds the promise of smooth sailing ahead.

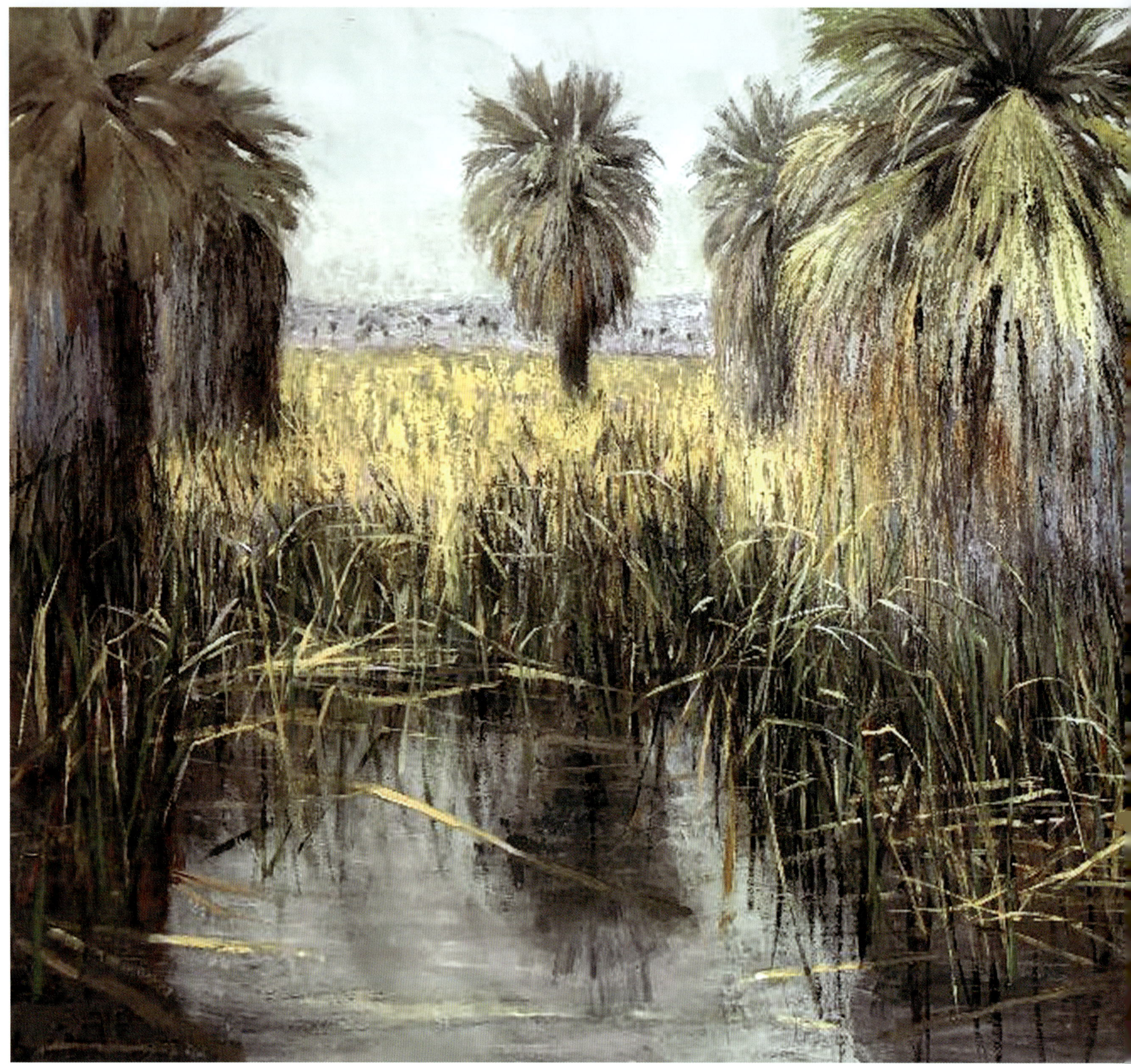

WATERWAYS—MARSHLANDS

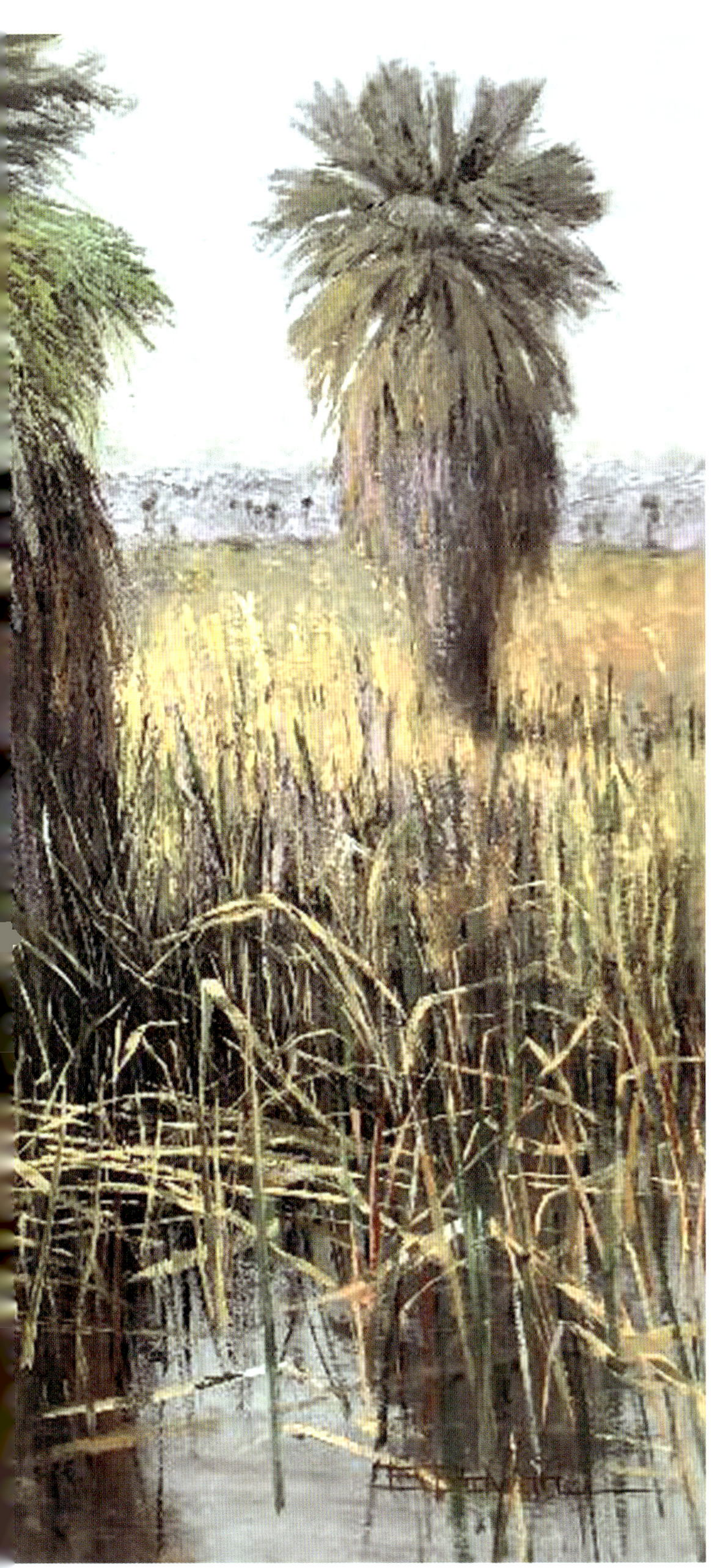

Brenda Boylan, Oregon

REFLECTIONS OF THE PAST

In the Coachella Valley of California, there sits an ancient oasis that has been percolating on the famed San Andreas fault-line. The fault forces underground spring water up to the surface and sustains desert life upon the treacherous abyss. It is estimated that this beautiful oasis landmark has been pooling for 1,000 years or more. It is said the palms have lived through drought, disease, and are now threatened by mankind. To reach this oasis I hiked through deep, hot sand with my painting gear and set up onsite to create a beautiful pastel study. As I created it, I contemplated how life has had to adapt, perish, or suffer on the Earth. The pastel study was my inspiration for this large-scale masterpiece. It is more poignant to me now than ever before, how our time on Earth is so short. I also wonder how this stand of palm trees will carry on for another 1,000 years?

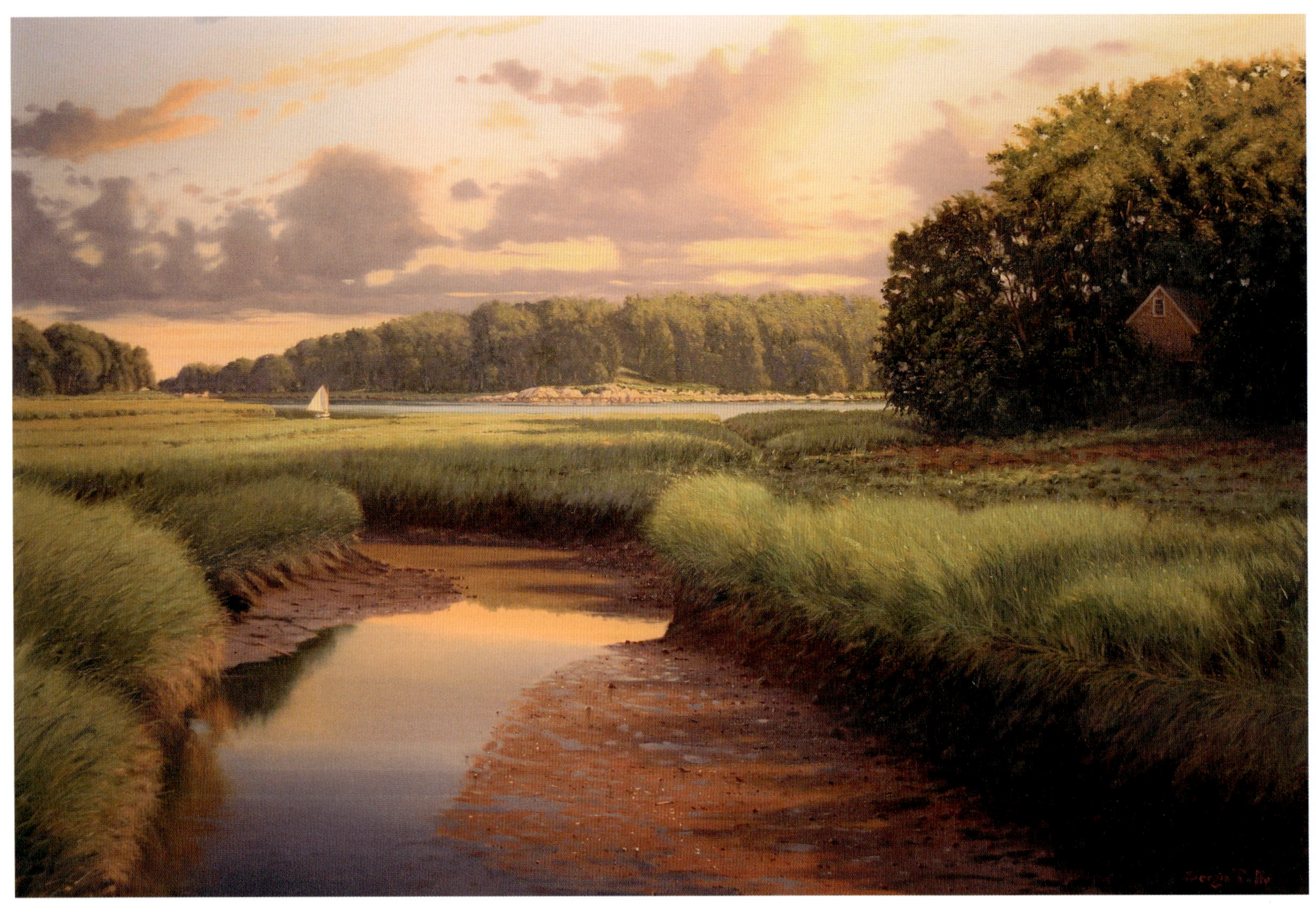

Sergio Roffo, Massachusetts
THE MARSH

The early morning light of *The Marsh* was inspired by a plein-air painting. In the early 20th century, Irish immigrants would congregate on the south shore of the Boston marshlands to collect moss from the river banks to sell. It was used to heat homes as a source of fuel. The seacoast town of Scituate became known as the Irish Riviera.

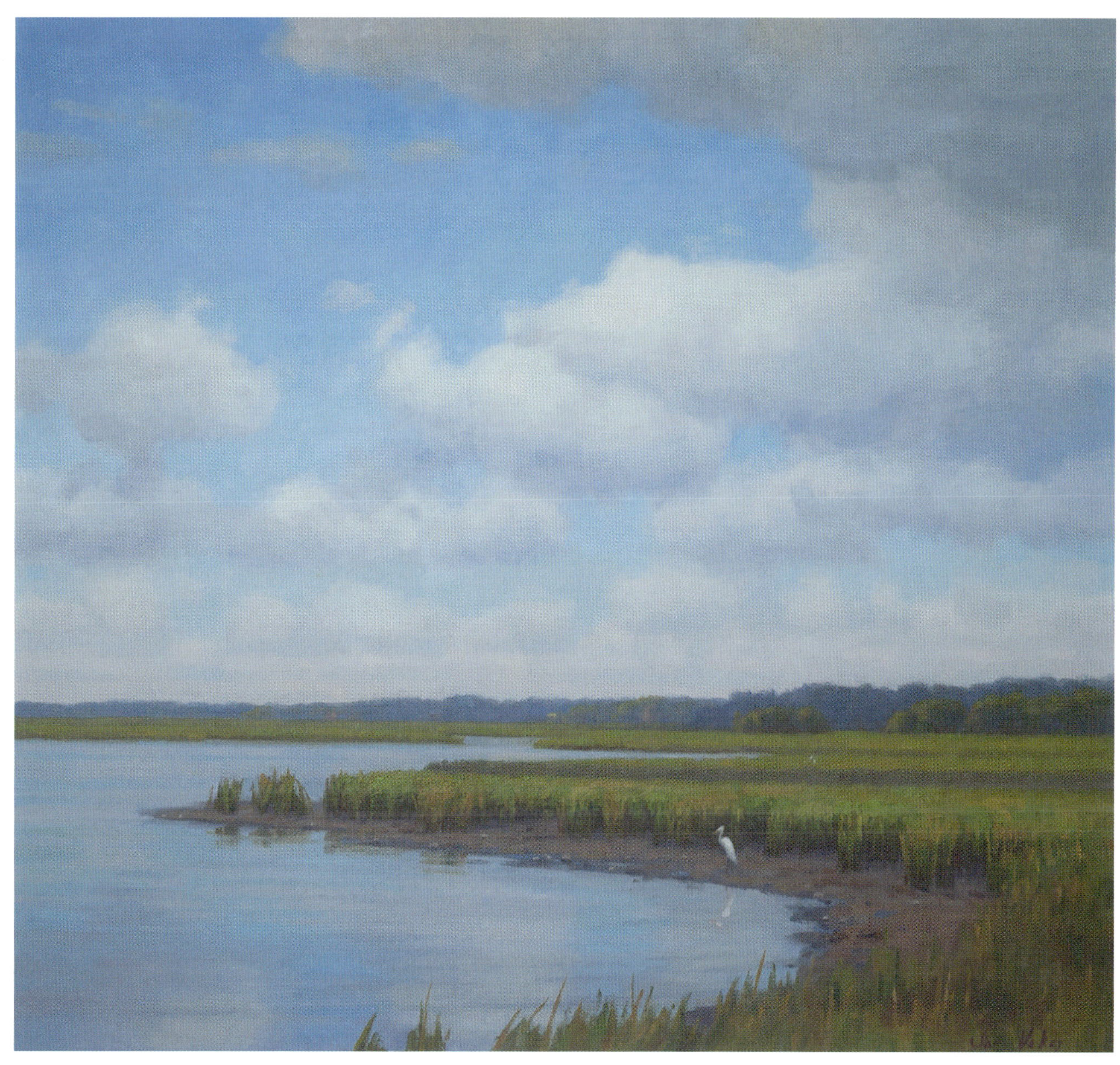

Sam Vokey, New Hampshire
SANCTUARY

A coastal marsh is a special place. We can find a real feeling of escape and peace in these out-of-the-way places that have their own rhythms of daily tides and changing light. And yet, if you stand in place long enough, like an artist who is quietly at work, the environment is alive with birds and fish and insect life. A whole ecosystem exists, fragile and beautiful beneath the dome of the sky.

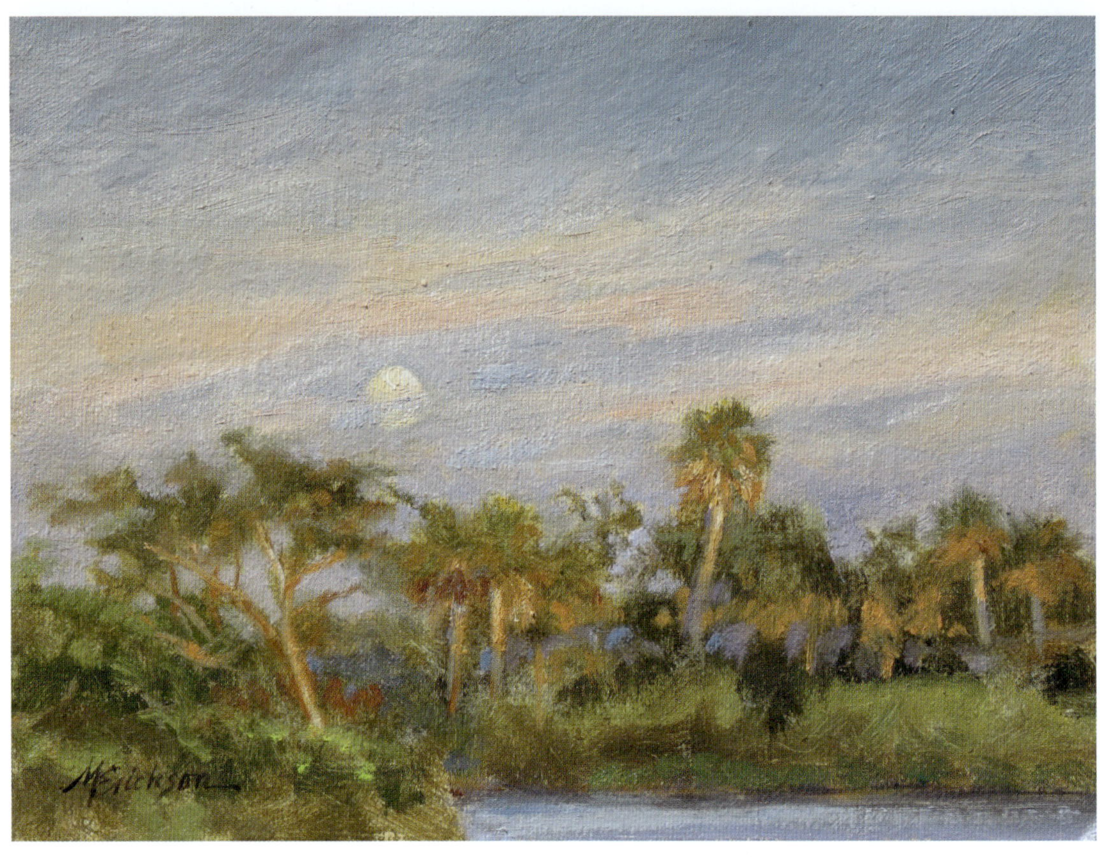

Mary Erickson, Florida

MOONRISE

After several weeks of solitary confinement in our studios, my artist friend Karen Weiss and I decided we were safe enough to get together to paint. I drove to Sarasota and we painted in her backyard in the afternoon. It was a beautiful, clear spring day in Florida, much like the previous days this time of year where, under normal conditions, we would be painting at the beach, downtown, and in the parks. After finishing our work, Karen's husband, Chris, made an enjoyable dinner, and we talked about everything non-stop, hungry for conversation with someone across the table. After dinner, we set up outside again to paint, knowing that the moon would be appearing around sunset. True to form, and on time, it rose into the evening sky. The last of the sunset light glinted orange on the palms across the water. And then I knew, all was right with the world.

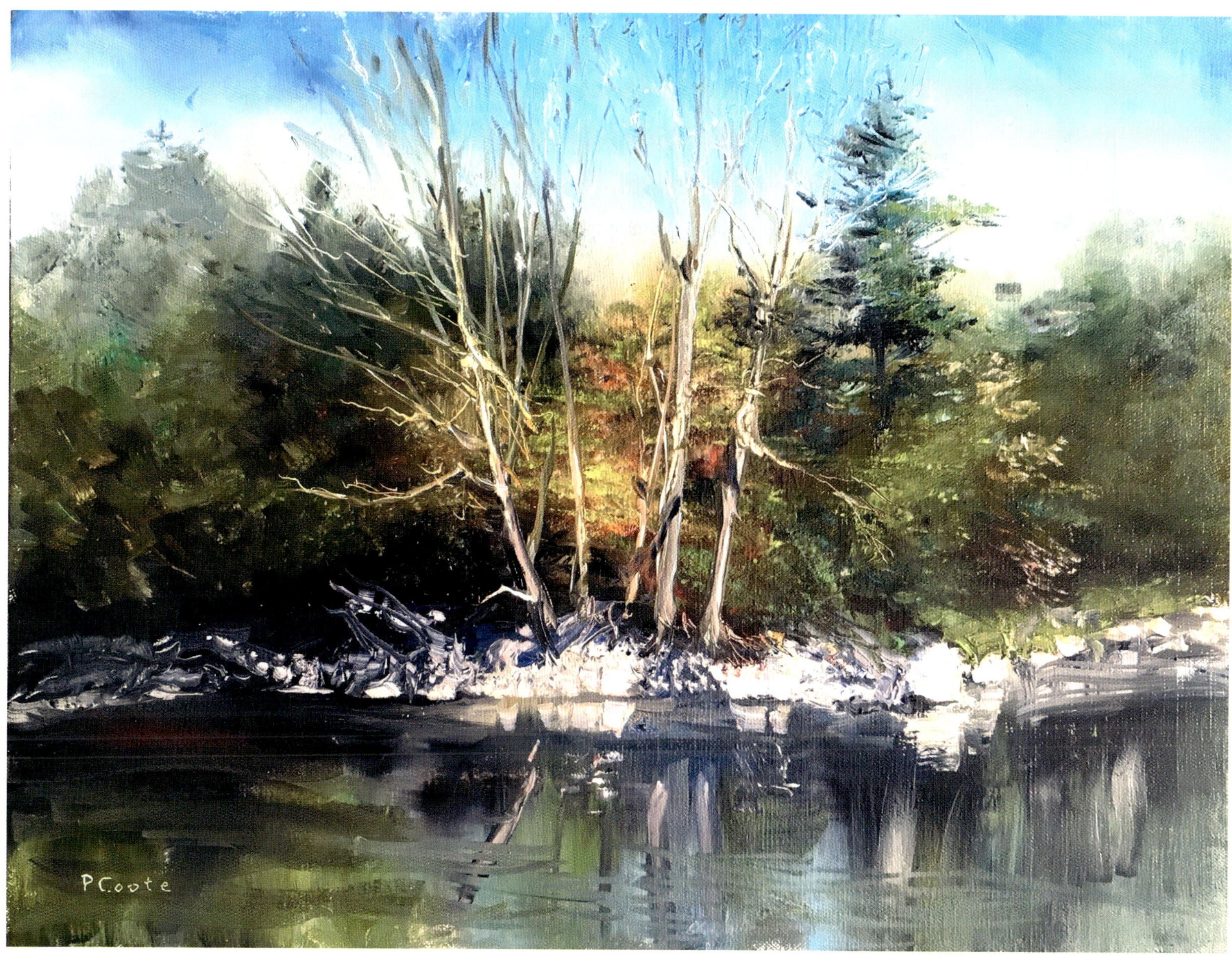

Priscilla Coote, Florida
CHOSEN

This was painted on my first venture out to paint beyond my immediate area, following completion of my required 14-day quarantine when entering the State of Maine. I drove for miles to reach this spot, just coming upon it by accident as the sun struck the rocks and trees, lighting up a part of the riverbank that you would otherwise not even notice. I called it *Chosen*.

9 LANDSCAPES

The natural landscape, with its quiet beauty and breath-taking views, has always centered me. I think that—perhaps now more than ever—all of us have witnessed the need for that centering place during these trying times of the pandemic, as our world has been shaken.

Living in upstate New York, I have always enjoyed the outdoors and the comfort the majestic Adirondack Mountains provide to all in their presence. They have been a huge inspiration to me in my work. During the pandemic, as all was shutting down and so much was being taken from us, I was so thankful that the landscape is something that can't be taken away. It was truly a saving grace for me. As I hiked on trails so familiar to me, I saw a vast increase in the number of explorers. As I savored these trails, taking mental pictures in my mind that would be used for my next paintings, I smiled silently at the people I passed, sensing that they, too, were here to find a quiet escape from the turmoil of the world.

Through the struggles of the pandemic, I try to be reminded that there have been amazing stories of human kindness, and perhaps even some positive change. Elisabeth Kübler-Ross once said, "Should you shield the canyons from the windstorms, you would never see the true beauty of their carvings." It has been quite a windstorm, but through it all, fully experiencing the landscape in life and in art keeps my lens focused on beauty and hope.

Rita E. DiCaprio
Saratoga Springs, New York

Jeff Williams, Oklahoma
SECTION ROAD

The year 2020 was a very strange year for all. As a plein-air painter, I began the year like gangbusters: being juried into every event I entered, selling work, and winning several awards. Spirits were high and in early March I began my first road trip, driving over 10 hours to my first event only to learn that the event had been canceled minutes before my arrival. Shocked, I turned around and headed home, hearing more about COVID-19 and the various closures and cancellations as I traveled.

Like everyone else, I was trying to process what was going on. The stock market was dropping rapidly, government programs were being discussed constantly, news reports and updates varied daily, if not with greater frequency. As they began to identify the "at-risk" population, it seemed like they were specifically identifying me. As every event and exhibition that I was part of struggled to determine what was possible, I began to see more events and exhibitions canceled, with sales opportunities slipping away rapidly, and I was trying to process what was happening to friends and family in New York City and the New Jersey areas. Hearing the residents of New York City applaud the healthcare workers every evening literally brought tears to my eyes.

How was I to earn a living? How important is art and beauty in a world that is becoming more and more focused on basic necessities? How do I concentrate on my painting when I am not sure whether we can pay our mortgage or buy food? When will this end? Like everyone, I struggled to process it all, and I became unable to concentrate on my painting.

Plein-air painting has always been a way for me to get totally immersed in my work, setting the outside world aside as I focus on how to communicate a particular place and how I feel about it. Being outside has always been cathartic, and painting has been my "happy place," as well as a way to earn a living. Instinctively I knew that I needed to stay positive and keep moving forward, but I could not find a way to do that through my painting, so I began to work on many things painting-related. I tried to think of this as a gift of time and worked on documenting my work, working on my website, finding new ways to market my work, learning online skills, setting up the studio to do online teaching, applying for grants, exercising, gardening, etc.

I also began posting to social media, engaging with multiple artists' work each day in the hope that I could help provide something positive and beautiful to those exploring social media as well as, in some small way, perhaps help those artists reach new followers and find new sales opportunities. I posted the work of hundreds of artists over an almost five-month period, and I found that I was learning about new artists, as well as making connections with many new art lovers. I stayed very busy, but every time I tried to paint, I found that I was distracted and found it difficult to focus on my paintings. As a result, I became dissatisfied with my work. As the end of August neared, I decided I needed to push past this by challenging myself to paint every day. Each day I ventured out to find something new to paint, and while this had to be done within the limitations of the pandemic, I was able to explore in isolation many areas nearby.

Step by step, I began to find myself in my paintings again. I have always tried to be a very optimistic person, and I am very glad to report that I feel like a new person (or, perhaps, my old self again)! As that has occurred, my painting quality has returned, and several commissions have come along, as have other successes in the art world! Through these paintings of simple, local places that are often passed by and never thought about, I have found a beauty around myself that has inspired me, and that I hope inspires others. This particular painting was done about a week ago on a lonely section of the road only a few miles from my home. Where is the road leading? It certainly has its ups and downs, and in spite of a virus meandering through our culture, and environmental issues affecting us regularly, there is a resilient, meandering landscape that stretches out before us. I like to imagine myself somewhere out in that landscape, enjoying the cooler air that is coming and the sounds of nature that surround me as I explore my way forward, acutely aware of the beauty that surrounds me. It is my sincere hope that paintings like these can help others as well, to find their way in these unfamiliar times.

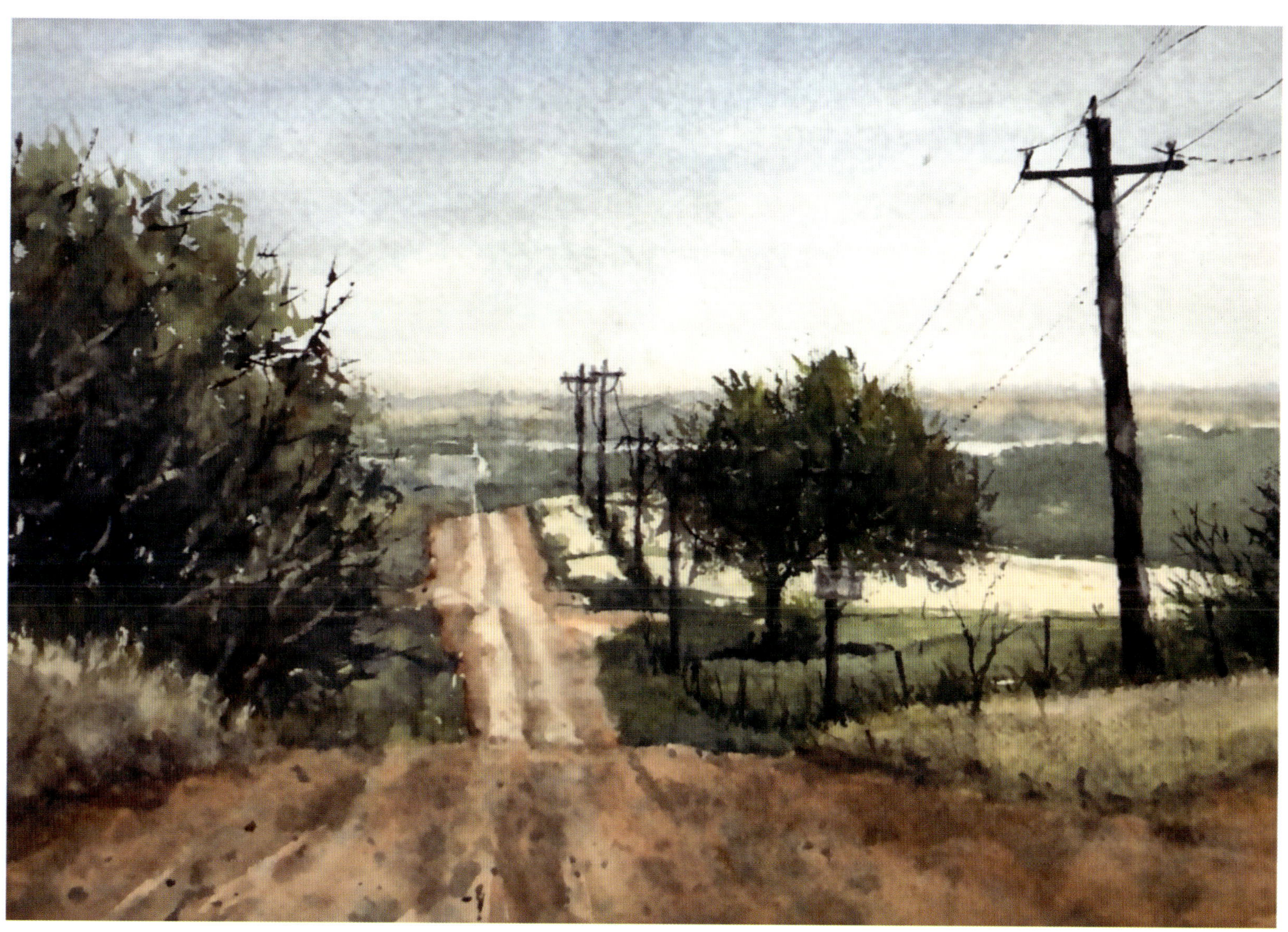

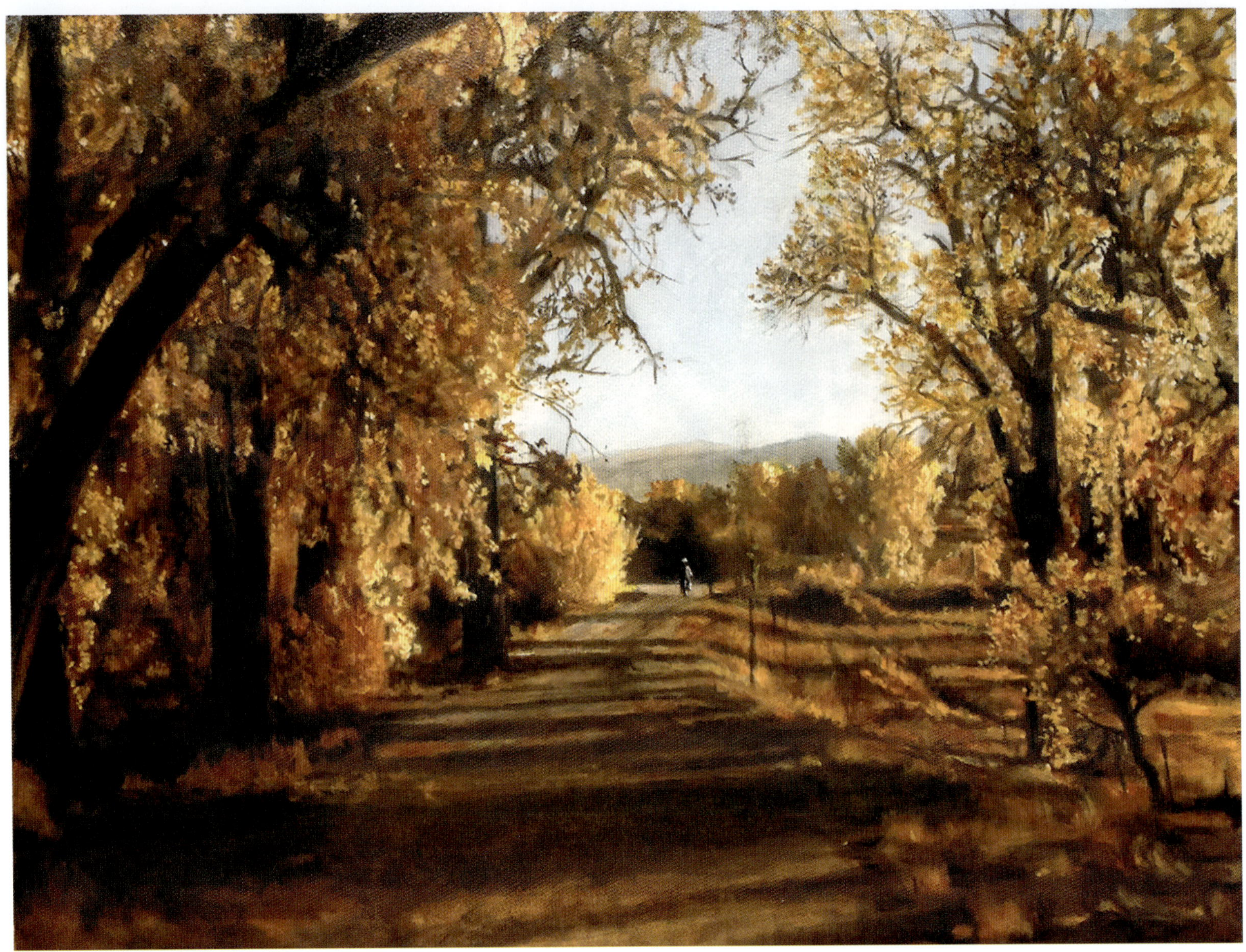

Tom LaRock, Texas
THE HIGHLINE IN THE FALL

This is a painting of the road that runs beside the High Line Canal in Denver, Colorado. The inspiration for this work is the sunset and the late afternoon light that show off the yellows and golds of the cottonwoods and aspens lining the pathway. This was one of our favorite paths to run and bicycle since it provided long traffic-free distances.

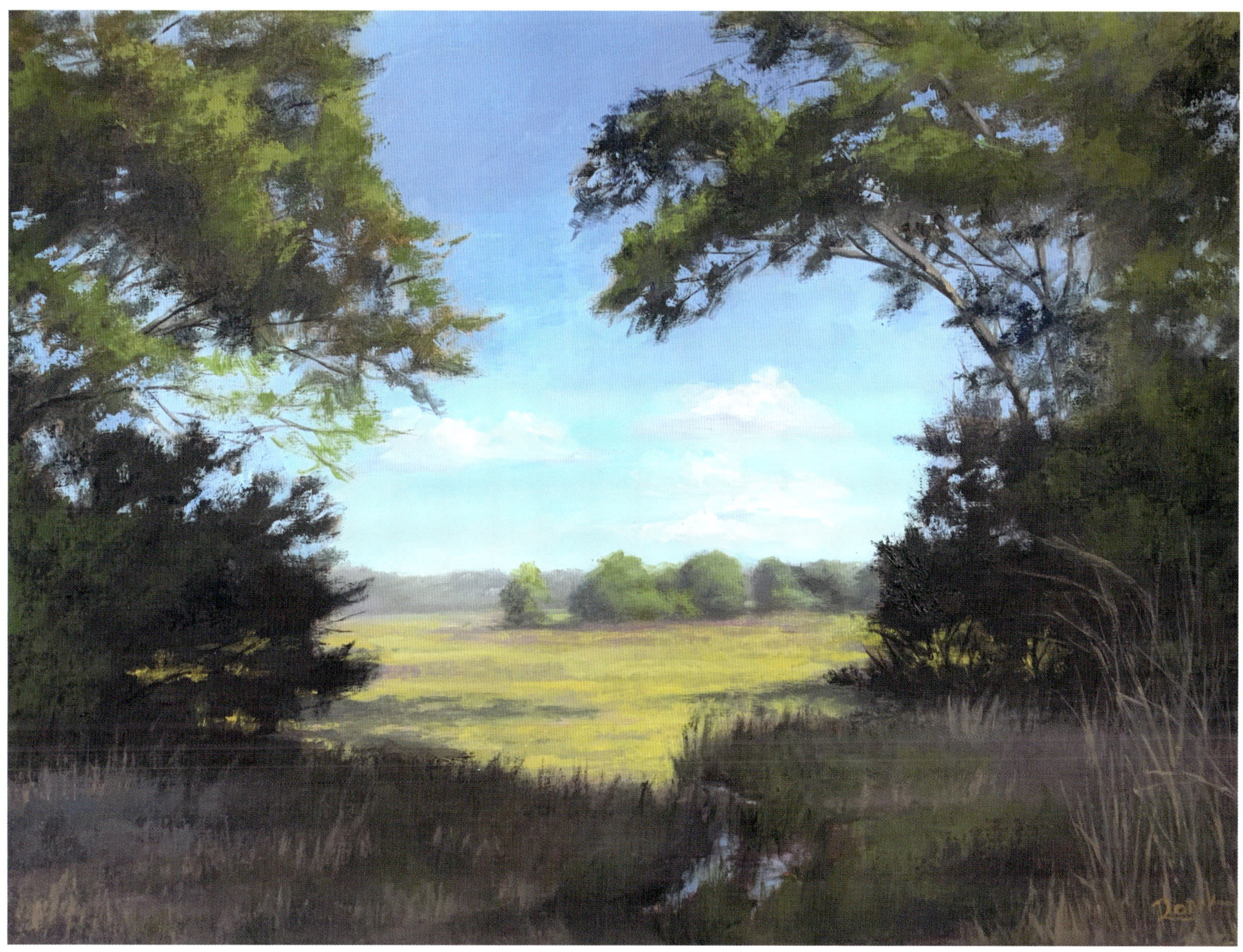

Carol Roark, Mississippi
BUTTERCUPS THROUGH THE TREES

As an artist in the remote Mississippi Delta, social distancing is somewhat normal in my world. As much as I love the beauty of our farm and the southern landscape surrounding it, I realized during the pandemic how much I have taken this life for granted. While I enjoyed sheltering in place to some degree, I began to realize just how blessed I am to live where I live. As I watched stories around the world where people were sequestered in their homes, my heart broke for those who longed for the spaces I was enjoying every day. As I brought my plein-air studies back into the studio to transform into larger paintings, I kept the faces of these strangers in my head. I painted in the hope that, as I posted my finished paintings on my website and social media, maybe I was bringing a bit of the peacefulness of our countryside to those who otherwise could not experience it. I also hope that, as people view my work, it can bring more attention to the natural world and its importance to overall well-being.

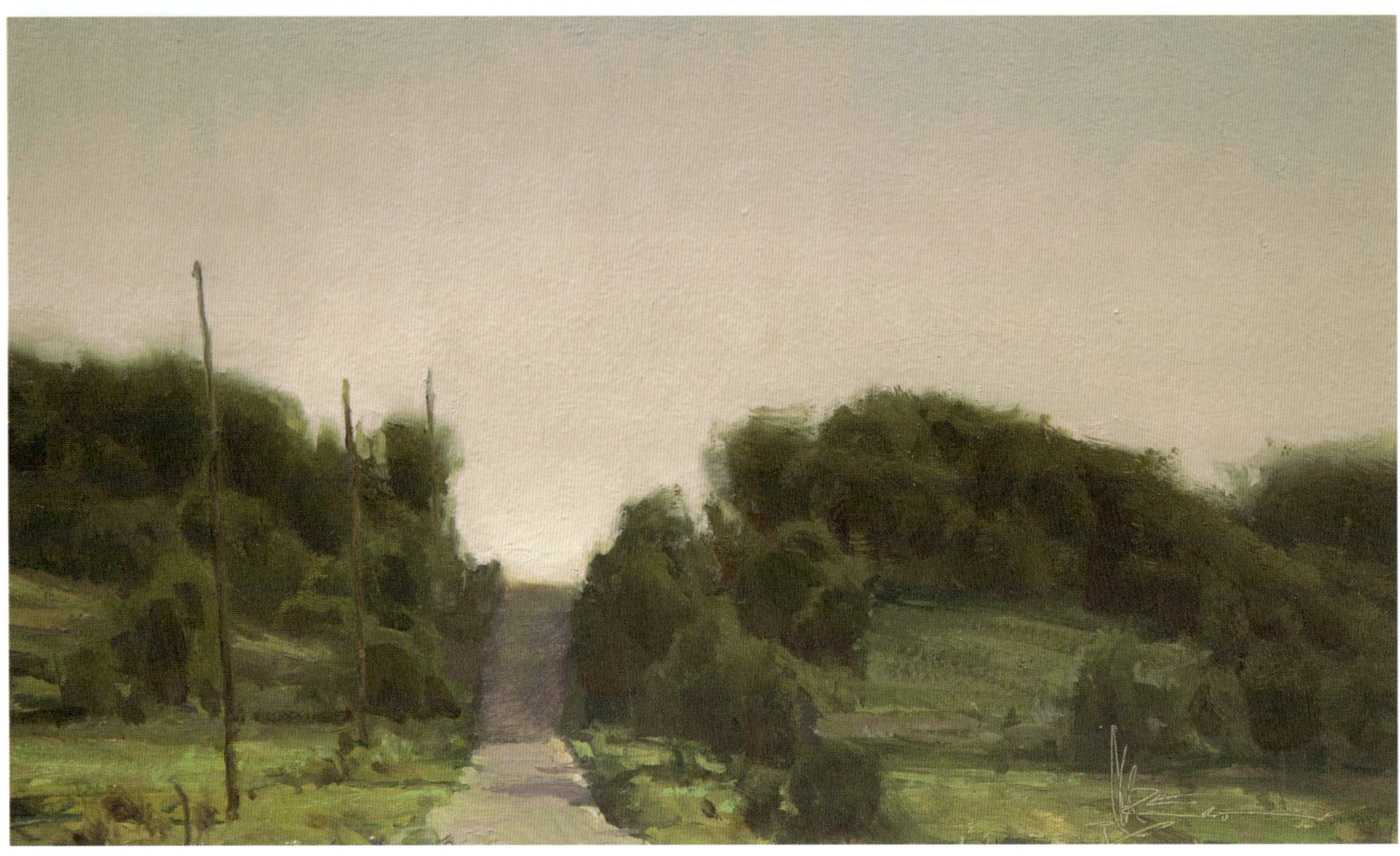

Josh Clare, Utah
BACK ROADS

I participated in a very meaningful show in 2016 with two of my very good artist friends. The reference for this piece was gathered on a trip we took to Ohio together. It just felt like the right time to revisit that moment.

John Whytock, Missouri

WAPITI WOLF PACK

Even though my life as an artist is a fairly solitary one, the lockdown has affected me. For the past several months, I've feared for my country, friends, family, beloved wife, and myself. Like the rest of the world, that fear has motivated us to stay inside for many weeks, venturing out only a couple of times to get necessities. I was in the process of painting *Wapiti Wolf Pack* when the COVID-19 threat descended. The hours I spent painting allowed me to reflect on the content of the work. Yellowstone National Park is less crowded in winter, so the domain of the wolves is wider and they are able to roam more of its expanse. My friend, Chris, is a guide working in the park. He spotted the pack near Old Faithful geyser and took some wonderful photos. With his permission, I used those photos as the reference from which I created the painting.

There is a human presence at the geyser all year long, so the wolves tend to steer clear. It was a pleasure to imagine how the pack might have appeared before the crowds. I envied the wolves' tight little community and their former freedom to go wherever they pleased. It made the loneliness and my feelings of confinement more acute. There's also something about winter and the silence of a snowdrift that added to my sense of isolation. But this painting will always hold a special place in my heart. I will always remember my desire to experience the sensations the wolves were feeling: the cold air in my face; the freedom to run through the snow; the closeness and familiarity of my tribe; and the unique experience of a life without borders, boundaries, and face masks.

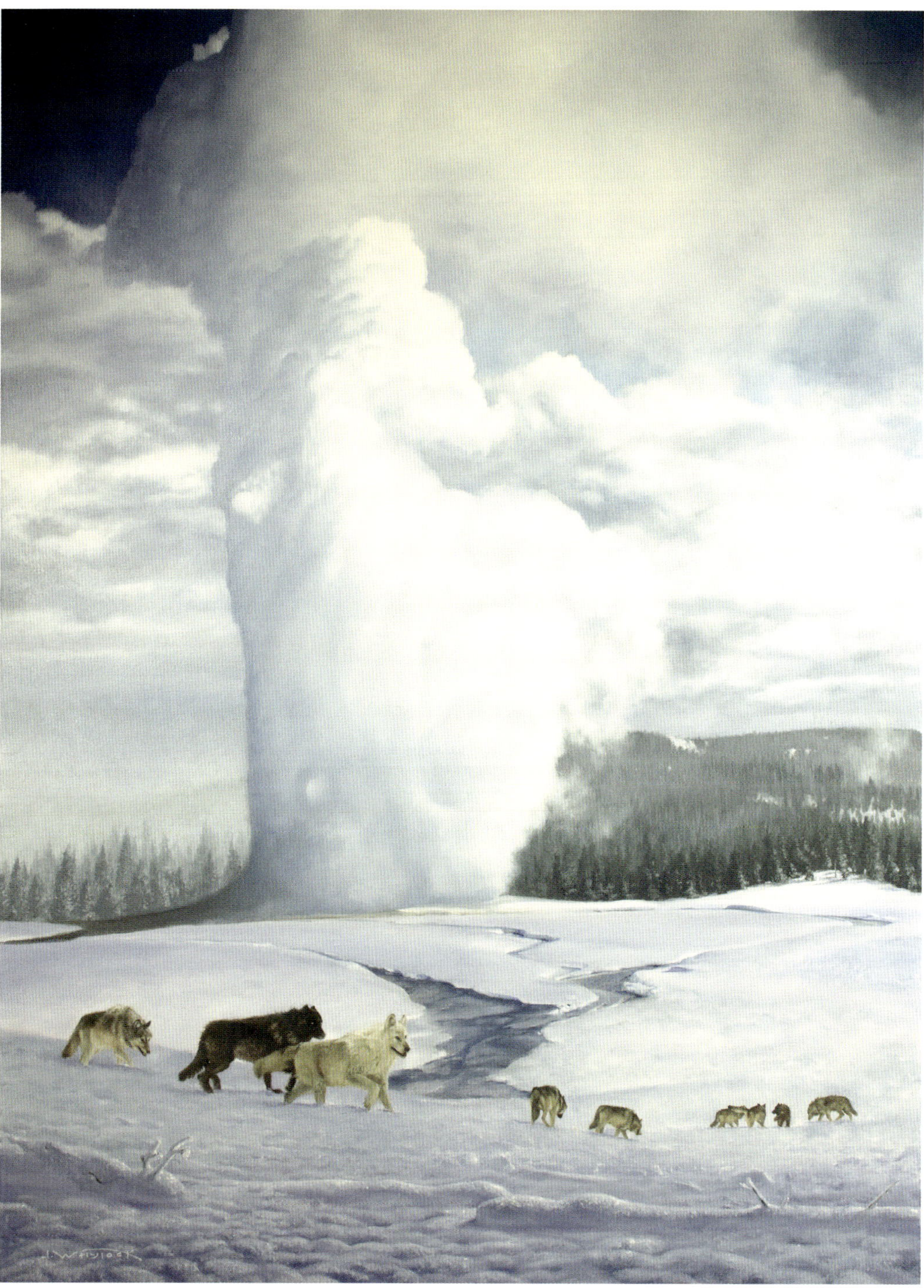

S. Gary Frisk, Texas

WEST TEXAS PUMPJACK ACCESS ROAD

My painting of the oilfield excursion in February seems like a long time ago. It was to be my last major plein-air outing before the virus hit. All of my plein-air events have been canceled or postponed. During that week, I found this access road and took a break from painting the pumpjacks. It was so peaceful, and I was delighted with the vanishing power poles as well as the quiet serenity. While painting this on-site, it was the only time during the trip that a company man drove up and suggested that I leave. He was extremely polite; we talked for a spell, and he took some pictures of me. Nevertheless, I was not able to finish the painting so, during the quarantine, I put it up and went through a period of just looking at it; reflecting upon the trip and how I felt about staying in my studio. This painting is so calm, I remember standing there, painting in the silence, absorbing the beauty of this crisp cool February afternoon, not knowing the events to come. Working on the painting in my studio was bittersweet but I am absolutely thrilled with the result. And, the icing on the cake? My wife likes it.

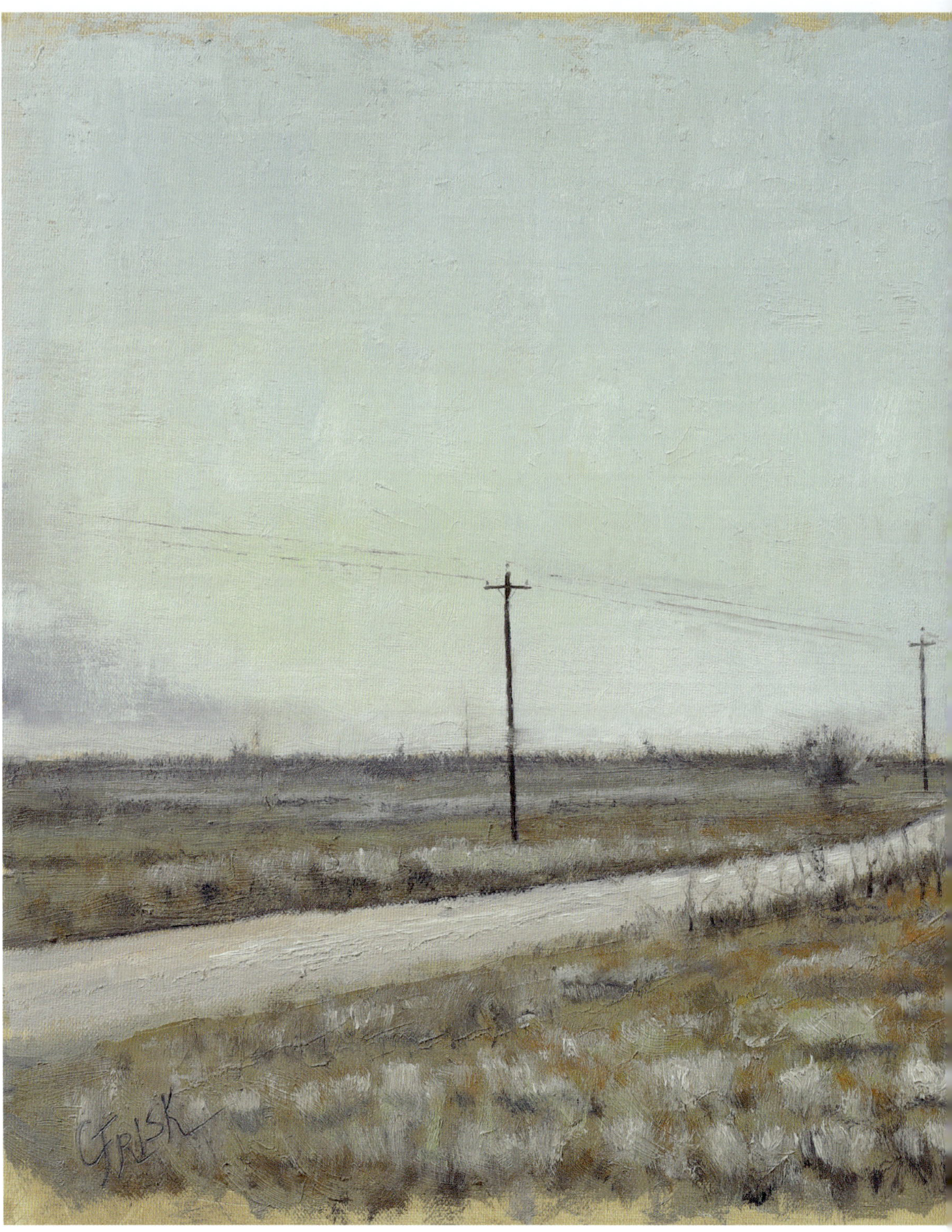

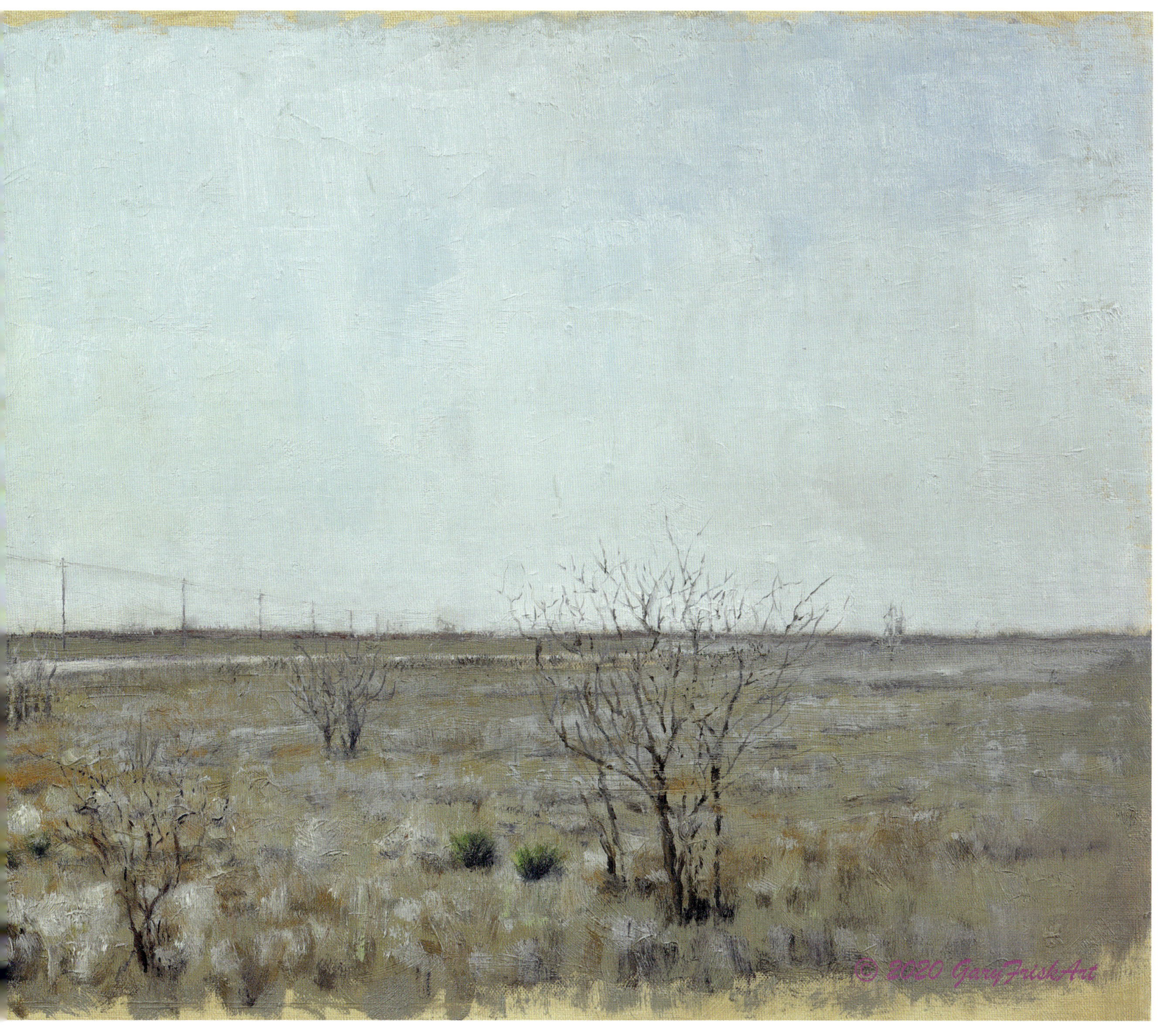
© 2020 GaryFriskArt

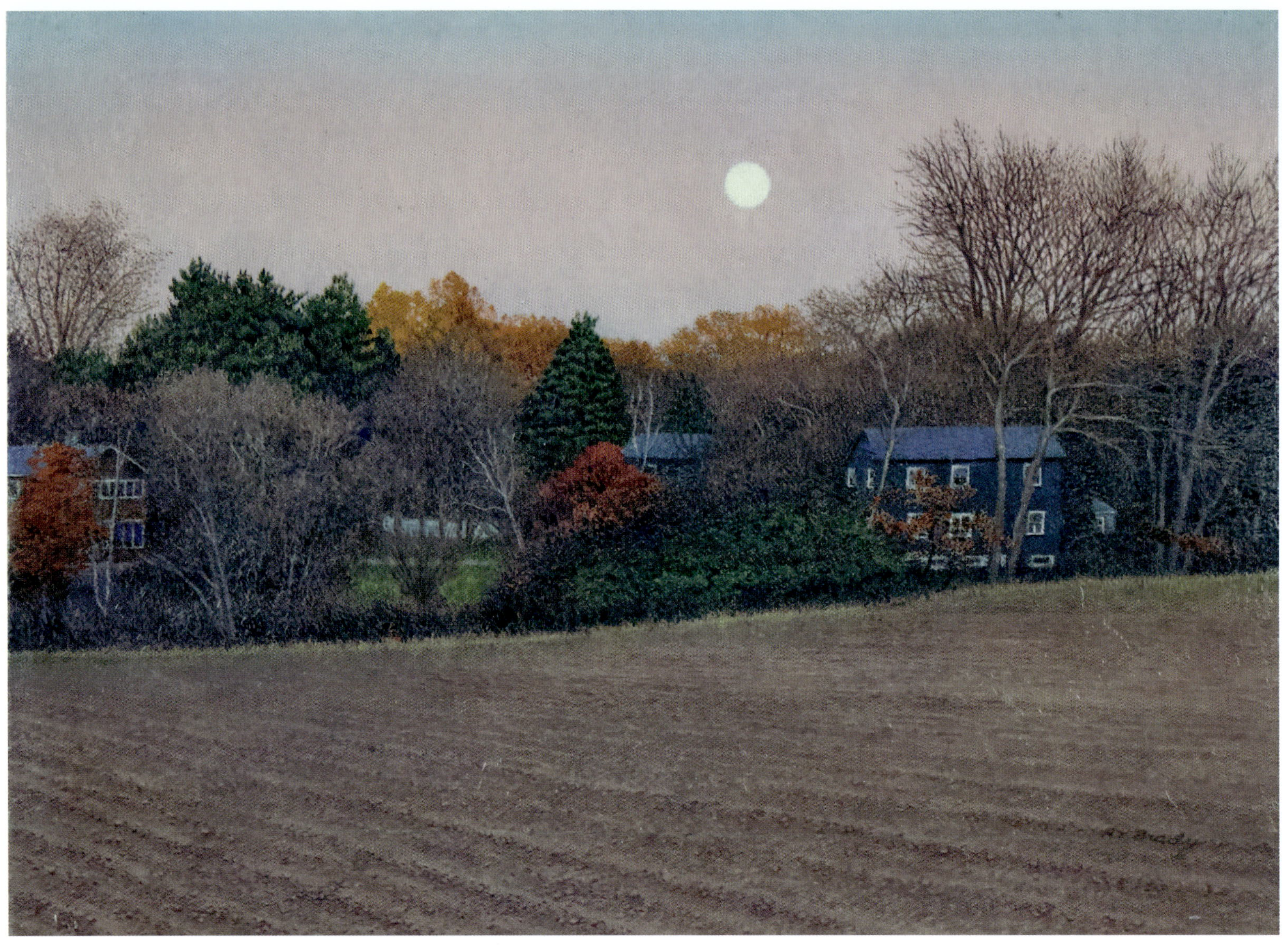

Richard T. Brady, Massachusetts
TILLING THE LAND

Sheltering in place, staying home, avoiding crowds, is not a terrible thing to me. I love working at home and occupying myself with the study of nature, finding beauty and connectedness. As such, my paintings have not changed during the quarantine. Each painting is challenging, requiring multiple layers of glazing. I delight in living with a painting as it develops, before considering it finished. When I do go to town and see people, the social distancing and protective gear is a reminder that we are under threat. Knowing some people are dying nearby is very disturbing. I appreciate that these measures are as much about protecting others as they are about protecting ourselves. The painting *Tilling the Land* is a landscape with a freshly ploughed field. It can be seen as an analogy to the process of reinventing oneself, preparing the ground for new life within ourselves and our society. The rising new moon suggests this practice is universal and far-reaching.

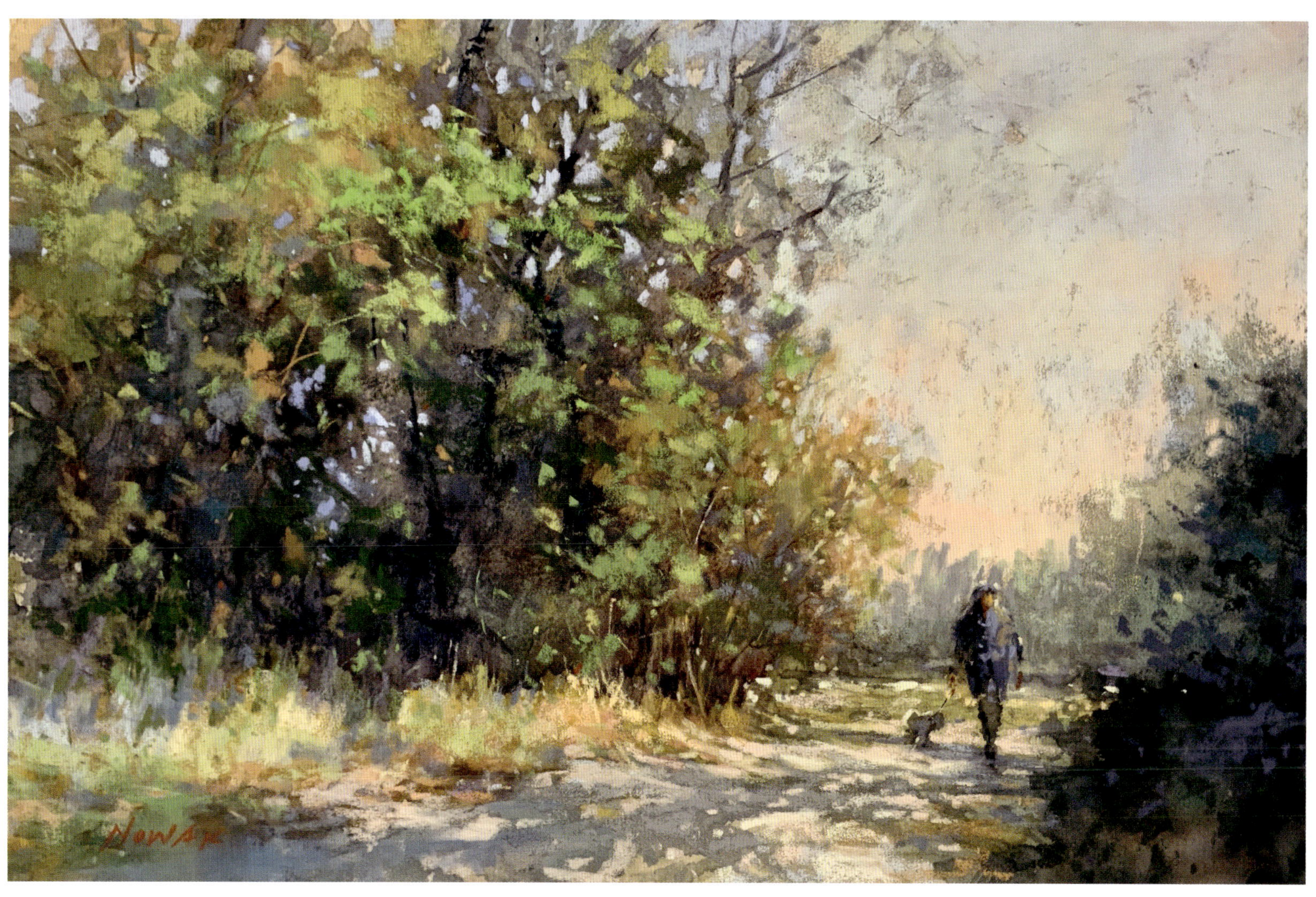

Nancy Nowak, Georgia
NATURE'S RESPITE

A nature walk is not only good for the body but essential for my mental health during this time of seclusion. Luckily, there is a local park where I find myself drawn to renew my spirit and breathe in the fresh air while reconnecting with the natural world. This was the first time I brought along my husband, Don, and our little dog Beaux. It was one of those gorgeous Georgia spring days with the sunshine beaming through the trees and on the paths. The perfect respite for the three of us. I like to think during these uncertain times, it's important to stay positive, keep putting one step in front of the other and move forward.

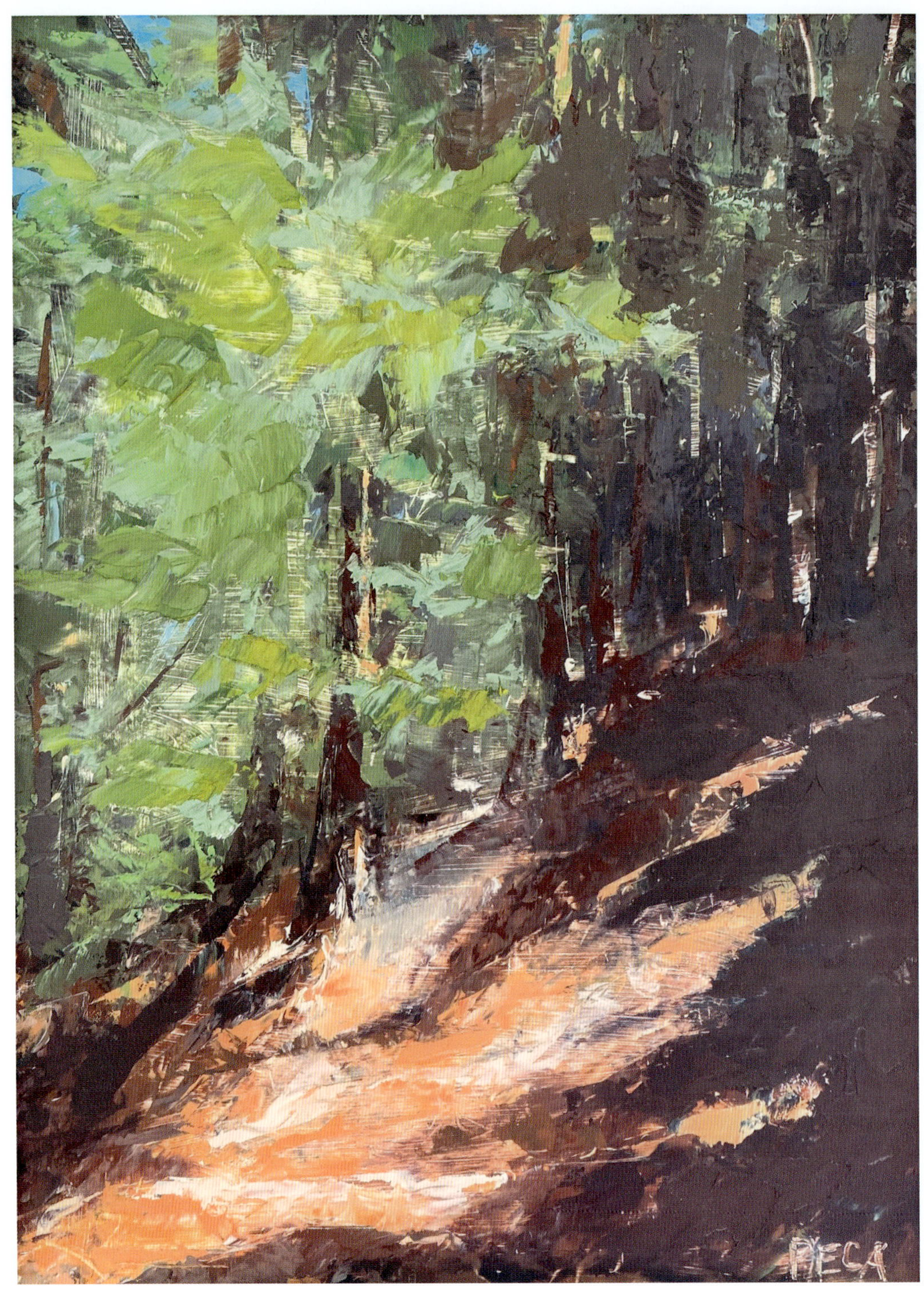

Terry Peca, New York

SUNLIT

I am always seeking the light; a reason to be grateful or hopeful, or both. This is especially important during this challenging time when it is easy to feel discouraged and disconnected. This painting represents light. Inspired by a small piece of the landscape near my home in the foothills of the Adirondacks, this painting reflects the light that has the power to illuminate even the darkest corners.

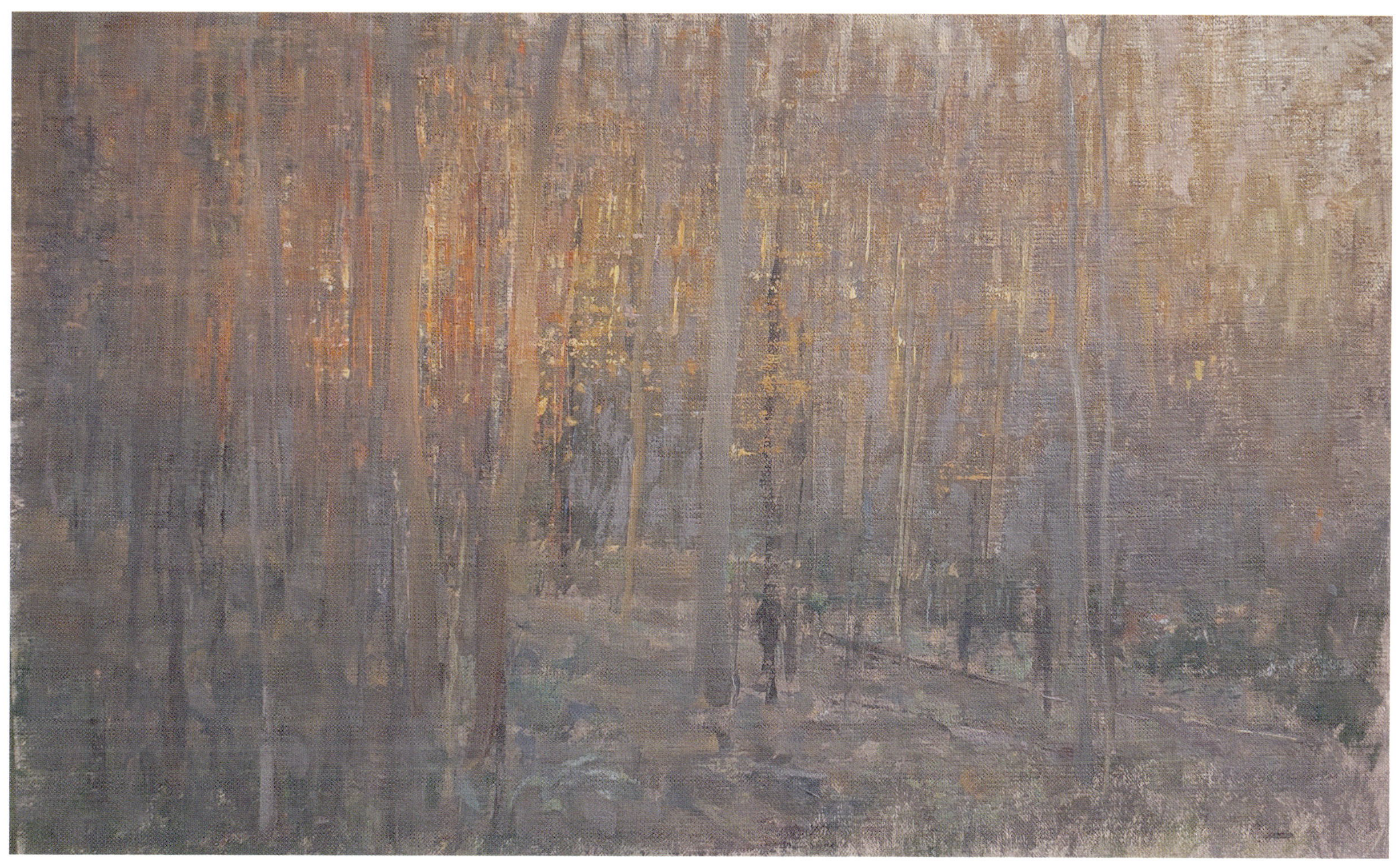

Seth Tummins, Tennessee

LIFE ITSELF

As I stood in that doorway, I was watching time pass; light grow, slide down, fade, only to light up another section. And it seemed to me like a dance, something fast made slow, a silent song, a drama. I didn't make mental notes, I didn't make a sketch. I made time to see it. I gave it time. From all these layers—the drama with no audience, my eavesdropping upon the performance, the beauty of the colors, the warmth given to a chilly morning, the short time it would last—from all of this bubbled up the idea that this was life itself. Not only what was happening on the stage (so to speak), but also my standing there so grateful for this silent stage. The light would fade from the scene, but now I carried it within me. Such is life. What we surround ourselves with matters. What we take into ourselves really matters. What we can give others is from the overflow of the heart. And so, now there is a painting in the world that would not have been—a product of the heart's overflow for quiet beauty that contains ancient lessons, ancient lyrics, made into a present melody.

Cecilia Brendel, Ohio

RUBY WOODS

Five years ago, I did a study for six months on Post Traumatic Stress Disorder (PTSD) and depression. I discovered that the high chroma colors in paintings, as well as painting itself, helped these individuals to overcome their situations, especially when colors are combined with a contrast of intense darkness. I have spent the past couple of years painting simple landscapes with light as my subject matter, creating a euphoric feeling to help individuals feel the presence of God and to provoke images of peacefulness. I have had many people tell me that these recent paintings have given them feelings of hope and serenity. They feel the presence of their lost loved ones when they see the light in my paintings. I am honored to be able to help people during this COVID-19 situation; to feel more at ease by looking at the light as a means of meditation. COVID-19 has brought out depression and anxiety in people and I feel compelled to use my skills to better society using light as my subject matter. Thank you for allowing me this opportunity to share.

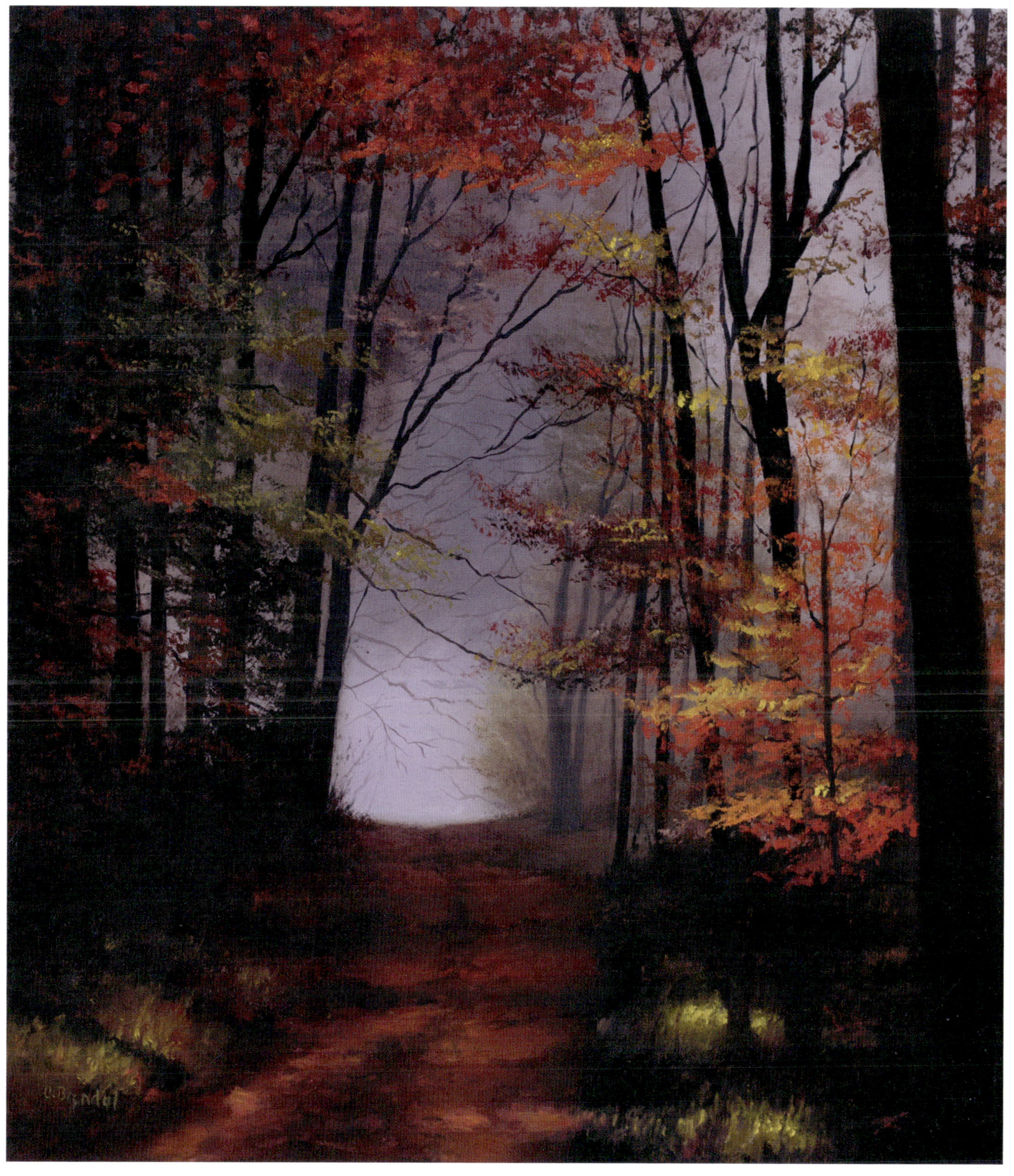

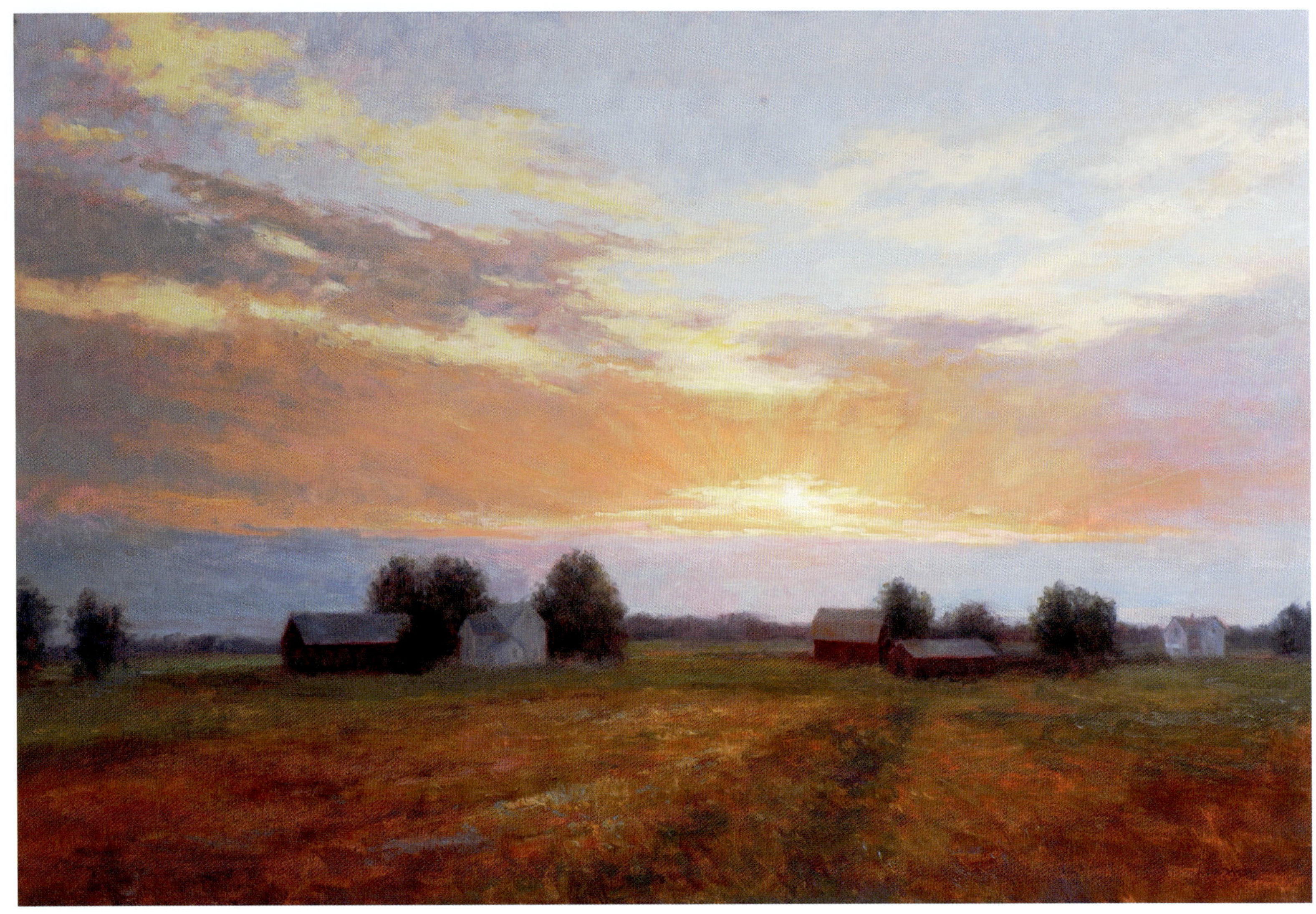

Kathleen Kalinowski, Michigan
NEIGHBORS

These last few months of staying close to home have opened my eyes to the potential of the landscape around me. Driving through farm countryside has me noticing the homes, barns, and fields in different ways. I often wonder how long people have lived there and who tills the soil. Do they know each other? The neighbors live further apart than most, though they are together in their dependence on the soil. While driving one evening, the last rays of the sun gave a glorious crown to an otherwise average setting in the country.

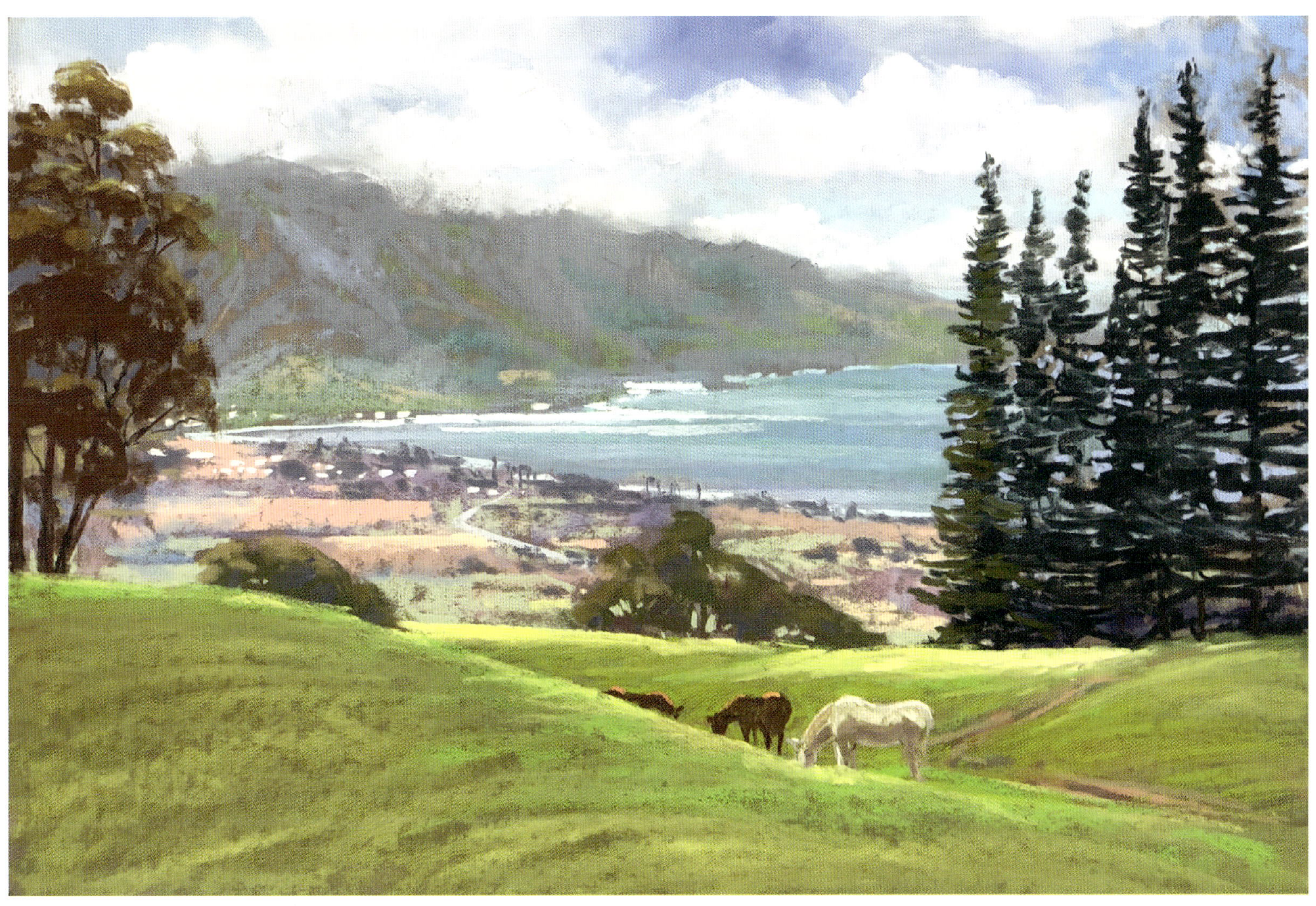

Michael Clements, Hawaii
SUMMER UPCOUNTRY MAUI

Living on Maui in the Hawaiian Islands for the past 33 years has been a beautiful experience for me. Growing up in the Midwest, I never contemplated where my life's journey would take me. As fortune would have it, I have been blessed to live in some beautiful places, but nothing compares to Maui, my island home. My art career started late in life and I'm happy to say that it is never too late to fulfill your passion. I have been surrounded by a very encouraging and fraternal community of artists and a vibrant community of art galleries catering to visitors, of which we have many, and residents alike. Until recently, that is.

After COVID-19 spread throughout the world, here in Hawaii we have been affected in ways that most states have not. Being the most geographically isolated place on the planet, we are dependent on ships and aircraft for nearly every essential item. Our economy is nearly 70% dependent on tourism. As expected, the shutdown of the economy has had tragic consequences for many businesses.

The good news is that the island's natural beauty has not diminished one iota. Being a plein-air painter by choice, I have the uncommon opportunity to paint outdoors all year long. I eagerly and passionately do just that. The locale where I live is at a 3,000-foot elevation on the slopes of a 10,000-foot volcano. While most of the area we refer to as "Upcountry Maui" is rural farm and ranch land, it is also home to Haleakalā National Park. I wander the roads and pastures looking for scenes to paint and to find more inspiration and compositions than I have time to paint. Deep gorges, green pastures, forests, horses, farms, ranches, and livestock, all complemented by spectacular views of neighboring islands and the blue Pacific Ocean, are enough subject matter to last me a lifetime. If I tire of that, minutes away lie the beaches, cliffs, crashing surf, waterfalls, palm trees, and historic island architecture. Everyone comments on how beautiful the sunsets are where they live, but trust me, ours are just a touch more magical. So, while the world now is surely in a different place than it was at the beginning of 2020, I remain optimistic that brighter days are ahead. As a representational landscape artist, I feel compelled on a daily basis to record the beauty and tranquil serenity that nature provides me. It feeds my soul. If my paintings evoke that feeling in you, then I've accomplished my objective.

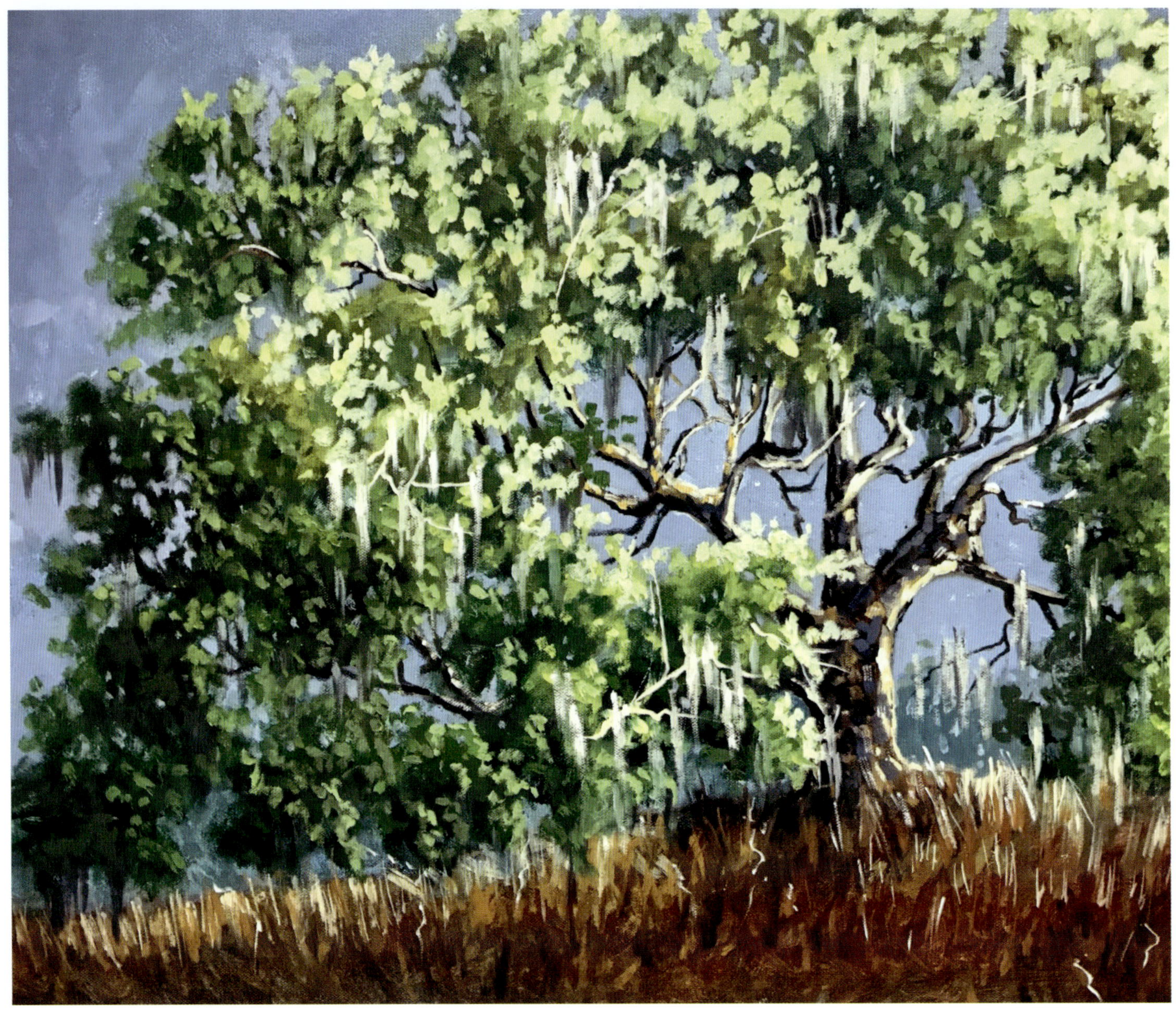

Linda Blondheim, Florida

STORM AND SUN

This live oak tree lives in Evinston, my favorite painting location in Florida. It is on a day of sunlight in front of storm clouds. Evinston is in north Florida, and I've been painting there for many years. I've had the pleasure to paint on a private pristine old estate with native flora and fauna. And so, the story goes that the oldest home in Evinston was built in the 1880s when William Drayton Evins, a captain who served in the Confederate States Army, moved his family there from South Carolina to start a new life. Evins became the founder of Evinston, having surveyed the land when it was just Florida brush. Oh, if this tree could talk! On this day, the sunlight streamed in front of the brewing storm clouds. It may have been telling us what was yet to come with the uncertainty and storm of the pandemic.

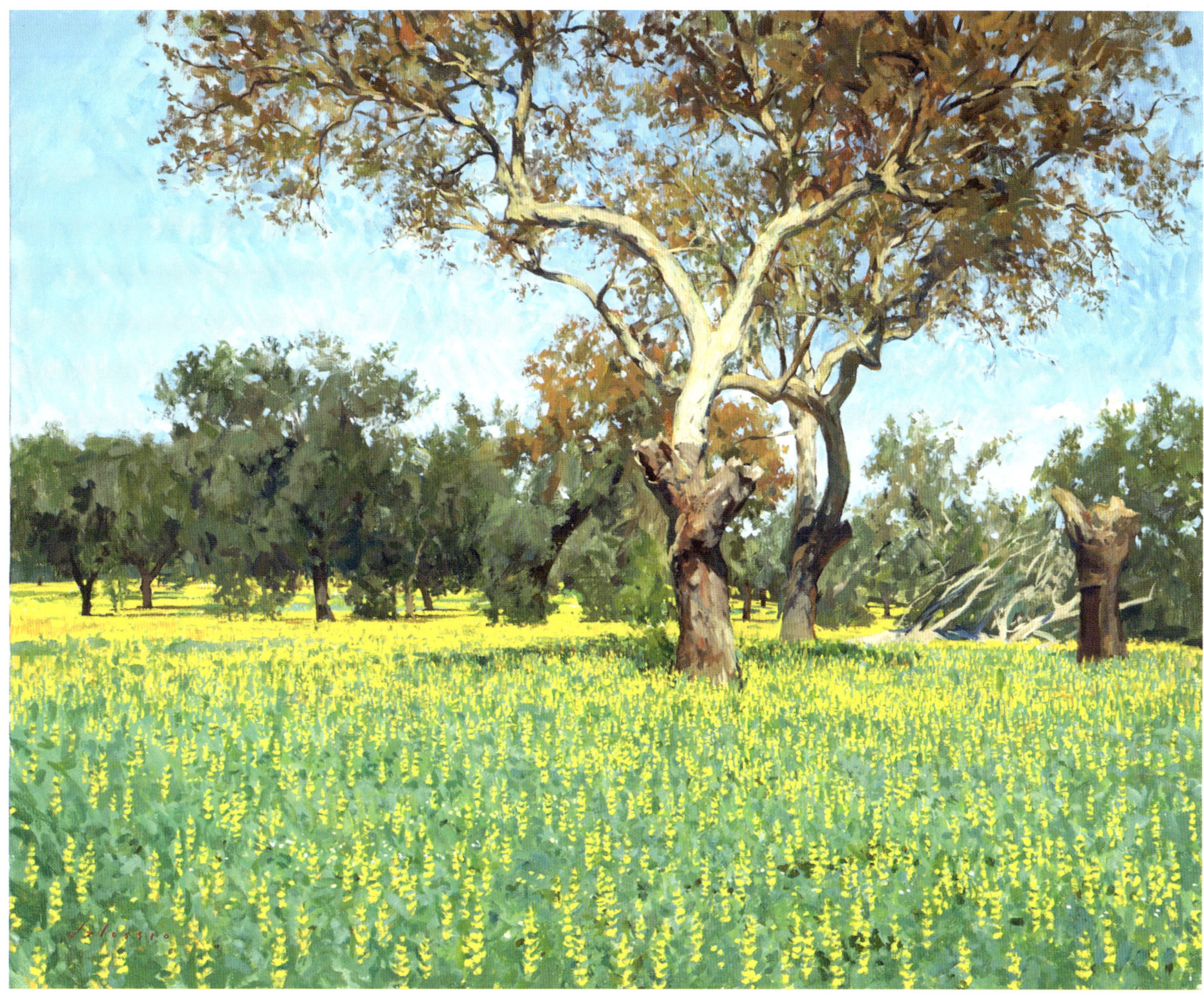

Marc Dalessio, California

YELLOW LUPIN IN A CORK OAK FOREST

I am currently residing in Estremoz, Portugal. We were very much looking forward to painting the beautiful spring colors of the Alentejo while news of the virus was getting worse. We have a young friend in Italy who caught it early on and was hospitalized, so we were taking it very seriously. Still, while we were allowed out, we scouted for days in the countryside. We found this field of yellow lupin in a cork forest about 20 minutes from our house and painted there for a week as the virus began to hit neighboring Spain very hard.

When I was about halfway finished with the painting, we were asked to work from home and the country began to lock down. I finished the painting in the studio from photographs, and it worked out well. Both from the point of view of being able to travel mentally to this wonderful field while being stuck inside, and also technically, as the unfinished part of the painting was mostly the flowers. As I made the final touches to my creation, I soon realized that I preferred the pattern I invented in the studio compared to the actual design in nature.

Andrew Orr, Vermont

A SUMMER VIEW

Living on the Vermont/Canadian border has given me countless opportunities to explore a quieter area of the state of Vermont. The beauty of the Vermont landscape and, in this case, the lovely views of Quebec, are all part of the many joys of living in a more remote location of the state. This painting depicts a scene with a view that is located on my property. I live on a 12-acre parcel with a variety of subject matter from which to find inspiration for my paintings. A pond, large perennial gardens, meadows, woodlands, and woodland streams are all part of the material from which I am so incredibly fortunate to be able to compose many of my paintings. I would say this copse of trees and brush is one of my favorite places here on the property. I have loved watching this area through the seasons. It is simple and unassuming but rich and lovely with diversity. Every season, different times of the day, and even lighting conditions seem to offer new inspirations. The shapes of the clusters of foliage and brush, the colors of the leaves, and the beauty of the wildflowers is peaceful to me. There is a mystery in this cluster of trees as under the brush and growth are remnants of an old stone wall. It always feels this part of the property is trying to tell me a story.

Stopping by this vignette has become part of my ritual when walking the property. It is like visiting an old friend. Witnessing the seasonal changes throughout the year is almost like that point in a conversation with a close friend when the lovely, open-ended question "So, what's new with you?" arrives. Every time I seem to visit this stand of trees, there is more sharing, more learning; there is always something new. During this time of isolation, social distancing, and uncertainty; being in the middle of 12 acres on the border of Vermont with few people around has provided for much reflection and opportunities of quiet gratitude. In the stillness of this time, I am grateful for the opportunities to be with nature and to have nature as something ever-present, strong, and sure on which to rely upon. I hope in some small way, with the completion of this painting I have been able to share a little of what nature is trying to communicate to me.

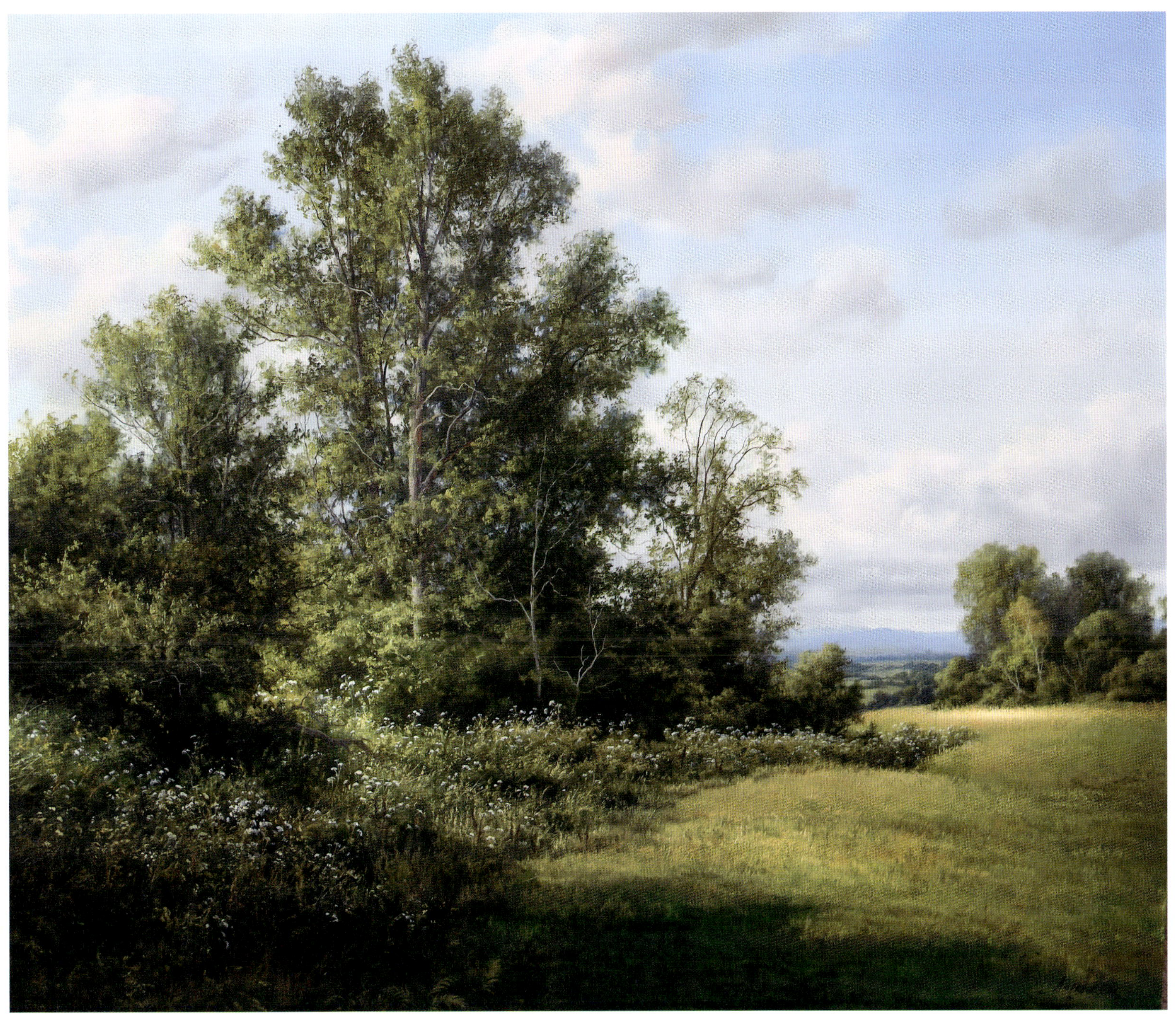

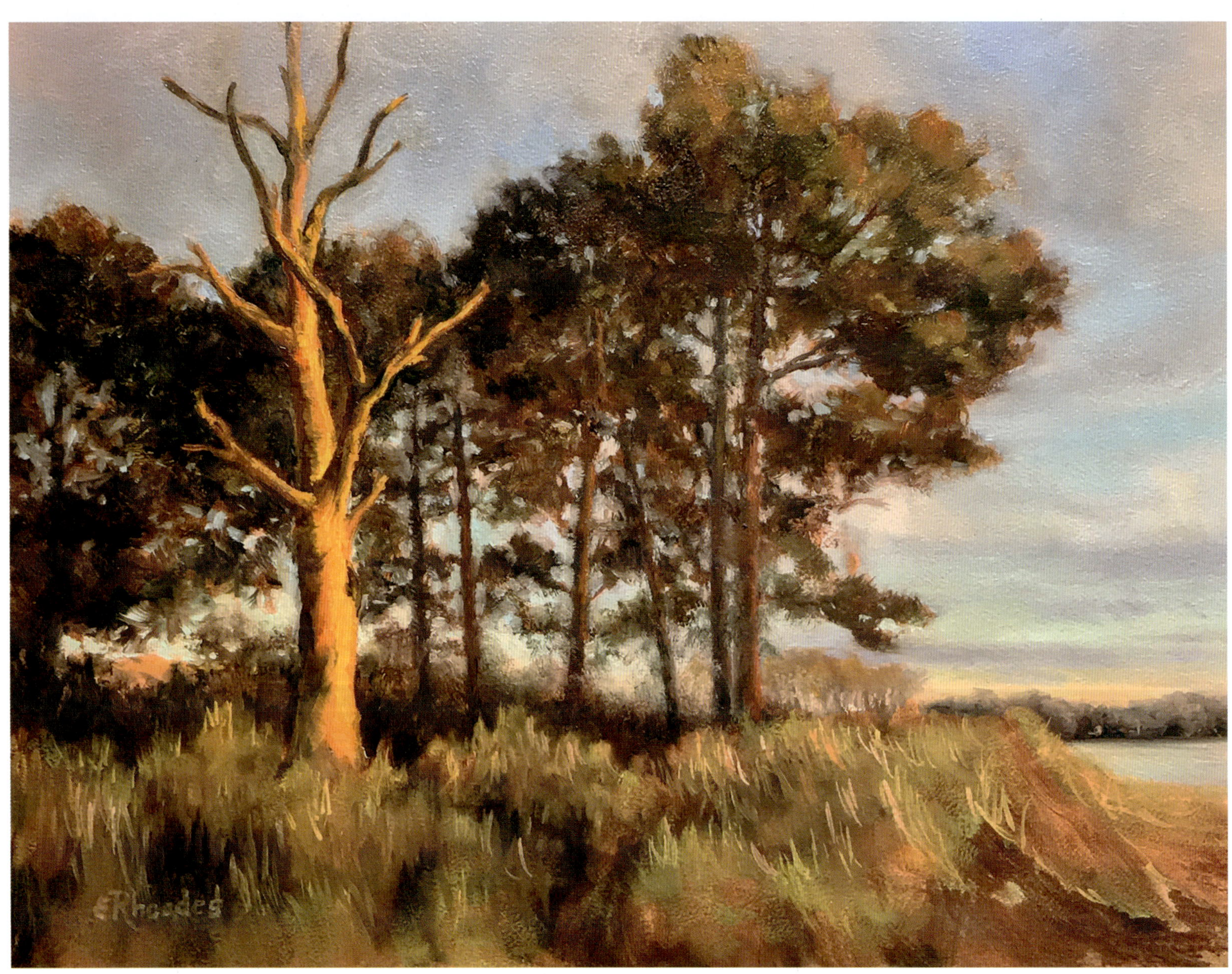
ERhoades

Elizabeth Rhoades, Virginia

UNITED WE STAND

Throughout the past three years, I have felt completely disheartened by the huge political divide in our country between polar-opposite factions. The anger and violence that erupted have made me quite scared. It seems that we cannot find the truth in anything we hear. We hear news from a source that validates our belief system, without listening to what is being said by other sources. We have come too far from the ideal of being a united country and having a common goal of working together for the good of all of us. The landscape tells us everything we need to know about how to coexist in a diverse environment. In this painting, *United We Stand*, I tried to show that by standing together we could survive. When isolated, we are exposed to the harsh elements and are not buffered from them. By standing alone, we deteriorate and decay. By standing together we thrive. This painting depicts the healthy, strong stand of trees in the middle ground, behind the decaying dead tree before them. The golden light of the setting sun casts a hopeful glow to the future and indicates that the predictability of the future is clear.

Kari Ganoung Ruiz, New York

KEEPER OF THE HEDGEROW

During this time of terrible uncertainty, I've found myself struggling with indecision, sadness, frustration, and guilt. What should I be doing right now? Use this time to better yourself and get organized! Why aren't you in the studio? Overwhelmed and exhausted, I threw on a jacket and stepped outside. Our seven-acre meadow is surrounded by hedgerows; strips of brush and trees separating old farm fields. I had always looked at these wooded areas from the outside, never having stepped inside their shady midst. A different world awaited me there; sheltered from the early spring wind and misty rain, I found an almost magical mix of textures, muted colors, earthy smells, and inspiration. As I ducked under branches and climbed over forgotten piles of field stones, slowly a calm took over. I was just looking and wandering and exploring; taking time to just be.

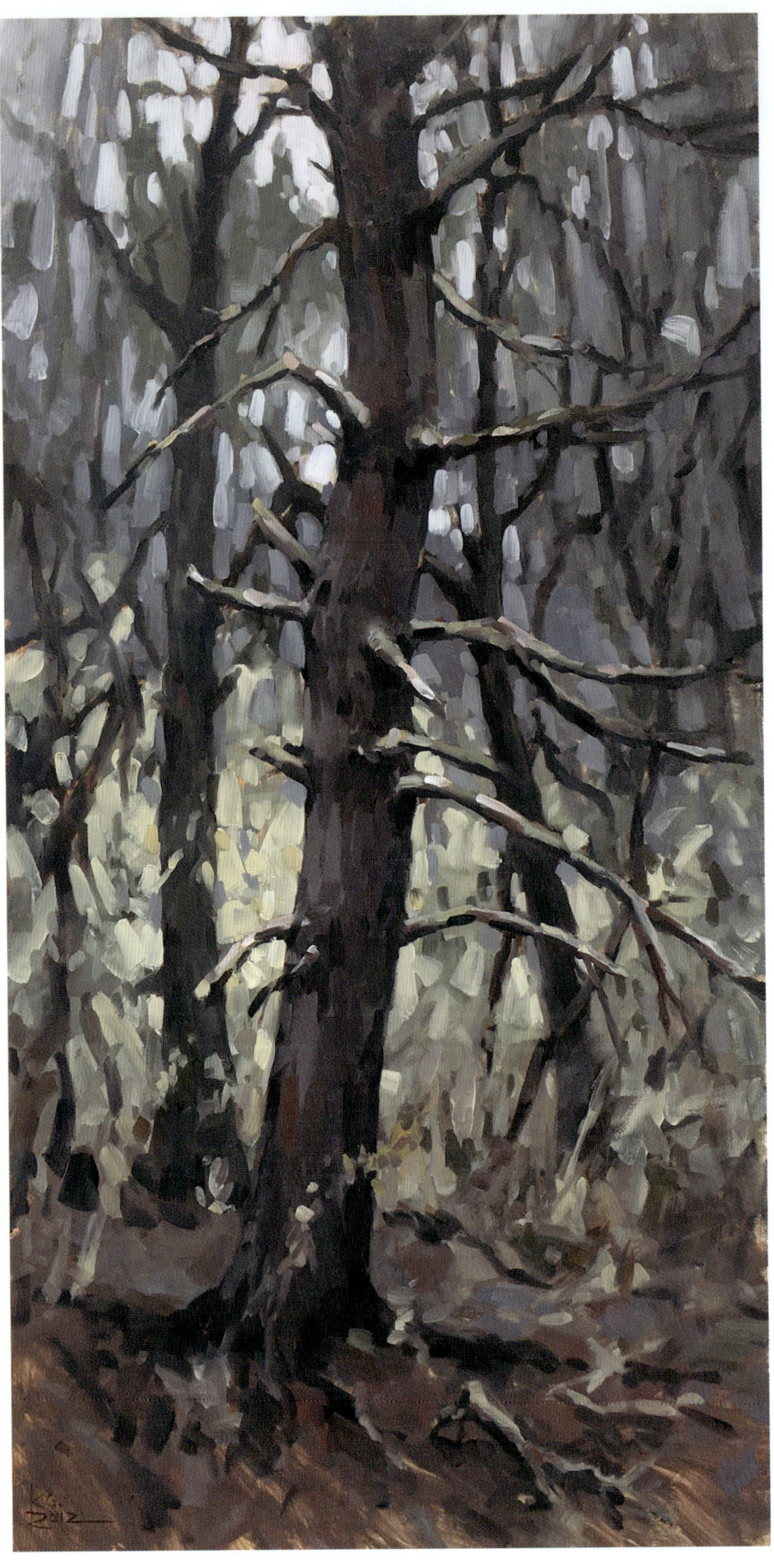

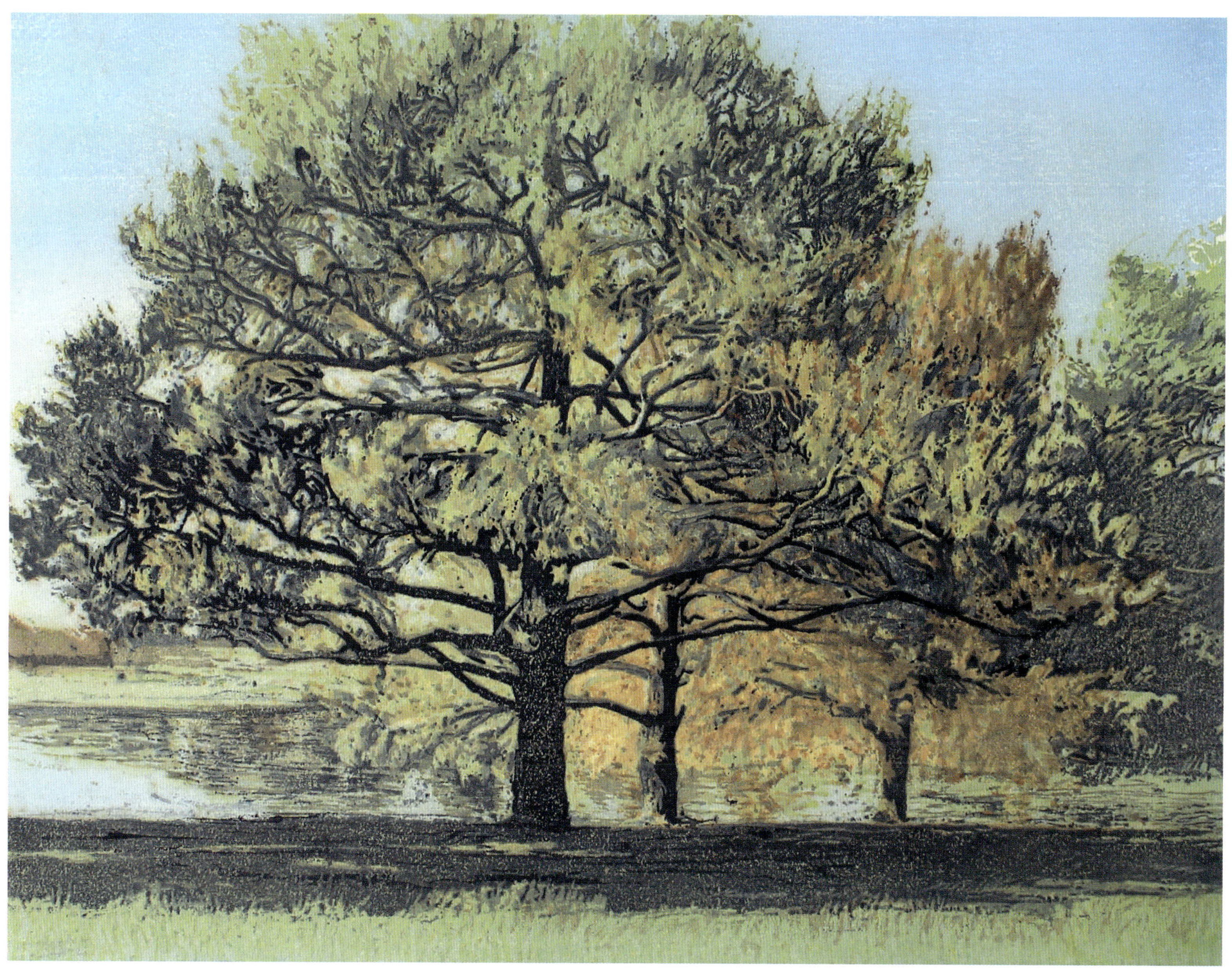

Jennifer Worsley, Utah
TREES IN OCTOBER

The spring of 2020 has been like a new version of spring 2017, when my partner had emergency open-heart surgery. Both years seem to have been carried by frightening events completely out of my control. Happily, 2017 went on to be a year of extreme gratitude for me; the surgery was a success. The interesting difference in 2020 is that anxiety and uncertainty are not just my own private worry—it's being experienced throughout the world in everyone's lives. I ended up making elaborately carved woodblock prints of trees during both springs—both with quite a bit more stillness and quiet than is usual in my work. I didn't plan these to be ways to take my mind off events, but the carving and printing process—in both situations—felt like a calm current of stability; needed and welcomed.

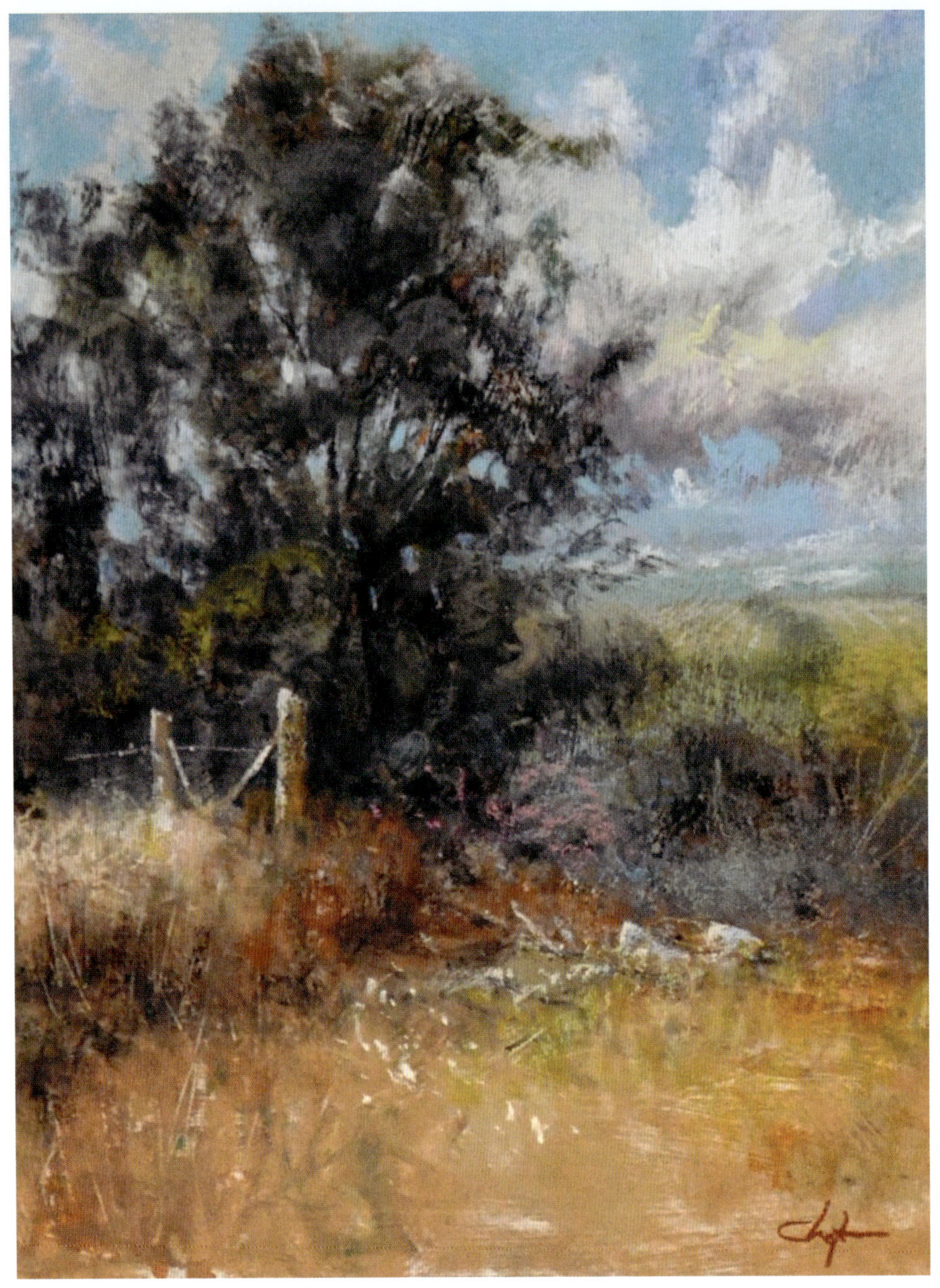

Tom Christopher, Iowa

HARDIN COUNTY

This pastel depicts the landscape near my home in Central Iowa when the grasses and foliage begin to show the first signs of autumn.

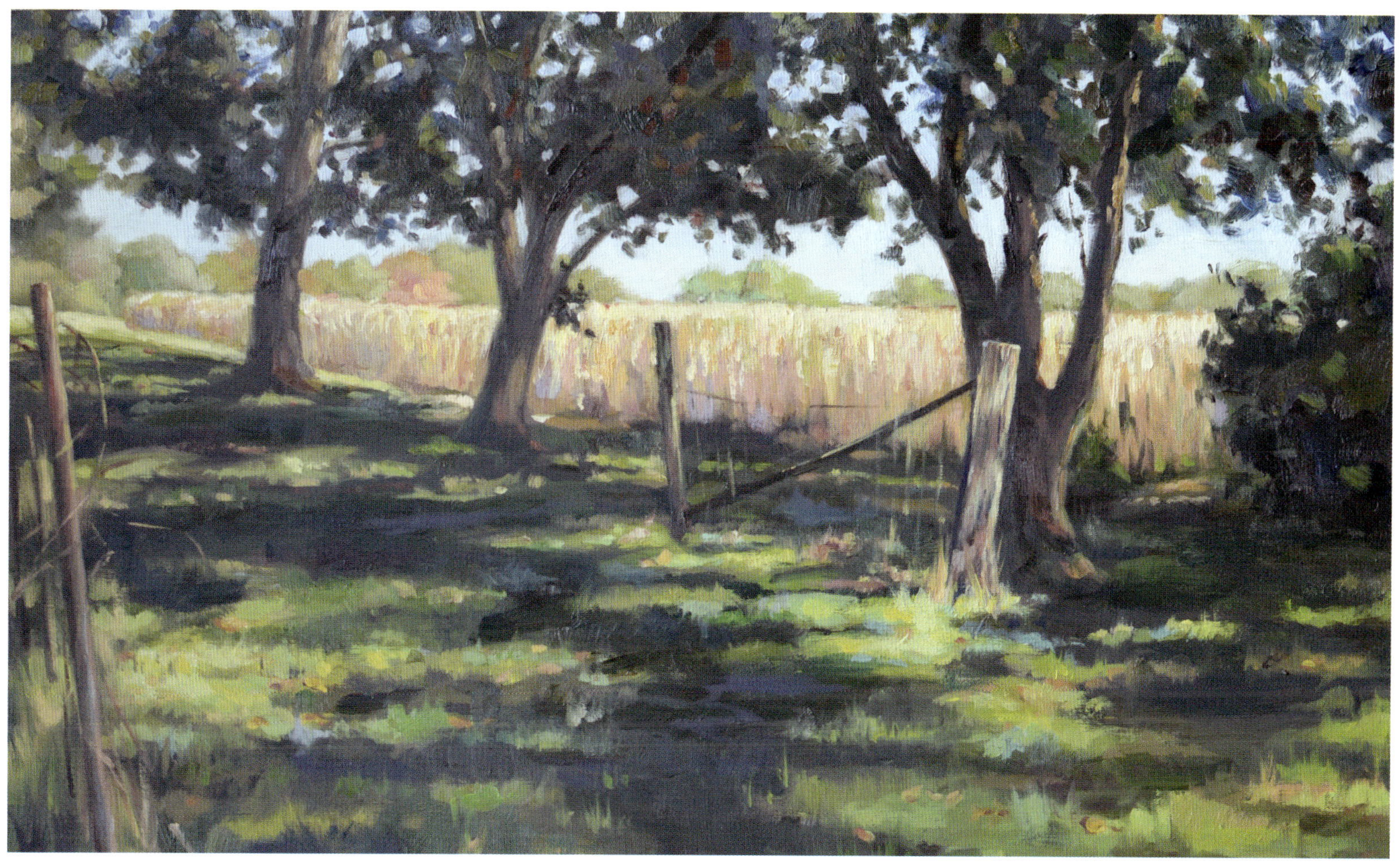

Katharine Taylor, Michigan
ALMOST HARVEST TIME

During the pandemic, I return over and over to the idea that our surroundings are what ground us. This land, these trees showing the cycle of seasons, these farms sustaining families, is what provides the soil into which we stretch our roots. I find great comfort in painting the scenes around my rural home, and that comfort endured when the pandemic shook all my assumptions. The declining late summer sun on the gold of my neighbor's cornfield reminds me that it's a long wait for harvest, but it will come all the same. The remnant of an ancient fence has been there for no one knows how long, perhaps left by a previous farmer. There is a permanence to the way we relate to the land around us that gives me hope.

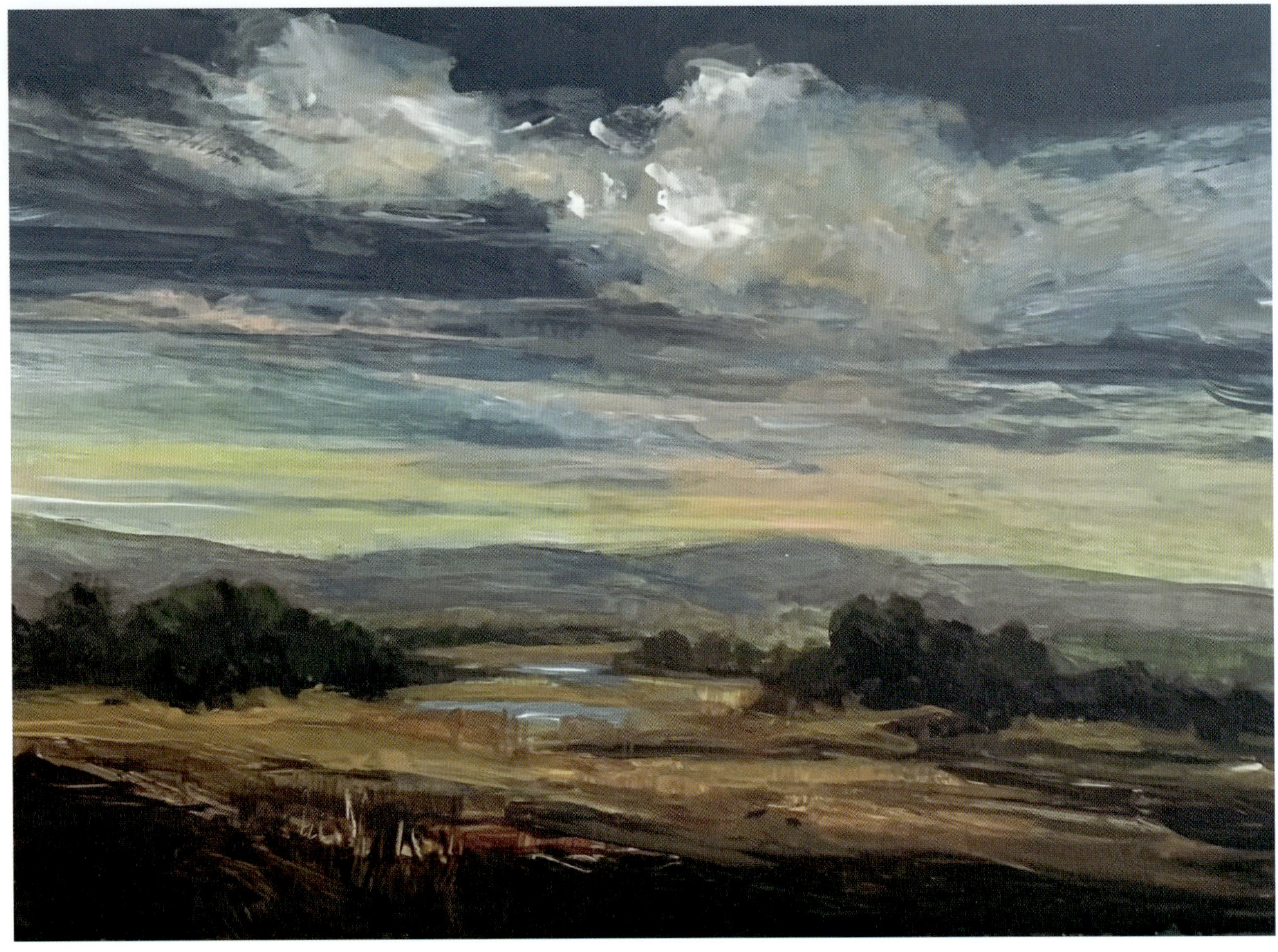

Rita E. DiCaprio, New York
AWAKENING

As I go through these trying and uncertain times, I am so grateful to live in upstate New York, near the Adirondack Mountains, where the beauty constantly astounds me. During the pandemic, I have been able to hike and explore various parts of this region which is so vast and remote that social distancing and masks are often not an issue. The mountains center me, bring me peace, and literally take my breath away no matter how many times I see them. With the recent limitations on inside activities and events, I have taken advantage of the outdoors and created opportunities to see the mountains at various times of the day and in changing light. This piece was created during one of my favorite times of day: dawn. Morning light breaking through the darkness is always beautiful but seeing it over these past months, it also seems symbolic. No matter how dark a day, the light always comes if we are patient. For me, it's God's reminder of hope.

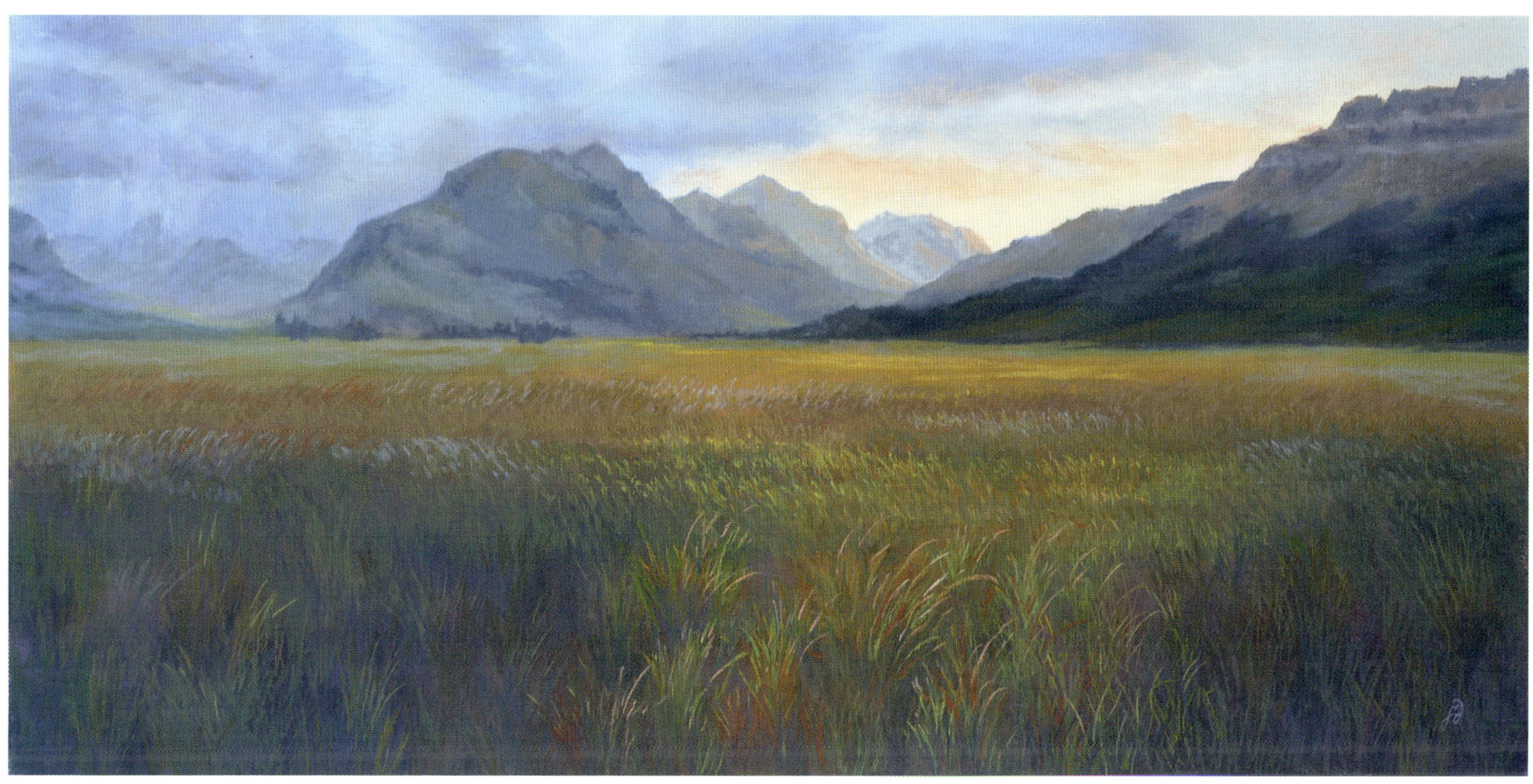

Francesca Droll, Montana

WHISTLING GRASSES

The scene was inspired by a trip to the east side of Glacier National Park during the summer of 2019. My art partner and I were plein-air painting in the park, and we left in the evening just as a storm was blowing over the mountains. The dramatic sky and colorful grasses attracted my attention, and we pulled over so that I could take some photos. As I stepped out of the car, I was almost blown over by strong wind gusts. I regained my balance, quickly took a few shots, and hopped back in the car just as heavy raindrops started to splash down. The storm chased us all the way to the cabin where we were staying for the night. Although this painting was not inspired by being quarantined during the pandemic, it represents my anxiety levels during this chaotic time when questions were not answered, and one worried about how our society was going to weather this particularly frightening storm. The pandemic was bearing down on us this past spring just as these storm clouds were sprinting across the sky toward us that day in the park. The sunset in the distance represents our hopes and dreams as they are being overtaken by the pandemic's dark clouds. The swaying grasses in the foreground correspond to our oscillating emotions as they have been blown to and fro in the conflicting reports coming from our leaders. The storm still has not cleared, and we continue to wait for the time when we can enjoy life without fear of contracting COVID-19. At some point, the sun will burn through the dark clouds of the pandemic, and we will be free to pursue our hopes and dreams once again.

Allison Spreadborough, California

AUTUMN HIKE BY LEMBERT DOME, YOSEMITE

This original watercolor was painted from a reference photo of the imposingly beautiful Lembert Dome, Yosemite. My husband and I were fortunate to win the High Sierra Camps lottery in the Tuolumne Meadows area of Yosemite around Lembert Dome. It was an incredible experience to hike in beauty each day and stay at six different campsites. Although I won't be traveling to Yosemite this year, I can draw on memories of the adventure.

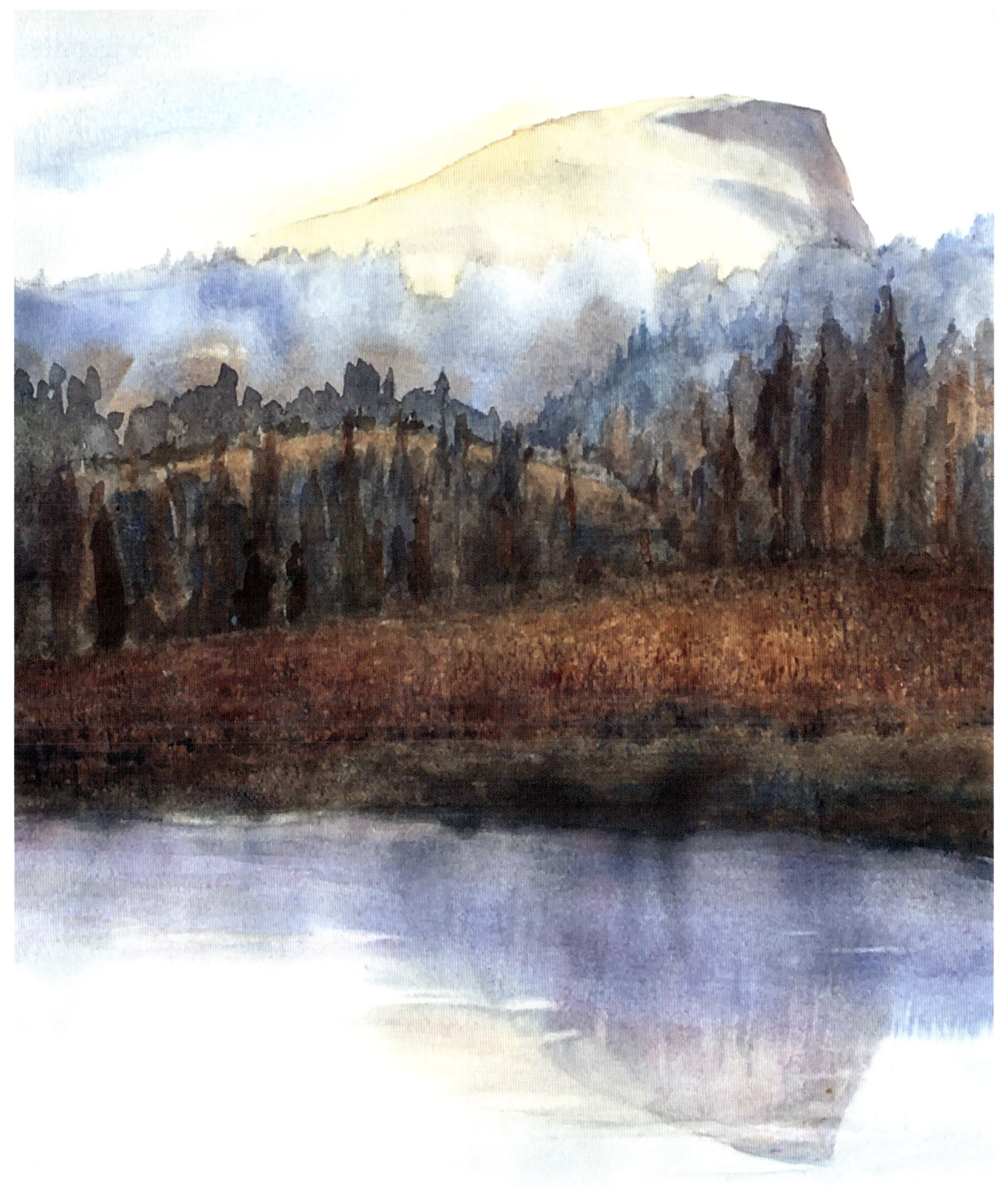

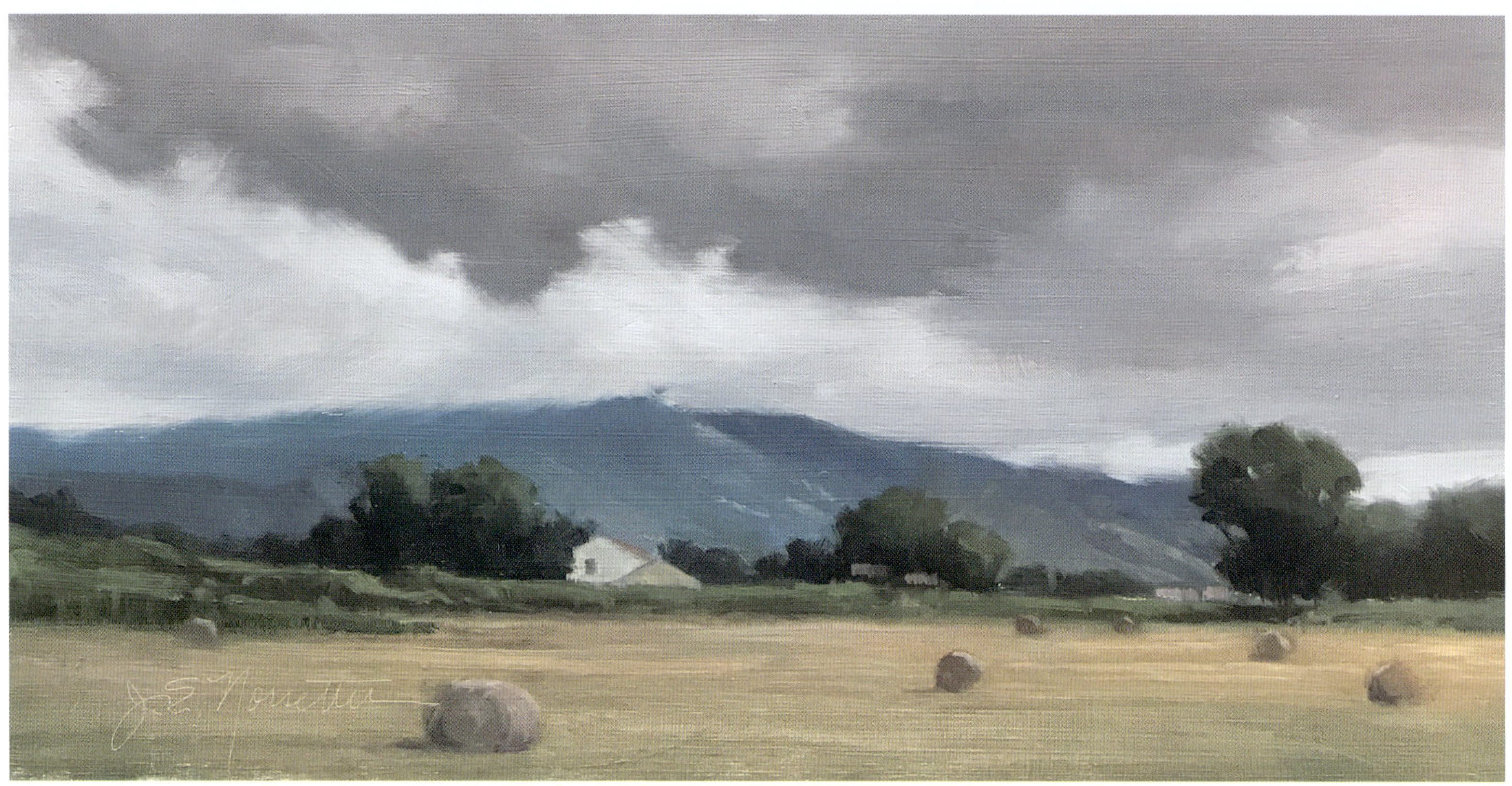

Jan Norsetter, Wisconsin

SOMEWHERE IN UMBRIA

The stay-at-home order for me translated into painting even more than before. I've always been quite motivated to paint, but somehow the lack of in-person contact with friends and family served to concentrate my efforts further. I've done a lot of plein-air painting in all seasons so painting from travel photos hasn't been a priority for me. While thinking about the places I've traveled to and painted in, I had the chance to participate in a Zoom plein-air event and the photo reference was somewhere in Umbria. I've spent a fair amount of time in Umbria so the photo spoke to me. Umbria is the breadbasket of Italy where literally tons of food is grown. This one allowed me to travel virtually while not traveling at all!

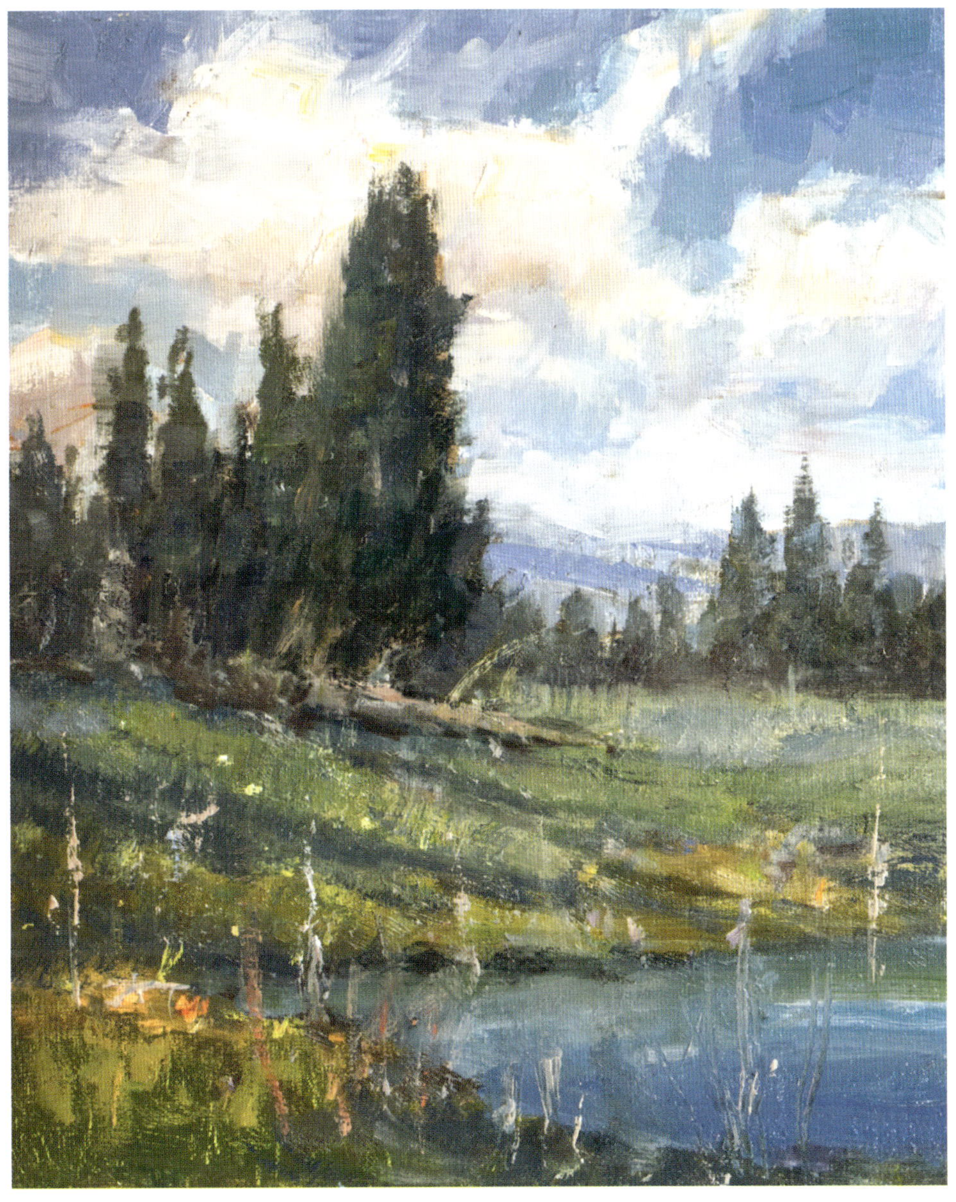

Howard B. Friedland, Arkansas

HIGH MOUNTAIN PASTURE

Most painters live a pretty solitary work life. When we are in our studios, it is just us and the canvas that are "socializing." I am lucky to have a wife who is also an artist, but when it comes to the choices we have to make in our artwork, we each fly solo. For folks who work with fellow workers on a regular basis, I am sure the "stay at home" orders have been a burden. With deadlines for galleries and shows put on hold (for who knows how long), I now have the incentive to play more with my paintings in the studio. I have taken to reimagining some plein-air studies where I see room for improvement. I have found that it has been very freeing! *High Mountain Pasture* was painted en plein air before the pandemic, when getting in the car and driving to lovely panoramas was the thing to do. I pulled the on-location painting out of my stack of studies and reimagined it in my mind's eye. No photos, sketches or any other reference were used. This allowed me to stretch my creativity. It is more like a dream now, not reality. I love this method of working because it gives me permission to follow my muse and not cede all the power to what was literally there in front of me on location. This is a positive exercise and I plan to continue using it even more in my larger studio work. It is important to try new and different approaches to keep growing and to keep our work fresh.

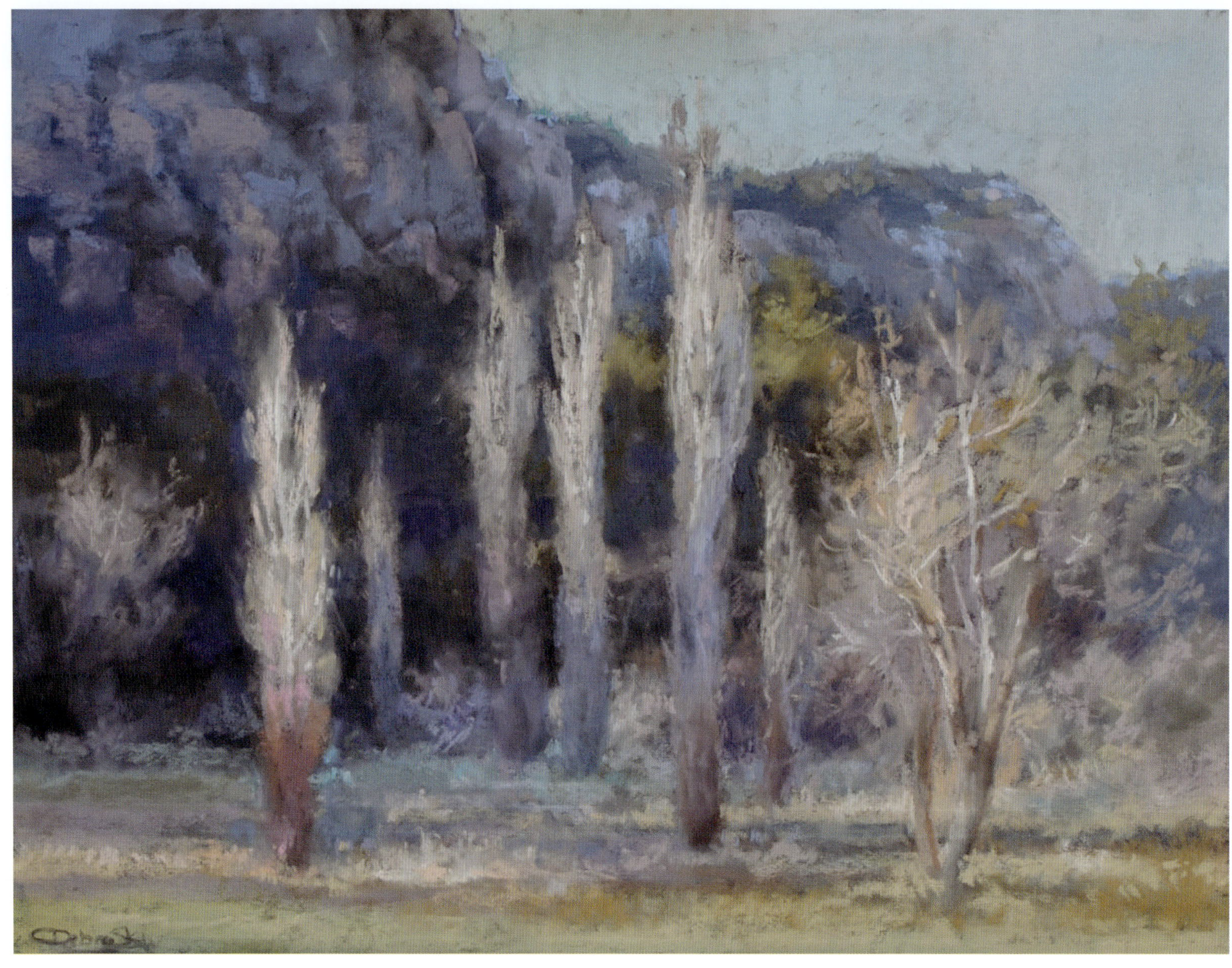

Christine Debrosky, Arizona
SILVER FLAME

When the pandemic became severe, I had been getting ready for a solo exhibition. Realizing I had to cancel, I stopped work on my red rock paintings and turned towards pieces I have always wanted to paint. I have plein-air painted in this location many times, but I had some images from a late afternoon when the trees were bare, yet with the subtle color of the low sun. The location work certainly helped me to realize this piece. This is how *Silver Flame* came to be. I sequestered in my studio, played classical music, and worked on problem-solving, which was just how to render the delicate branches. As I worked, I realized that the focal point—the isolated tree to the left—had become a metaphor for what we were starting to go through. Isolation, and a "cutting off." This is one of the first paintings I did during this period. Little did we know that the crisis would continue the way that it has...so I have done many pieces since.

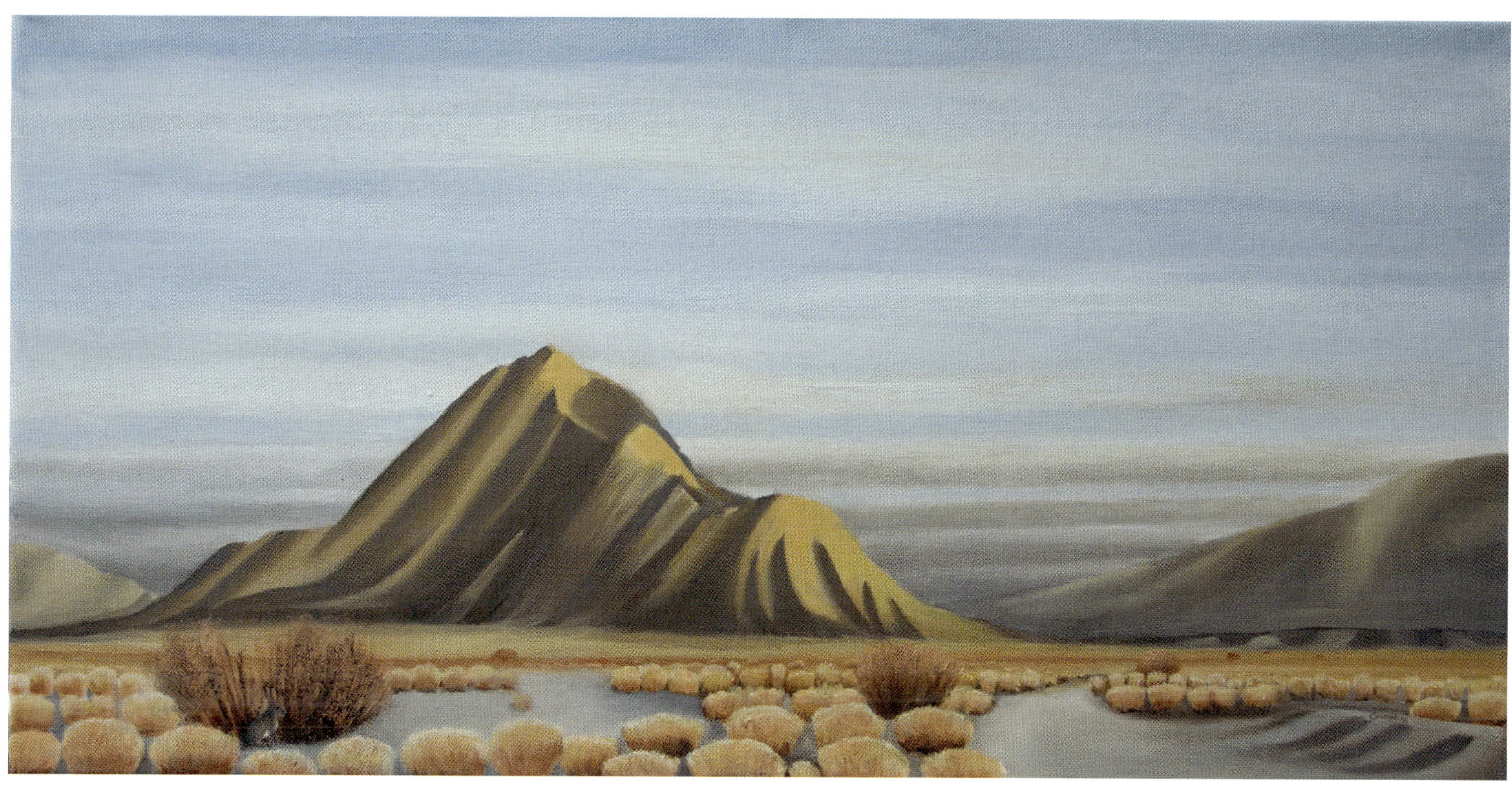

Don Cornelius, Alaska
DESERT SENTINEL

My wife and I have recently been taking late winter vacations to the southwest, where we like to thaw out from our Alaskan winters. This year the Coronavirus put a halt to a 2020 trip, so I opted to virtually return to one of my favorite desert areas, the area around Death Valley, California. There is a geologically sculpted mountain, south of Death Valley Junction, which particularly intrigues me. Every angle from which we view the mountain at any time of day seems to inspire a new painting subject. *Desert Sentinel* depicts an abstracted version of that unnamed mountain.

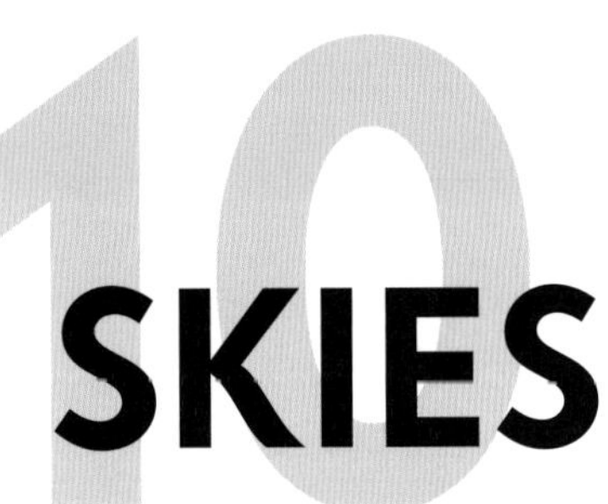

10 SKIES

The painting I submitted to this project was my first painting created during the COVID lockdown. It represents the feeling of isolation experienced by many, but also the feeling that the show must go on. There are dances going on in the sky. The sun rises and sets, creating color-filled canvases of memories. Beauty never ceases. Our routines will continue but may be changed in some way forever.

Charles Muench
Gardnerville, Nevada

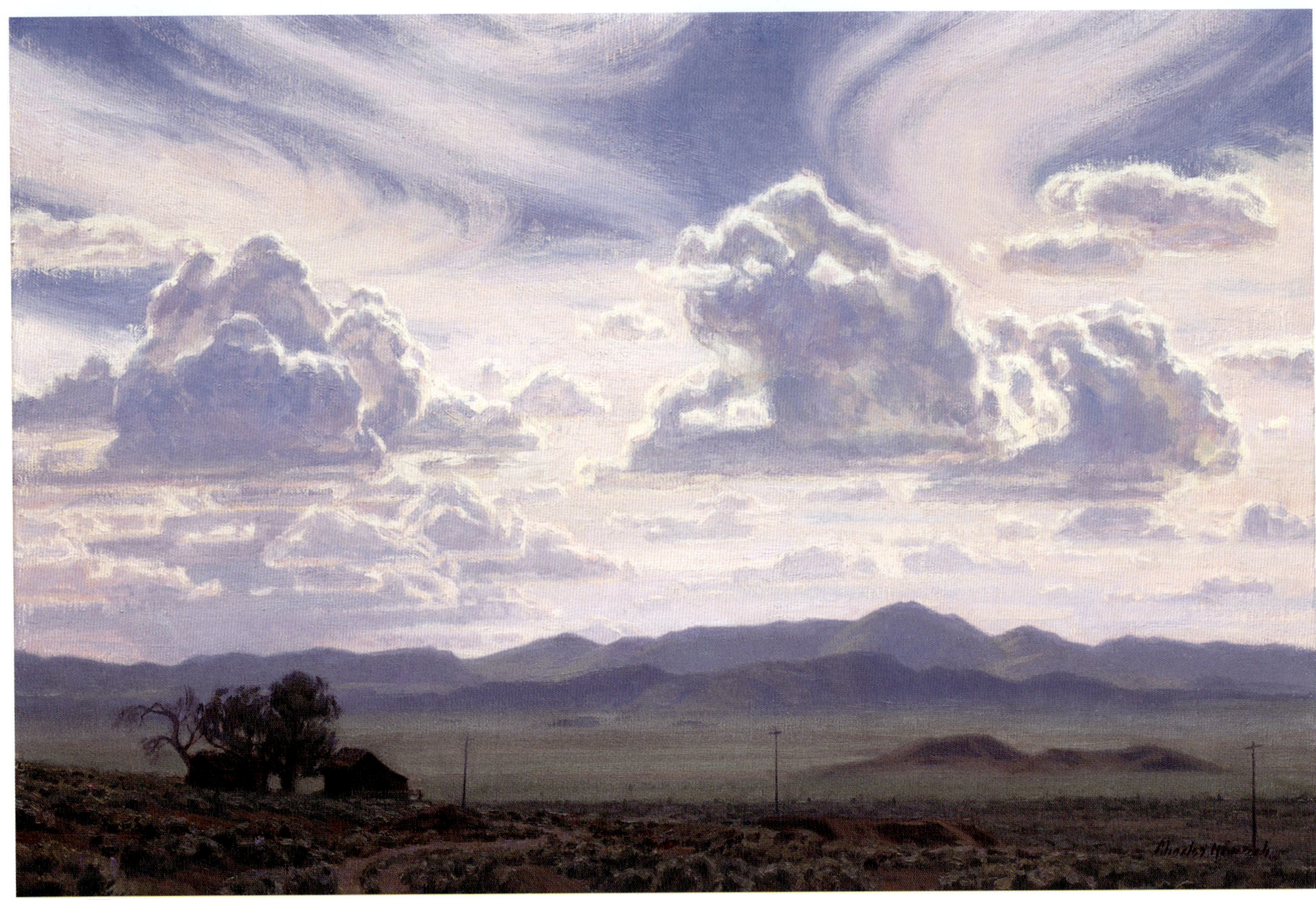

Charles Muench, Nevada
NEVADA CLOUD DANCE

This was my first painting created shortly after the country shut down. It is an expression of the isolation and loneliness that is imbued in the stark Nevada landscape. In contrast to these emotions and empty space, the clouds are dancing to baroque and serpentine rhythms, oblivious to the turmoil below.

Sara Linda Poly, Maryland

A SILVER LINING

Since March I've had more time in the studio because I have not been able to teach as I usually do. It's actually been nice to have more time to think about new ideas. During the summer we had a series of storms passing through. I am always excited by storms...especially as they approach or depart. I love painting clouds and I am always interested in the changes in the sky. Watching this storm pass reminded me of the chaos and order we live with. This cloud formation reminded me of hope for the future and to look for the proverbial "silver lining" in it all.

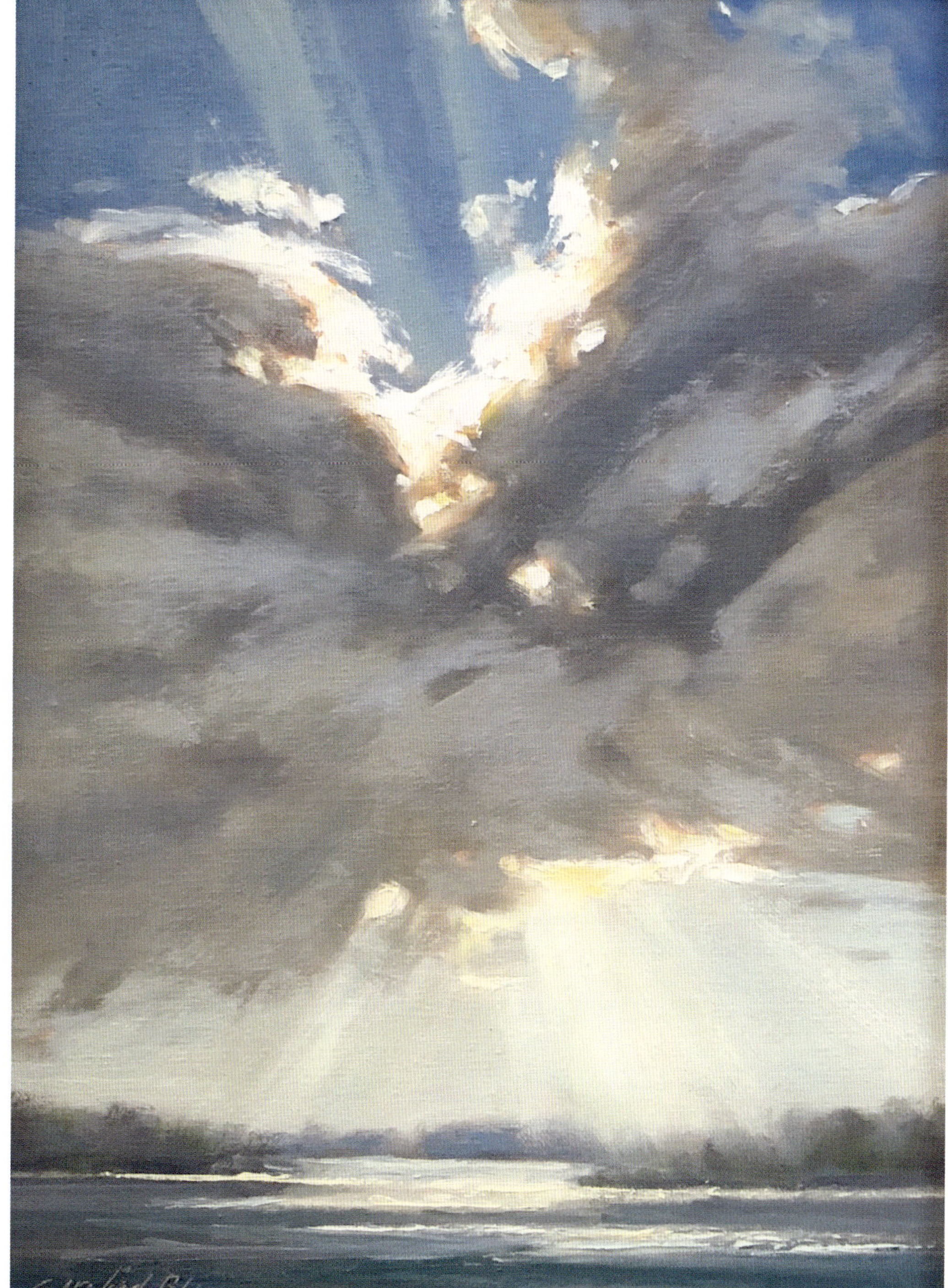

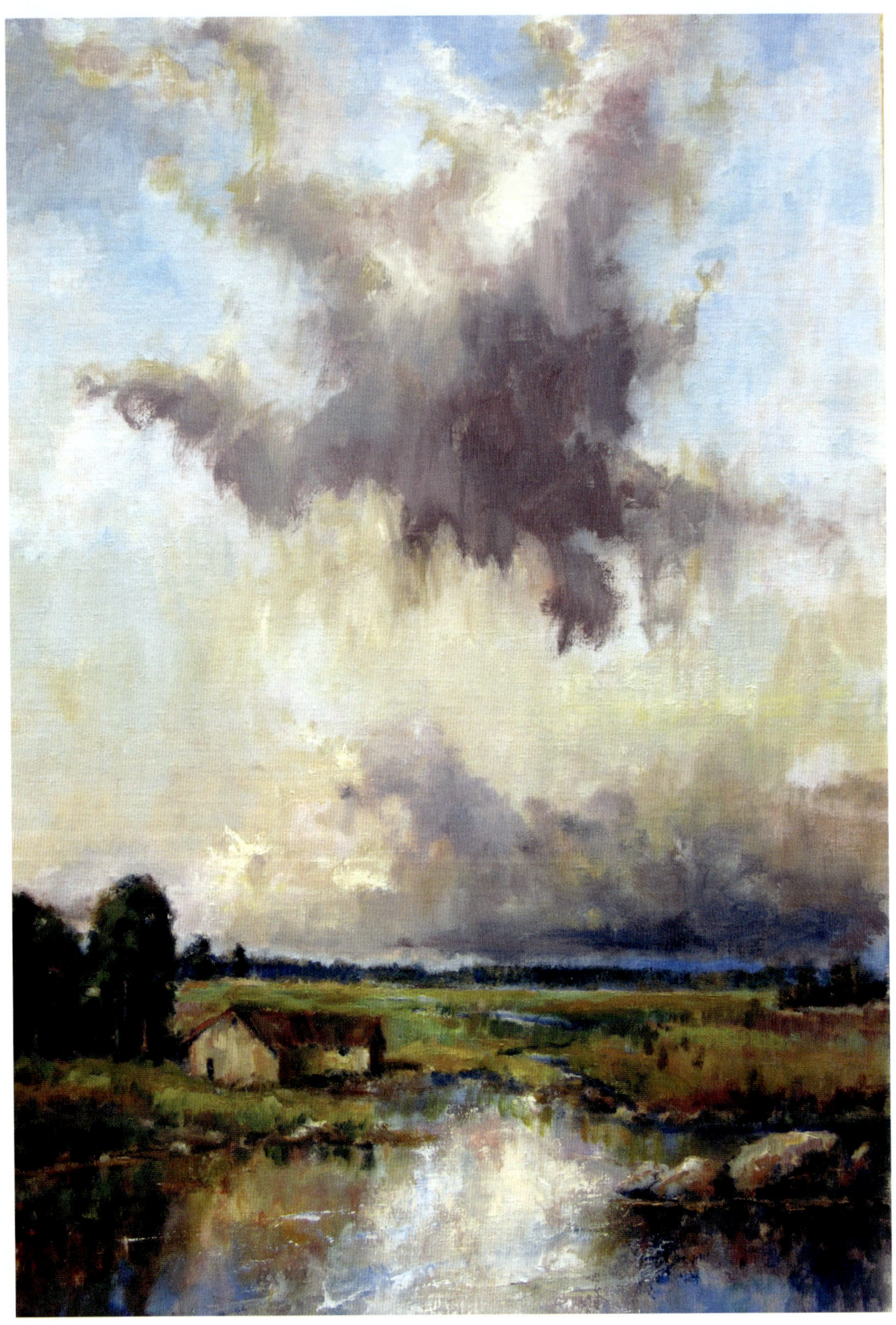

Joe Palmerio, Florida

THE BLUE HORIZON

The scene depicts the isolated residence of this house just outside of Everglades City, Florida. The dark cloud, coupled with the isolated structure, is in reference to the present condition we now find ourselves living in. The blue color of the sky's horizon on the right references the blue period we are now experiencing, but the light is still trying to burst through, referencing hope for the future.

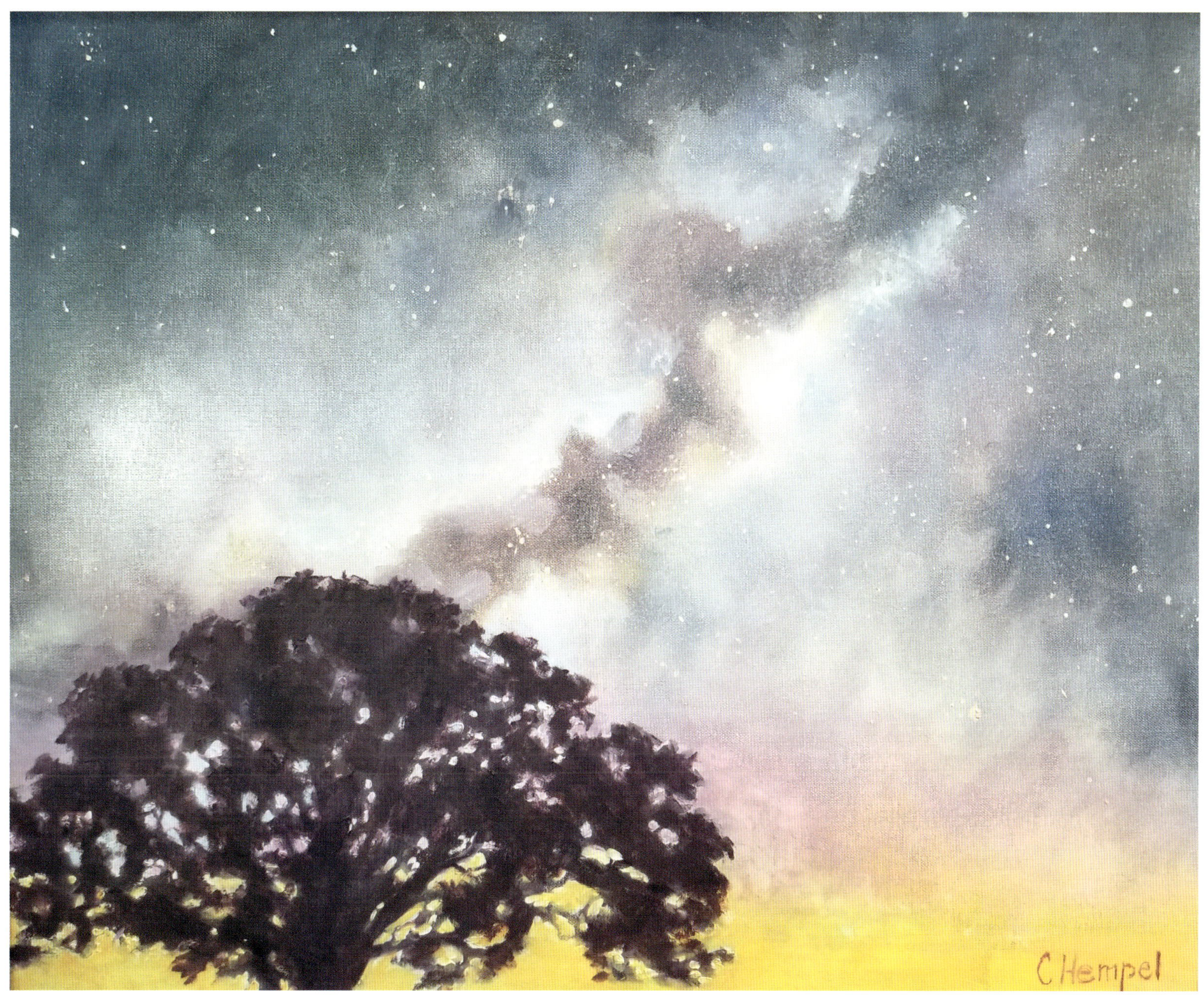

Catherine Hempel, Florida
THIS TOO SHALL PASS

Living in Central Florida with all its light pollution, I was fascinated to be able to see the Milky Way while kayaking at the Merritt Island National Wildlife Refuge a few summers ago while there to observe the bioluminescent plankton in the Mosquito Lagoon. Sometimes we just need to stop and remember that the world is indeed a magical place and will continue to be so.

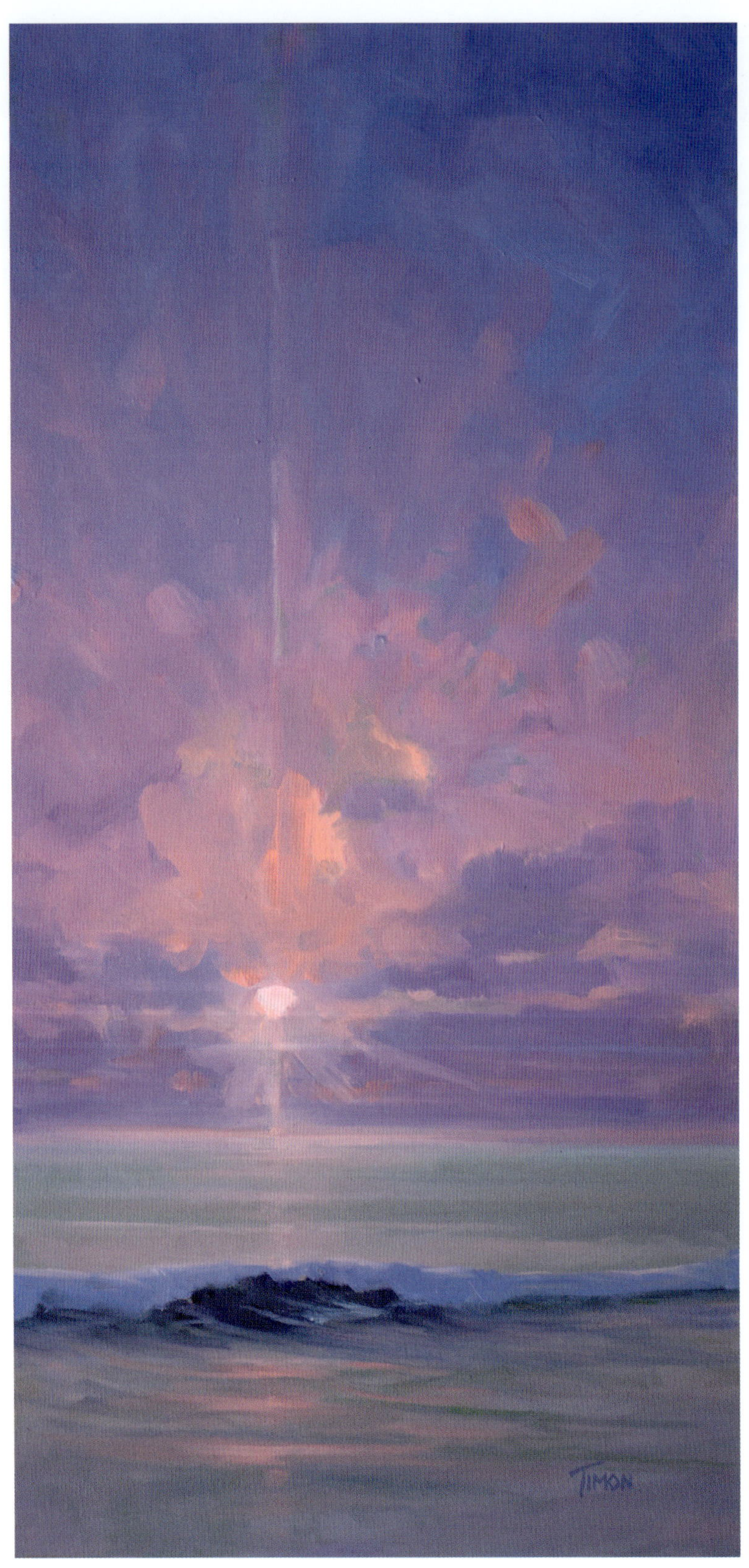

Timon Sloane, California

SLICE OF SUNSET

Slice of Sunset is a piece from my *Broken Sky* collection, a series centered around capturing the essence of light while simplifying and deconstructing its surrounding landscape. I describe this work as a balance between abstraction and internal illumination.

As an artist based in California, I am constantly inspired by the natural beauty of the western coast. My work seeks to highlight luminosity in everyday scenery. Finding the charm in what may seem commonplace is especially important nowadays; quarantine has compelled me to look for enjoyment wherever possible, even in the most mundane parts of the everyday. While *Slice of Sunset* was painted in 2019, I feel it still highlights the necessity of finding beauty in ordinary life. I hope this piece allows viewers to have a moment of quiet splendor in these uncertain times.

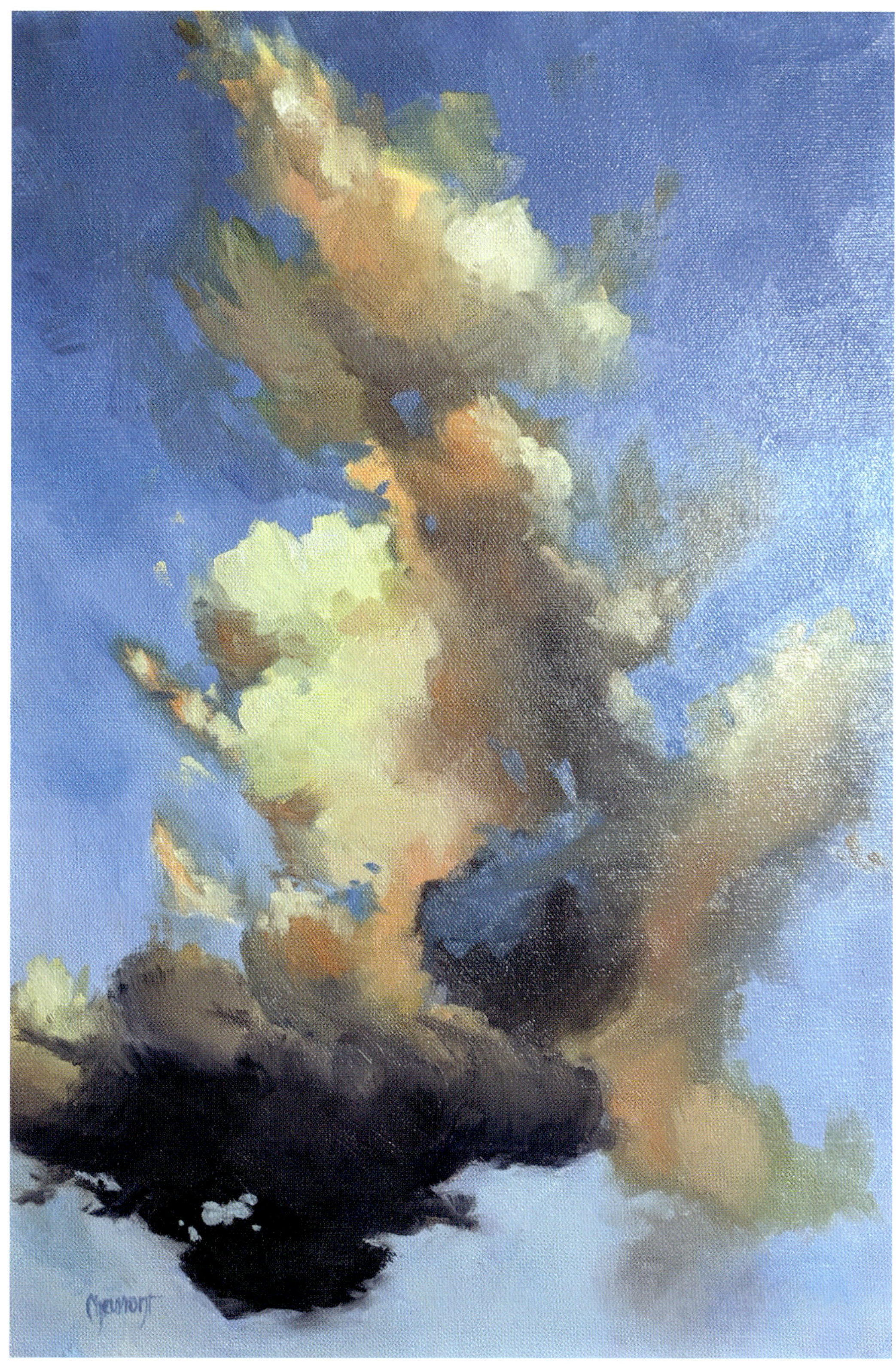

Casey Cheuvront, Arizona
DESERT SKIES

Unparalleled drama in the Arizona skies is what draws me to painting clouds. This particular evening's light show did not disappoint! This painting took second place at an annual art exhibition and sale.

I chose this work because it is dynamic, happy, expansive, colorful—things I sorely missed, particularly during the pandemic's earliest days when we were surrounded by so much constant bad news. It represents these things to me not only because I used to fly hang gliders—well, it's the sky, after all—but because I have been fascinated by skyscapes and clouds for many years. This painting represents openness, expansiveness, freedom, and hope for those things to return. When I painted it, I was in a "zen" place, using big bold brushwork and strong color; it's a fearless piece. I hope we can return to that mindset soon.

11 FLOWERS

"Where flowers bloom, so does hope."—Lady Bird Johnson

Uncertainty and darkness spread amongst us during these pandemic times. What a reminder that I am not in control, and to hold on to my plans loosely. Plans change, dreams evolve, but no matter how dark or confusing things may become, nature always reminds me that the dark night will pass, a promise of spring bursts forth, and joy comes in the morning; our promise in Psalms 30:5.

Getting outside and exploring the beauty around me helps to refocus my thoughts, calm my mind, and quiet my soul. Birdsong carries me away as the breeze blows gently through my hair. I take a deep breath and let the cares of the moment wash away. "Trust," I am reminded. "All will work out, all in its perfect time. Let go," I hear...

I walk through the desert, the valley before me, thankful for the hope and gift found in wildflowers. Seasons change...we cannot avoid life's struggles and pain. Yet our journey is one of hope and light in spite of, and maybe because of, our times in the desert. How much sweeter the beauty, the vibrance, the joy, when spring comes once again.

Vibrant blooms draw my attention nearby. Flowers always bring me such joy; each one a special gift. These blooms cause me to smile; my heart warms and joy blossoms within me as everything becomes new.

Out of the darkness, beauty emerges. Her buds push forth stretching into the early morning light, reaching for the sun. Vibrant petals unfold one by one, shifting in color and form. She is radiant, contrasting against the darkness below. The long night in the desert is slowly coming to an end. Amidst the thorns and harshness, beauty cannot be contained. She always breaks through, bringing hope and promise. I love to see the joy and rebirth on the other side of darkness. Be patient; it will come. One day you will blossom again too, I am reminded. She welcomes the morn, smiling into each new day.

Each hopeful bud, developing into a breath-taking flower, is a unique creation. One by one, these blossoms open, reaching for the sky, warmed by the kiss of the sun. We are all special and unique as well; meant to bloom fully right where we are, regardless of our circumstances. There is no competition, just a compelling from within to shine brightly; we all have a different story to share. Bloom on!

Rise Up is the first painting I completed after stay-at-home orders were put into effect. Honestly, it was weeks before I could even bring myself to pick up a paintbrush, which was frustrating and confusing. I chose these blooms as a symbol of hope and a call to "rise up." Each of my paintings has an accompanying story and this is hers.

Desiring to bring light and hope during our stay-at-home orders, I chose to capture these vibrant prickly pear blooms rising into the sky. Nature reminds us of the promise that spring will always come again as the darkness passes away. Beauty, love, hope, and light are what we all need right now and always. I choose to step into the beauty. While painting prayerfully, the song *Rise Up* by Andra Day came on. This painting seemed to call for this title as we all "rise up" together during these difficult times. Long ago, I felt called "to be a bringer of light and beauty;" to strive to make an impact in the lives of others through my paintings and words. This is what I choose to do. I will create, I will write, I commit to bringing hope and encouragement to others.

Lucy Dickens
Carefree, Arizona

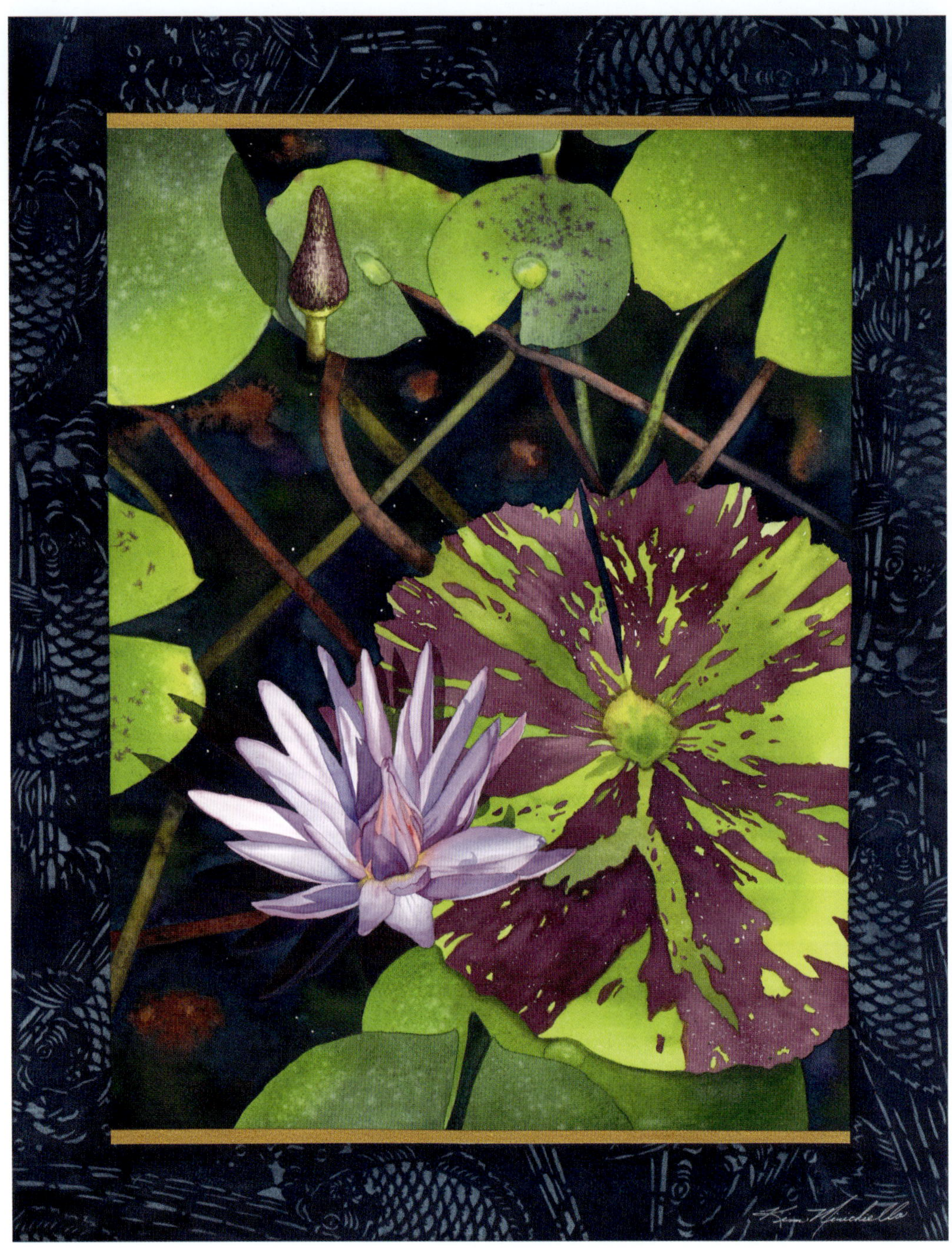

Kim Minichiello, Florida
A CALMING INFLUENCE

With the unsettling time we are living in, due to the current COVID-19 crisis, I am returning to a subject I love, water lilies, painting a larger series of works. The title of each painting in the series reflects how I am feeling during this unprecedented time and how I feel while I'm in the process of creation. The beautiful, calming subject matter puts my mind at ease and while working on them, I lose myself into a meditative state. In many ancient cultures, the water lily symbolizes rebirth and peace. I'm conscious of working on this series, and it is my hope that, as we come out on the other side of this global pandemic, we have renewed hope for a better future.

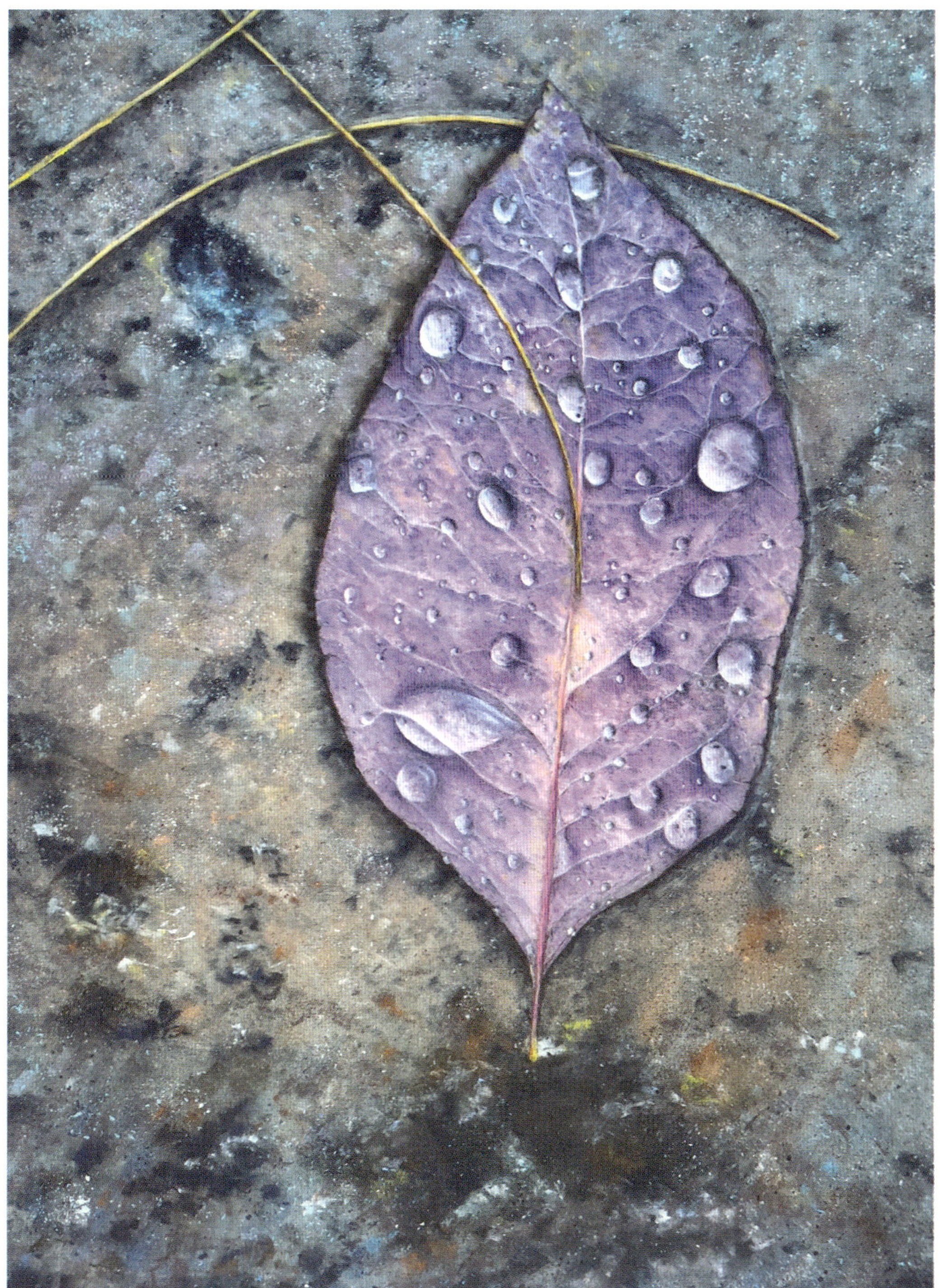

Tracy Klinesteker, Michigan
SPRING LEAF

I started this painting in December of 2019, before the lockdown. It's inspired by a photo I took on my way to work in the spring of 2018. I loved the lilac color and the shape of the water drops on the leaf. The texture of the sidewalk also got my attention. I was about a third of the way through when we were locked down. I couldn't settle down and concentrate for a couple of months, so I left the painting sitting on my board for quite a while. I didn't paint at all. Gradually, I relaxed a bit more, got used to the isolation, became inured to the fear. I kept looking at the unfinished painting, knowing that it was going to be a good one if I could only get back at it. One day, I couldn't come up with any more excuses to put it off, so I picked up a pastel stick and began again. The concentration for a painting like this one is very important. I began to get into the "zen" of it again, a little more each day. Finally, I finished! Now I need to find a framer that is open for business!

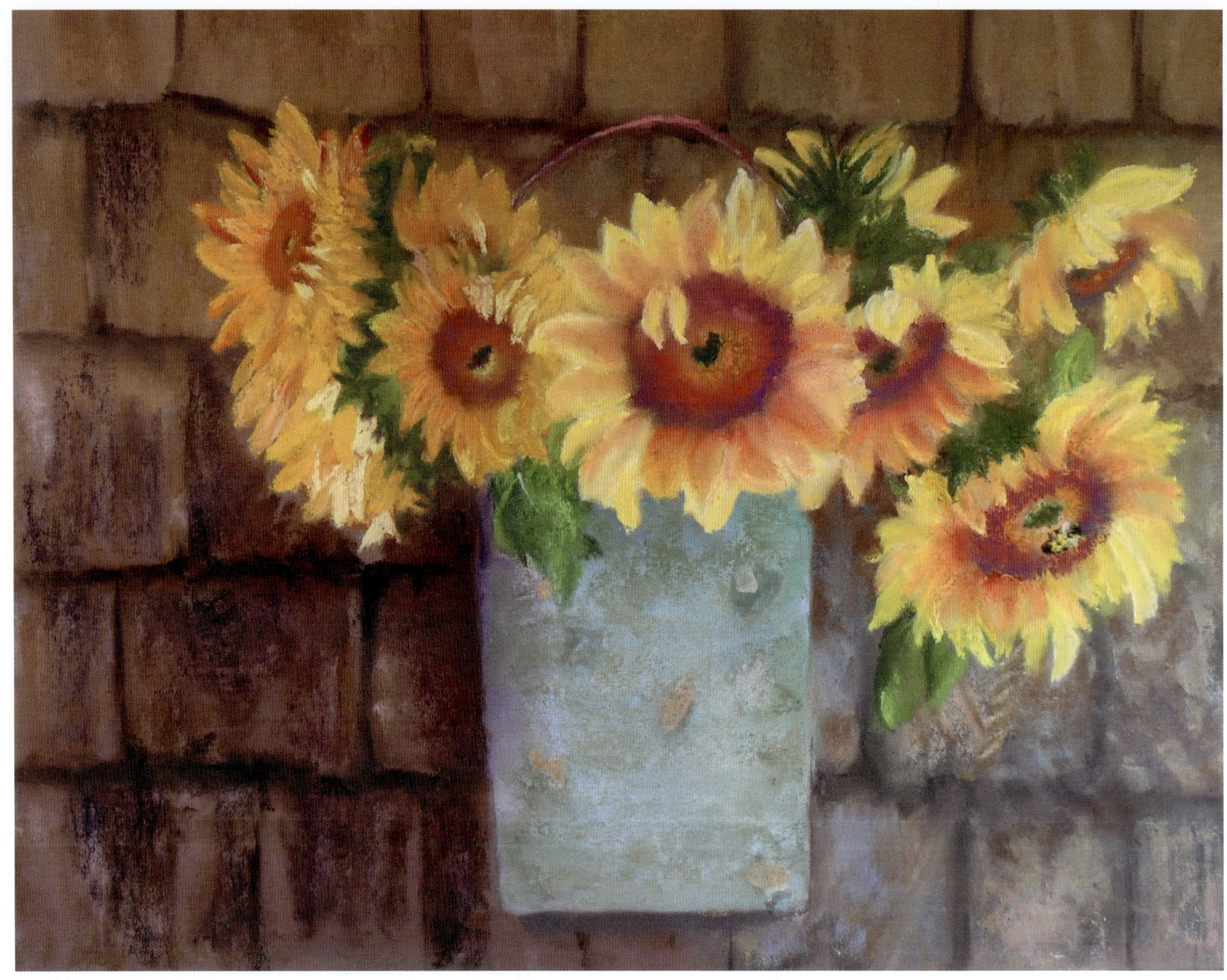

Carol Frieswick, Massachusetts
SUNFLOWER DECOR

Sunflowers always seem to brighten up a room and bring joy to those in it. I usually paint smaller pieces but as I had the 16x20 inch frame to fill, I chose this to paint. New England winters are cold. This year was made worse by being in a state that was an epicenter for the Coronavirus. We were in total lockdown, with few retail shops open and unable to socialize with friends and family. I'm hoping these sunflowers will bring a ray of sunshine to anyone still feeling lonely and hopeless in the face of today's escalating troubles.

Lucy Dickens, Arizona
RISE UP

Desiring to bring light and hope during our "stay at home" orders, I chose to capture these vibrant prickly pear blooms rising into the sky. Nature reminds us of the promise that spring will always come again, and the darkness passes away. Beauty, love, hope, and light are what we all need right now and always. I choose to step into beauty. While painting prayerfully, the song "Rise Up" by Andra Day came on. This painting seemed to call for this title as we all "Rise Up" together during these difficult times. Long ago, I felt called "to be a bringer of light and beauty," to strive to make an impact in the lives of others through my paintings and words. This is what I choose to do. I will create, I will write, I commit to bringing hope and encouragement to others.

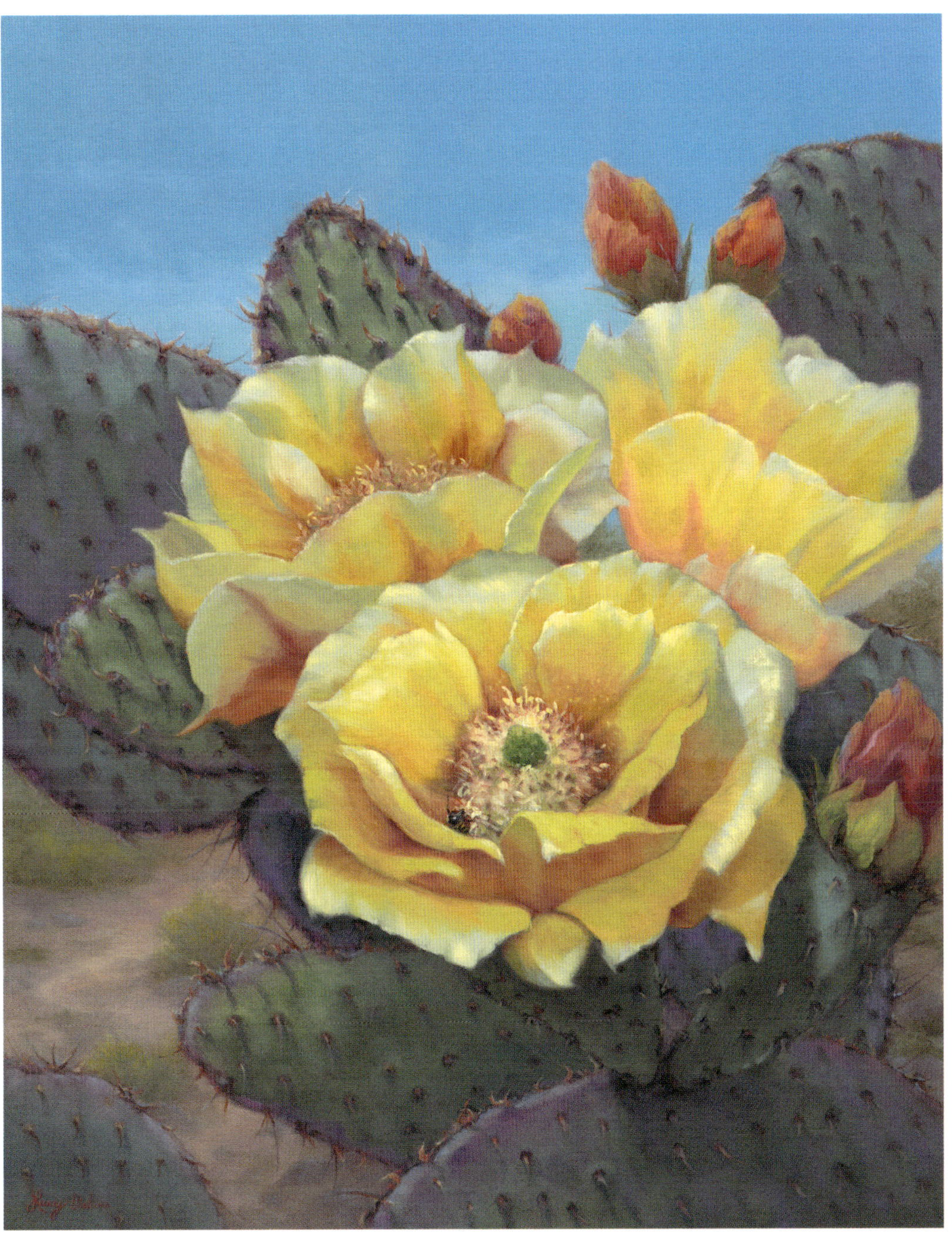

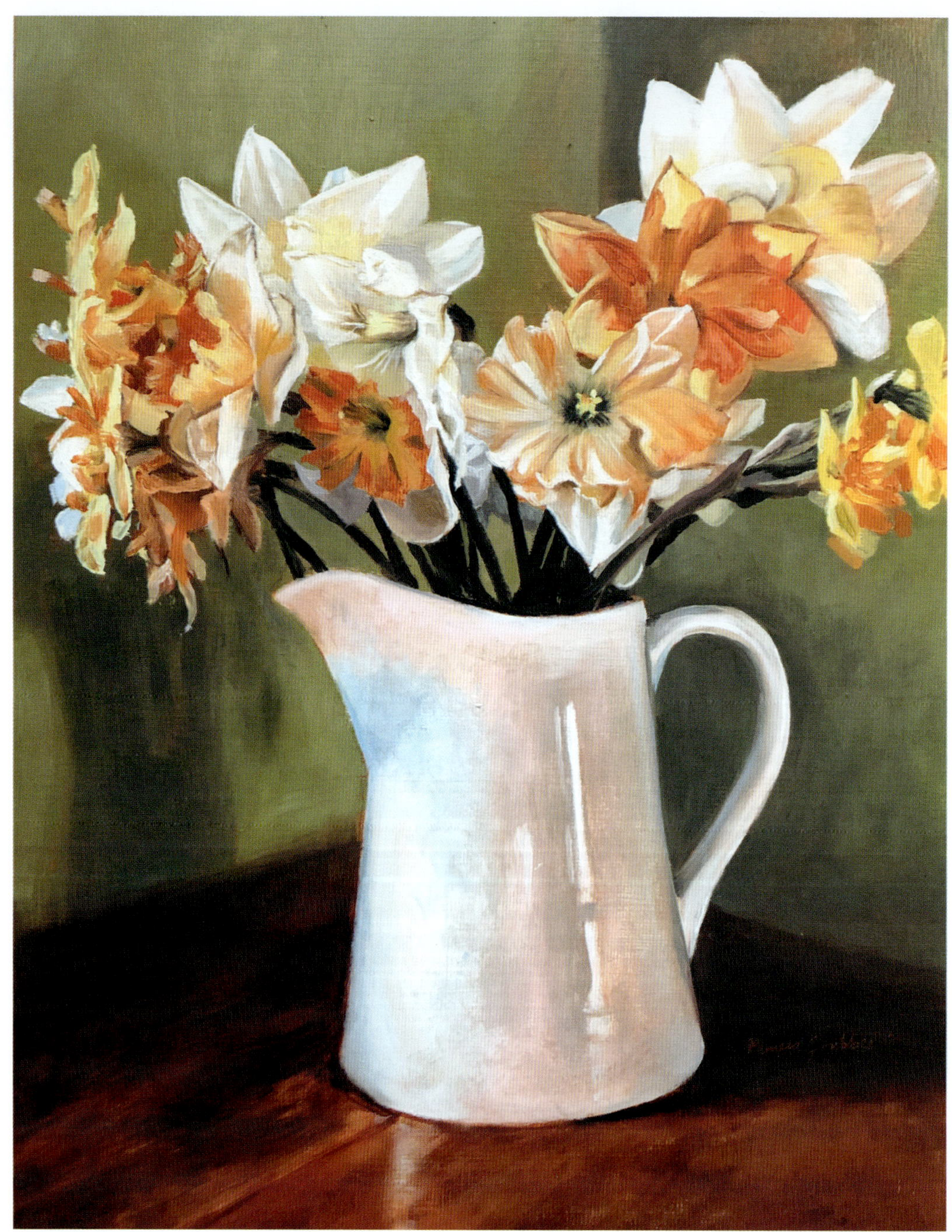

Pamela Grabber, Wisconsin

RESILIENCE

Two autumns ago, my husband John and I planted 100 daffodil bulbs in anticipation of a glorious spring bloom. They didn't disappoint! With COVID-19 canceling so much this year, the arrival of these beauties served as a reminder of all that was NOT canceled. What we hadn't anticipated were the three hard freezes that came after their blooming. One night, John hastily picked this bouquet as a means to enjoy their beauty should the frost cull the rest. The frost did its damage, but John won the day! I painted these daffodils as a tribute to the resilience God gives His children in troubled times.

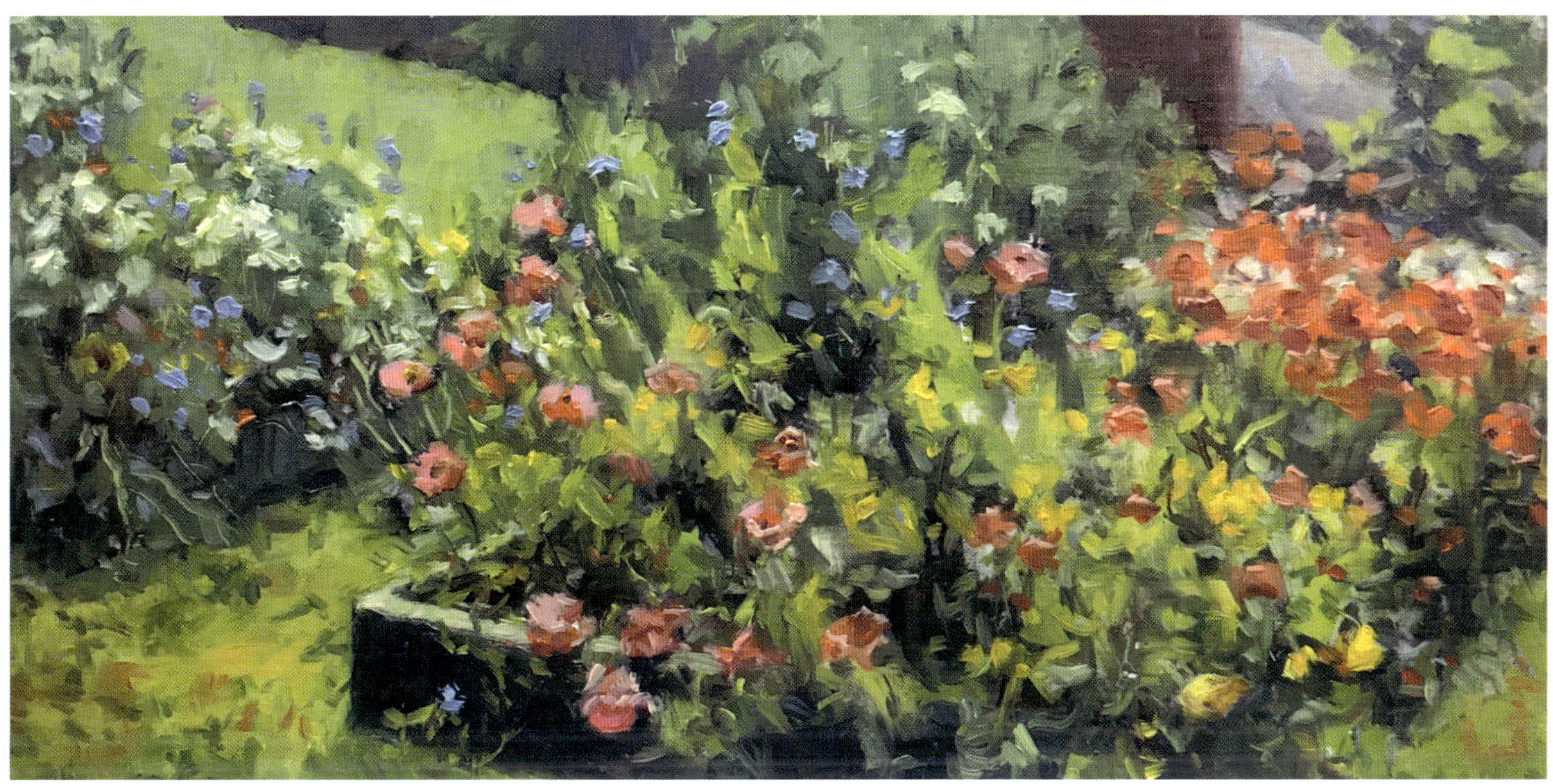

Pamela Lussier, New Hampshire

ISLAND GARDEN

I painted this in the tiny studio space I set up in my apartment for sheltering at home. I am missing flowers so much and Monhegan Island. I found painting this to be very uplifting. I hope the collector who buys this painting will feel the warmth and joy and will also be uplifted. I was looking forward to spring/summer 2020. I had made a full, but balanced, schedule of plein-air events, art shows, and painting workshops for both my husband—plein-air painter David Lussier—and I. Our oldest daughter was getting married on Monhegan Island in June and our first grandchild would be born in Missouri in July. I was looking forward to meeting her and hoped to help take care of her for a few weeks. Then, in a heartbeat, everything changed! All our carefully laid plans were postponed or canceled. The grandbaby will still be born of course, but when will I ever see her? I admit to being in a panic for a few days and feeling grief at missing those special life events. Then a picture began to form. Why don't we form some online critique groups? We could include the people we work with within the area, and we could even invite our friends from other workshop locations. Thus, David Lussier's Art Circle was formed. It has been such a blessing for us and for the people who are participating in it. The paintings people have been making are amazing and provide a great support system with a purpose.

Jim McVicker, California
PEONY

In California, we have had the shelter-in-place order for the past two months. I have been painting each day out on the landscape as well as in my studio, painting still lifes and a couple of self-portraits. As sad and as tragic as this has been for so many people, I have felt so fortunate to be healthy and to be an artist. I have found that the quiet time at home and in my studio, without any commitments, has been something I have been longing for, for a while. I am mostly focused, and excited to immerse myself in my work. Part of that focus has been spending more time painting still lifes, and this piece—*Peony*—is one of my works from this May. It's the first peony to flower in our garden after planting more than 10 years ago.

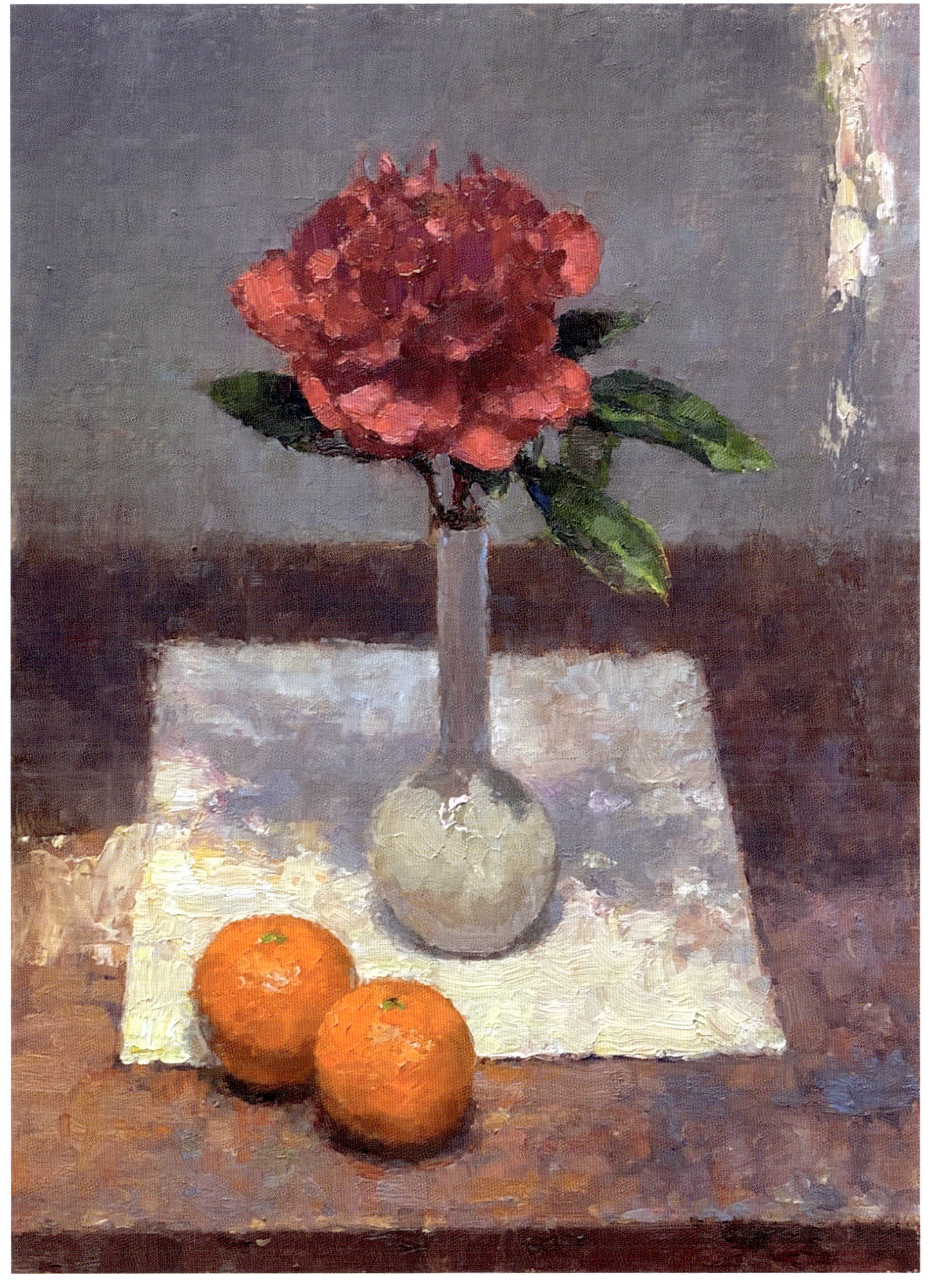

12 STILL LIFE

For me, the great gift of painting is that it not only requires me to take time to reflect but also simultaneously offers a constructive outlet into which I can channel those reflections. When the pandemic hit, I had a full calendar of painting commissions and workshops lined up, all of which suddenly fell away. Although the transition was a bit of a shock, I grew to become deeply grateful for the opportunity to reconnect with and steep in my own immediate surroundings. Through painting, I have weaved those surroundings into a visual tapestry that resonates with me personally, and that hopefully will resonate with the viewer as well.

Joseph Daily
Vestal, New York

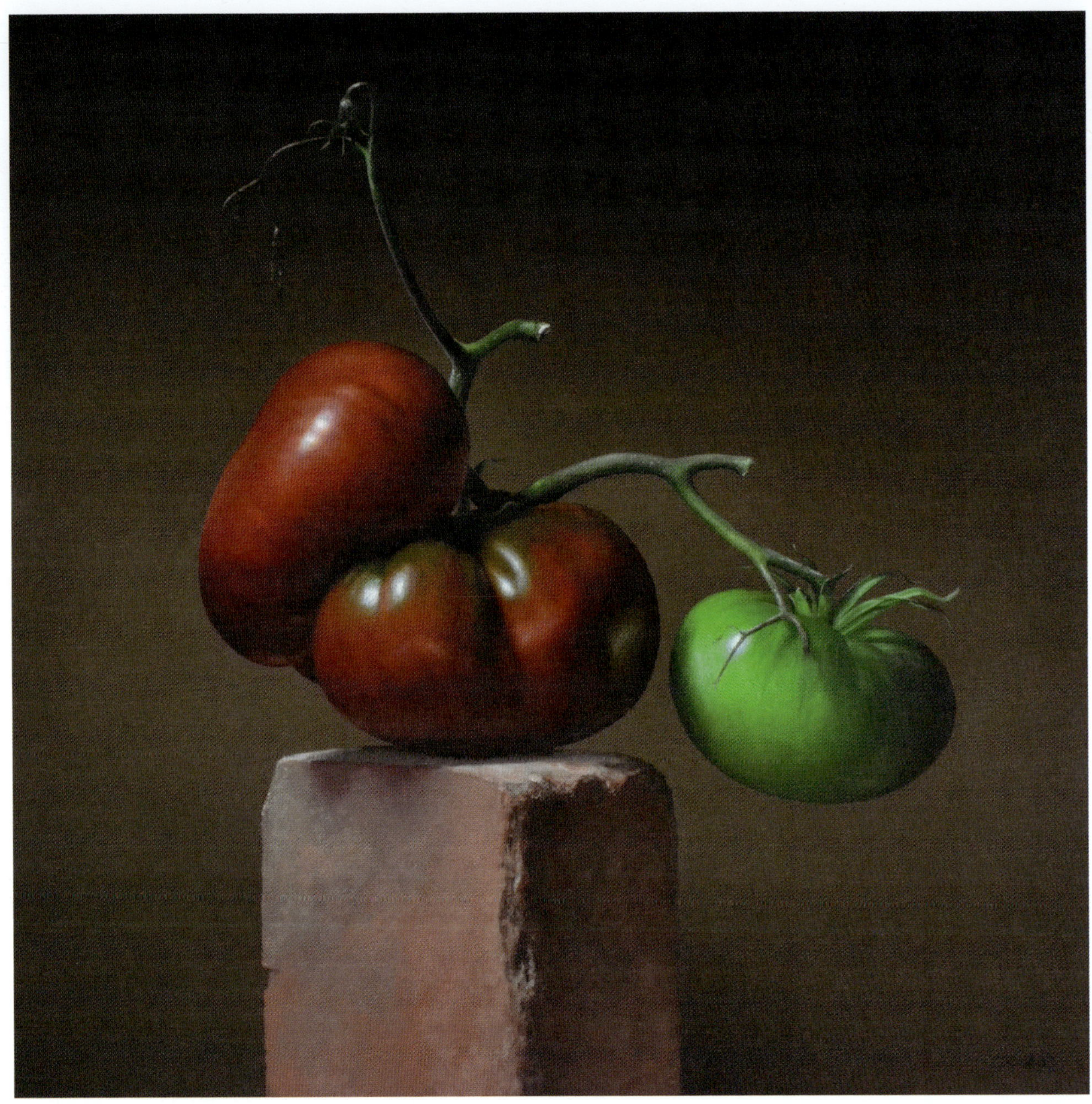

Trish Coonrod, New York

HEIRLOOM TOMATOES

I grew these particular tomatoes in my garden last summer. When I first noticed them, something about their shapes and how they're connected got my attention; I picked them still green and brought them to my studio. Over the next few days, as I was thinking about composing them, the larger one started to ripen quickly. This change in color brought to mind the idea of time, while their connection got me thinking about human connections. To me, this painting hints at a potential family dynamic. The larger, more mature fruit holds up the younger one, protecting it; and they are balanced there with care on a rough, but solid brick. This painting symbolizes the shutdown for me because I've been fortunate enough to spend these last three months with my family, and I believe that that time together will be a lasting memory for my husband, children, and me.

Roger Firestone, Virginia

LOOK THROUGH THE RAFTERS

While walking through the old mercantile building on the grounds of the Farnsworth estate, I found myself looking up at these rafters and the abstract geometric shapes that were constructed years ago. The shapes and sizes really intrigued me and caught my attention, along with the window in the distance giving the composition even more depth. The hook and pulley hanging down added an even more surreal abstract sound to the overall composition.

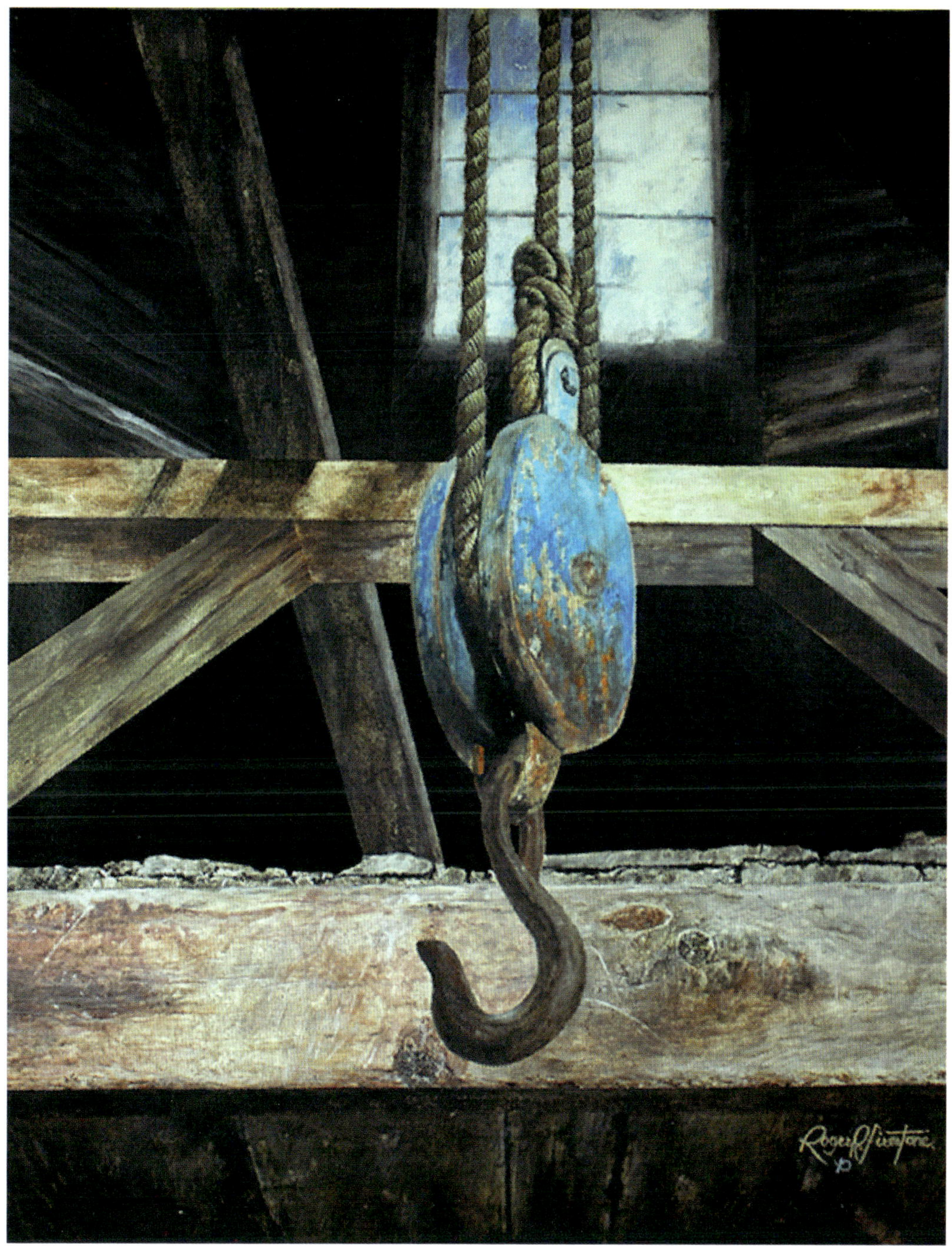

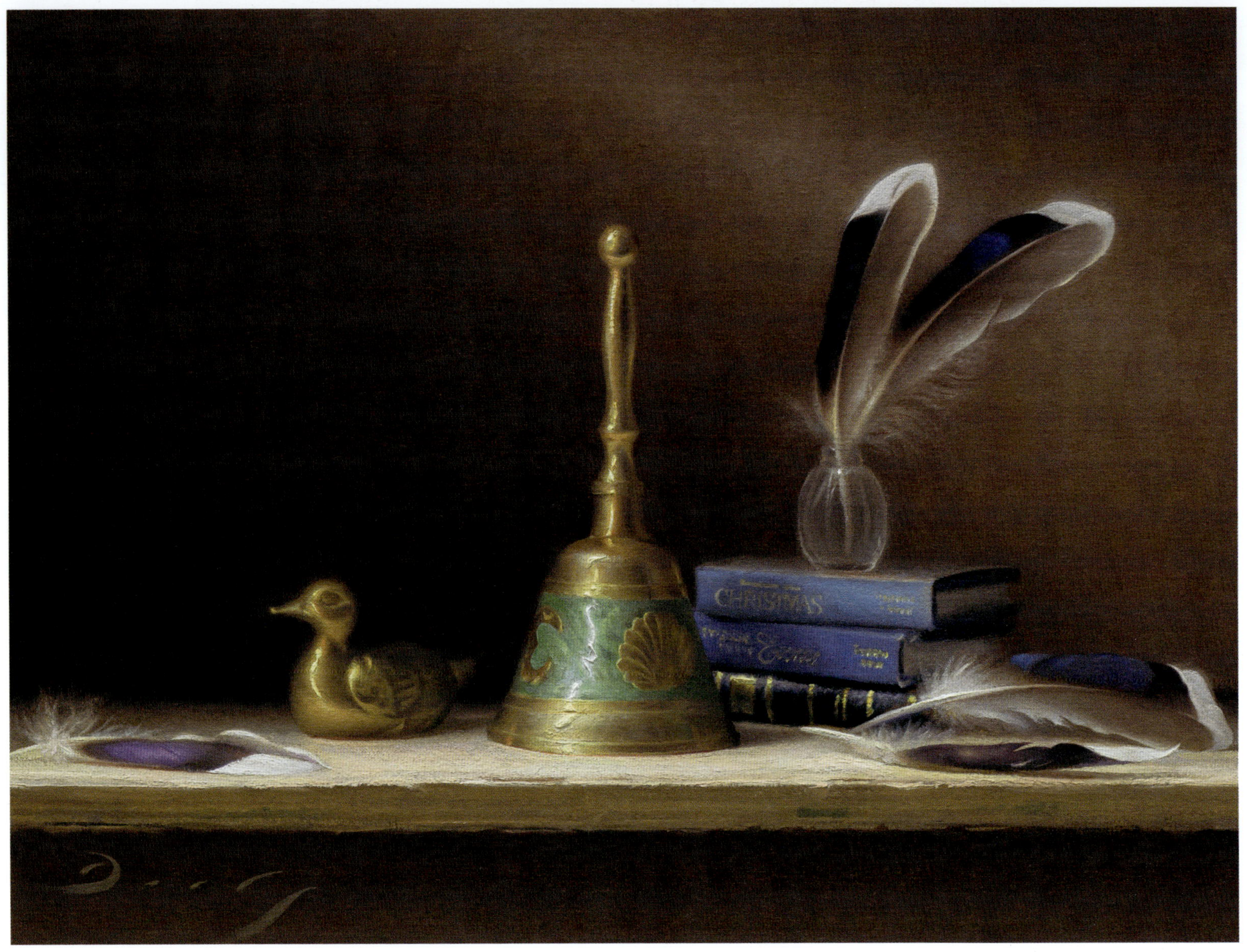

Joseph Daily, Pennsylvania
CALLED AWAY

With several painting commissions postponed during the COVID-19 lockdown, I suddenly found myself with time to pursue personal works. This still life is the first to come out of this period. It is a tribute to Schnappi, a duck who brightened up our property for almost nine years before recently disappearing. Schnappi was the last duckling in the nest to hatch, and when my brother-in-law discovered her, she had been abandoned. My mother-in-law quickly stepped in as Schnappi's surrogate mom—for a time, Schnappi would only fall asleep while resting in her hand—and it was beautiful to witness the bond that grew between them. All we have now are our memories, which are a joy to reflect upon; and her feathers, which were a joy to paint. I'm so grateful to my wife for having collected some of these feathers when Schnappi molted so that I could bid her a fond farewell now through this painting.

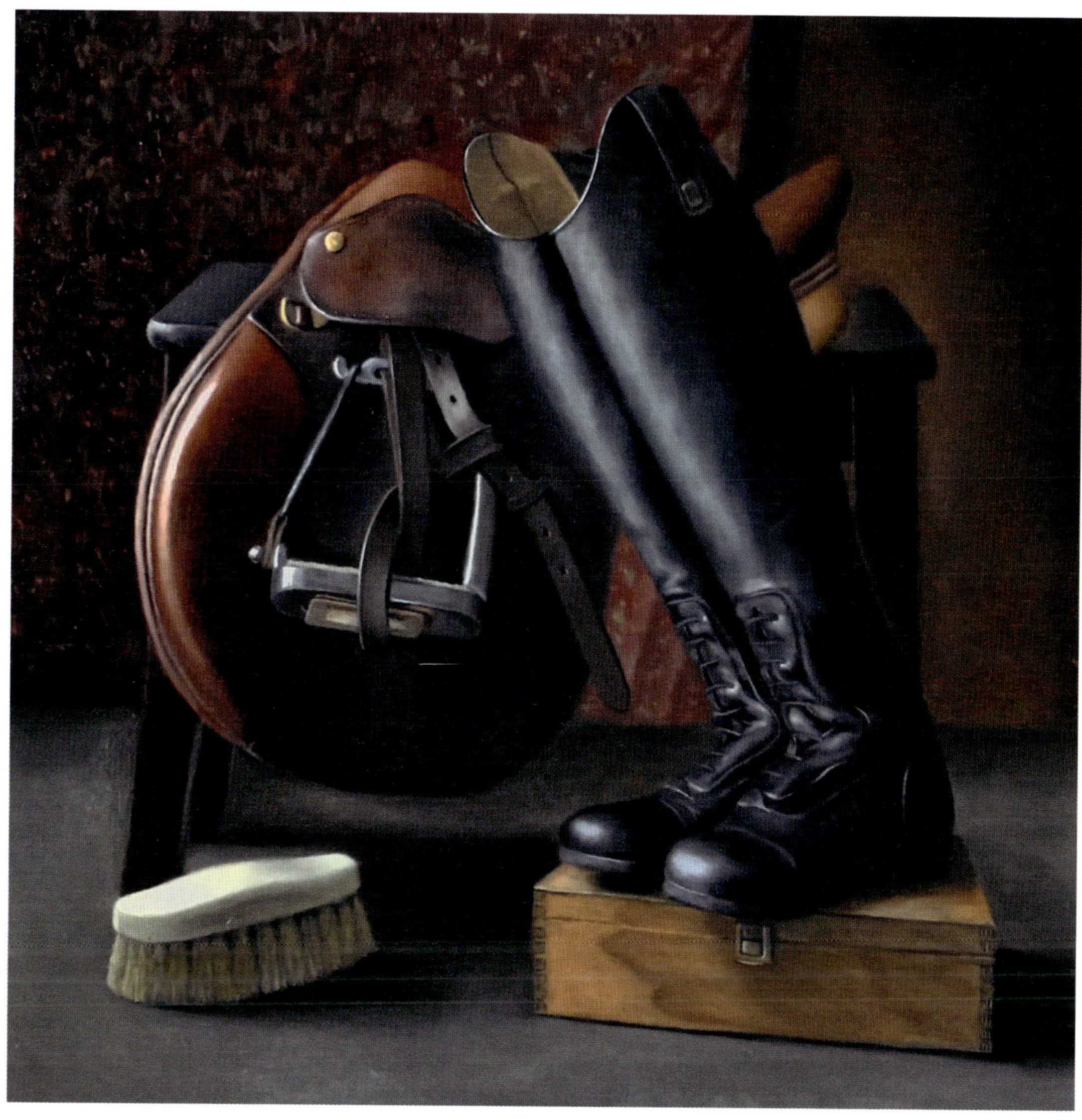

Claire Taveras, New York
EQUESTRIAN ATTRIBUTES

When I was younger, I was an avid horseback rider, and my saddle was and still is one of my most prized possessions. The unique experience of riding a horse, as well as the aesthetic of the sport, have always been major inspirations of mine. It's a sport that strives to keep the tradition alive, like I do when I paint. When the quarantine began, I felt incredibly inspired to begin to undertake more ambitious projects that I had been excitedly planning for a while. I painted this prior to moving into a studio, so I set up this still life in a cramped corner in my room, with the frustratingly inconsistent natural light from my window as my only light source. I found myself painting right up until the sunset, squinting at the painting in the dimming light. Despite the uncomfortable conditions, my experience painting this work was of deep meditation and calm. This painting taught me a lot about rhythm, composition, and atmosphere; and the lessons I learned from it have helped me with every painting I have done since.

But most importantly, the act of creating this painting was an incredible source of comfort to me while I grieved the death of a family member resulting from COVID-19. In a way, this painting has been a culmination of everything I love about art: the technique, the craft, its ability to soothe in the toughest of times, and its permanence in a time when everything is changing.

The frame for this painting was also handmade by me, as I strive to master the craft of creating a piece of art from the beginning through to when it is hanging on the wall. The frame was inspired by Italian cassetta frames of the 16th century.

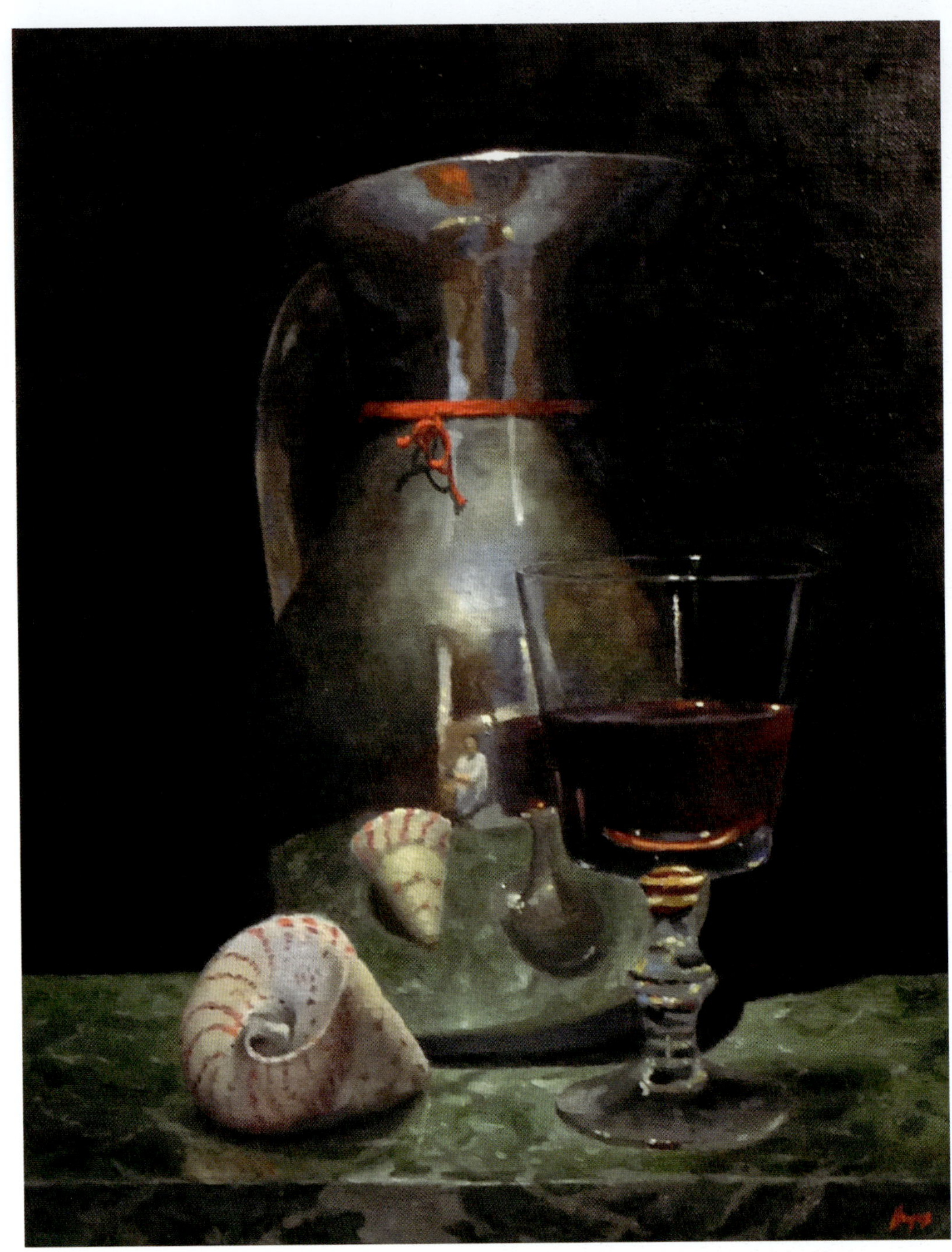

Jeffrey Hayes, Massachusetts
RED CHERRIES, SILVER CUP, 2020

When the darkness surrounds us, we come together and reflect each other's light.

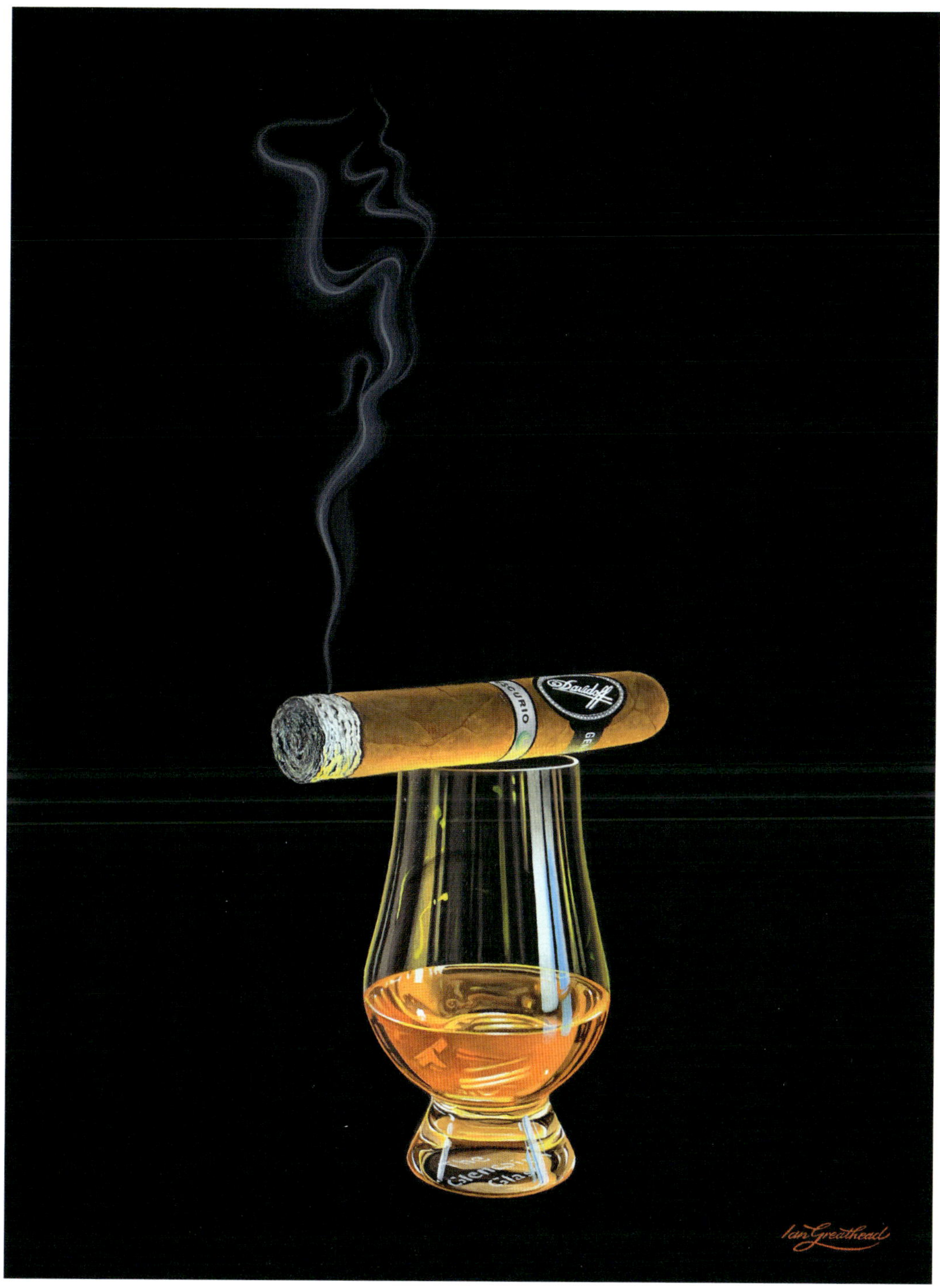

Ian Greathead, Georgia

DAVIDOFF AND BOURBON

As an artist, I feel fortunate to be able to work during the pandemic. Though I am painting daily, the rest of my life has changed drastically. No more restaurant meals, a trip to Paris has been canceled and get-togethers with friends have been put on hold. A weekly trip to the grocery store is a carefully managed event using a face mask and plenty of hand sanitizer. The one bright spot for me and my wife is that we get to see our two grandchildren daily. Our daughter is working remotely and needs help keeping the one-year-old and 4-year-old from joining her client Zoom conversations! Day care isn't an option because of the risk involved in passing on the virus to our son-in-law, who is immunosuppressed; so we get to help out. Even though the world has been turned upside down, this painting reflects the satisfaction I get at the end of each day relaxing with a good bourbon and reflecting on how fortunate I am to enjoy painting daily and spending time with a loving family. Life is good!

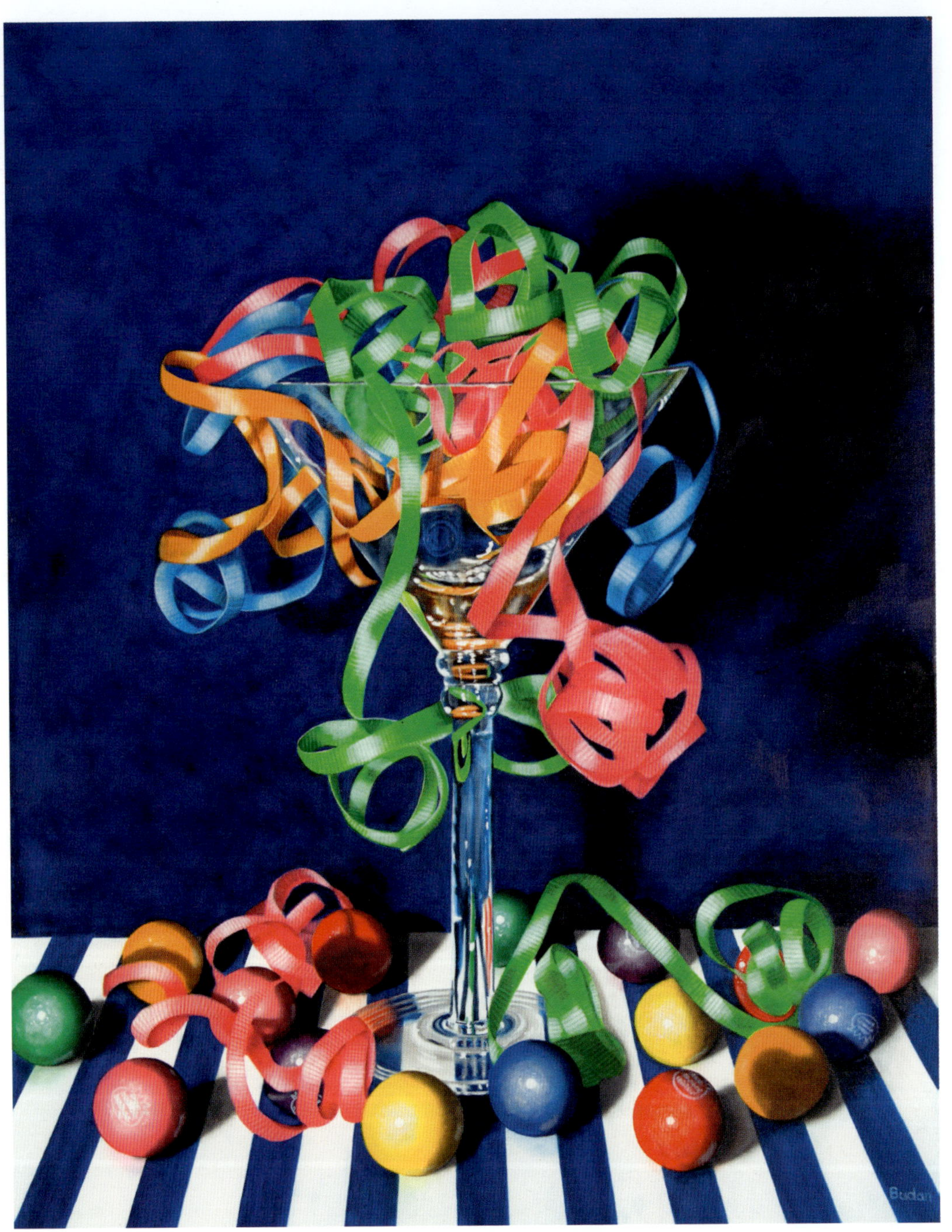

Karen Budan, Arizona

MERRY MARTINI

I decided at the start of this COVID crisis that I needed to paint something happy. As I looked through my collection of still life objects, I was drawn to the bright colors of my bag of gumballs and curly ribbons. The result was this concept, which does make me smile. From the start, I was calling it *Merry Martini*. However, a good friend saw what I was working on and suggested I call it *Quarantini* or *Quarantini Blues*. I thought her suggestions were actually kind of neat and wondered if I should change my title. I decided to ask my followers on Instagram and Facebook which of the three titles they preferred. I got a lot of responses and comments.

After tallying the votes from Instagram, Facebook and Messenger, it was a near tie between *Merry Martini* and *Quarantini*, with *Quarantinid* being two votes ahead. But I decided to stay with *Merry Martini* for two reasons. First, I realized that without my intro as to why I was painting this piece, there is absolutely nothing in the painting itself that says quarantine. This was brought home even more to me when people suggested I add a mask or something. If someone just saw the painting itself without my intro, and saw the title of *Quarantini*, I can see them saying to themselves, "I don't get it." Second, many comments spoke to how bad this crisis has been for them as they have lost friends and relatives or suffered financially. They did not want a reminder of this very sad time, which is understandable. After all, my original intent was to paint something happy that would make me, and other viewers smile. So *Merry Martini* it is. I agree...I hope to leave COVID-19 behind in the future.

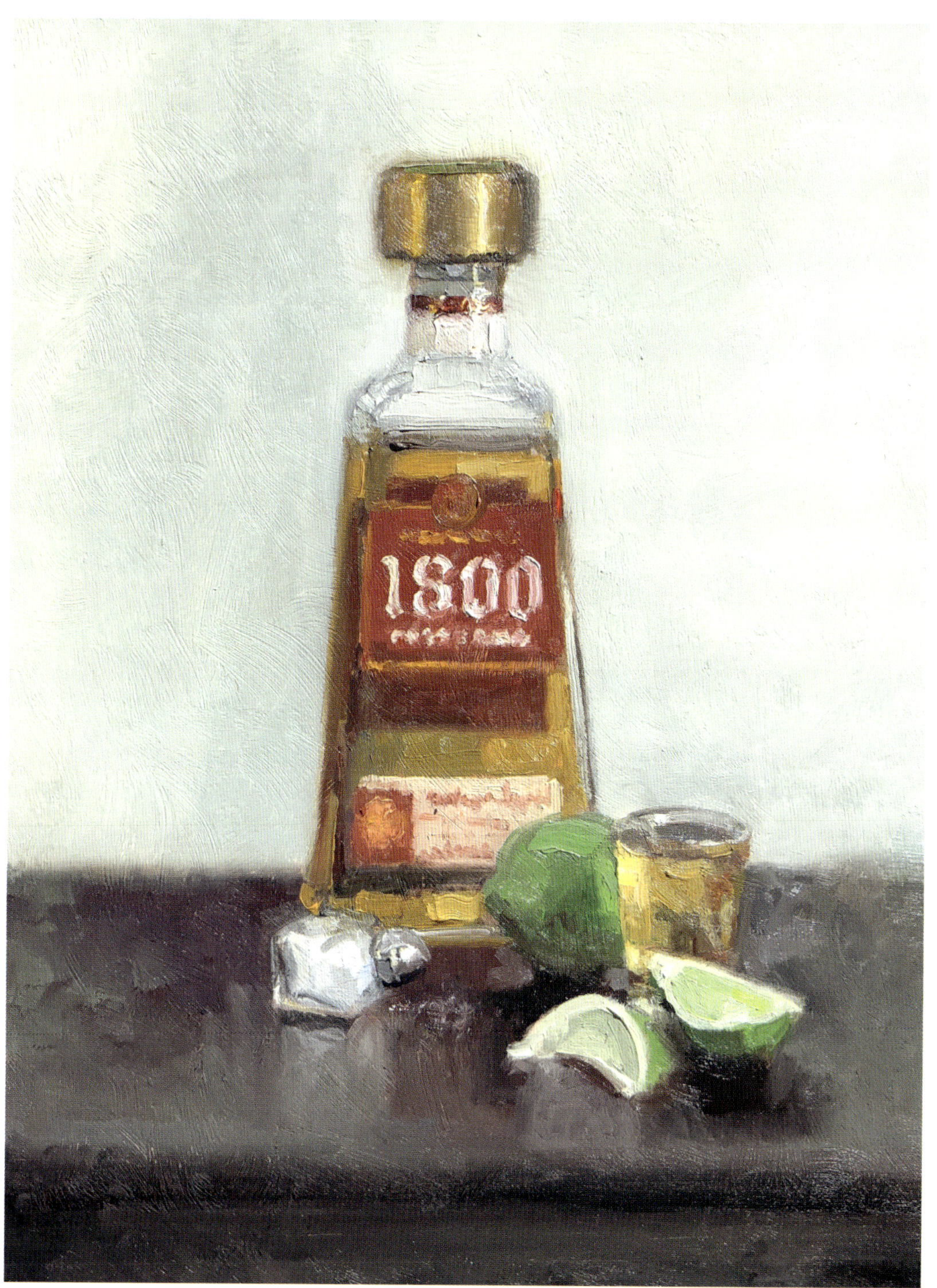

Mitch Kolbe, North Carolina

CURE FOR THE CORONAVIRUS

This painting, entitled *Cure for the Coronavirus*, is quite a personal story, as I had vowed to give up drinking alcohol in January 2020 as part of a movement I had heard about on NPR [National Public Radio] to abstain for one month. January slid into February, no problem. I didn't miss alcohol one bit and was surprised at how easy it was for me to give up the habit. March came and I had been following the news about this virus starting to come into our country and decided to take action myself by first canceling a workshop that I was to give toward the end of March. I went out with friends for the last time on Saturday, March 14th to celebrate my and my wife's birthday, as we are only six days apart in age. You could see people in the restaurant already eyeballing one another suspiciously.

Since then, my wife and I have stayed at home. Being an artist, it wasn't that difficult for me to stay at home anyway, as I do it all the time, painting from my home studio. I felt sorry for the rest of the people who had no clue how to work for themselves at home, and for the long lines of people that I saw on the news, waiting in their cars for food. I couldn't believe this was America. This painting is dedicated to them.

On April 13th, the day after that story broke, I was inspired to paint the liquor bottles that were now accumulating dust in my pantry. First, because I had never seen a still life of the ingredients that go into a cocktail, and second, because liquor bottles are just so colorful and interesting looking; not to mention the more obvious but also deeper meaning that lies in maybe imbibing during this time of fear and uncertainty. I painted them as honestly and simply as I could, striving to suggest the scene, rather than paint them literally. I painted the first *Cure for the Coronavirus* and it sold almost immediately on Facebook. This one is the third in the series and one of my favorites because I love tequila, and I love the shape and design of the bottle. Oh, and did I mention I'm drinking again?

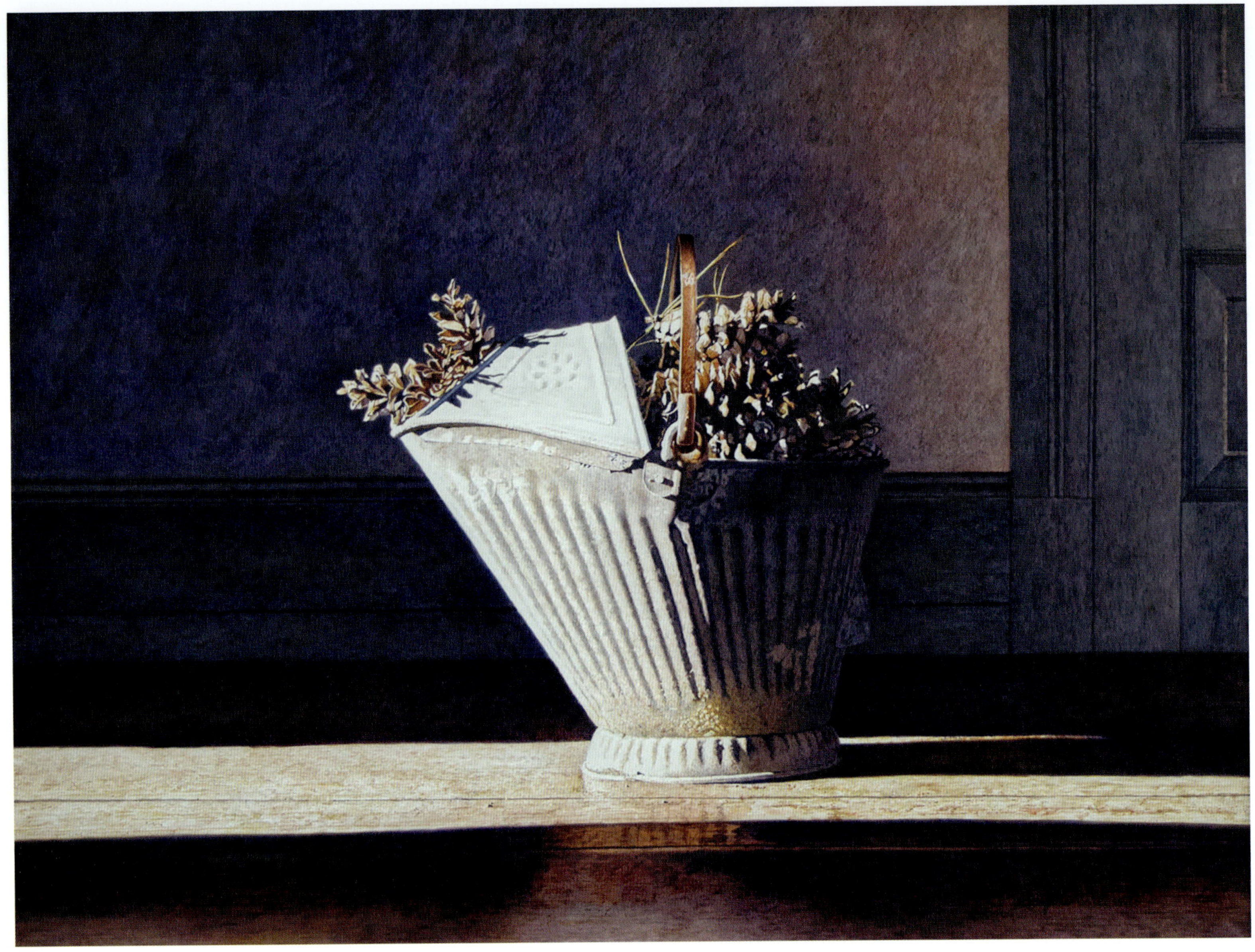

Douglas Wiltraut, Pennsylvania
SCUTTLE BUCKET

Collecting pine cones is something I have done since my childhood, beginning with family vacations to the Great Smoky Mountains and to Maine. We have also heated our home with a wood stove for over 40 years, so the ash bucket gets a heavy-duty workload during the winter. Here in the off-season, the "scuttle bucket" finds another use, as it holds the firestarters for the upcoming season. The pine cones, normally found outside, are now, like us, residing inside due to the pandemic.

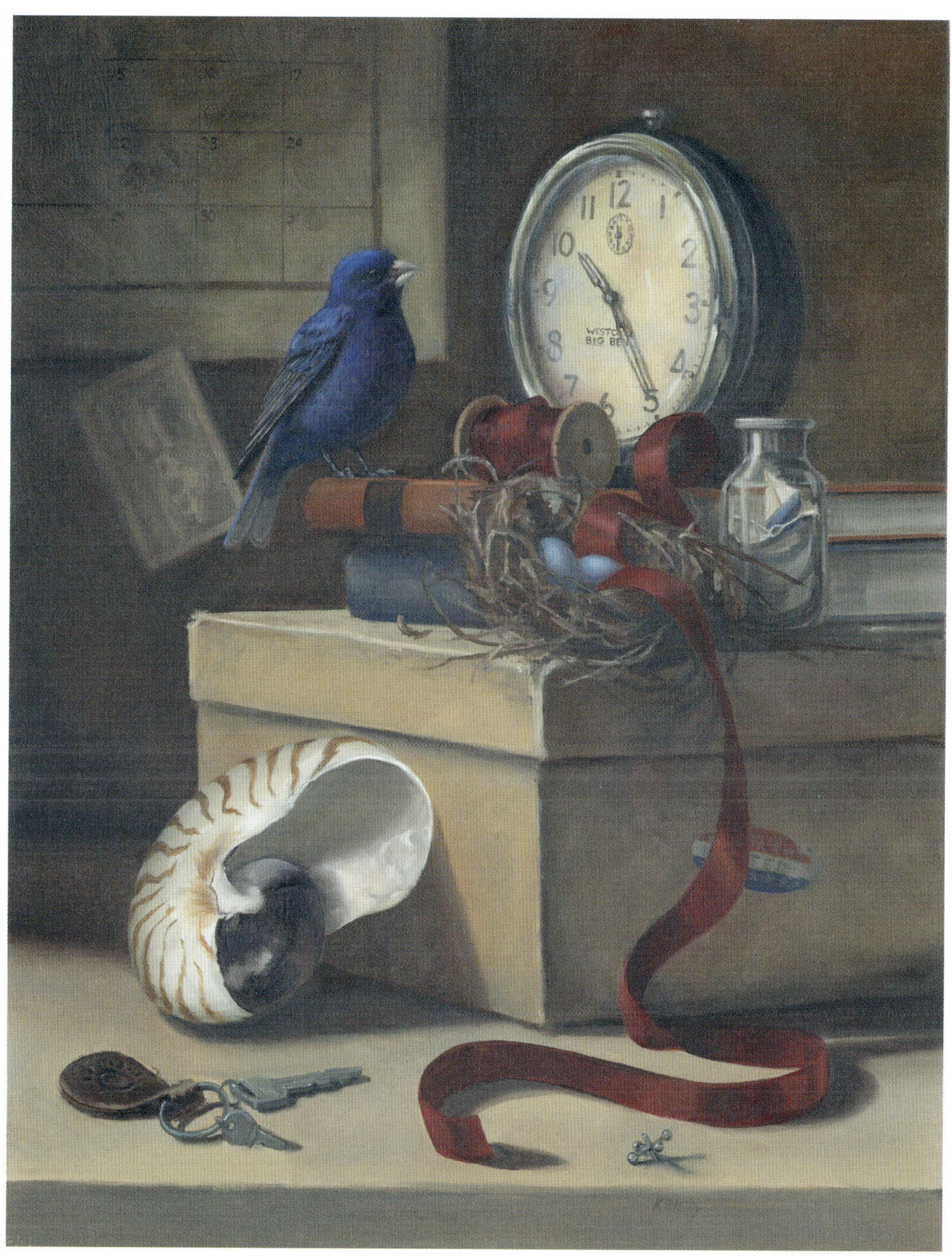

Katharine Krieg, Pennsylvania

TIME CAPSULE

My works of still life tend toward the more reflective, quiet side of me and this piece is no different. In troublesome times, I prefer to concentrate on looking ahead and imagining what will be said after steering through the mess. So much of quarantine in 2020 has a "suspended in time" feeling—jobs, classrooms, calendars were left, in many cases, without much warning. As the quarantine continues, it allows for speculation on how this time will be seen and how it was spent. Finding a message in a bottle, or discovering a time capsule, seemed to fit with all this. Color and value were controlled to mimic the feel of an old photo. The unhatched nest, the car keys, the voting sticker, and the turbulent sea in the bottle, are all overseen by an old alarm clock and a patient indigo bunting—a springtime migratory bird. This unique time can be when lessons are learned from experience, but intentions and actions are directed toward the future.

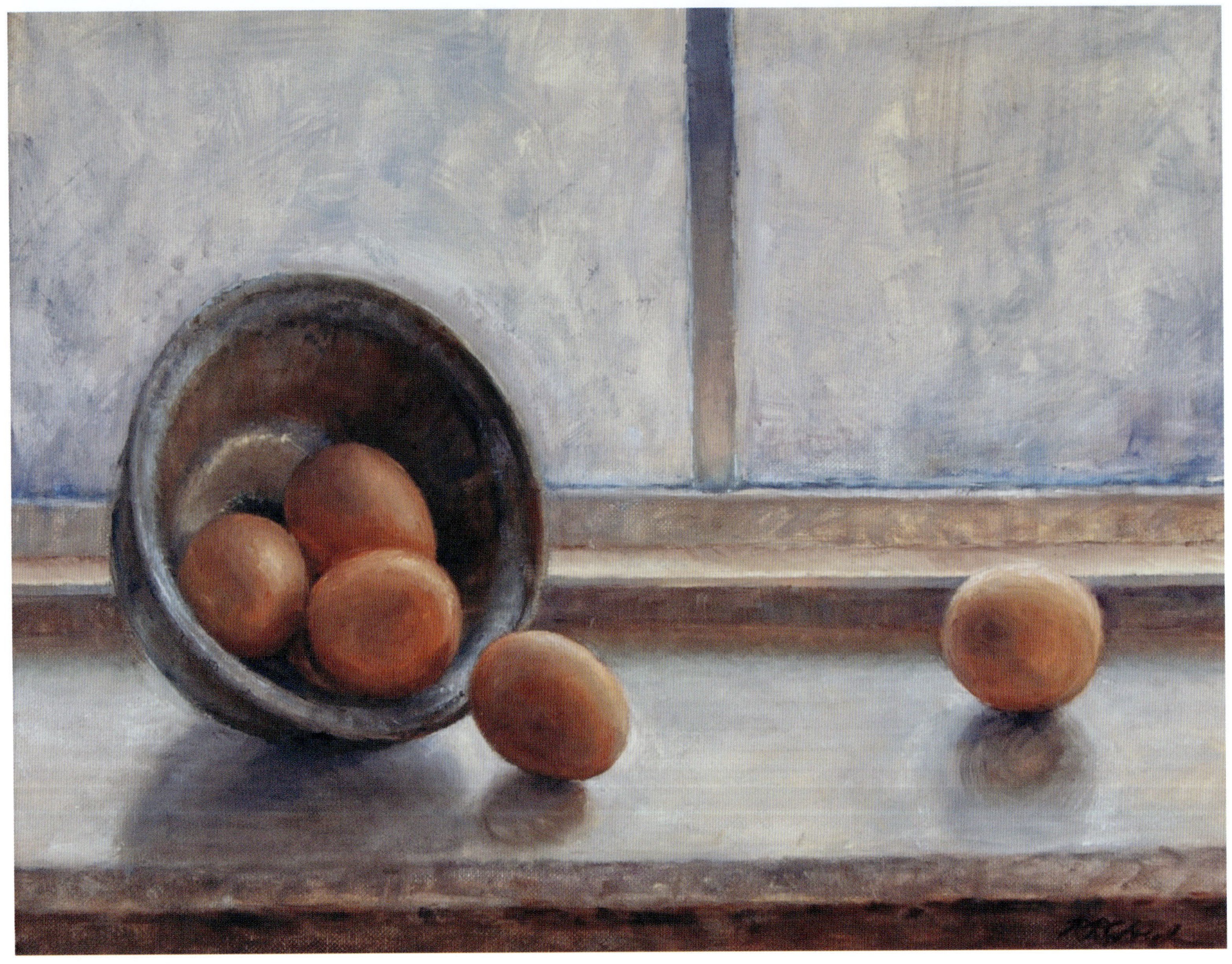

R.R. Christensen, New Mexico
INSIDE LOOKING OUT

I love portraiture and figurative work, but when it became impossible to safely paint from live models due to COVID, I began setting up still lifes in the large windows of my studio. Even though I missed interacting with my subjects and other artists, I found so much joy in contemplating the simple beauty of a farm-fresh egg and gazing out the window at the world we're all trying to keep safe.

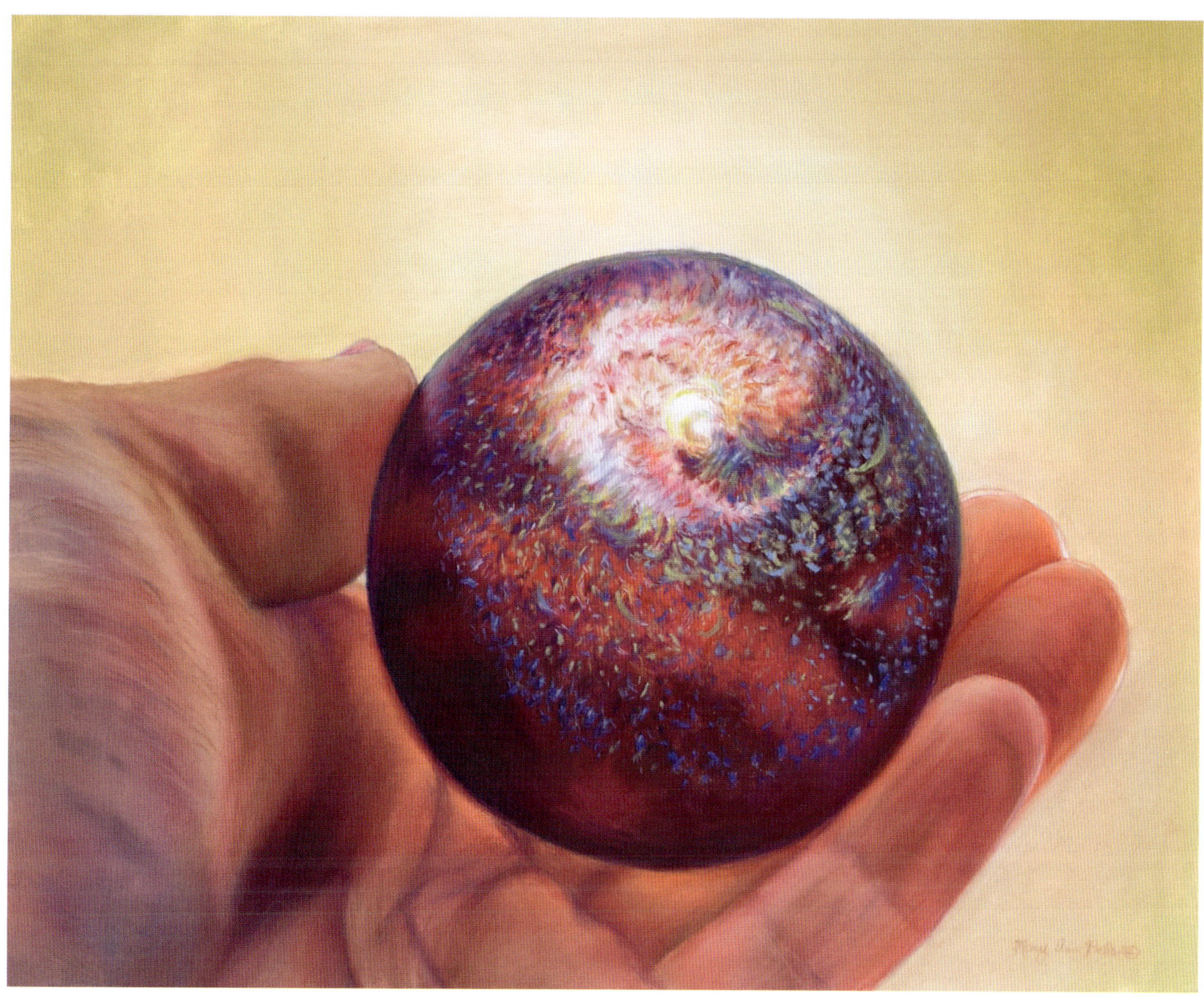

Mary Ann Pals, Indiana
POMEGRANATE GALAXY

Once the shelter-in-place order came during this pandemic, I became increasingly filled with a sense of dread about the future. How long will this last? How is this going to affect my art career? As it turned into many weeks of sheltering at home, and a "new normal" started to emerge, an even more poignant question arose in my mind: Going forward, how am I going to recreate myself as an artist? How will I market my artwork now? How will I go about teaching my art classes and workshops? I was left with even more questions, not less.

It all left me feeling very small. I sifted through my hundreds of reference photos for a possible painting to start, and one image floated to the top of the stack. It was a picture I took of my hand holding a large glass galaxy marble that I purchased last fall from a glass artist friend. I absolutely love playing with the marble, watching the shimmering stars dance in 3-D spirals of deep space. Yes, that was the painting I chose to tackle while sheltering in place. What a catharsis for me! I was able to totally immerse myself in the work and I imagined that I was in charge of a whole galaxy, turning it in my hand and exposing its beauty to changing light. The process of creating this work gave me the confidence I needed to start thinking about recreating my art career and forging ahead with some new plans. Most of the questions are still there, but my self-confidence is now gaining speed again. The process of creating a galaxy has revived me.

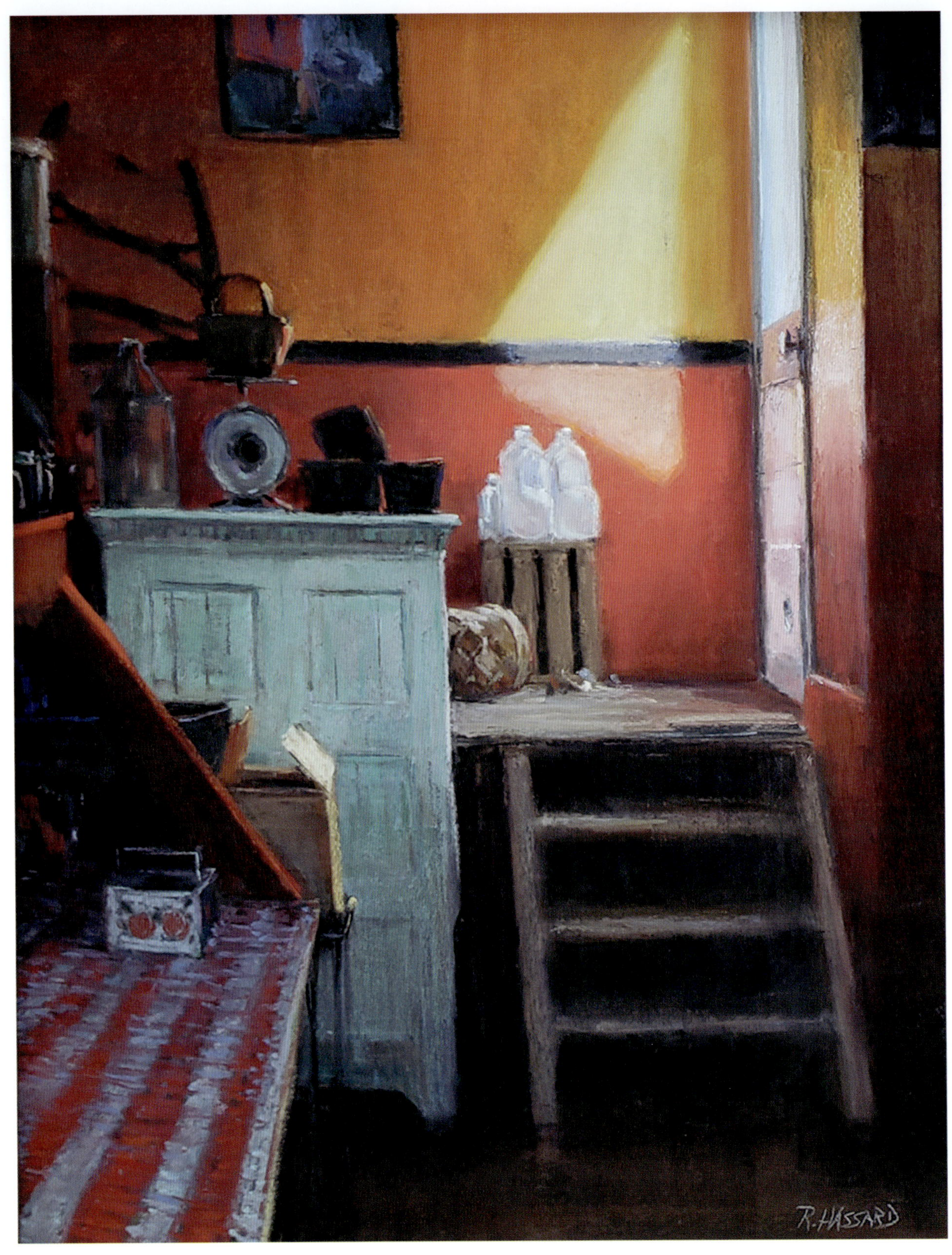
R.HASSARD

Ray Hassard, Ohio

MORNING LIGHT

For many years, I have painted at a nearby farm in Western Cincinnati. The farm is very large, with several ponds and acres of fruit trees. Ron, the farmer, has always been very welcoming and allowed me to bring artist friends and even classes there to paint. It is one of the most beautiful places I know in this area at all times of the year, and I consider it one of my "spiritual homes." Of course, 2020 was rocked in March by the pandemic and lockdown. Two friends and I decided to get out and paint at least once a week. On our second visit there, Ron was inside the small building that serves as the farm's produce outlet during the summer. I went inside to speak with him, and as we talked about the future in the dark, empty store, sunlight suddenly streamed in through the rear door onto the back wall. It seemed like a good sign; an omen of light in the darkness (literally) and hope. I took a few photos quickly; it moved on and disappeared shortly afterward. I showed them to my friends, and one said: "You should paint that!" *Morning Light* was done in my studio from the photos and from the memory of that moment. As the lockdown continued, we returned to the farm to paint the fruit trees in bloom and other scenes, and always felt peaceful contentment in being there.

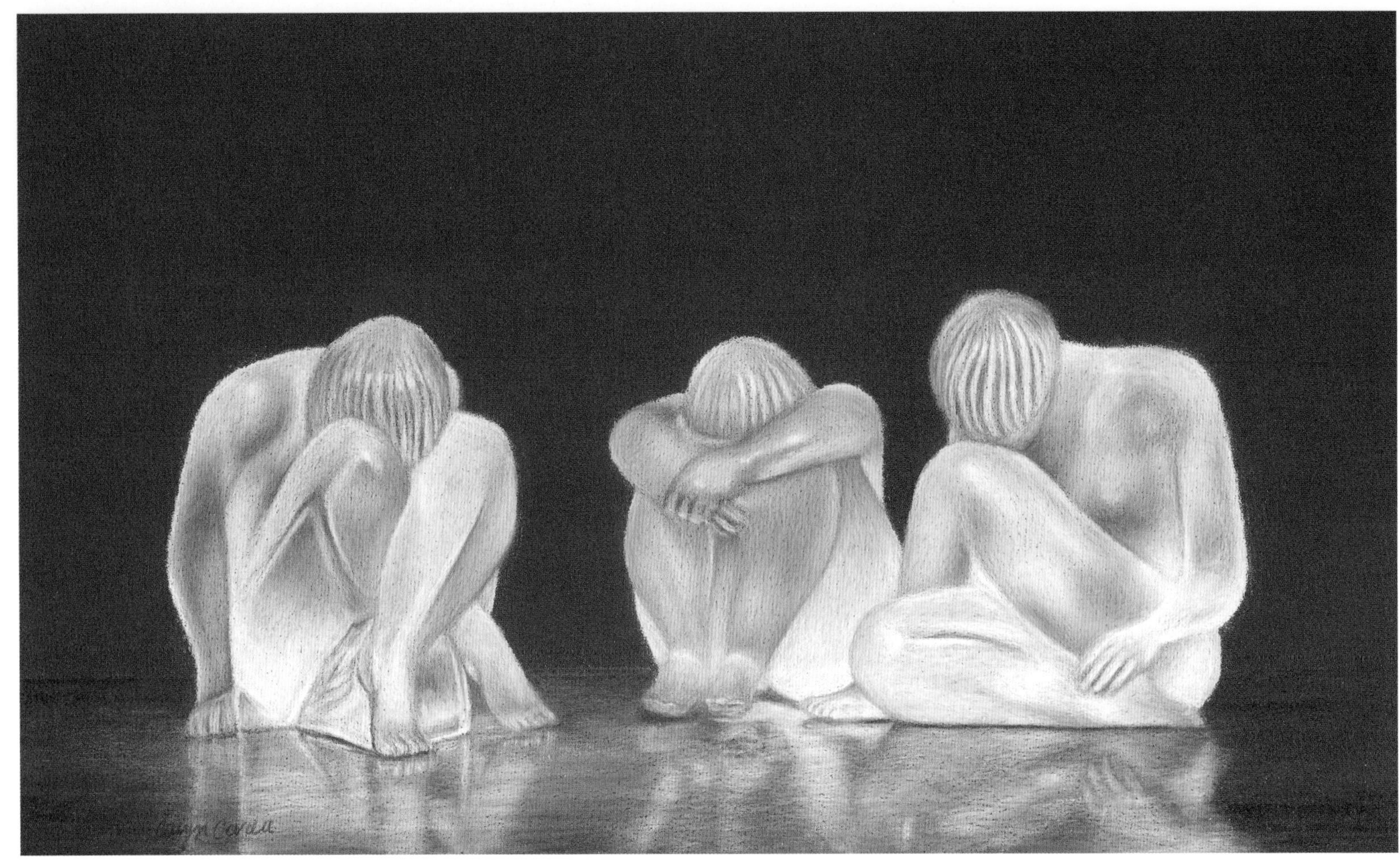

Caryn Coville, New York
ISOLATION

From the start of the pandemic, my mother, who is 87 years old and lives in an independent living community, was put into complete lockdown for three months. She was not allowed to leave her apartment. Her meals, packages, etc. were delivered to her. When I would talk to her, my mother's loneliness broke my heart. People moved to her community for socialization, and now they were completely isolated. I did this drawing to convey the isolation that my mother and the world we are living in were experiencing.

Stephanie Amato, Georgia

SPRING GODDESS

How has the Coronavirus and quarantine affected my life? It has given me the gift of time. With all shows, events, and workshops put on hold, I have taken the opportunity to look at the world that exists just outside my front door; to appreciate being close to my family, and to immerse myself completely into my work. With this year's mild winter and rainy spring, the flowers were bursting with blooms. I spent many days painting the irises in my own garden. This statue of the Greek goddess, Hebe, was never installed so I was able to move her into the flower bed and surround her with these flowers. This pandemic has put many things into perspective for me. I realize how lucky we are to live in a time where we can reach out to friends and family online. I appreciate that I live in a beautiful town where the shelter-in-place order is not a burden. And I am fortunate to capture the world through my artwork.

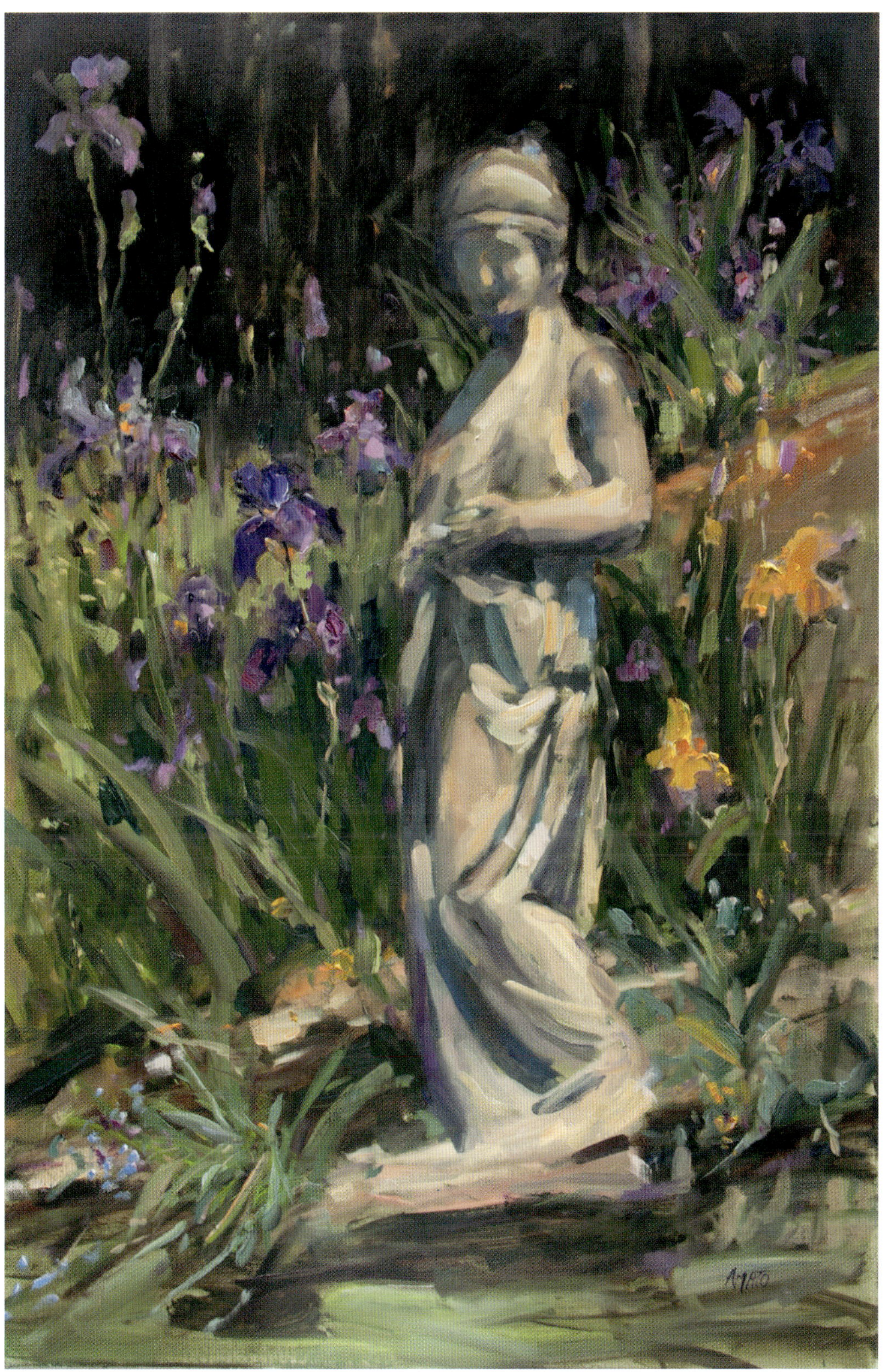

13 ABSTRACTS

I feel like I was raised on abstract art, and whenever possible I would go see exhibits in museums in New York, Boston, and Washington, DC. I enjoy modern and abstract art and really am a product of the '60s. This period of art is considered mid-century modern or modernism. I feel like my abstract collages nod back to this period.

At the start of COVID, I was so nervous. I didn't know what to do. Do we go out? Can we go to the grocery store? Can we see our family that has been out? Do we need to wash the exterior of our groceries? I was a nervous wreck. The only thing I found that would center me was to dive into some abstracts. I found that the abstracts were like solving a puzzle. I was engaged in the process and, for a time, could forget about the pandemic. They had a calming influence on me.

I began a series of pieces, adding more—and varied—ephemera. I was working with sculpting paste and coins from other places as well as my antique and mono-printed papers. I soon found that there was a critical situation with a loved one. I could not work in my studio on larger pieces and I had shorter blocks of time available. Because I found the process of creating abstracts so healthy for my brain, allowing it to create and solve, I decided to make a series of small abstracts on the covers of journals. I had to keep using my brain in a way that allowed me to be fully engaged. It is still the process I use to self-soothe and create calm. It is completely therapeutic for me.

Nina Chatham
Maitland, Florida

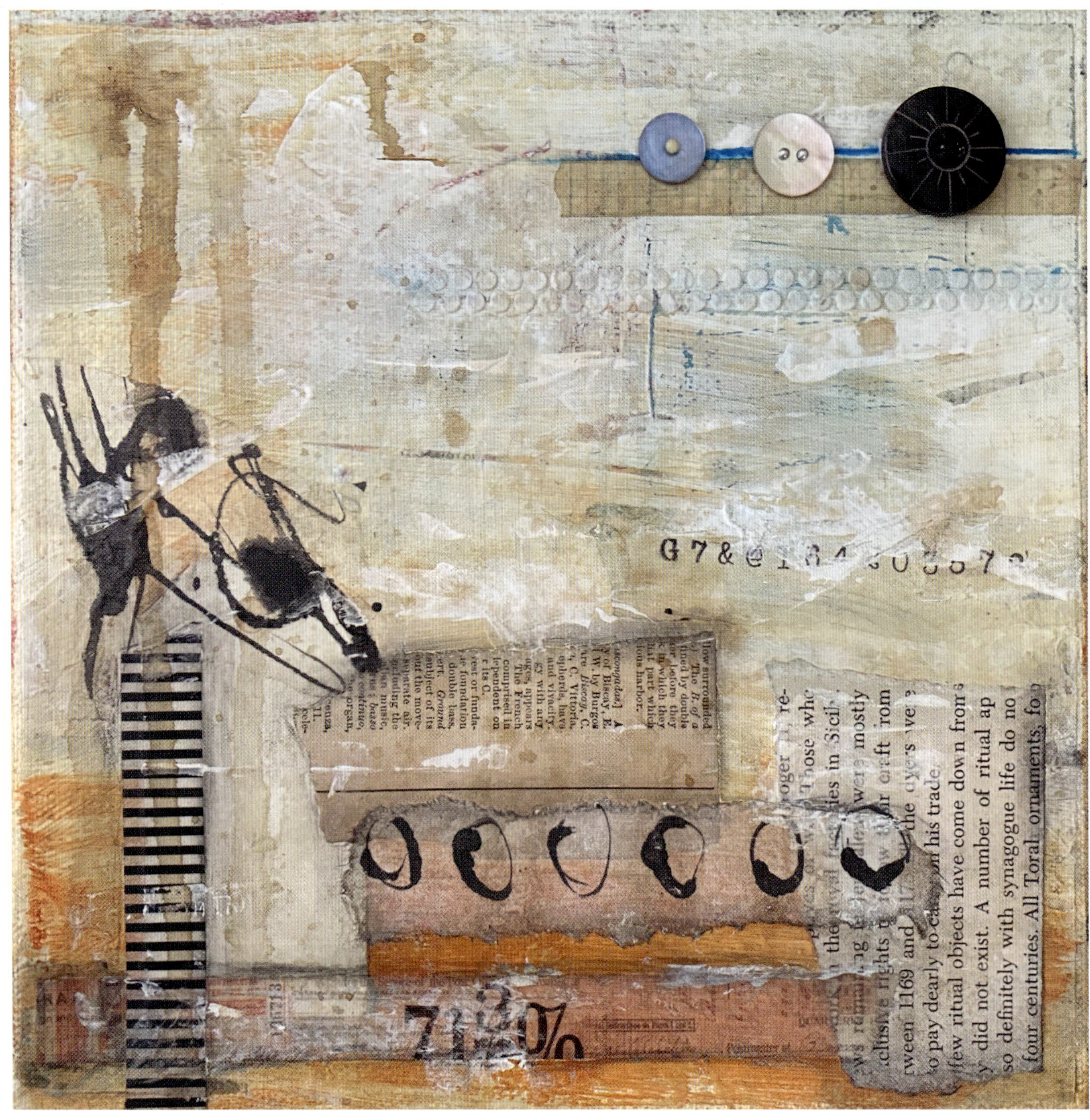

Nina Chatham, Florida
ENGAGEMENT

I have been very concerned during this pandemic because I have had pneumonia twice and am easily prone to bronchitis, so I started isolating early. I was productive at first and then became out of sorts. I knew I needed to start creating art. In general, I find that the process is always engaging and therapeutic for me. I decided to try something different; to make art for myself and to enjoy the process. I have discovered a variation of different techniques and this painting is the first and my favorite so far. As this crazy pandemic goes on, I got a call that my 92-year-old mother had a horrible fall, but I could not be with her, even though she was COVID-free. With my nervous energy, I did what I could and went right back to my drawing board. A month later, I am able to be with my mother and we are hoping for the best. During this unprecedented time, my art continues to comfort me as we continue to wait for a cure.

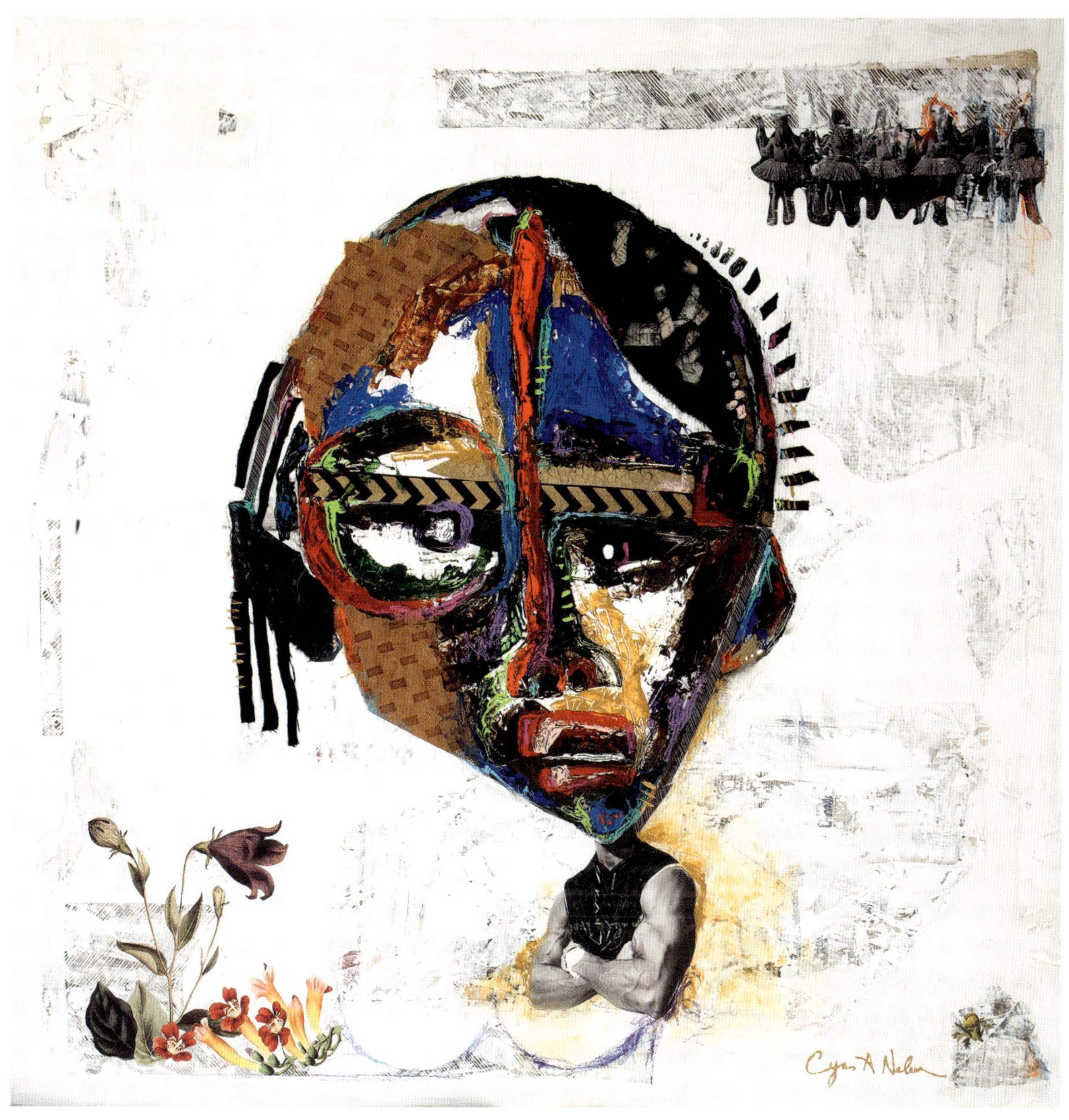

Cyrus A. Nelson, Georgia

BLACK SHEEP

Black Sheep was quite personal for me and many others have told me how relatable the piece is. Feelings of loneliness and isolation from loved ones during the pandemic can take a toll on one's mental health and wellness, and mine were both affected.

In spite of that, COVID-19 has been an unexpected blessing. One consequence of the pandemic was being furloughed, which eventually led to me leaving my corporate job. Not knowing what would happen next, I stepped out on faith, deciding to truly focus on my art. I was filled with anxiety and palpable fear, but I followed my heart.

Fortunately, I have been able to sell my work nationwide, and even overseas. I thank God for allowing me to be able to share my creativity and passion during this unfortunate time.

Black Sheep is about hope. We are all unique and special. Tap into your potential and flourish. Believe in yourself and the beauty that shines within you! Keep going!

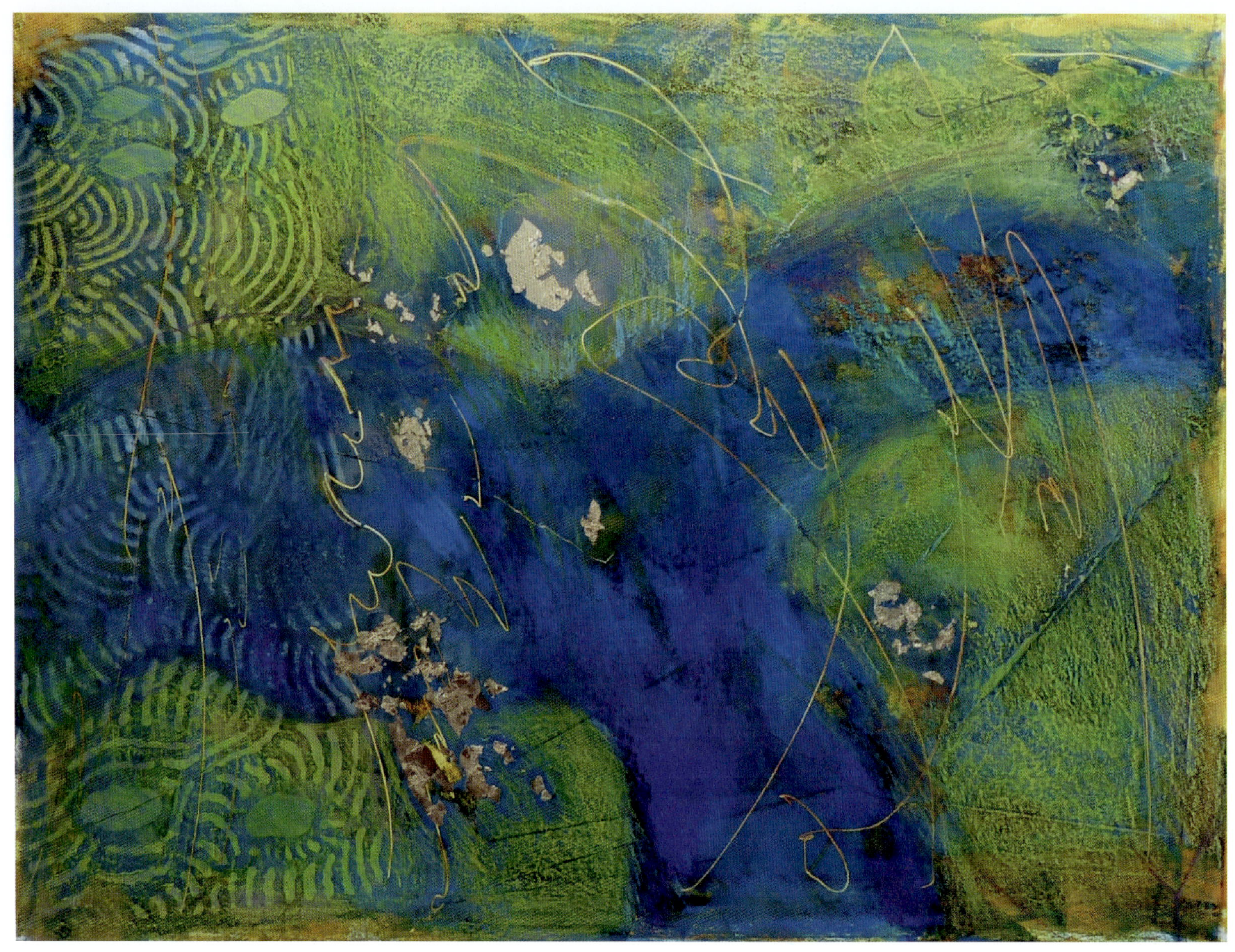

Bobbi Miller, Wyoming
HER SEARCH

Being sequestered in Florida during the winter months of the pandemic allowed for daily walks on the beach and time with my inner life. Dolphin tails breaking the ocean surface reminded me of mermaid tails and tales of mermaids. These fantasy stories ignited artistic inspiration.

Kathleen Quinn-Leslie, New York

MEDIATIONS IN THE GARDEN: THE ABERNATHY SERIES

The "Abernathy Series" is a group of paintings exploring the sensory experiences of the Abernathy family in the 1800s. Admiral Abernathy, his wife, and his children lived their lives traveling with the British Navy to India and the Far East. This artwork was ready to be shown at the "Member and Volunteer" show at the Tri-County Arts Council when the show was canceled because of quarantine.

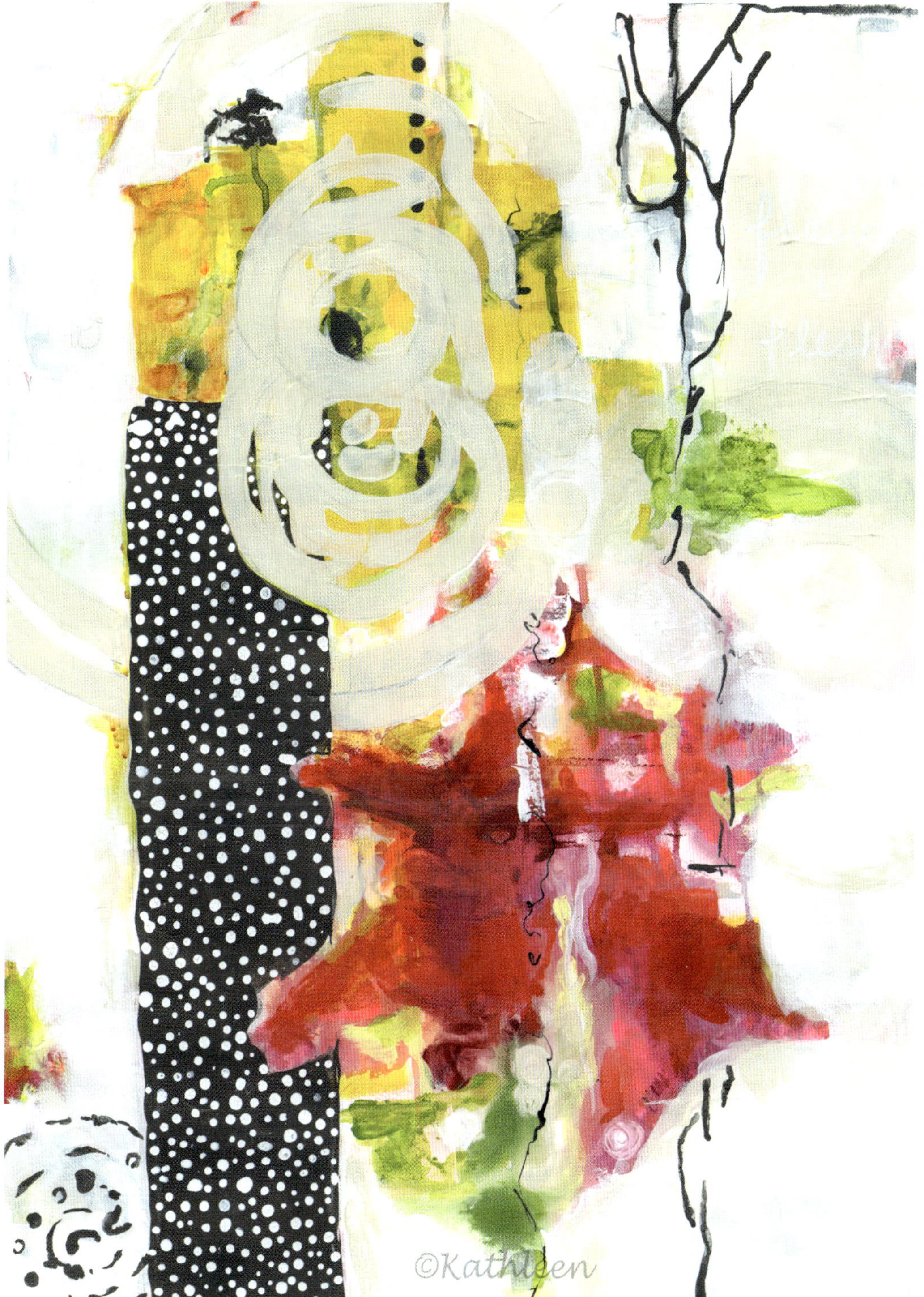

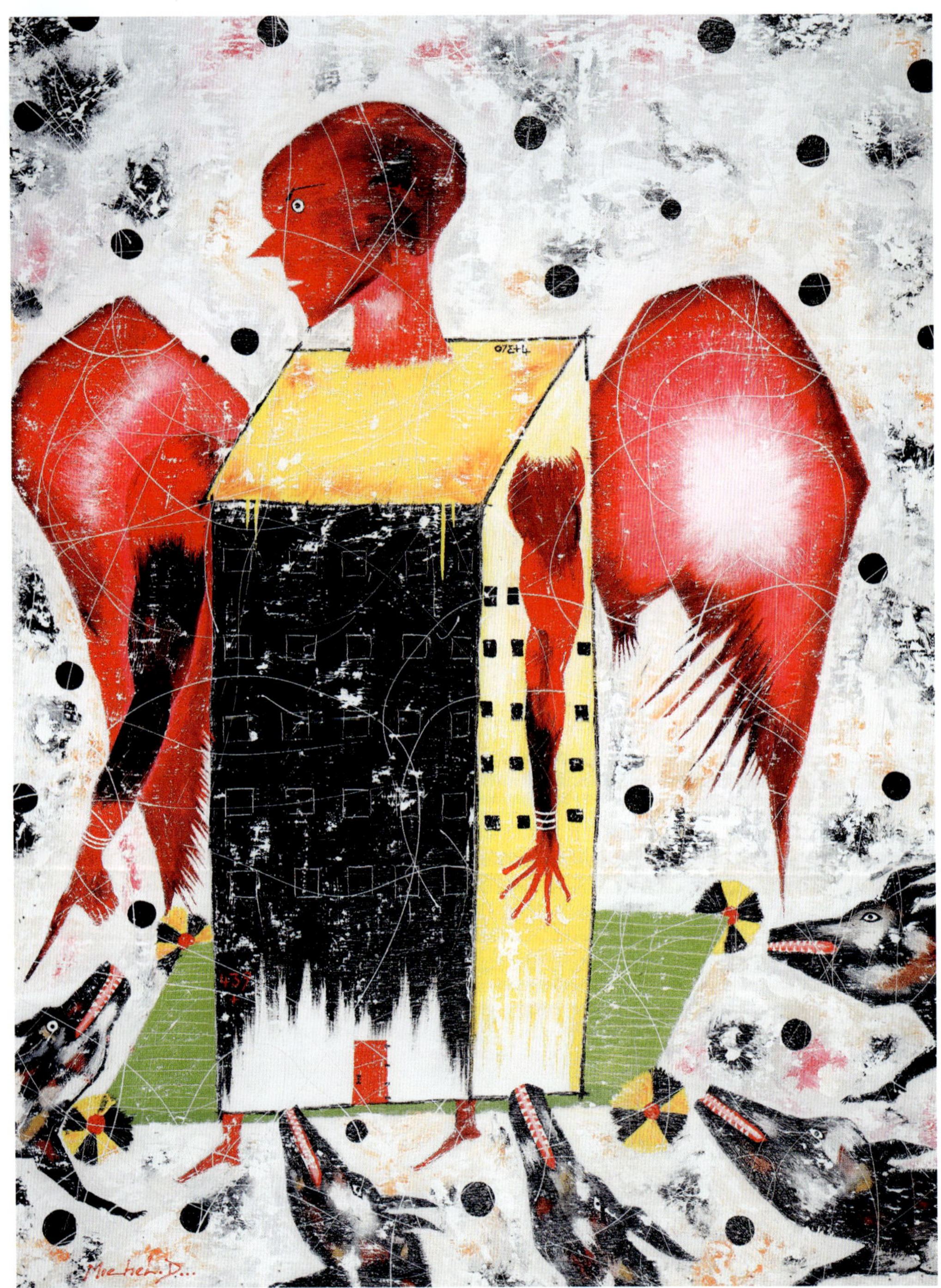

Michel Delgado, Florida

GROWING WITH CONFIDENCE

This painting was made at the beginning of the pandemic. At the time, I felt unwilling to accept what my reality was about to face. I was consumed with thoughts about how best to adapt, going forward. This unpredictable experience was vivid for me on every level: physically, emotionally, and spiritually. How will I embrace my new world, with all of my existence, and secure my own confidence in it?

As I began working on the composition of this piece, the visual elements came to me very strongly and clearly, guiding me with what I needed to know: the attitude I have to carry moving through this new situation and beyond. All of it comes together—the wings, the building, the person with a confident gesture of his hand—to keep this external force at a distance for a peaceful unfolding, until we move to the next experience that this beautiful life and this world have to offer. I cannot be more grateful to be here. This meaningful painting came to me in order to make sense of this difficult time; allowing me to stay strong and to remain determined that this will pass.

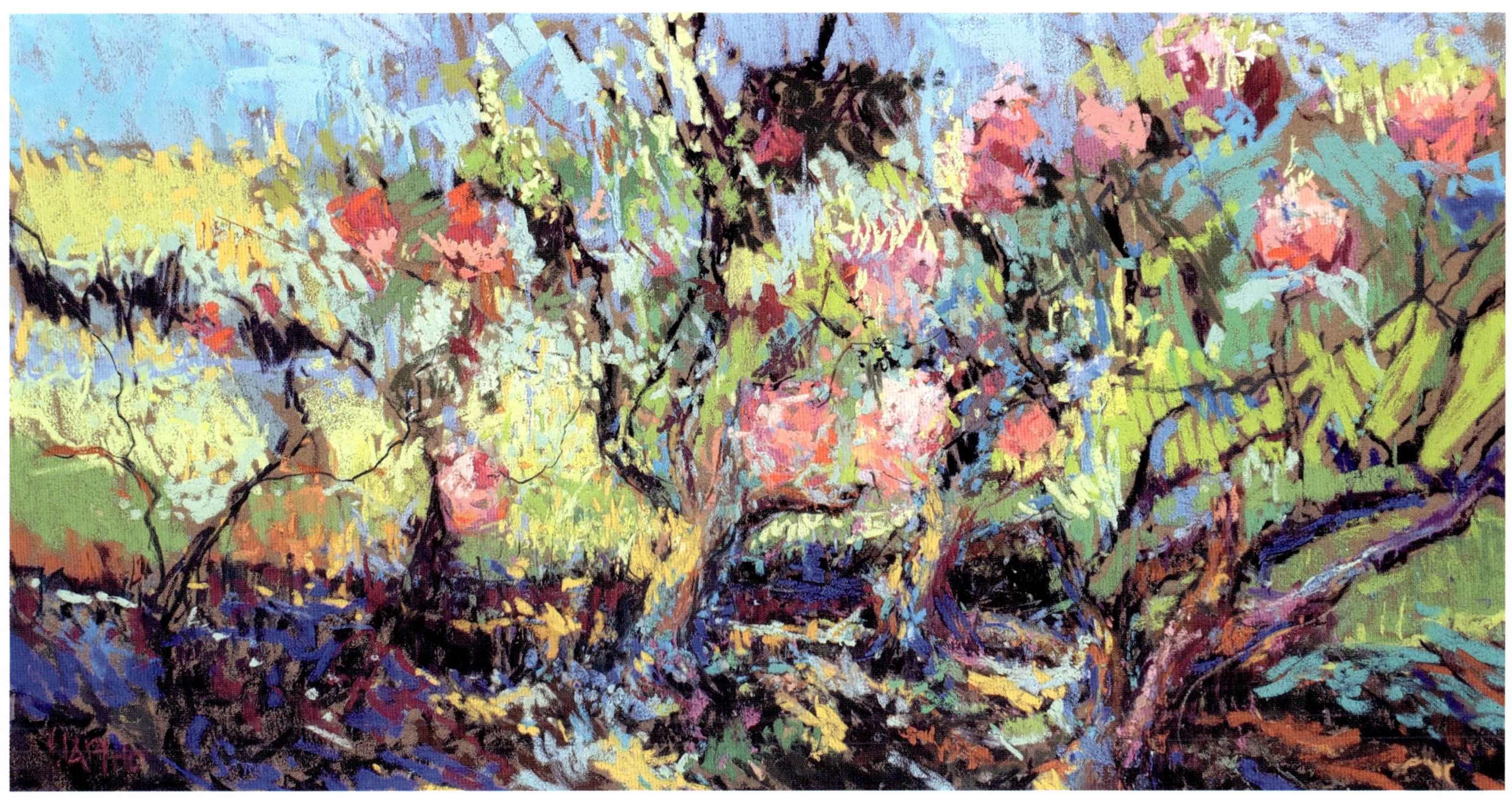

Maria Marino, Maryland
EVENING IN PORT SALERNO

Evening in Port Salerno was painted from a small plein-air painting completed at Lighthouse ArtCenter's 7th Annual Plein Air Festival. That particular evening, light filled the waterway with beautiful color at Manatee Pocket. It reminds me that, even though there are travel restrictions in place, the memories of special places live on!

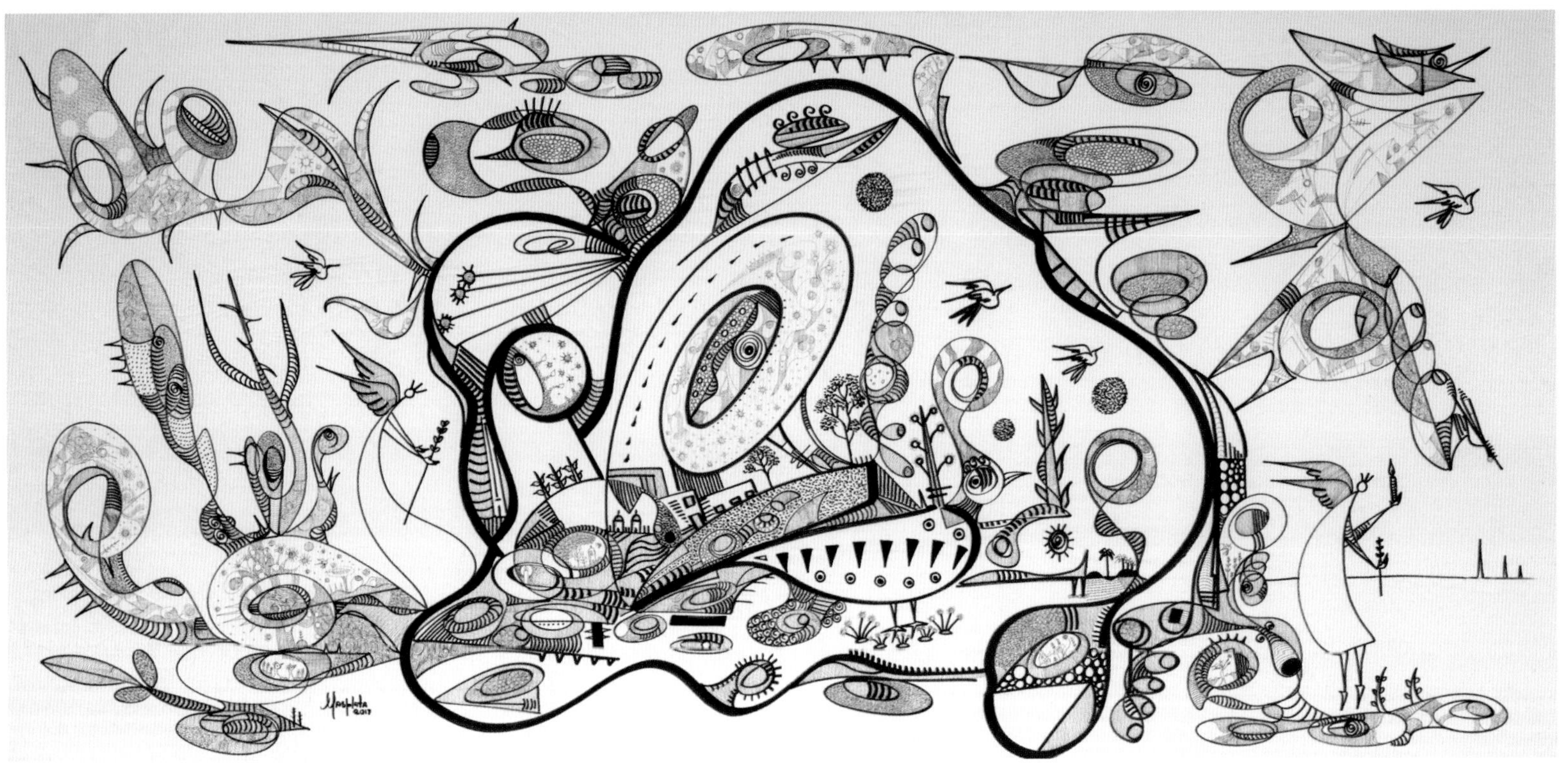

Masplata, Florida
A GUARDIAN PORTAL

I have always understood that my talent is a gift entrusted to me by God. My responsibility is to share this gift and communicate a message of hope. Prior to the pandemic, I found my inspiration by connecting with locals and tourists while drawing at various establishments throughout the city of Miami Beach, Florida. Sheltering in place made it impossible for me to share my gift. I knew I needed to establish an online presence, so I began to photograph and to make an inventory of my work. This activity proved to be very cathartic, and it was this piece in particular, completed in 2017 and titled *A Guardian's Portal*, that brought immediate comfort in a time of significant grief.

The artwork documents two worlds, with the visible world encapsulated by one thick black line. The candle beyond the church is lit with prayers and opens the portal to the invisible world in times of disorder. The guardians arrive to maintain order, restore balance, and provide protection. I have hope that this same scenario is occurring now and the balance in our universe will once again be restored.

Everett L. Spruill, Florida

THE PROBLEMS OF SEGREGATION AND DISCRIMINATION

Growing up in Birmingham, Alabama, during the '60s, I've always felt that I was a part of the "movement." As a visual artist, I've always felt it is an honor and a duty to use my platform to bring about change. I hope it will expand and enrich that dialogue. The African-American experience is much more than most people can imagine: images of pleasure and leisure, images of family, images of empowerment, images of hope and freedom. America has always portrayed Black people in a negative, stereotypical way. I hope that my work shows people a different view of what it means to be Black. *The Problems of Segregation and Discrimination* is filled with symbolism and metaphors. I use a wide range of recycled, reclaimed, and repurposed materials to illustrate the resilience and diversity in African cultures. What was discarded as worthless is, and always was, a valuable resource...just like African people.

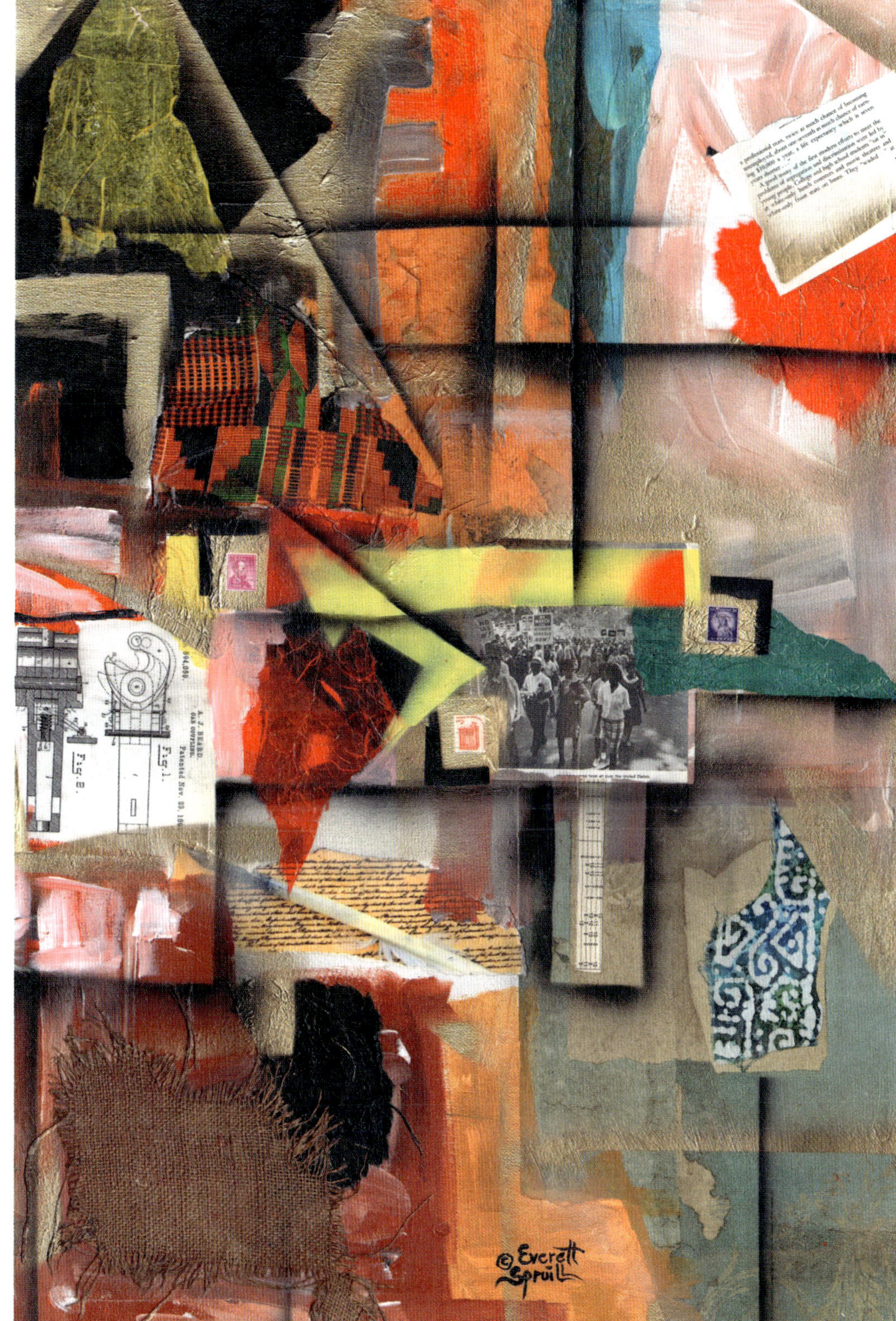

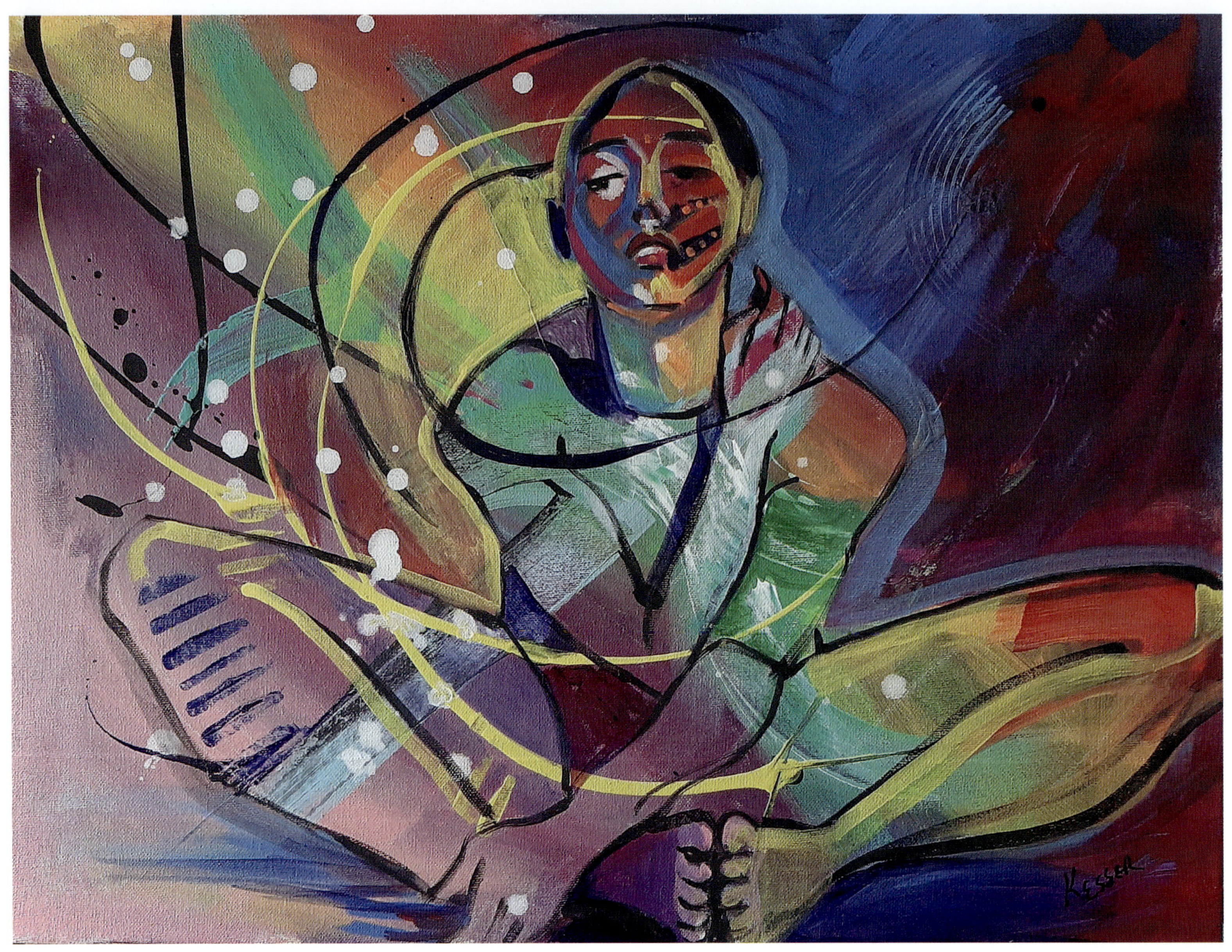

Kaytee Esser, Florida
SITTING IN THE MIDDLE

It is a struggle to make sense of all the information that is thrown at us. This is a representation of what it feels like to have to process it all.

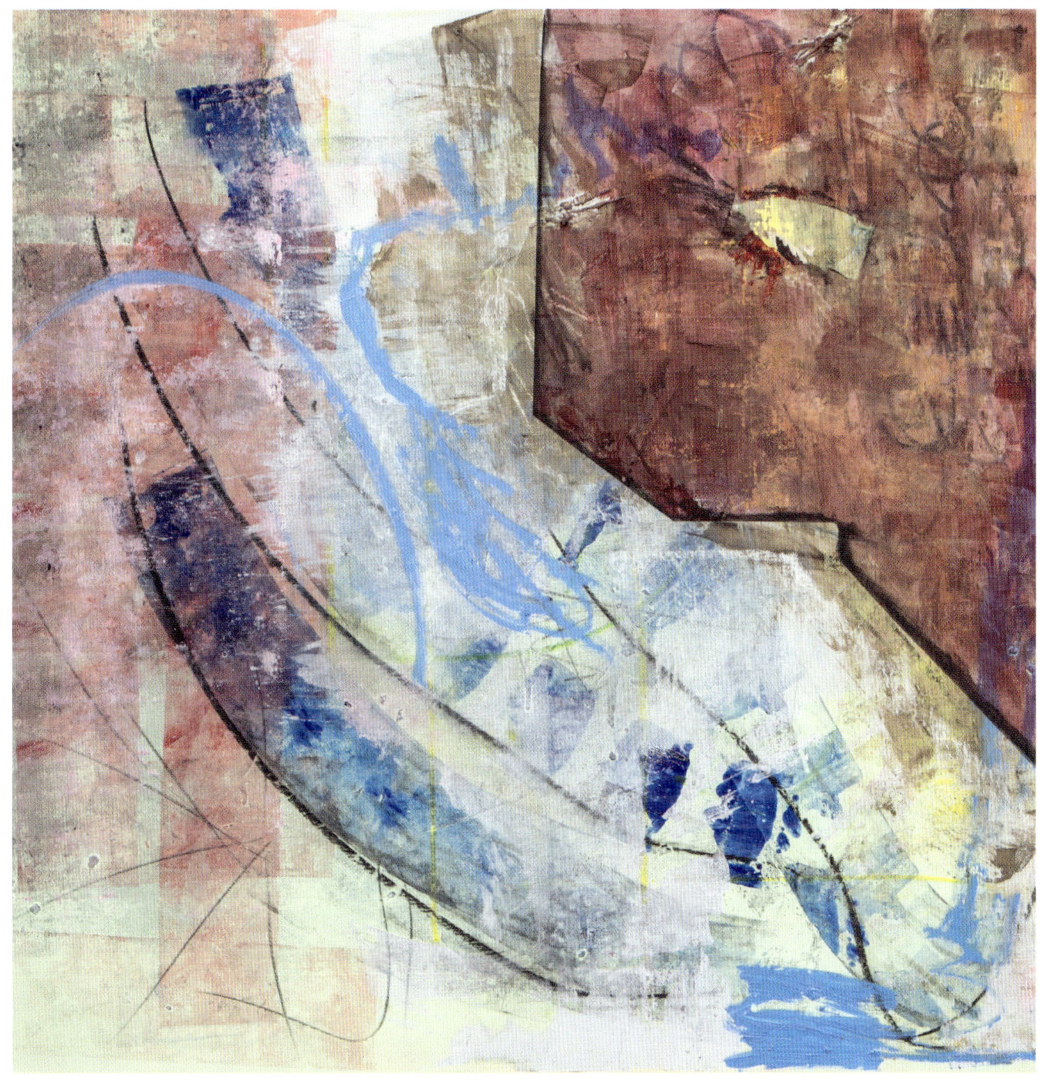

Kent Broadbent, Illinois
CONNECTED

During this time of isolation, the thing that I miss most is the feeling of being connected to other people by just sitting down and talking about life.

14 ARCHITECTURE

I am primarily a painter of rural Pennsylvania and coastal Maine—regions that I know well; regions that have special meaning to me. Many of my subjects can be found close to my home and studio in Hoppenville, Marlborough Township, in Montgomery County, Pennsylvania.

My Pennsylvania paintings depict the rural community and a way of life that is quickly fading into the past. Many of the timber and stone barns and mills, the houses and outbuildings, which are part of the Pennsylvanian heritage, are rapidly disappearing. I'd like to feel, in a way, that I have preserved them in my paintings.

In Maine, I paint the rugged shoreline of the mid-coast region and Monhegan Island where I enjoy the smell of salt air and the feeling of sea spray. I've always loved the sea, probably due to a combination of things—the boats, the energy of the surf, the rocks, the storms, and the romance of it all. I hope this comes across in my paintings of the weathered clapboard lobster shanties and the granite towers of the lighthouses.

I believe that a photograph, however well composed or whatever the atmospheric conditions, can only show what is physically present. However, through a painting, I believe that I can help the viewer "feel" the lighthouse and its past, thereby preserving its image and character for eternity.

My work depicts the stone farmhouses and barns of Pennsylvania and the granite towers of the lighthouses of Maine, which are very enduring and stoic, and will remain through—and long after—the pandemic. And so will we.

Bradley Hendershot
Green Lane, Pennsylvania

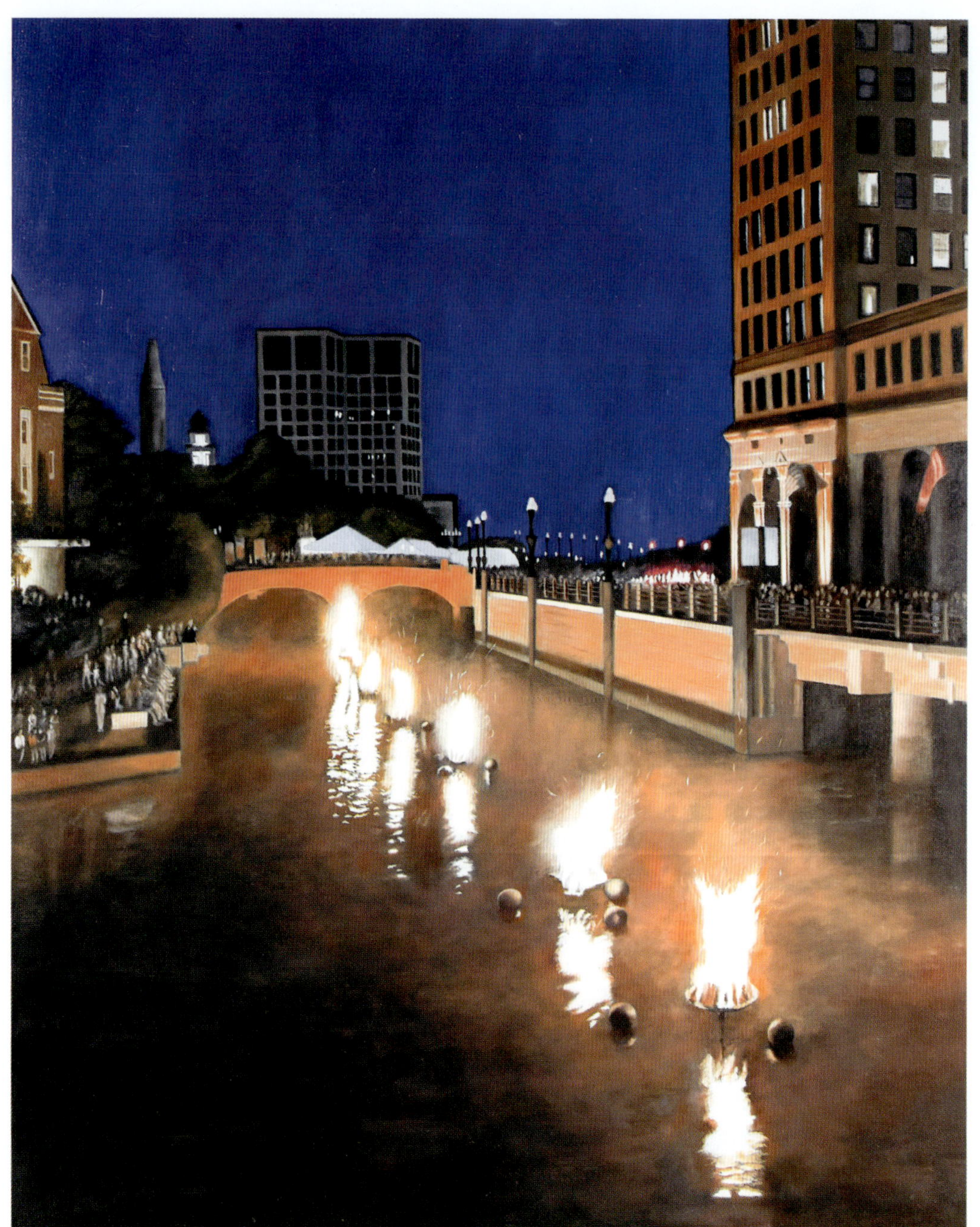

Nick Patten, Rhode Island

FIRE ON THE WATER

"However vast the darkness, we must supply our own light"—Stanley Kubrick

Light has been the focus of my paintings for the last 30 years, so it was only natural that I would be drawn to the iconic event called WaterFire in my newly adopted home of Providence, Rhode Island. This is a happening that was created here 25 years ago. There is a river that runs through the city. Once a month, during the six warm months of the year, small bonfires are lit in spaces placed in the middle of the river over the course of a mile. The event usually draws between 50,000–100,000 spectators on warm Saturday nights. Combined with the scents from the fires and the music that is piped in, it is a multi-sensory experience.

I made this painting at the end of 2019 before the pandemic was dominating our lives, and we were all sheltering in place. The dancing light and the symmetry of the fires were irresistible to me. In my painting, using a photograph I took for reference, I was trying to capture the magic of seeing these beacons glisten on the water, and the atmosphere created by the smoke. This spring, as the news was getting darker, businesses were closing, and events were being canceled, I was looking at this painting one day in my studio and I had the realization that we wouldn't experience WaterFire this year. It would be impossible to even consider gathering this many people together. Initially, the painting made me sad, as I felt the loss of the experience. But as the pandemic grew, my feelings changed. The motto of Rhode Island is HOPE. Now, as I look at my painting, and visually spend time there on the river, my hope grows. So, too, do my feelings of resolve—that we will get through this; that we will prevail. My hope and my belief is that, here in Providence, we will come together again to celebrate and experience this mystical event on the river, and watch the fire dance.

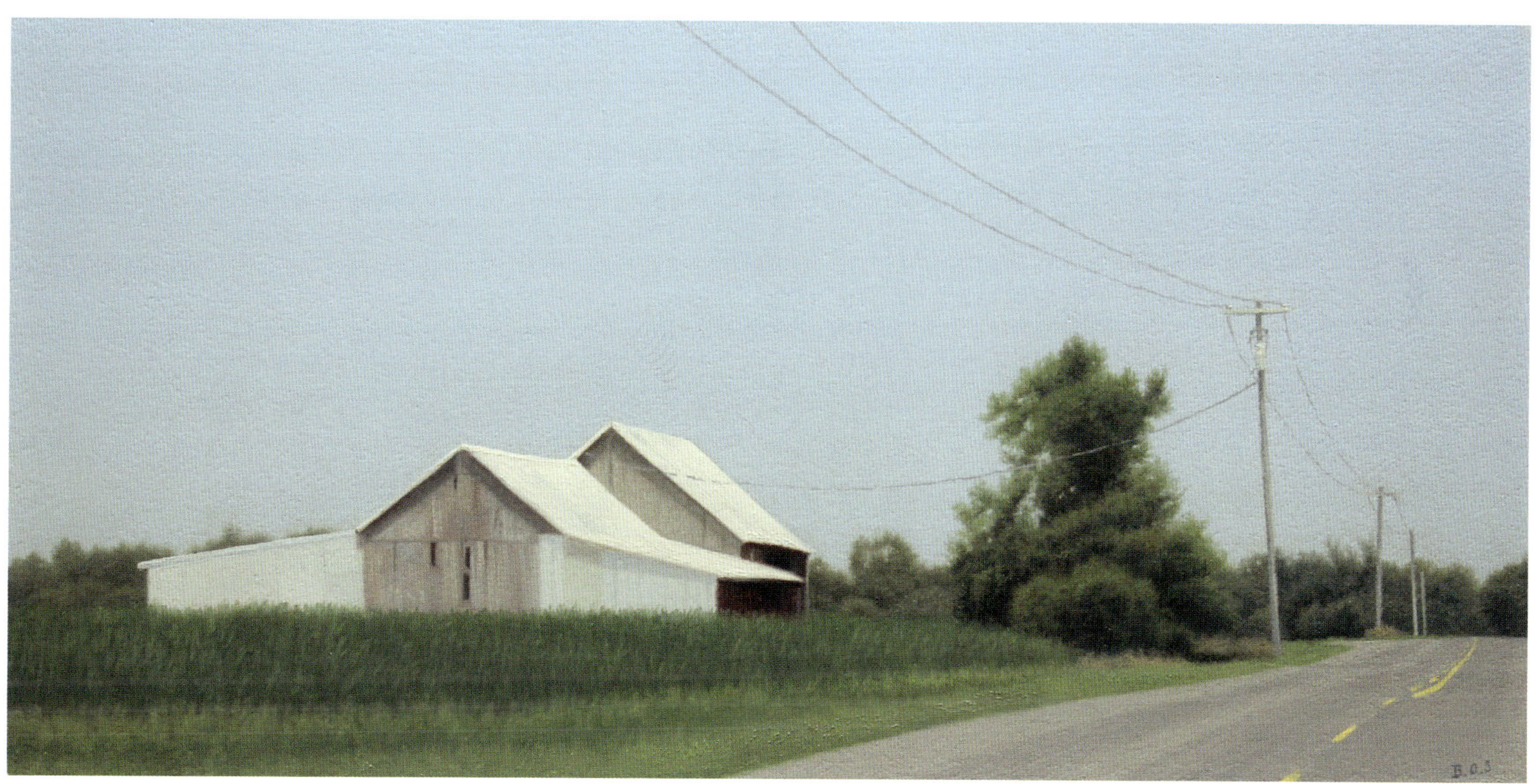

Brett Scheifflee, New York

FARM COUNTRY

During the Coronavirus shutdown, we kept hearing in the media about what is "essential," so I decided to paint a little bit of what is essential in my community. We thank our farmers for their commitment and access to a local continued food source during this pandemic.

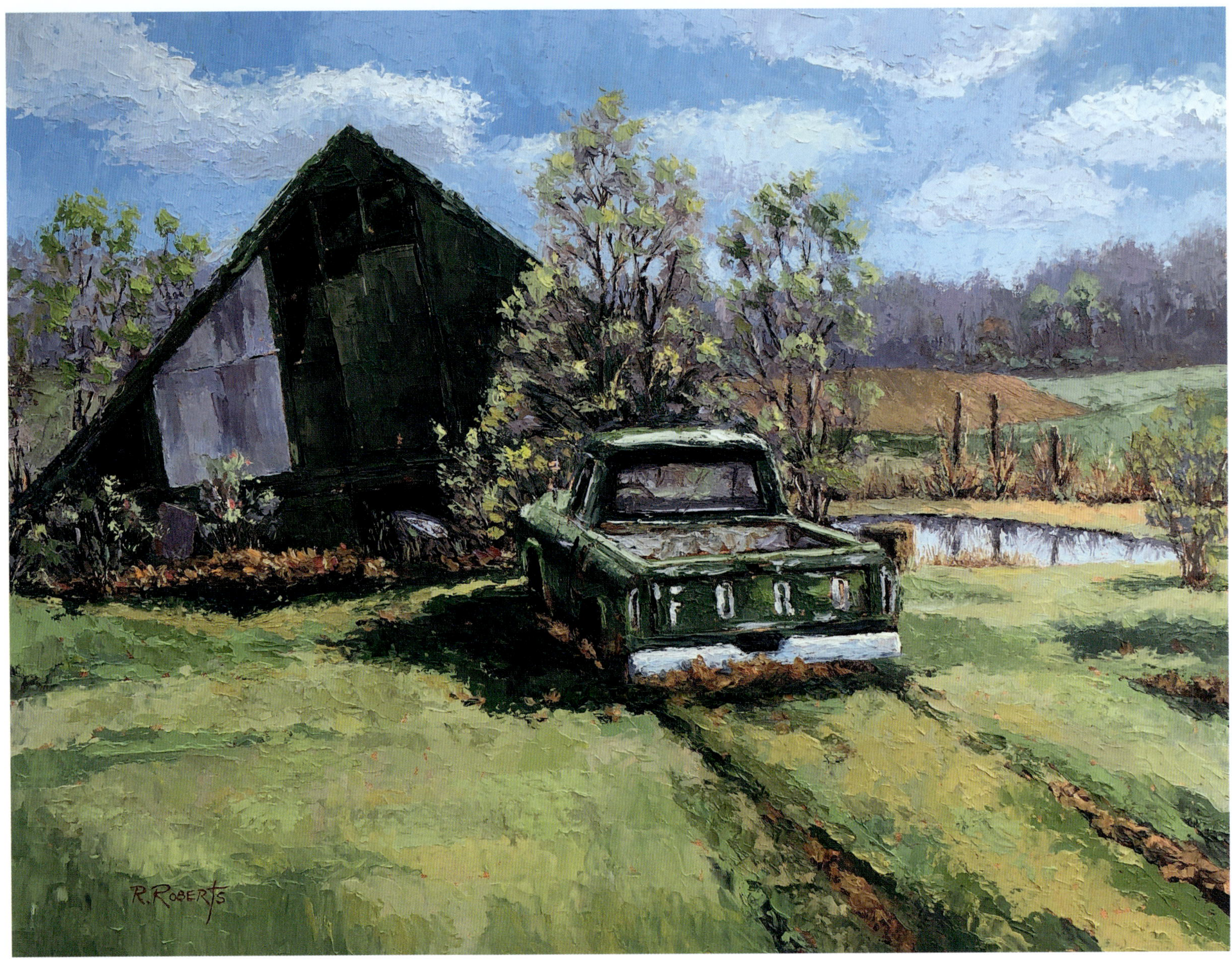

Robin Roberts, Ohio
DILAPIDATED

This painting was done as spring was beginning to awaken in my part of the world. It is a reminder that God is everywhere, making things new and giving hope for renewal, as we ride out the effects of the pandemic.

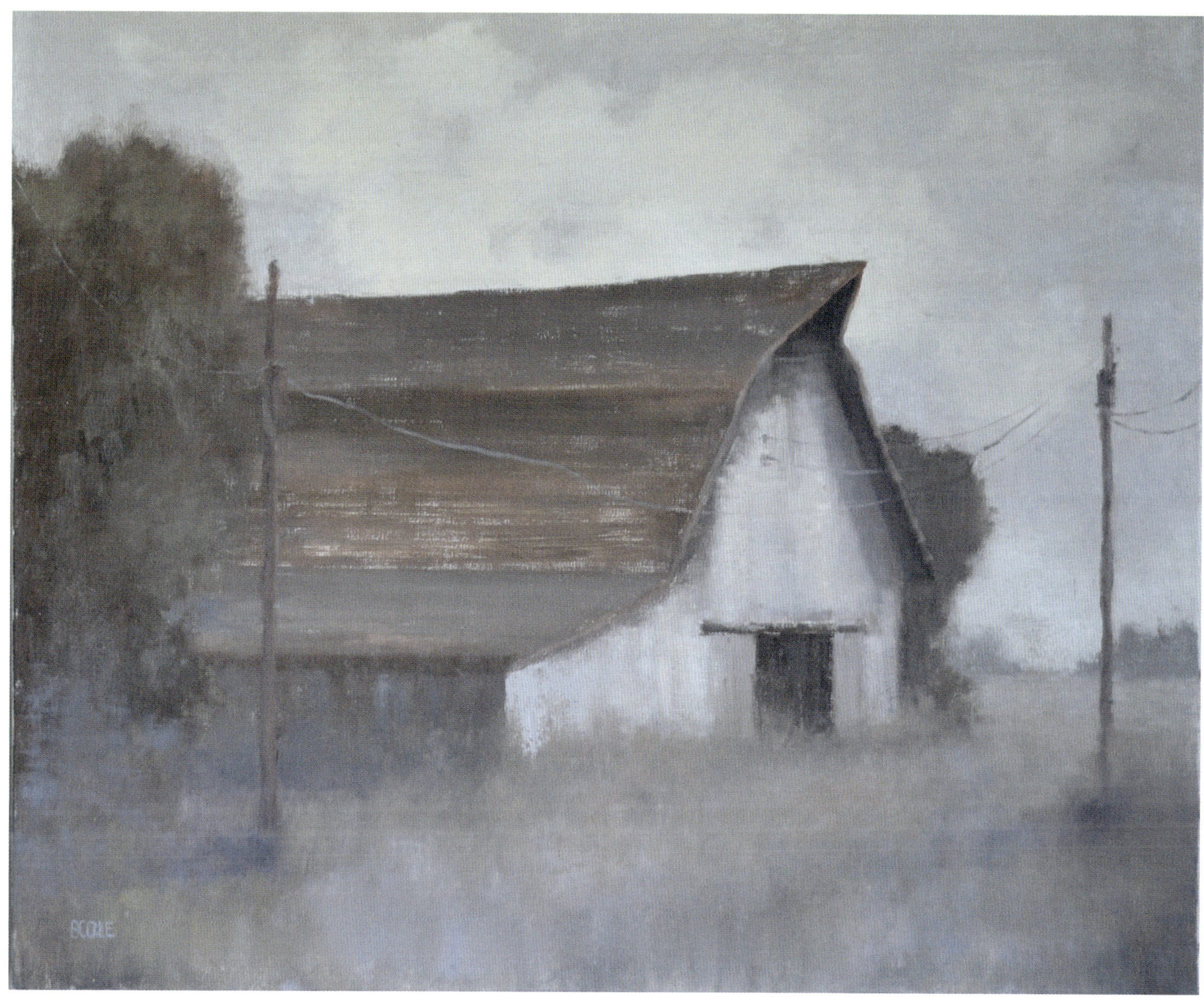

Beth Cole, Nebraska

CONSTANCY

I've always heard you can't hide from the paint, that what you are feeling as you paint will always come out on canvas. This painting is titled *Constancy*, and as I consider the swirl of events we have experienced in 2020, it may be my way of symbolizing things that don't change. Some things you can depend on in life. The sun will rise, and it will set. The sounds of life around us and the beauty of the natural world remain, continually rejuvenating, no matter what is happening around us. The barn embodies constancy in a sense. It is a place on which you can depend to keep, store, nurture, and protect what has been entrusted to you. I like thinking about the stability and stewardship that a barn represents, as well as how it ties into the whole idea of the unchanging natural world.

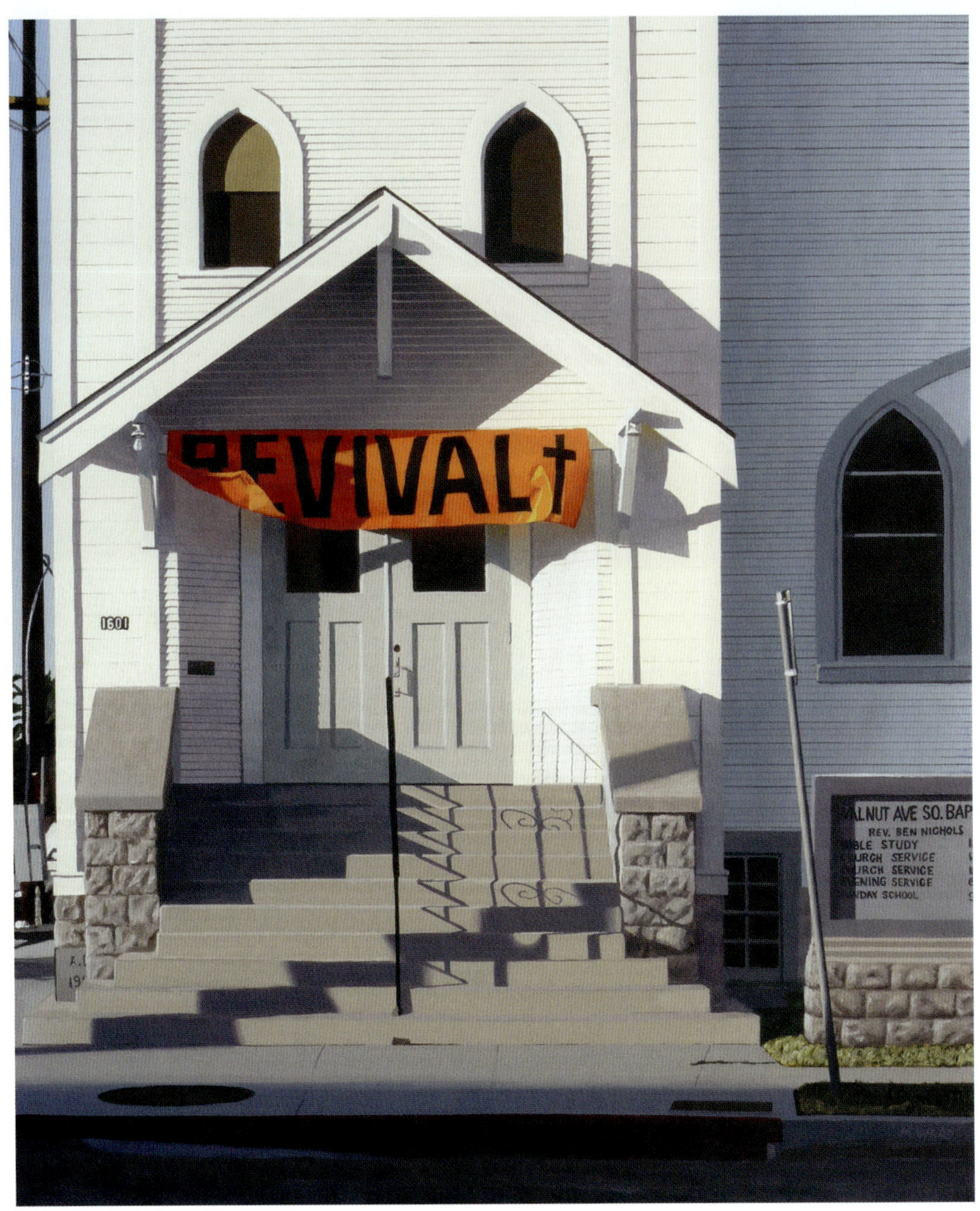

Michael Ward, California
REVIVAL

Revival depicts a modest wooden church near where I once lived in Long Beach, California. It was on my to-paint list for many decades. In the time of the pandemic, it seemed an appropriate subject, with a message of hope and redemption.

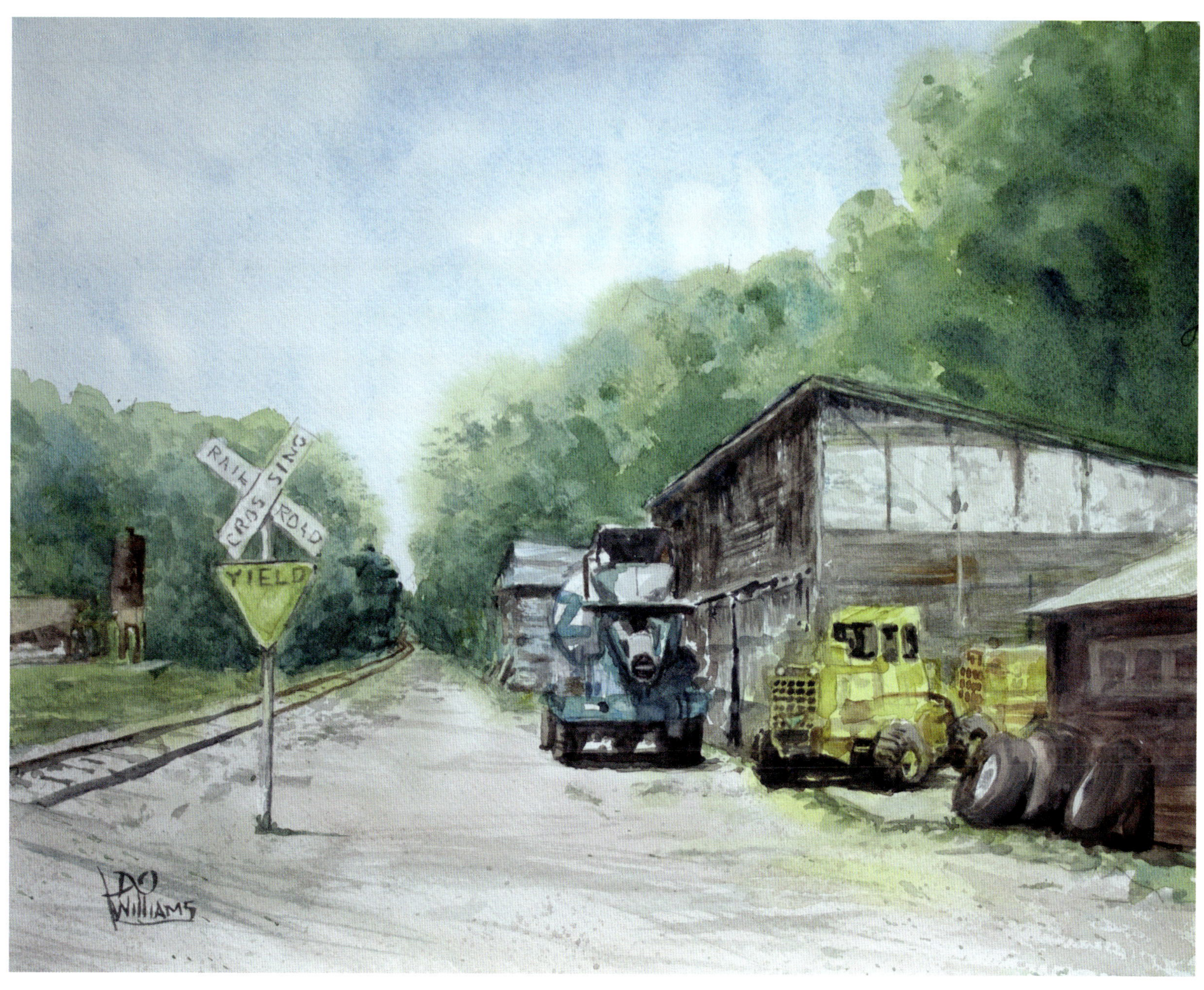

David O. Williams, Wisconsin

AT THE CROSSING

Living alone with few safe places to go, I went for a drive to explore and get out of the house. Just past business parks and newly constructed housing, the road opened up to a patchy country highway. At an oblique railroad crossing, a number of idle construction vehicles were parked around dilapidated buildings. Likely this business is still operating but the sense of isolation and desertion is an illustration of our world today. We are at a crossing.

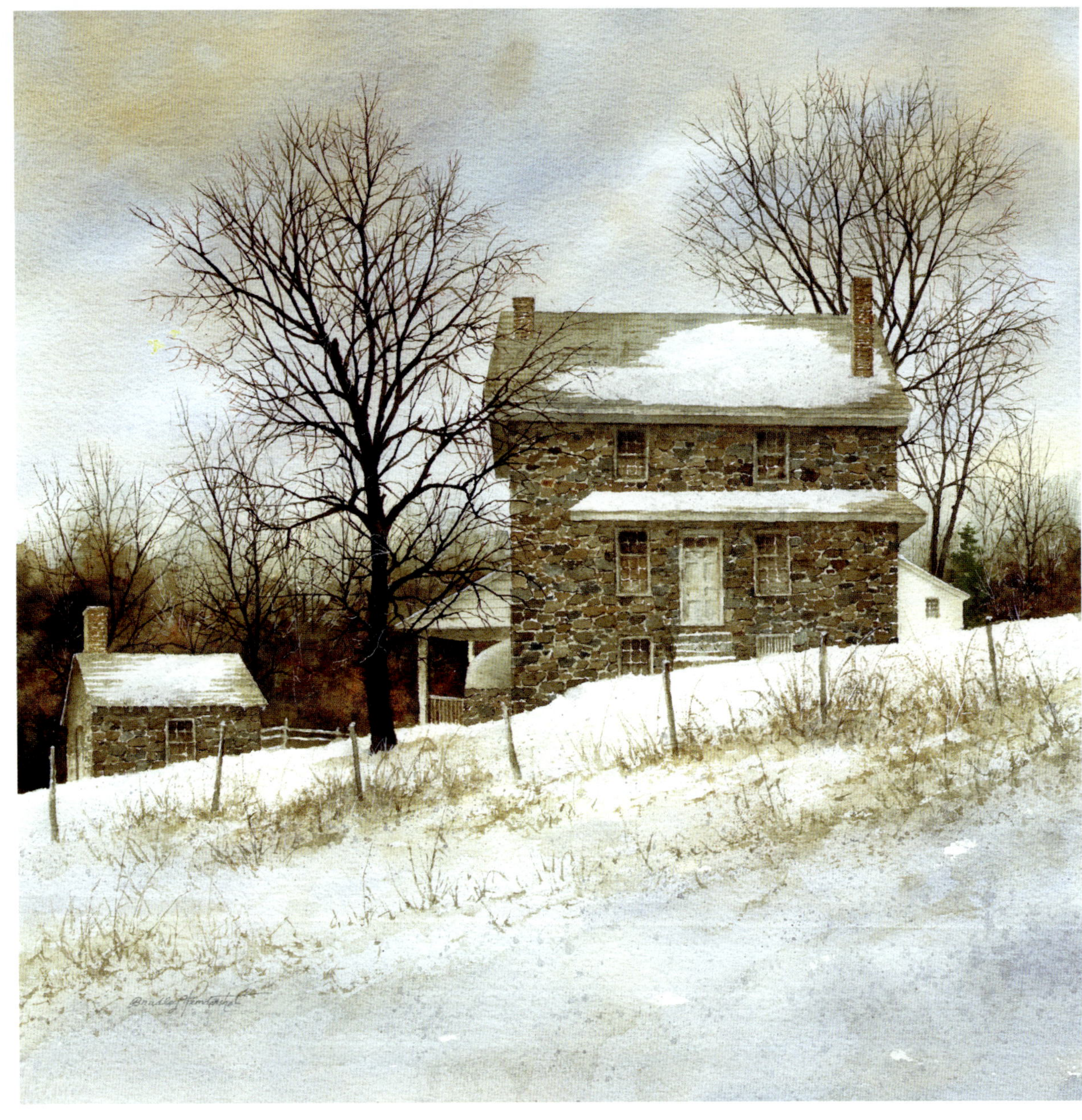

Bradley Hendershot, Pennsylvania
WINTER AT THE CHAD HOUSE

Quarantine and isolation have grown to be words that may be uncomfortable for many in our mobile society. But, when viewed as a positive, the nature of being in the studio allows for self-reflection and the development of one's craft without the normal distractions of everyday life. In my case, the quarantine has not altered my life much other than the temporary closures of galleries and suppliers. I am still here in the studio every day, and I have enjoyed the personal journey in my surroundings and continue to develop my artwork. Some may view the snow and the stone house in my painting as cold, desolate, lonely, and isolated. But I see it as a warm, cozy place to hunker down with family while the blizzard of the current situation is raging in the world. This charming stone building, c.1726, was the home of John Chad—ferryman, farmer, and tavern-keeper for whom Chadds Ford, Pennsylvania, was named. Now restored, it is located along Creek Road in Chester County's Brandywine Valley.

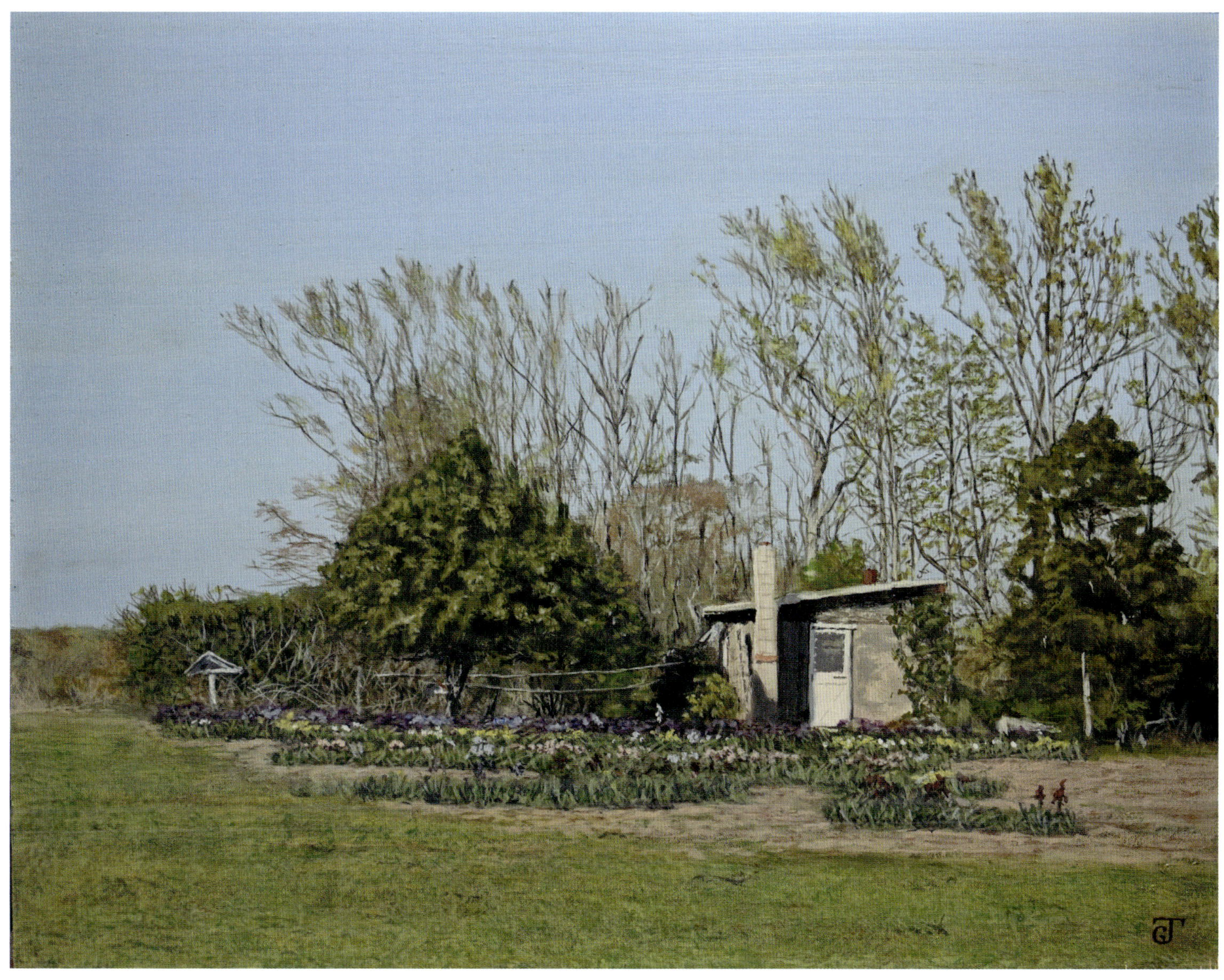

Jeff Gola, New Jersey
IRIS FARM, SOUTH JERSEY

I went into March of 2020 with no art deadlines or commitments, and I stuck with my plan: simply spend the spring and summer painting what I wanted, using my backlog of photos I'd taken in the area over the years, and taking short trips to further explore and sketch. I also looked forward to painting some springtime subjects for a change, as I had previously focused on winter scenes. So, when quarantine hit, not much changed for my process except for putting aside thoughts of outdoor trips until later.

I started *Iris Farm, South Jersey* based on the sights and memories of my local farm landscape, with the garden plots and their stands of multicolored German irises. These plants last for years, often providing a direct link to family and neighbors long gone, and for a time no farmhouse or small-town yard was without some. While I often focus on structures and sights which seem ordinary, I'm mostly attracted to those which seem to have an ephemeral nature and will be changed beyond recognition or will be completely gone soon. Egg tempera, my chosen medium, is a slow process given to introspective thought, as the image is built with one layer of paint at a time. Lately, while working on this and other pieces, my thoughts tend towards wondering how our common sights will be changing as we proceed through this pandemic, and how much more rapidly we will see the disappearance of many old remnants and businesses that have been taken for granted.

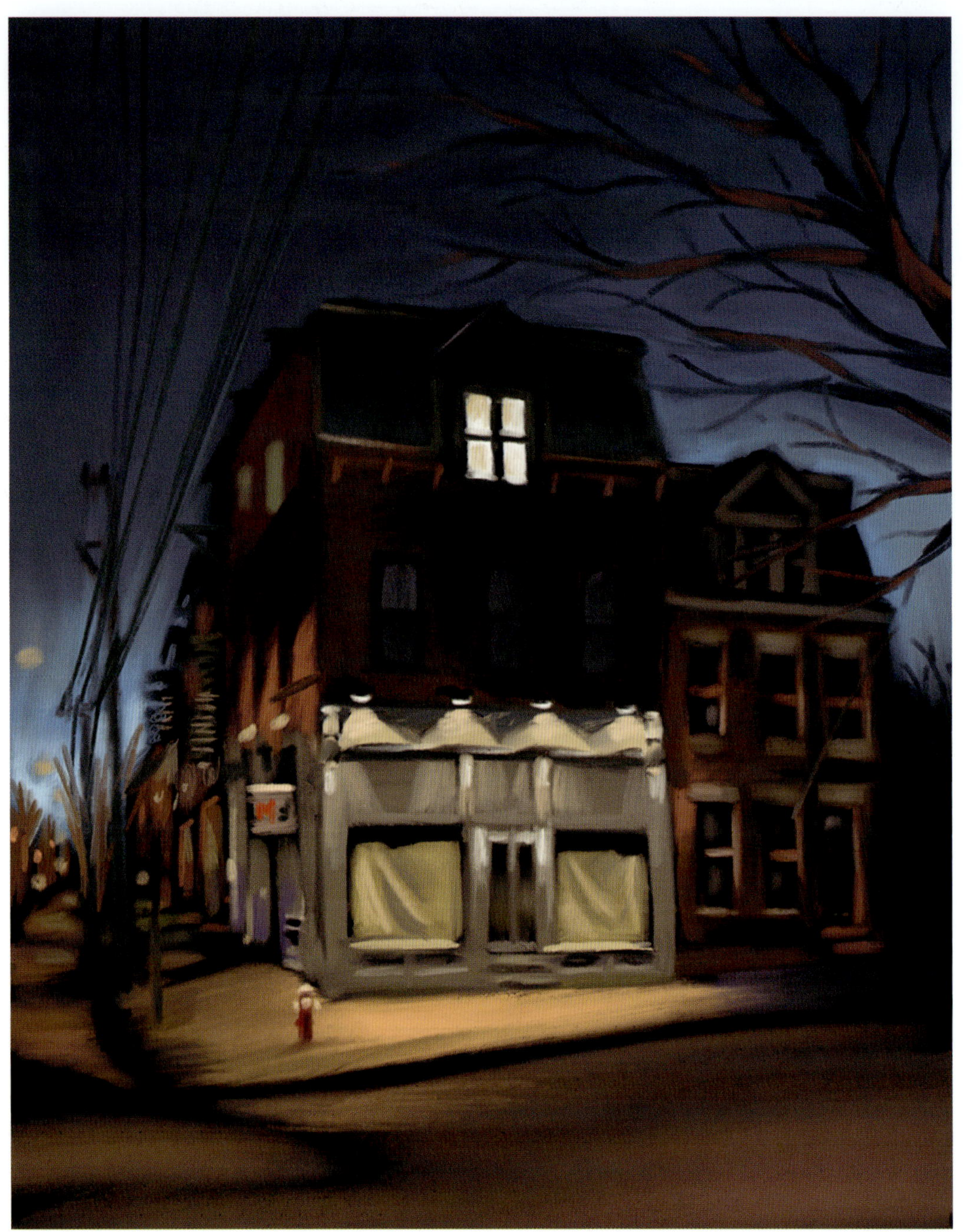

Dan Wintermantel, Pennsylvania

LATE NIGHT INSTALLATION (1/25)

I live and work in the historic Mexican War Streets neighborhood in Pittsburgh, Pennsylvania. It is comprised of late 1800 Victorian row houses, saved from demolition in the 1970s by a dedicated band of enthusiastic preservationists. The neighborhood and many of the street names were given by General William Robinson, who owned the original tract of land, and refer to significant battles and generals from his experiences in the Mexican–American War. Renowned for the architectural detail, materials, and appealing human scale and charm of the era, the Mexican War Streets brings visitors and history lovers from far and wide.

Once, storefront businesses were on nearly every corner: groceries, butcher shops, pharmacies, dry goods, taverns, and professional services provided everything residents needed within easy walking distance. Many storefront details are still in evidence but are now largely residential, or in the case of the building in this painting, an installation art gallery, caught between exhibits. The neighborhood retains the feel of a walkable small town in the city. What is normally a festive, bustling social atmosphere, with impromptu get-togethers, stoop-sitting, sharing wine, laughs, and stories, is now eerily subdued. The architecture, shuttered and lit by unforgiving light throwing long shadows, now suggests isolation, distance, and loneliness in an uncertain world. I've been trying to use this time to observe and capture the timeless look and feel of this neighborhood that was here long before me and will certainly be here long after me. Adding solitary figures seems almost to call attention to the isolation and sense that everyday life is currently far from normal. Most of this current work is digital and painted on an iPad, which also seems to suggest an incongruously modern take on this old neighborhood.

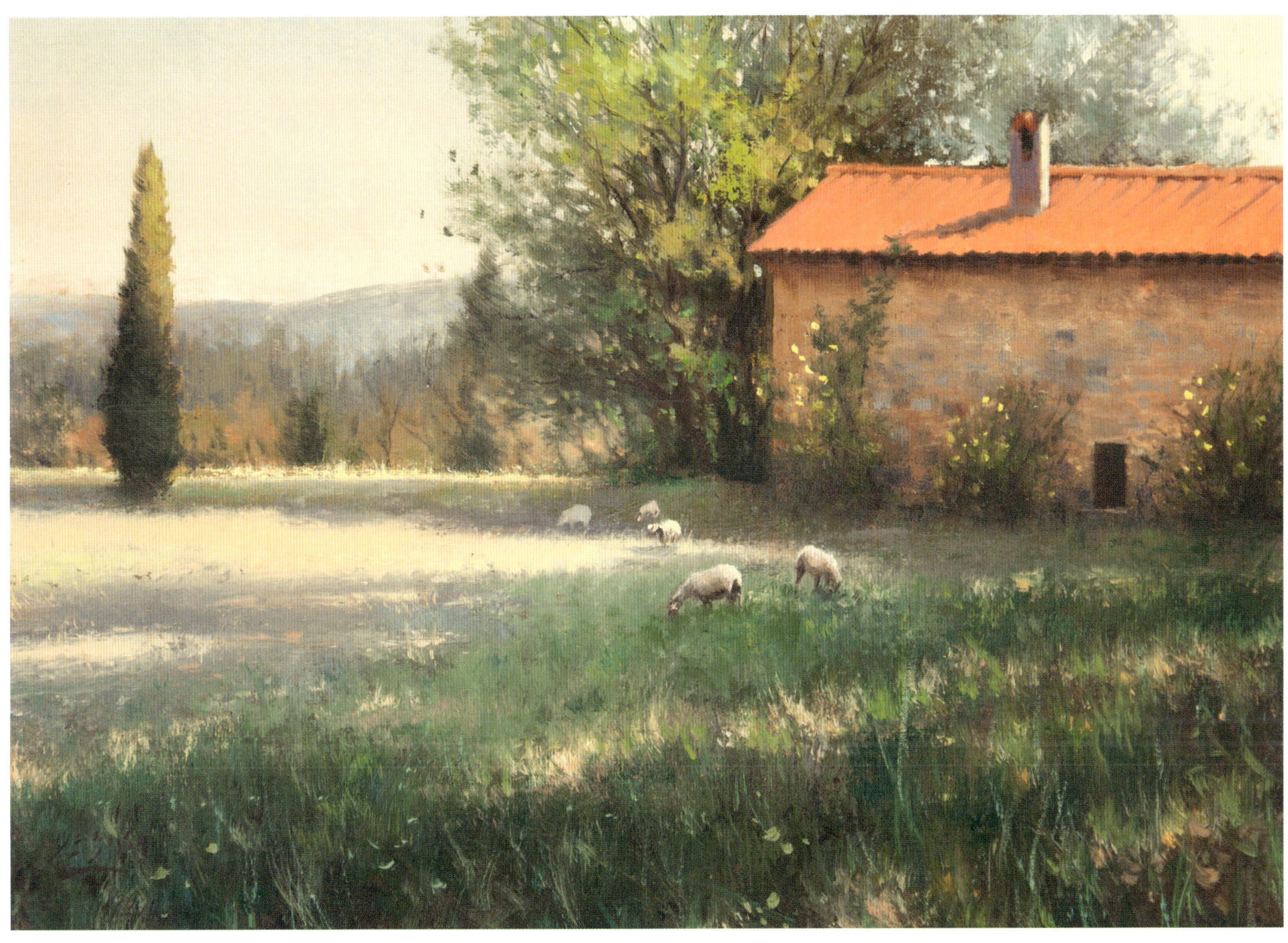

Eleinne Basa, New Jersey
AFTERNOON IN PROVENCE

During the COVID-19 lockdown, I was looking for a way to revisit my traveling days while in Provence in south-eastern France, bordered by the Mediterranean Sea. I wanted to work on paintings that brought me back to the happy times and memories of plein-air painting in Provence. This piece simply reflects the serenity of that peaceful time.

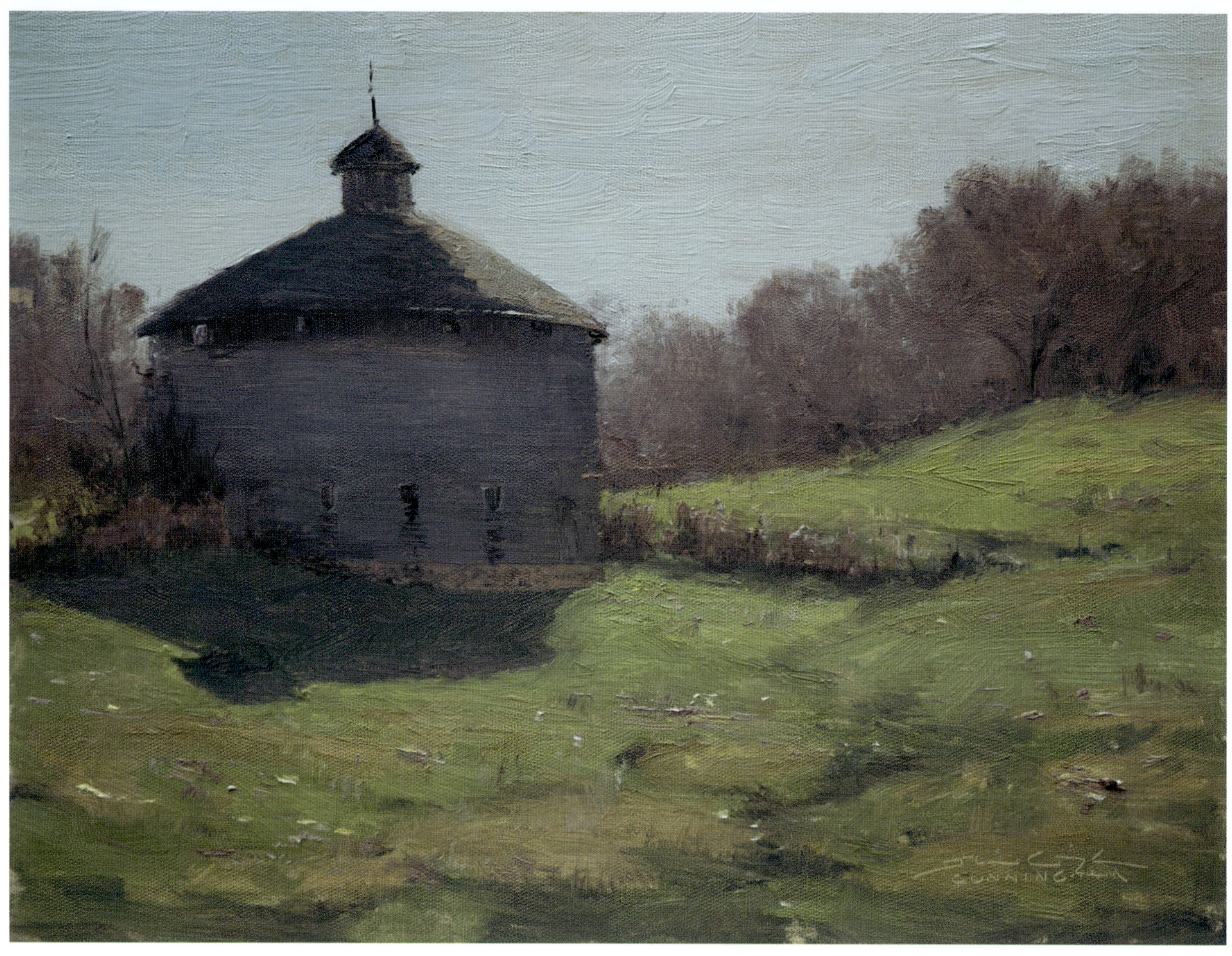

Joshua Cunningham, Minnesota
SLIPPING AWAY

Slipping Away is the first painting I created on location after a month of being home in the studio during the early stages of Minnesota's lockdown. It was good to be out on a chilly morning with the bright sun and a sharp breeze in one of my favorite valleys. There is a farmer who owns most of the valley. He is a one-man preservation society. The valley and surrounding bluffs have been his home for all his life. His ancestors immigrated from the British Isles on a ship to New York. A train to St. Louis followed by a riverboat up the Mississippi to Winona, Minnesota, and from there they marveled at how they walked for weeks without ever leaving the woods. He knows his fields better than most people know their neighbors, and manages them accordingly. When painting this piece, the farmer explained that he didn't own this beautiful round barn, but that his father had helped build it for a fellow farmer. He added, with notable sadness, that it isn't long for this world. "It's good that you're painting it. People need to know; they need to remember."

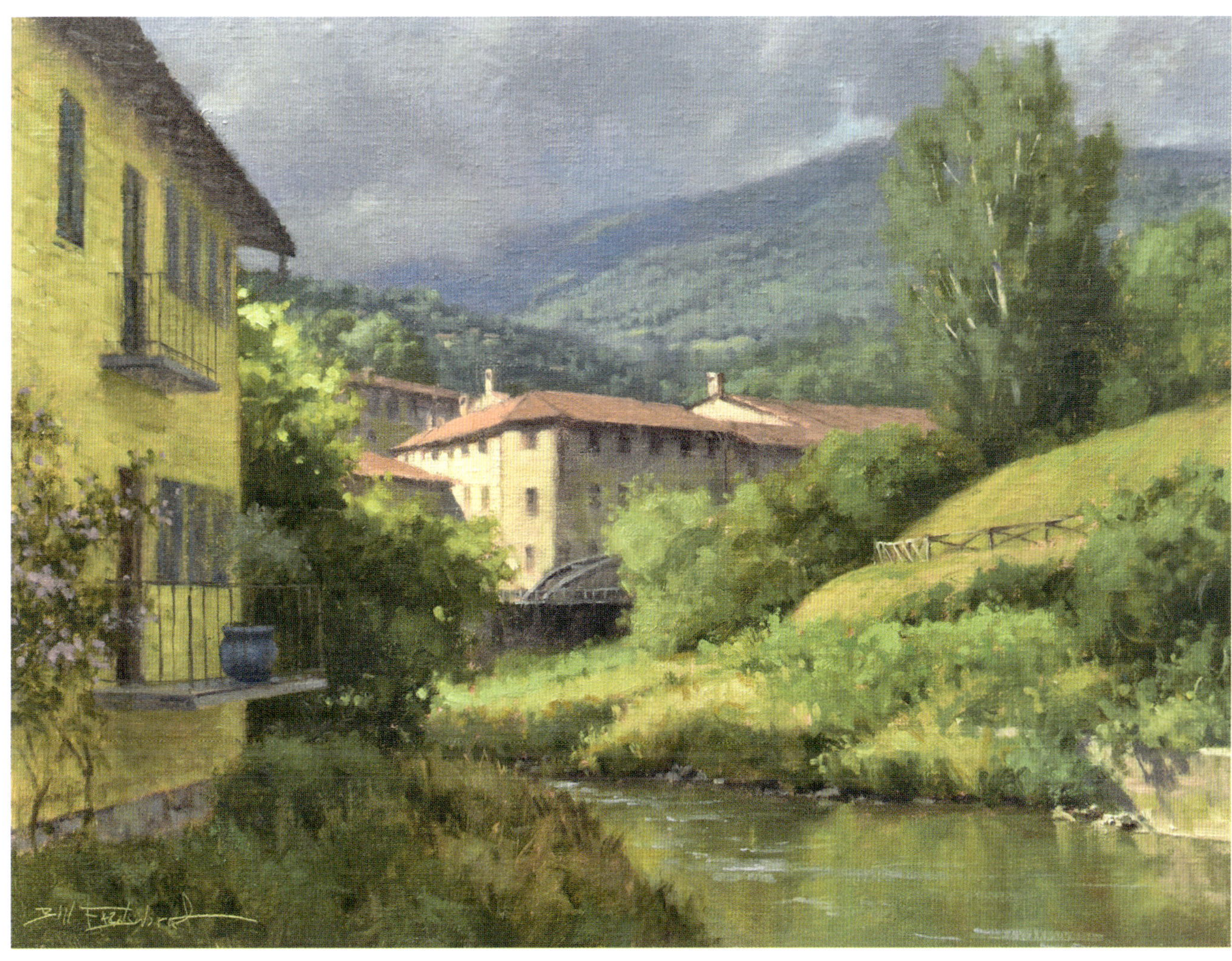

Bill Farnsworth, Florida
HEADWATERS

This studio painting was inspired by our trip to Tuscany in 2018. The view is from a small bridge that arches across the headwaters of the Arno in the little village of Stia. The mountainous terrain, texture, and light were what caught my eye that late afternoon. I painted this during our quarantine and felt sympathetic for the people in Italy. This painting took me on a trip to a happier time, a remembrance of a place I hope to return to one day.

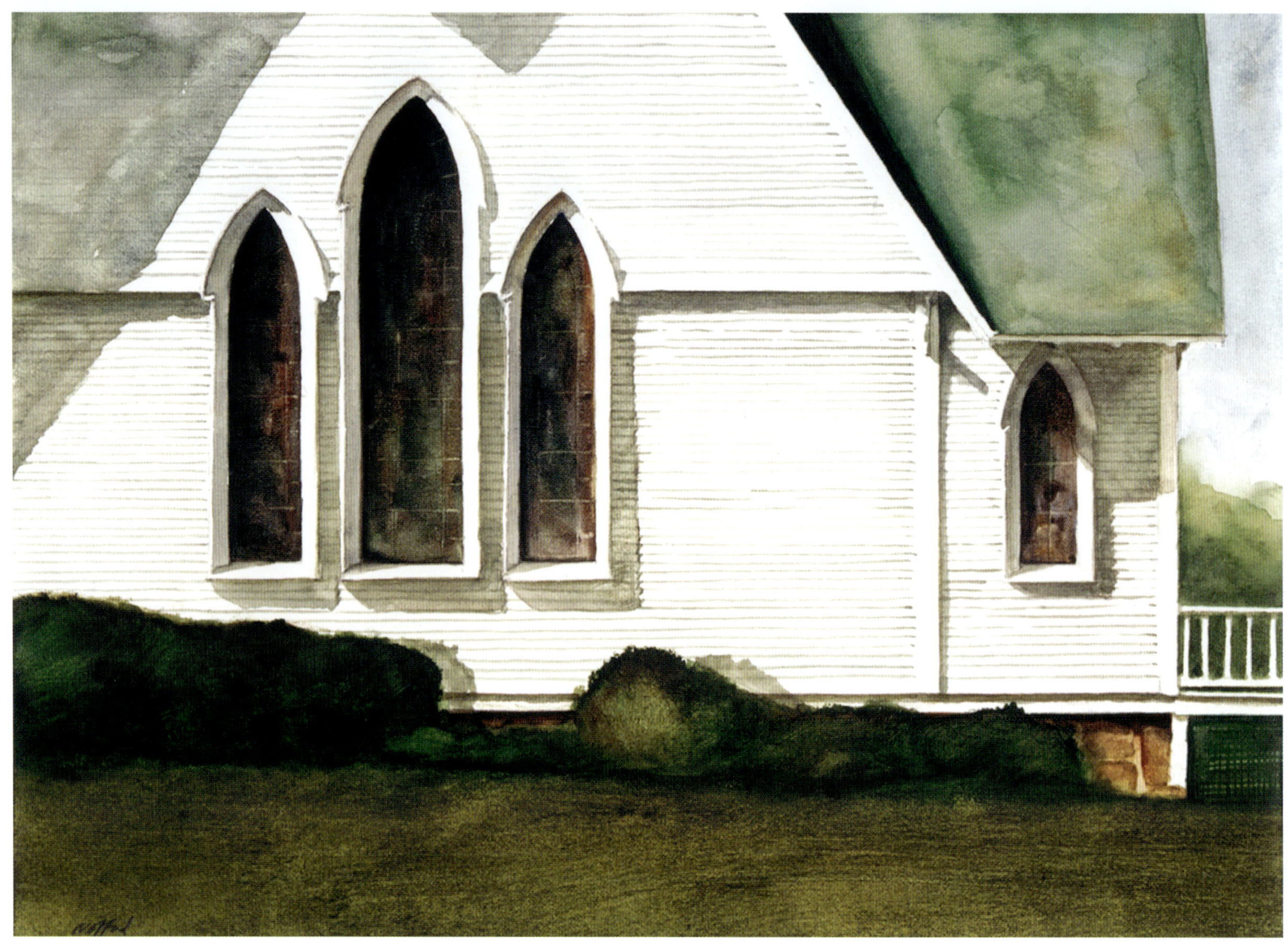

William Wofford, Florida
CENTENARIAN

In September 1990, on my first trip to Maine visiting a friend and fellow artist, I drove by myself from his studio/gallery in Northeast Harbor for a day trip to Stonington. Since it was my first visit, I didn't really know where I was going but was in no hurry. Everything was so beautiful and unique to this native Floridian. On my way, I came across this church. As any tourist and artist will do, I photographed every interesting subject I could find and collected every local paper and map. After returning home, I discovered a newspaper article mentioning the fact that the church was celebrating its 100th anniversary the weekend I came upon it. Thus, the title.

For the most part, I have an affinity toward subjects, and objects, with which I have daily interactions. Subjects that are personal, whether they be animate or inanimate, take on a life of their own. They often have more private meaning than many would assume at first glance, and the more you can relate to any subject, the more of yourself you can put into it. There is also a case to be made, however, for a pure interest in light and shadow, abstract design, simplicity, balance, and subjects that can more easily relate to a larger audience.

Rather than select a subject from my immediate surroundings, which I so often prefer, and as a means of going back in time and revisiting not only friendships but happier and healthier times, I have chosen *Centenarian*.

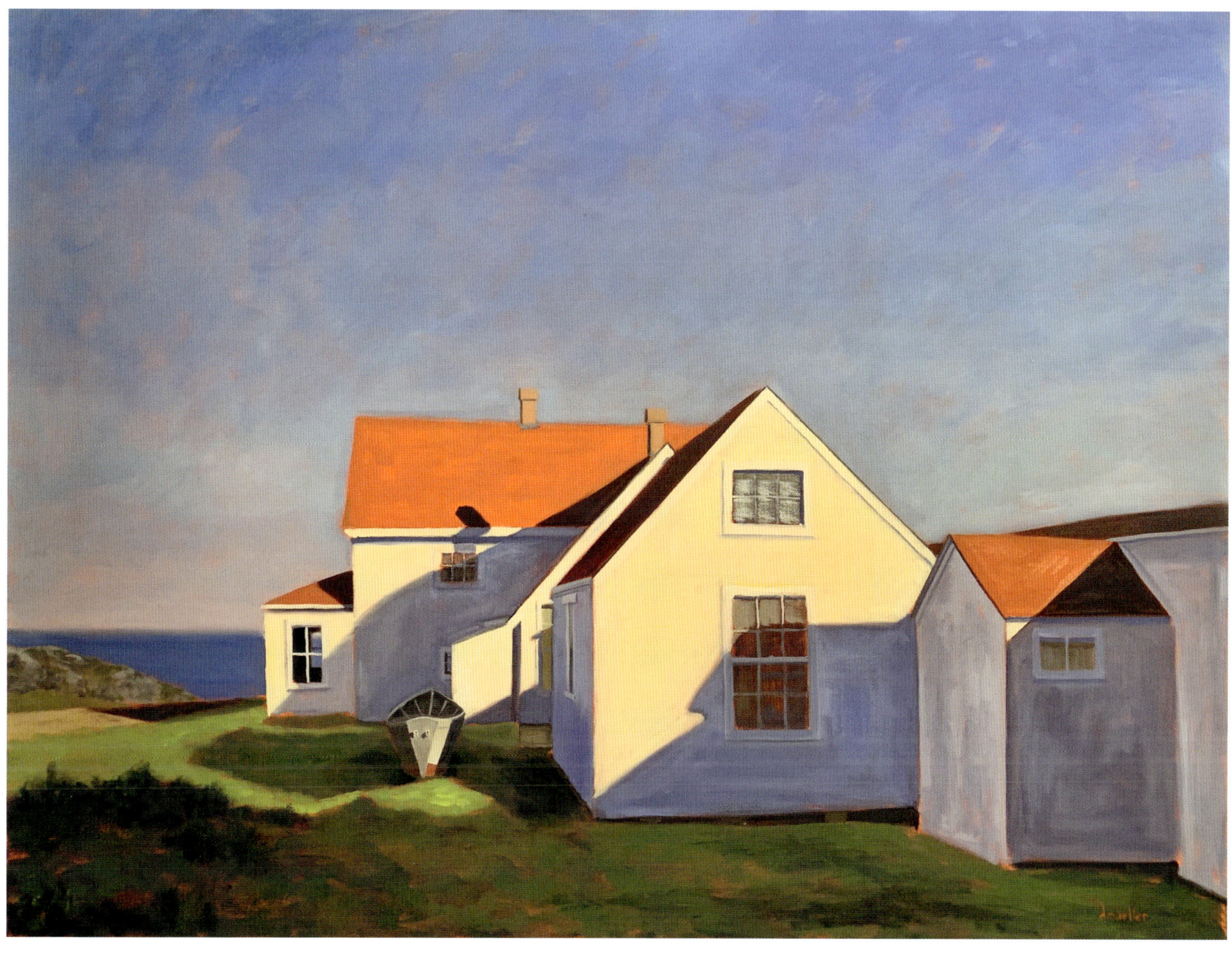

Debbie Mueller, New Hampshire
MONHEGAN BLUES

Monhegan is my touchstone. I traveled there for the first time in 2018, and the experience was life changing. Being in the same place, and seeing the very same vistas, such as Hopper, Kent, and the Wyeth, as my painting "ancestors" and heroes was a powerful experience. Each time I have visited the island since, besides being infused with a sense of peace and belonging, my painting ability has advanced, almost as if the air there is magic. This year, Monhegan is grappling with the very difficult decision of how to transport visitors to the island safely on what are, typically, ferries packed with people and their luggage. A trip to the island this year, the thought of which has sustained me during the stressful months of dealing with the threat of COVID-19 for my pregnant patients and their babies, now seems quite uncertain. Gazing at *Monhegan Blues* brings me right back to the feeling of peace and optimism that I feel when I have stood looking at that majestic view. I feel the solidity of the island and its timelessness. The world and its problems feel very far away.

15 FEATURED STATE

With a focus on America, the project team always wanted to feature at least one artist from each of the 50 beautiful states. It was no surprise that the first artist to sign on was Mikel Wintermantel, who is the project lead's childhood friend from New York State.

William Weinaug and Mikel have a lot of history, as Mikel's grandfather delivered William, and living on the same block, they were childhood friends since they could walk! Mischievous, yes, but their creativity through art and science, specifically, was always at the forefront.

> *The spring of 2020 was when Bill's local project in Florida, Wekiva Paint Out, was finishing up. I came to support the project as I do every year, but the onset of COVID-19 was beginning to surge by the end of the event. My wife Cheryl, a nurse, and my daughter Aline, a student at UB studying Public Health, had been discussing the outbreak in Wuhan, China, for months. As the weeks passed and the pandemic worsened with shutdowns beginning, Bill and I had conversations about how the pandemic would affect people and businesses overall, worrying about how the shutdown would affect artists and musicians in particular. Bill wanted to create a way to support them and express their stories of how they were affected personally. Through those conversations, The Great American Paint In® project was born.*
>
> *New York was one of the hardest-hit cities early on in the pandemic. I could see from social media posts how it was affecting people. Our family was quarantined early on when my wife was exposed to one of the first COVID-positive patients in our county. My artist friends closer to New York City lived in isolation, and while some thrived on their creativity, others withdrew, feeling cut off as the reality of a pandemic darkened their spirits.*
>
> *As the weather warmed up, many plein-air artists took the opportunity to go out and paint, finding that being out in nature and creating safely outdoors lifted their spirits. New York State has a wide array of intrinsic beauty: from Niagara Falls, the Great Lakes, the Finger Lakes, and the gorges and waterfalls of central New York, to the Mohawk Valley region, the Adirondack Mountains, the Catskills, Hudson Valley, the Thousand Islands, St. Lawrence Seaway, Lake George and Lake Champlain.*
>
> *The city of New York, arguably the country's creative cultural center, was devastated by the virus. With Broadway going dark, and galleries and museums shuttered, the dense population made the isolation even more restrictive.*
>
> *Artists withdrew and cloistered themselves, glued to their easels. Their works reflected the myriad of emotions so many were feeling. Musicians had their Zoom concerts and were able to commune, whereas it was harder for artists to express themselves.*
>
> *This project (and book) was a way for the artists to commiserate and contribute together in one community countrywide. Some found solace in their studios, while the human condition tormented others. This art is representative and reveals the artists' state of mind.*
>
> *Mikel Wintermantel*
> Allegany, New York

This last chapter is dedicated to New York State and its artists. This state is notable not only for being the state where the pandemic first spiked, before raining down its fury over the rest of America and the world, but it is also one of the top states with the largest artist submissions for this project. It also happens to be the birth state of William Weinaug, co-owner of Gallery CERO.

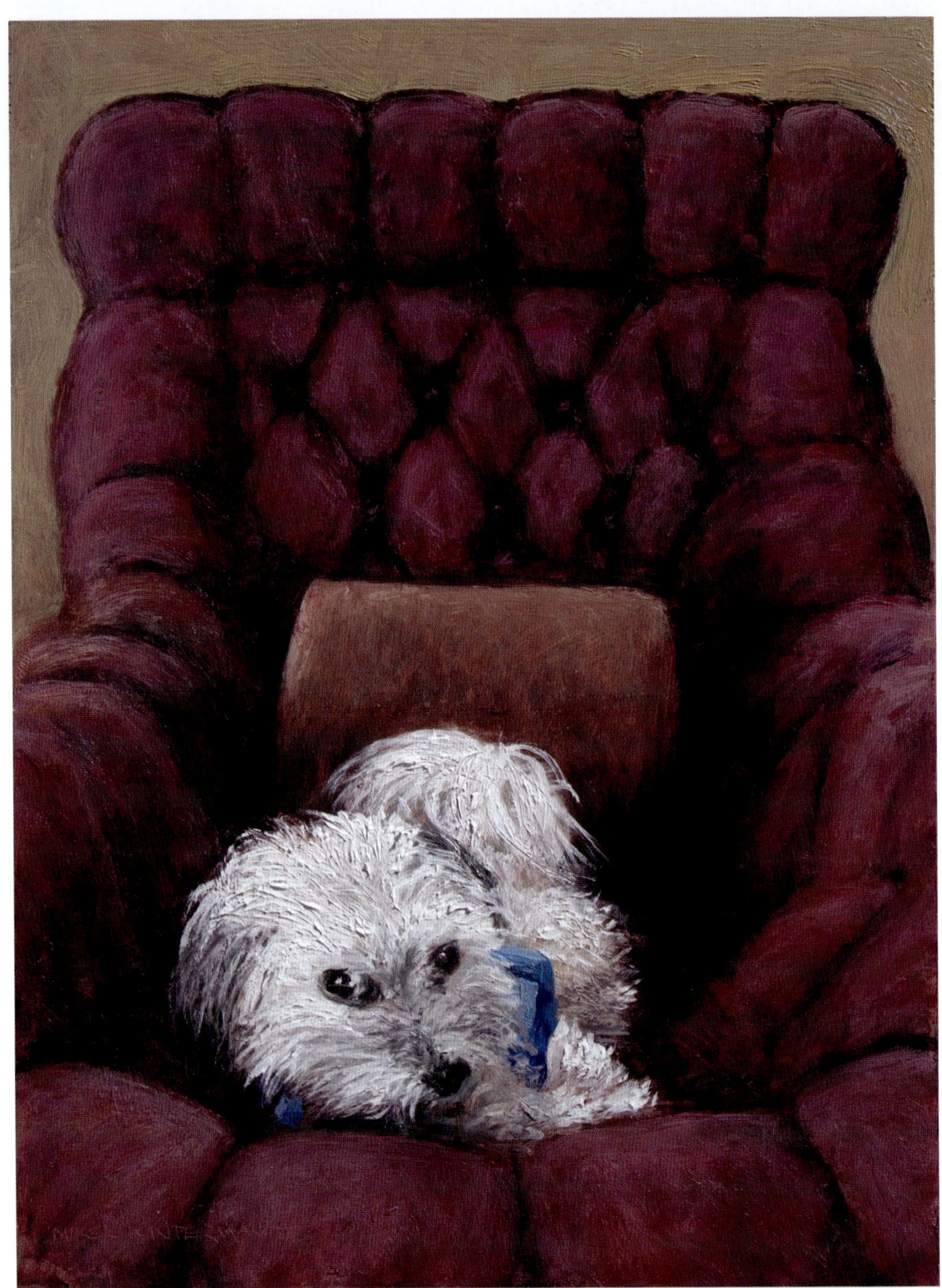

Mikel Wintermantel, New York

THE SURVIVOR

We will survive this pandemic. *The Survivor*, a portrait of my pup, LJ., was painted one week after he was attacked by a pit bull and survived. He was resting in my grandfather's reading chair as I painted him.

My grandfather, Dr. Joseph Adam Wintermantel, was a graduate of the University of Buffalo School of Medicine where Dr. Roswell Park once taught. Roswell Park Cancer Institute is where I was treated for stage-four throat cancer seven years ago, which I survived. I was treated with radiation. You can see there are still research papers that my grandfather had published with the Radiological Society decades ago on the treatment of cancers with radiation. He also treated a woman for throat cancer in his office with open tube radiation, shortly after he delivered her only son, who quickly became one of my best friends and has been my whole life. In addition, my Grandmother was a breast cancer survivor, and my grandfather actually operated on her. They both served in WWI during the flu of 1918; he was a medic and she was an Army nurse.

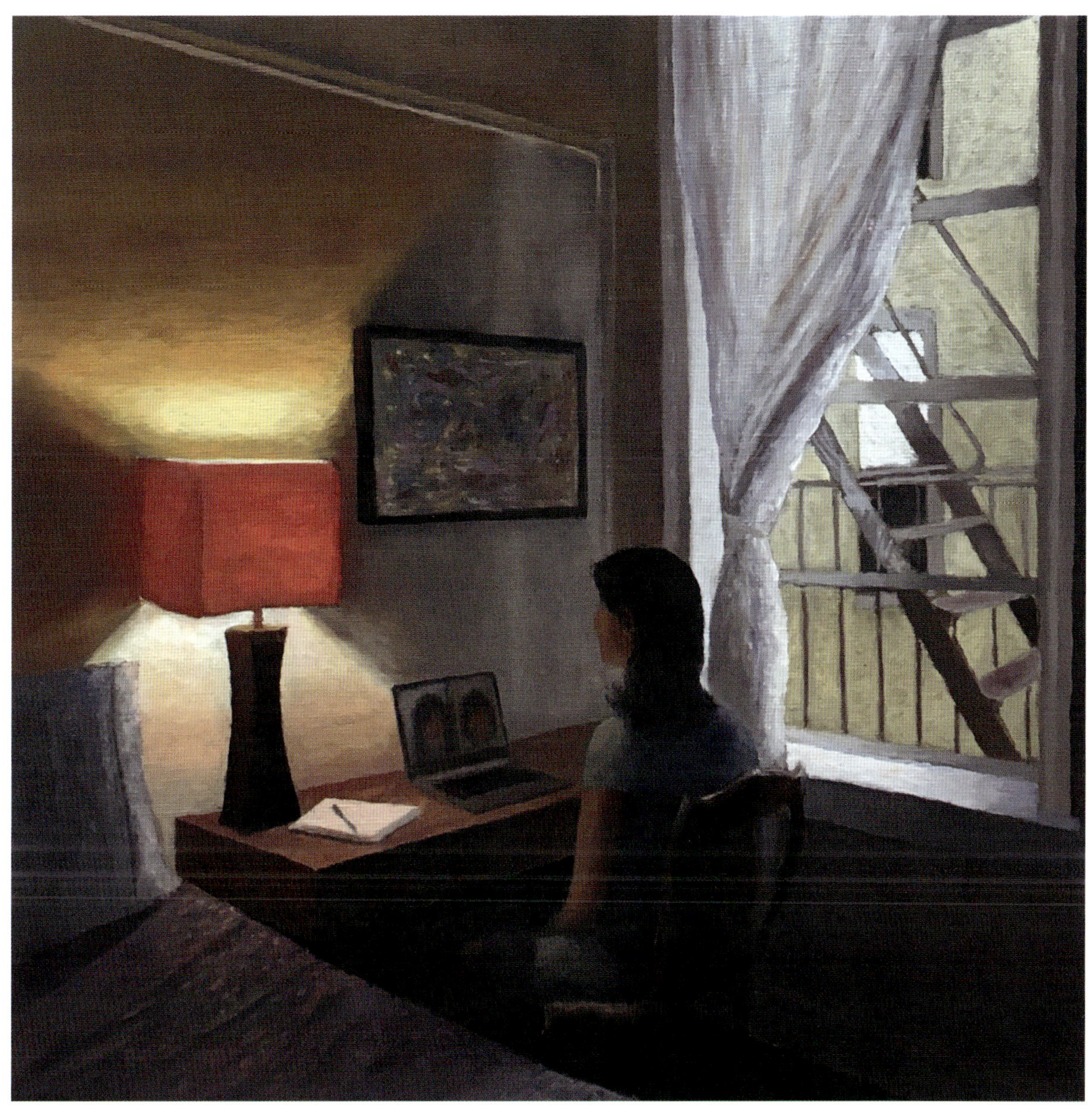

Robert Buckwalter, New York
PANDEMIC OFFICE

Of the multitude of ways in which the pandemic profoundly affected people's lives, in this painting I wanted to capture how it impacted home life. For those fortunate enough to maintain employment by working remotely through the pandemic, that often meant the quick improvisational creation of a home office; in this case, my wife working out of our bedroom. But more than that, I was interested in capturing how this new existence created a world of "connection" and isolation simultaneously.

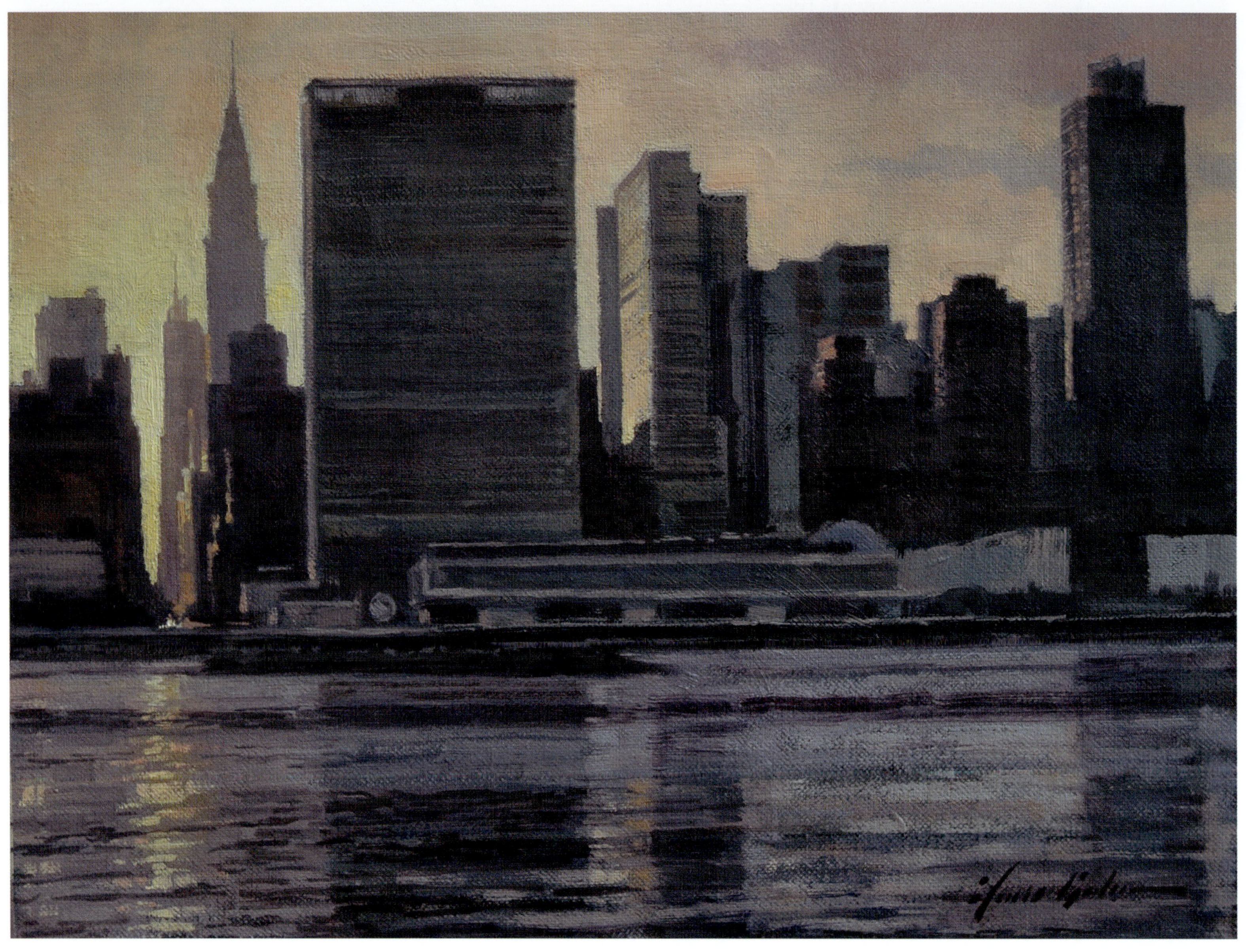

Garin J. Baker, New York
NYC COVID-19 7PM

While the COVID-19 pandemic rages on, this captures the scene painted along the Queens side of the East River, facing west during sunset. Gazing across and through Manhattan Island at 7 pm, the cheers and clapping ensues from all the windows of apartment dwellers throughout New York City, acknowledging their support for today's real heroes...our healthcare workers.

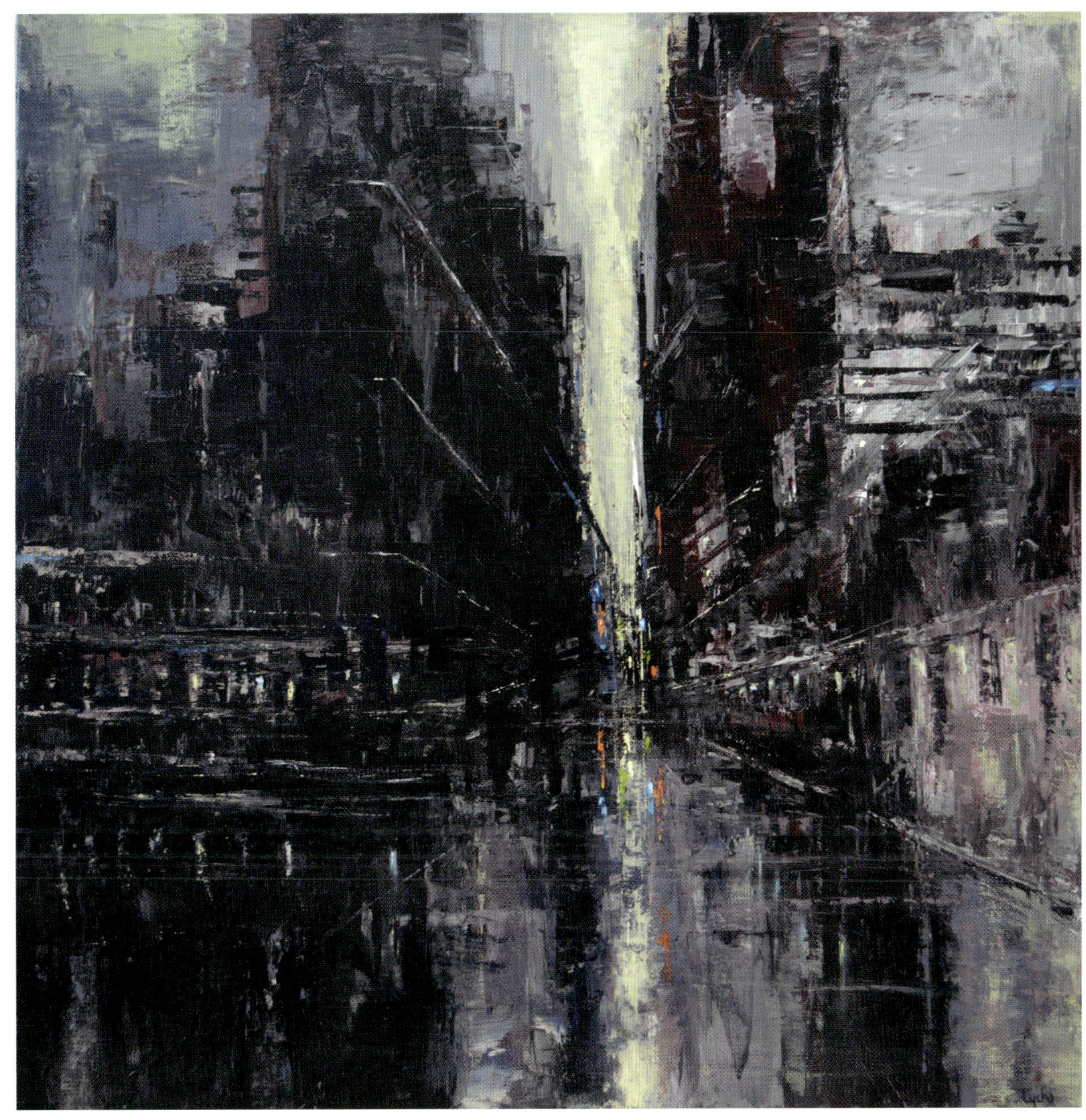

David Tycho, Canada

URBANIA #3

This is a painting I completed around the time Coronavirus was first making the headlines, and the possibilities of a pandemic and subsequent lockdown were fast becoming very real. The photos I used as reference material were ones I had taken in Manhattan two years before when I marveled at the dynamism of this bustling metropolis. In this painting, however, darkness has descended upon the city, and the cars, bicycles, and citizens have all but vanished. The city that never sleeps has slipped into a state of hibernation, and the hustle and bustle have been supplanted by an atmosphere of silent tension. The painting is not, however, an elegy or requiem for New York, nor any city for that matter. As one looks down the urban corridor to the end of the proverbial tunnel, there are indications of activity, and flickers of neon. In this sense, the painting is not so much about the darkness, as it is about the light. It is a painting of hope and a testament to the resilience and resolve of humankind in the face of adversity.

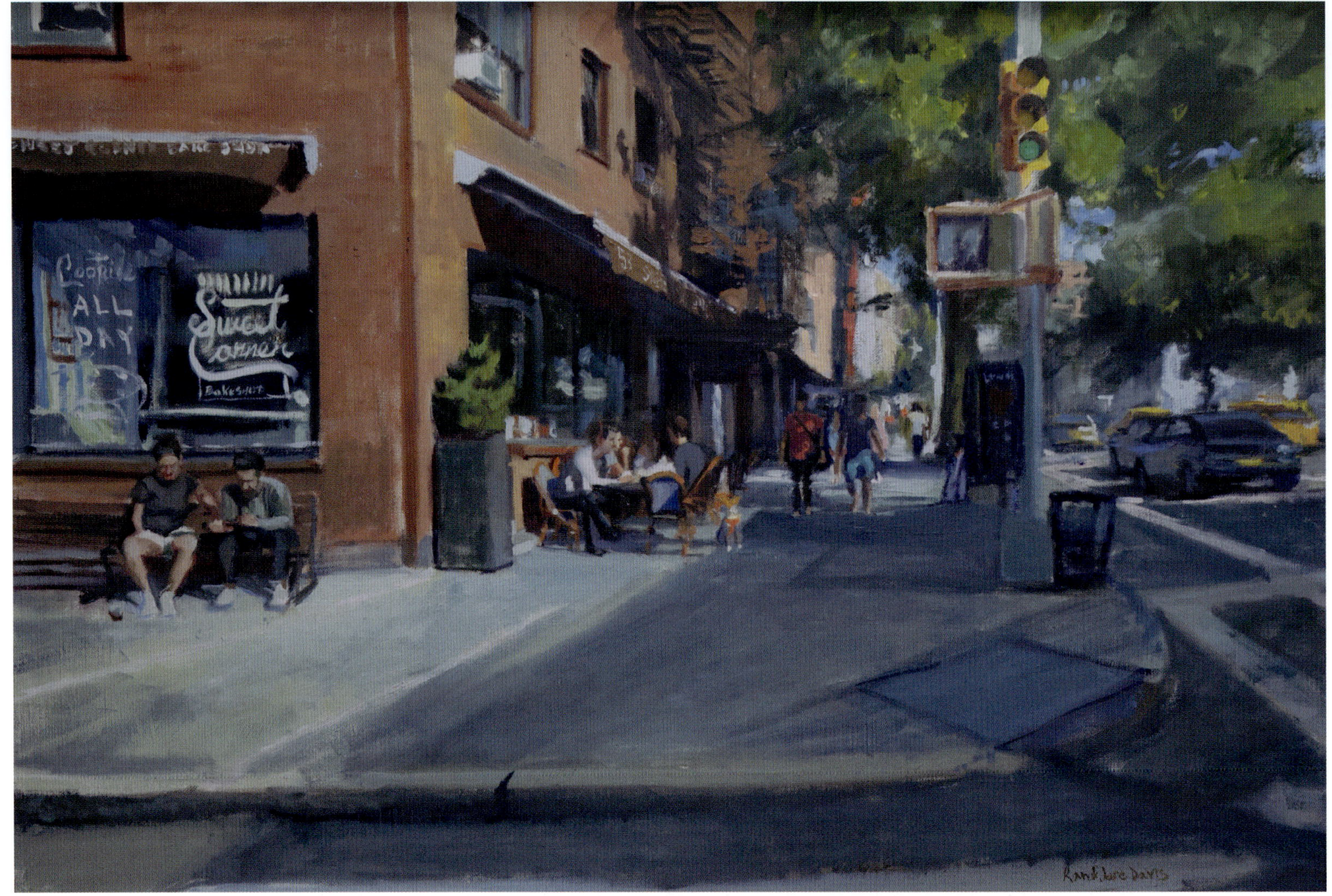

Randi Jane Davis, Connecticut
BEFORE SOCIAL DISTANCING

I spent the day walking around New York City, trying to photograph scenes that describe the vibe of the West Village. I found this corner and the strong compelling graphic that the light created. When COVID-19 started, I found myself drawn to the story that once was: A simple Sunday morning, having coffee or breakfast; people watching and enjoying the vitality of the city.

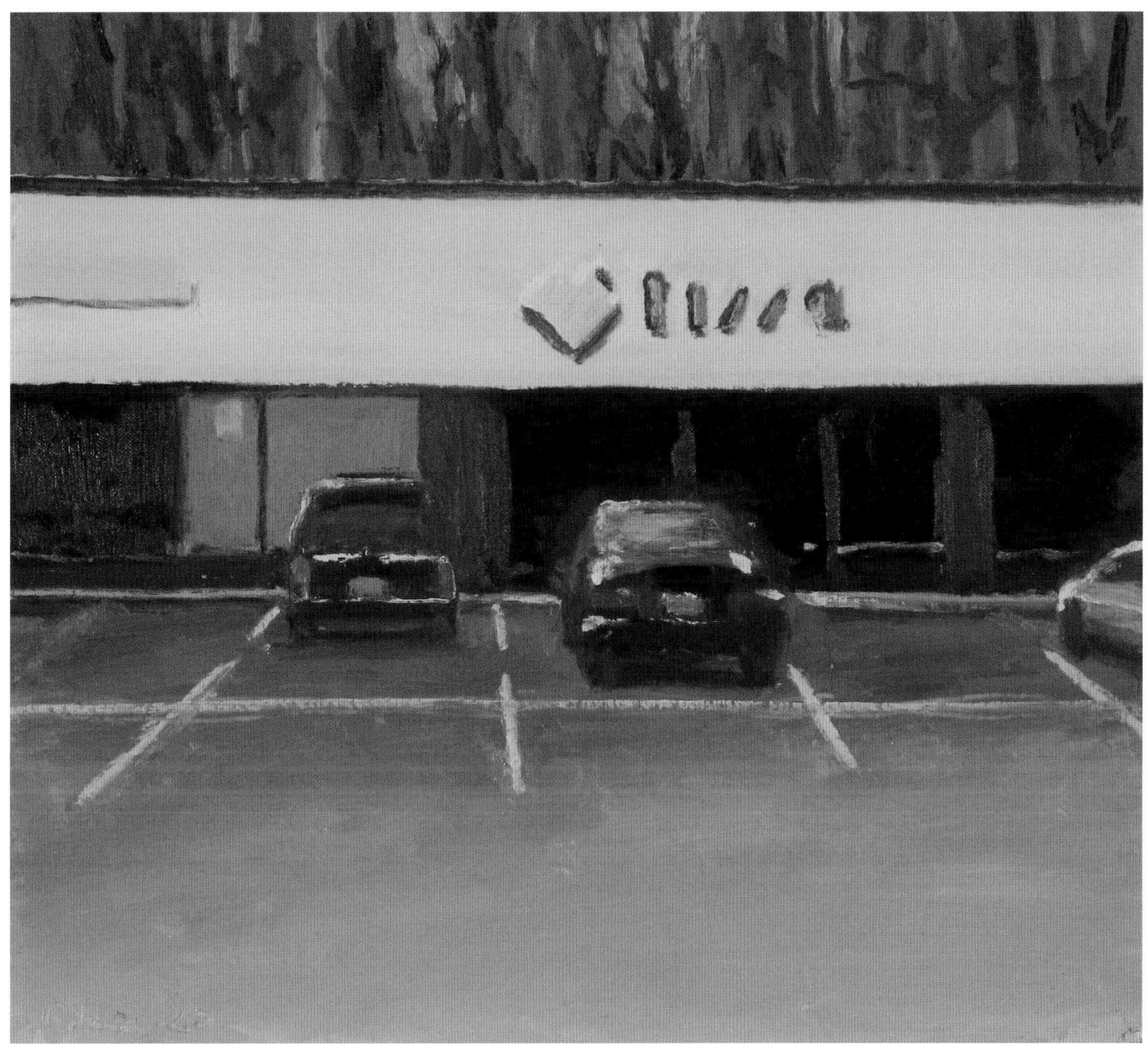

Matt Chinian, New York

#1600 JAY'S PIZZA

The plein-air version of this painting was done the first week that the state of New York officially went on "pause." The realities and emotions that accompanied this seemed to live in the air, the zeitgeist of the day without even looking for it! This scene shows a nondescript plaza and parking lot with a few random cars; a place you'd pass by, or stop in if you needed something. The narrative of the painting casts the unseen players and their mysterious ways.

THE PARTICIPANTS